EMIL AND KATHLEEN SICK SERIES IN WESTERN HISTORY AND BIOGRAPHY

With support from the Center for the Study of the Pacific Northwest at the University of Washington, the Sick Series in Western History and Biography features scholarly books on the peoples and issues that have defined and shaped the American West. Through intellectually challenging and engaging books of general interest, the series seeks to deepen and expand our understanding of the American West as a region and its role in the making of the United States and the modern world.

RECLAIMING THE RESERVATION

Histories of Indian Sovereignty Suppressed and Renewed

ALEXANDRA HARMON

CENTER FOR THE STUDY
OF THE PACIFIC NORTHWEST

in association with

UNIVERSITY OF WASHINGTON PRESS
Seattle

Reclaiming the Reservation was made possible in part by a grant from the Emil and Kathleen Sick Fund of the University of Washington's Department of History.

This book was also supported by a grant from the Tulalip Tribes Charitable Fund, which provides the opportunity for a sustainable and healthy community for all.

www.tulalipcares.org

Printed and bound in the United States of America
Composed in Minion, typeface designed by Robert Slimbach

23 22 21 20 19 5 4 3 2 1

CENTER FOR THE STUDY OF THE PACIFIC NORTHWEST
http://cspn.uw.edu

UNIVERSITY OF WASHINGTON PRESS
www.washington.edu/uwpress

COVER DESIGN: Katrina Noble
COVER PHOTOGRAPH: Closed area of Quinault tribal beach, September 1972. Photograph by Gene Daniels. Identifier 545248, Record Group 412: Records of the Environmental Protection Agency, 1944–2006, National Archives at College Park, Maryland.
INTERIOR MAPS: Ben Pease, Pease Press Cartography

LIBRARY OF CONGRESS CATALOGING-IN-PUBLICATION DATA ON FILE
LC record available at https://lccn.loc.gov/2018047475

ISBN 978-0-295-74586-2 (hardcover)
ISBN 978-0-295-74585-5 (paperback)
ISBN 978-0-295-74587-9 (ebook)

The paper used in this publication is acid free and meets the minimum requirements of American National Standard for Information Sciences—Permanence of Paper for Printed Library Materials, ANSI Z39.48–1984.∞

CONTENTS

ACKNOWLEDGMENTS

During the six or more years of my intermittent work toward the publication of this book, many busy, generous, thoughtful people have given me invaluable assistance, information, constructive criticism, and encouragement. Their contributions to a challenging project deserve acknowledgment. I am deeply grateful to them all.

Alvin Ziontz, Alan Parker, Michael Taylor, Daniel Raas, Charles Wilkinson, Francis Rosander, Pearl Capoeman Baller, and the late Harold Patterson and Justine James, Sr., did me the honor of sharing their memories in face-to-face interviews. Rodney Lewis, Richard Belmont, Barry Ernstoff, John Echohawk, and Bennie Armstrong kindly answered questions and offered insights about their experiences in telephone conversations, e-mail correspondence, or in-person conversation.

I had essential help arranging access to Quinault tribal records and personnel from Larry Ralston, Karen Allston, and Justine James, Jr., and to Suquamish records from Michelle Hanson, Marguerite McKnight, Janet Smoak, Leonard Forsman, and the Suquamish Tribal Council. Thomas Schlosser and Richard Reich searched law office records at my request, and Tamara Broadhead made her late father's papers available to me at her home. From David Wilkins and Robert Walls, I received documents and a lead to publications, respectively, that I would otherwise have missed. Larry Workman's rapid response to a late request for photographs was exceptionally considerate.

Knowledgeable, obliging archivists were indispensable to this project: Lydia Sigo at the Suquamish Museum and Archives, Ken House and Patti McNamee at the National Archives in Seattle, John Jacob at Washington and Lee University School of Law, and employees of Princeton University's Seeley G. Mudd Library, the National Museum of the American Indian

Cultural Resource Center, the Library of Congress, University of Utah Archives and J. Willard Marriott Library Special Collections, University of Washington Libraries Special Collections, the Center for Pacific Northwest Studies, Washington State Archives, National Archives in Washington, DC, Seattle Municipal Archives, and the Seattle Museum of History and Industry. Financial assistance from three sources—Friends of Marriott Library, Friends of the Princeton University Library, and the Center for the Study of the Pacific Northwest—covered costs of traveling to several of these institutions.

Seven people did the great favor of reading the entire manuscript and providing much-appreciated comments, corrections, and suggestions for improvement: Leonard Forsman, Justine James, Dennis Lewarch, Colleen O'Neill, Sherry Smith, and two anonymous scholars recruited by University of Washington Press. Other discerning colleagues read and critiqued portions of the work or related conference papers: Jamie Allison, Jean Dennison, Katrina Jagodinsky, Tsianina Lomawaima, Josh Reid, Paul Rosier, Cassandra Tate, and Christopher Teuton.

Finally, I thank the conscientious, genial team at my hometown press for making the last, potentially stressful steps in this project enjoyable, particularly editors Larin McLaughlin and Julie Van Pelt and editorial assistant Neecole Bostick.

RECLAIMING THE RESERVATION

Introduction

IN 1969, THE RESPONSE OF A TINY AMERICAN COMMUNITY TO A local nuisance attracted a national spotlight. Quinault Indians were barring non-Indians from the scenic seashore that edged their reservation in the state of Washington, vowing to use force if necessary. The *New York Times* and *Washington Post* focused attention there on August 26; CBS television followed suit the next day. Quinaults told reporters they were "angered by the white man's littering ways." Tourists and campers left garbage behind, stole Indian fishing nets, removed large amounts of driftwood, and defaced towering offshore rocks, a subject of Quinault legends. Developers of private oceanfront lots dumped debris on the beach, destroying valuable clam beds.

Washington's governor and attorney general questioned the Indians' ability "to make the closure stand," but Quinault officials cited a lawyer's assurance that the tribe owned the land and could therefore exclude "nontribesmen." "He said we have the United States Supreme Court behind us," one spokesman exulted. That satisfied the county sheriff, who added, "We assume the reservation encompasses the beaches. Whites have no right to go in there if the Indians object. The Indian police can take them into custody." James Jackson, identified as "tribal chief," warned that police would also eject "nonmembers of the tribe" from private reservation roads.[1]

The Quinault announcement drew abundant, remarkably positive public comment. The *Seattle Times* learned that letters flooded the tribe's mailbox from around the world—more than a thousand by September 4—all reportedly applauding the Indian effort to protect a precious natural resource. Keep America Beautiful, a nationwide community improvement organization, bestowed an award on the tribe's governing council. Meanwhile, Quinault police did enforce the beach closure, in some instances by removing intruders bodily. They sent trespassers' names and addresses to the US attorney in Seattle, although a *Times* reporter deemed prosecutions unlikely. "While the Quinaults have jurisdiction over their land, their tribal court hears only cases involving tribal members," he wrote. "Because of jurisdiction questions, federal, state, and county courts have been reluctant to proceed with misdemeanor charges . . . brought by the tribe."[2]

Quinaults were unhappily familiar with such legal questions. Many had concluded that the only acceptable response was to disregard doubts about the tribe's jurisdiction. Why not assume and assert that the Quinault government had standard government powers over everyone, everywhere within the reservation? The general council and elected officers favored that strategy. They had resolved to govern on the premise that location, not affiliation with the tribe, determined whether someone fell under Quinault law. History had shown that they could not manage their own land and resources as they saw fit unless non-Indians on the reservation had to honor the tribe's decisions. Keeping unauthorized persons off the beach was one of several actions they planned, all aimed at confirming Quinaults' right to "run" their reservation.[3]

Quinaults were not alone in thinking that Indian tribes could extend their laws to anyone within reservation boundaries. More than a decade earlier, Oglala Sioux in South Dakota had successfully asserted a tribal government right to tax non-Indians who leased reservation land.[4] In December 1969, representatives of tribes in six Northwest states approved a resolution that "provisions should be established, by Congress if necessary, to allow non-Indians coming on an Indian reservation to be subject to tribal authority."[5] But Quinaults were among the first Indians since the 1800s to act on the belief that they needed no permission to bring non-Indians under tribal government authority. They had expelled non-Indian trespassers and regulated non-Indian fishing on reservation waters well before 1969. More recently, they had enacted a land use code for all property, reservation-wide, whether owners were Indian or non-Indian. A few years after the beach closure, another Quinault code gave the tribal court jurisdiction over non-Indians accused of criminal acts on the reservation.

In relations with other tribes, Quinaults encouraged and found encouragement for their inclusive conception of tribal government power. Thus, by the mid-1970s, jurisdiction over non-Indians was tribal law on almost three dozen reservations, and non-Indians were answering criminal charges in the courts of several tribes. Then on March 6, 1978, the United States Supreme Court declared such proceedings impermissible. In a case that arose on the Suquamish Tribe's reservation, the court ruled that Indian governments could not prosecute non-Indians. According to the six-justice majority, America's indigenous peoples might once have been fully sovereign nations with power over anyone in their territory, but they lost the right to punish non-Indians when they became dependent on the United States, which had always opposed "unwarranted" Indian "intrusions" on its citizens' liberty.[6]

That decree in *Oliphant v. Suquamish Indian Tribe* had far-reaching implications for Indian communities and their relations with other Americans, more and more of whom would soon have reasons to be on Indian reservations. The ruling became an essential consideration in any dispute or public discourse about the nature of Indian tribes, their relationship to the United States, their powers as political entities, and the significance of Indian reservations. The justices' reasoning cast doubt on tribes' ability to manage community affairs ranging from economic enterprise and natural resource use to domestic relations and public health.

Such questions continued to arise despite the court's decision because tribes persisted in asserting powers and property rights that directly affected non-Indians. Those claims both reflected and stirred deep-rooted, enduring fears and hopes. Indians, fearing erosion of the territorial and demographic basis for their tribal communities, hoped for acknowledgment of the tribes' inherent, continuing sovereignty. Many non-Indians, confused or offended by that insistence on sovereignty, remained fearful of subjection to laws made by Indians.

Indian territory in North America has not been non-Indian-proof since Europeans stumbled across the continent. Jurisdiction issues have been an inevitable consequence. The borders of US Indian reservations, like other geopolitical boundaries, have been porous and often contested. By crossing them, challenging them, and assigning them varying legal significance, non-Indians and Indians have triggered disputes with substantial and wide-ranging interests at stake. Such contests could decide who would manage or have access to land, water, and other vital or potentially lucrative resources; they could determine whose laws or customs controlled in specific locations and determine penalties for nonconforming behavior. The outcome of one dispute could set a precedent for resolving disputes in other Indian country.

Questions about tribes' jurisdiction over non-Indians became especially salient in the 1990s when casinos and other new tribe-owned enterprises drew thousands of non-Indians onto reservations for recreation, business, and employment. But by then, Indians had a four-hundred-year history of dealing with non-Indians in their territory. For decades after Europeans planted their first small colonies in North America, their forays outside those enclaves took them into indigenous nations that had the power to punish them for violating Native norms. Colonial authorities who did not want supposedly lawless Indians to decide the fate of offending colonists had to negotiate for their extradition to colonial jurisdictions, including the young United States.

During the nineteenth century, as colonial populations grew exponentially and spread geographically, the United States government gained bargaining power in negotiations with the people it called Indians. Increasingly able to take territory by violence, both military and paramilitary, the American republic displaced or surrounded and restrained indigenous communities, ensuring their impoverishment. By 1890, Indians' numbers and economic circumstances hit historic lows, their modes of self-government and ways of life were under direct American assault, and they had few means to contest additional non-Indian demands for land. The United States reserved some tracts for Indians' exclusive use, but when lawmakers authorized non-Indians to acquire property within those tracts, rebellion was not a practical option for dismayed tribes. Before long there were sizable, permanent non-Indian populations inside the original boundaries of many reservations, seldom with Indians' willing consent.

After several decades of oppressive US rule failed to dismantle reservations and disband tribes as intended, a federal government policy shift in the 1930s encouraged tribes to pin their hopes for community well-being on self-government and collective management of the lands remaining to them. World War II and postwar opportunities subsequently drew many Indians off their reservations, but US reversion to a goal of terminating reservations angered and alarmed Indians across the country. Termination opponents declared that the reserves were "ancestral homelands," essential to tribes' survival.[7]

When efforts to abolish reservations gave way in the 1960s and 1970s to a policy of US support for Indian self-government and "self-determination," tribe leaders took heart. Like Quinaults, some reasoned that self-government should and could rightfully entail reservation-wide regulatory power. By taking measures in keeping with that notion, tribes sharply raised the stakes in their mounting drive for meaningful political power. The rhetoric of that drive—its emphasis on the concept of inherent tribal sovereignty—added heat to debates about Indians' place in the American political system.

That a tribal prosecution of non-Indians soon incited litigation was not surprising. The surprise for advocates of tribal power was which tribe provoked the lawsuit that reached the Supreme Court. Instead of the Quinaults or another tribe with a record of exercising comprehensive government power, the Indians defending tribes' right to penalize non-Indian offenders were the Suquamish, whose disputed arrest of a white man came just three weeks after the tribal council first enacted a criminal code and established a court. On a small reservation near Seattle, Washington, a few dozen Suquamish lived amid several thousand non-Indians, and most of the land belonged to non-Indians. Yet Quinaults' example had given Suquamish leaders confidence in their right to govern the entire area and population within their reserve's boundaries. It was their bad luck—and as it would happen, the bad luck of other tribes—that a local lawyer was eager to dispute Suquamish claims of sovereignty, and an unruly white resident of the reservation gave him his chance by taking a swing at a tribal cop.

The tribes' bid for all-inclusive reservation jurisdiction was an important, bold move in American Indians' long history of resisting erasure by the settler-colonial nation-state that engulfed them. The terms of indigenous peoples' relationships to nonindigenous polities have been the subject of recurring negotiations since European invasions of North America began. Even after the United States extended its reach across the continent and imposed its laws unilaterally on weakened Native nations, give and take between the subjugators and subjugated continued. Indians have challenged US dictates in multiple ways, usually with determination to perpetuate indigenous identity and territory-holding, self-governing tribes.[8] The contention in the 1970s that US law entitled tribes to govern everyone on reservations was such a challenge. It reflected Indian memories of their historical autonomy and renewed confidence in their bargaining power, but it stopped short of disputing ultimate US legal authority.

This book about late twentieth-century Indian attempts to police non-Indians is a product of my desire to explain what motivated and encouraged tribes to assert such power after decades of more restricted self-government. I wanted to examine that development at the reservation community level, then trace the processes that linked community ambitions to a national-level Indian push for acceptance of broad tribal sovereignty. The account I pieced together does that and more. It is a rare case study of the promises and perils inherent in Indian efforts to ensure tribal communities' endurance by appealing to US law in US courts. It also offers essential historical perspective on issues of continuing practical import for relations between Indians and non-Indians.

The story climaxes with the Supreme Court ruling in *Oliphant v. Suquamish Tribe*, a pivotal event in a transformational phase of Indians' struggle for acceptable relations with the United States. Nevertheless, the book is not primarily a study of that litigation. Legal strategy, procedure, and doctrine are less important to the story than Indian experiences and actions outside of court—experiences and actions over many decades in tribal communities, at fishing grounds, in federal government offices and congressional hearings, at universities, at intertribal meetings, and elsewhere.

The principal protagonists are Indians who came to see themselves, in effect, as participants in a movement for qualified independence from colonial control and resource exploitation. Although they resented the adverse effects of US rule, they had reason to believe that some American principles of law could be a basis for relief from galling oppression. The doctrine of inherent tribal sovereignty confirmed their elders' stories of past nation-to-nation relations with the United States government. Lawyers and experiences in American courts had familiarized them with procedures and language they could use to assert their nationhood. They sought federal government acceptance of the meanings they ascribed to their treaties with the United States, their reservations, and the term "tribal sovereignty."

By their claims of jurisdiction, tribes challenged non-Indians to consider the concepts of Indian reservation and tribal sovereignty from Indian perspectives, both past and present. They particularly wanted acknowledgment that the concepts could be construed in contemporary circumstances to allow fair-minded tribal management of affairs in the places promised to them as tribal homelands. Their arguments persuaded judges and officials at some levels of American government, but in 1978, six members of the Supreme Court did not see the issue in the same light. Scarcely any of the Indian history related in this book came to the justices' attention. For them, Indians' experiences and conceptions of their tribes were mostly beside the point. Their opinion in *Oliphant v. Suquamish Tribe* emphasized US government law and policy. It did recite a history of nation-to-nation relationships, but from only one perspective—that of the United States.

Even so, tribes did not abandon the goals that prompted their bids for tribal government control of reservation affairs. Unwilling to drop all claims of jurisdiction over non-Indians, tribes continued after 1978 to make their arguments for regulatory power, with revisions, in various courts, institutions, and levels of American government. Nor did the ruling in *Oliphant v. Suquamish Tribe* deter tribes from adopting economic strategies that attracted non-Indians to reservations. Consequently, stories that explain why Indian governments sought to expand the powers they exercised had continuing relevance both for tribes and for their many existing and potential non-Indian neighbors, contractors, employees, customers, and visitors.

When I taught undergraduate university classes about law pertaining to American Indians, the subject of tribes' desire to police non-Indians sparked lively interest. Students were largely from Washington State, which encompasses twenty-nine Indian reservations, most of them near urban populations, crossed by highways, and home to non-Indians as well as Indians. Yet the fact that non-Indians can reside or own land on reservations surprised many students, as did the Supreme Court's decision in *Oliphant v. Suquamish Tribe*. Students remarked that they could travel into the jurisdictions of multiple governments—cities, other states, or

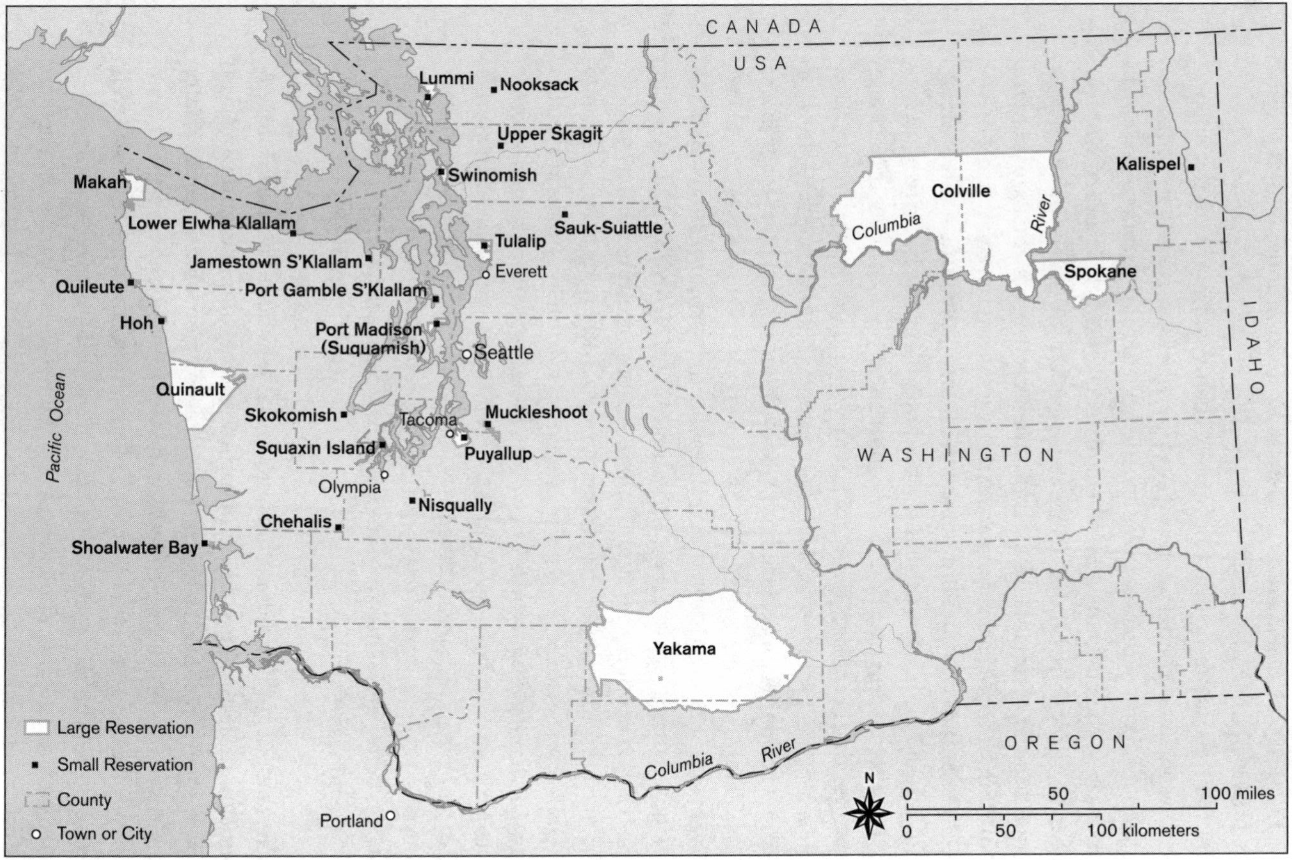

Indian reservations in Washington State as of 2000. Small reservations were subsequently established in western Washington for the Snoqualmie and Cowlitz tribes.

countries such as Canada and Mexico—and those governments could prosecute them if they violated local law. How were reservations for self-governing tribes different?

My students' initial ignorance of reservation jurisdiction issues and their reactions to what they learned—ignorance and reactions I also encountered among friends, relatives, and casual acquaintances—were incentives to write this book. Another impetus was my conviction that many people outside college classrooms needed the same information. Tribal governments were gaining stature in the American political system, developing economic clout, and in many instances adding to their land-holdings. As they did so, their reservation boundaries and the range of their powers acquired immediate or potential relevance for increasing numbers of Americans.

My attention to the subject of this book has even older roots. I worked as a lawyer for tribes in Washington beginning in 1973 and ending with a five-year stint during the 1980s as the Suquamish tribal government's staff attorney. For several of those years, Seattle Legal Services employed me to oversee a network of lawyers stationed on reservations across the state. Many of our clients' legal issues raised intriguing questions about Indians' distinctive history, but we undertook historical inquiries only to answer questions of immediate legal relevance. Wanting to explore such subjects more thoroughly without the goal of resolving issues in clients' favor, I made a transition from tribal attorney to history graduate student and then to professor. Eventually, it was the classroom discussions and conversations with friends that motivated me to study the deep origins and historical context of the tribal jurisdiction dispute.

My direct involvement in the book's central story was negligible. I had no role in the Suquamish litigation, nor did I represent tribes in other disputes about jurisdiction over non-Indians. I was not present at conferences, councils, hearings, or demonstrations that figure significantly in my account. Even so, I faced special challenges when writing about affairs that I had followed with keen professional and personal interest as they occurred. In the 1970s, I was not only aware of some tribes' intention to govern non-Indians; I sympathized with their desire to wield more power on their reservations, and I thought the legal arguments for tribal jurisdiction were sound. I knew several of the people whose actions and recollections the book would feature; I had collaborated with a few of them in matters tangentially related to my subject. One challenge was therefore to minimize the effects of my bias on my analysis. Another was not to let memories or extrapolations from my experiences control the direction of my research, fill gaps in the available records, or determine my interpretation of evidence.

I do not pretend to have achieved neutrality on the subject at the heart of this book—Indian tribes' struggle for survival and self-determination. I have not strived for neutrality. I remain an ally of tribes in their efforts to undo or rise above colonialism's dire effects on their communities. As such, I have an obligation to research and write in ways that foster understanding of those effects and empathy for Indian efforts to counter them. That obligation is not incompatible with my responsibility as a historian to depict all events and actions truthfully and all other actors with empathy. While recognizing that my scholarship is not disinterested, I have tried to consider all available sources of information with an open mind and draw on them judiciously for a frank, accurate account and fair-minded analysis.[9]

While taking non-Indian perspectives into account, I chose to focus primarily on Indian experiences little known outside Indian country. For too long, the great preponderance of historical scholarship on Indians reflected only non-Indian perspectives. Efforts to correct that imbalance are under way, but many more Indian-centered accounts are needed. A history can put Indians at the center without being one-sided, insensitive to non-Indian views, or blind to mistakes and misdeeds of Indian actors. My obligation to the tribes that opened records for me and tribe members who shared memories is to present their views of the past, as well as their history, as accurately as I can, in a way that acknowledges the full, complex humanity of all the historical actors.

A word about some words I use is necessary here. Histories of Indians cannot be written without several unsatisfactory terms. When I write "Indians," "American Indians," or "Native Americans" to designate key historical actors, I do it grudgingly. After all, those names originated with misinformed Europeans, and they are prevalent only because English speakers ultimately attained hegemony in the Western Hemisphere north of Mexico. I use them because English speakers generally know what they denote and have not agreed on better terms. Furthermore, by the historical period covered in this book, "Indian" and "Native American" were names the designated people used for themselves, at least in some contexts. That may not be true of the word "non-Indian," but Americans' racial diversity rules out "white" or "Euro-American" as inclusive terms. Besides, while indigenous ancestry is a common constituent of Indian identity, tribal affiliation rather than race has usually identified someone as Indian.

"Tribe" is similarly a problematic term for the political-social entities I write about. That word commonly connotes a relatively small, homogeneous social grouping or population and applies whether the group has a defined geographical territory or not. But "tribe" can also designate societies that historically had and may now have the characteristics of a nation, defined in the *New Oxford American Dictionary* as "a large aggregate of people united by common descent, history, culture, or language, inhabiting a particular country or territory." Some present-day "aggregates" of Indians, deeming that definition appropriate for them, do call themselves nations. Others retain the designation "tribe," as I do when writing about people for whom it was the accepted term at the time under discussion.

In this book, "tribe" often denotes more specifically the government of a distinct Indian population. Readers should bear in mind that ascribing actions to a tribe in that sense may wrongly imply group solidarity. Tribe members have been as likely as any other people to disagree with each other, and tribal polities have acted as units in political and legal affairs even while members were at odds with each other on the desirability of that action. My account of tribal government decisions and activity says relatively little about diversity or discord in the tribal communities, but both were common, especially in stressful circumstances.

Writing about tribes' assertion of jurisdiction and subsequent court proceedings requires words of another kind—terminology that some call legalese. I know from experience that much of the legal profession's specialized vocabulary is Greek to otherwise educated people. Fortunately, my work in two professions has given me practice explaining unfamiliar law and legal terms to lay tribe members and college students. Readers of the book will judge how well I have learned from that practice.

To paraphrase novelist Thomas King, we are the stories we tell, and stories are all we have in the end.[10] All the people known as American Indians have a shared story that begins with their descent from North America's original human inhabitants. By the time Europeans found the Americas, those first inhabitants were the progenitors of countless distinct nations, tribes, bands, and clans, each with its own set of stories. Even after Europeans came to stay, indigenous peoples' diverse experiences gave rise to additional separate lore. The subject of the story they all have in common is relations with the United States. It concerns ancestral nations engulfed by a colonial nation-state that classified them all as Indians for purposes of policy and law. As the United States expanded across the continent, distinct Native peoples became characters in the shared story region by region, decade by decade, each nation or tribe contributing its own variation on a tale of coping with the imperialist state's claims of supremacy.

Certain threads of that tale were central elements of the 1970s controversy about tribal jurisdiction over non-Indian lawbreakers. Two hundred years of contested settler colonization and US policies had determined the circumstances of the tribes' bid for jurisdiction, the language of negotiation, and the stories that negotiating parties were likely to tell. Here, a concise rundown of history that haunted those negotiations will provide essential background for the twentieth-century events that are recounted more fully in the chapters that follow.

From the 1770s to the 1870s, many Indians had relations with the United States that included treaties. In Anglo-American political-legal culture, the word "treaty" designated formal agreements between self-governing nations, usually memorialized in writing. The US government practice of making treaties with Indians thus acknowledged that the indigenous societies were independent political entities, comparable in strategic respects to European states. Although lawmakers, officials, and most US citizens expected that "civilization" would ultimately supplant or swallow and digest Indian societies, the United States in its first century had compelling pragmatic reasons for following the English monarchy's example of recognizing the tribes' sovereignty. As historian Steven Hahn observed, Indian treaties were "a reflection of the multiple forms of sovereignty that defined the American union and empire."[11]

More than five hundred such treaties went on record as United States law. Some were later annulled, but many were extant in 1871 when Congress prohibited further treaty making with Indians. That legislation preserved existing treaties, and the United States continued for decades to negotiate formal agreements with tribes that also became federal law. Meanwhile, the Supreme Court, responding in 1831 to Cherokees' insistence on their sovereignty, confirmed that federal Indian treaties did indeed constitute US recognition of Indians' preexisting status as self-governing nations. The next year, in a closely related case, the court identified an important jurisdictional implication of that 1831 ruling. Citing the US Constitution as well as the history of colonial states' relations with indigenous peoples, Justice John Marshall declared that the federal government's exclusive power over Indian affairs and its acknowledgment of Cherokee Nation sovereignty precluded Georgia's attempt to impose state law within Cherokee territory.[12]

The opinions in those two cases—*Cherokee Nation v. Georgia* and *Worcester v. Georgia*—established several foundational principles of legal doctrine now known as federal Indian law. The cases were the first of many in which Indian governments contributed to the doctrine's development. In the late 1800s and early 1900s, however, Supreme Court rulings distorted and deviated from those original tenets. Without expressly disavowing the conception of indigenous nations as sovereigns, the justices construed the federal government's responsibility for dealing with Indians as a license to discontinue consensual relations with Indian tribes.

The court borrowed language from earlier opinions to create excuses for changing the terms of relations. In the 1831 Cherokee case, Marshall likened the tribe's acceptance of US protection to a ward's relationship with a guardian. By the twentieth century, the court had converted that metaphor into a legal status for Indians akin to guardianship for children or incompetents, thereby justifying direct US control of tribal territory, tribal government, even tribe members' personal affairs.[13]

Similarly, justices in 1846 turned the words of an 1823 opinion into a basis for sweeping federal regulation of everyone in tribal territory. The earlier of the two cases—*Johnson v. M'Intosh*—was an ownership dispute between non-Indians who had paid an Indian tribe for the same land at different times. Justice Marshall, expounding on European law governing international competition for American land, declared that a colonial nation's "discovery" of territory "gave [it] title" to the land "against all other European governments." Nevertheless, indigenous people remained "the rightful occupants of the soil, with a legal as well as just claim to retain possession of it, and to use it according to their own discretion."

Elsewhere in the opinion, Marshall noted that rulers of the discovering nations claimed "ultimate dominion," which entailed the power to grant non-Natives underlying title to land that Natives still occupied. Twenty-three years later, another justice gratuitously expanded on that point, to the tribes' detriment. United States "title," he wrote, came with "dominion and control" over Indian-occupied lands.[14] The added word "control" encouraged the court to hold that a federal judge could try a non-Indian for murdering another non-Indian inside Cherokee Nation boundaries. (Racial ideology was a factor as well. The white defendant had become a Cherokee citizen, but the justices insisted that he could not "throw off all responsibility to the laws of the United States.") The 1846 decision became a basis for others that allowed state prosecutions of Indians for crimes against non-Indians on the premise that the states' creator—the US government—had ultimate control over the Indian land where the offenses occurred.[15]

For many Indians in the trans-Mississippi West, including Quinaults and Suquamish, direct relations with United States representatives began in the 1850s and led quickly to treaties by which tribes ceded most of their terrestrial domains but reserved much smaller tracts for homesites. United States expansion to the Pacific Coast had made it impractical to continue the policy in force since 1830 of removing tribes beyond western US borders. Officials turned instead to locating tribes on tracts within states or federal territories, thus establishing many of today's Indian reservations.[16]

In the 1880s, however, non-Indian dissatisfaction with the reservations and their corrupt administration prompted federal government adoption of a program to compel Indians' detribalization. For five ensuing decades, the professed goal of US policy was to "civilize" Indians and thus enable their assimilation as individuals into the American population. Key measures for achieving that goal were new laws that simply disregarded tribal sovereignty. In the General Allotment Act of 1887 and similar specific statutes, Congress authorized the subdivision of reserved tribal lands. They maintained that allotting the land to individual Indians as private property would stimulate intelligent selfishness, the basis for American progress, prosperity, and civic order. Conferring US citizenship on allottees would supposedly redirect their political allegiance from their tribes to the American government. After all eligible tribe members received tracts sufficient for family farms, the sale of surplus reservation land would appease the non-Indians who coveted it and give Indians civilized neighbors to emulate.[17]

The Allotment Act was not the first federal law that disregarded Indian nations' inherent right to regulate their internal affairs. Two years earlier, Congress had showed disdain for that right by authorizing federal court jurisdiction over Indians charged with certain crimes against other Indians within tribal territory. The Supreme Court upheld that Major Crimes Act, characterizing it as a measure to protect "dependent" Indians, often from hostile non-Indian neighbors. That many Indians would thenceforth be tried in alien forums under alien laws apparently did not trouble the court.[18]

The detribalization program initiated in the 1880s fell short of its stated goals. Ironically, it resulted in the establishment of a special legal status for Indians and an extensive bureaucracy with inherent interest in perpetuating that status. The Indians entitled to land allotments had to be identified, then supervised until fit for assimilation. In addition, supervised private landholding did not by itself promote the rapid assimilation that its ardent advocates predicted. Most Indians, while willing to make some life changes urged by American authorities, were not eager to abandon tribal ties. For their part, non-Indians were generally averse to associating with Indians, "civilized" or not, and they increasingly interpreted Indian resistance to thorough culture change as proof of inherent deficiencies.

Where land allotment entailed pressure on Indians to leave villages or extended-family camps for nuclear-family homesteads, tribal ties did become harder to maintain. And over time, the privatization of reservation land had another consequence that many proponents wanted: the wholesale transfer of tribal acreage (approximately two-thirds of it) to non-Indians. Even so, the allotment program did not eliminate reservations or dissolve all resident Indian communities. After a period of uncertainty about whether allotment or non-Indian acquisition of allotted land ended the land's reservation status, courts and Congress concluded that they did not.[19]

As policy makers hoped, a half century of efforts to break up tribes did undermine indigenous methods of self-governance, in some cases causing their abandonment, but on many reservations, meddling federal functionaries laid groundwork for new forms of Indian self-government modeled partly on Anglo-American practices. Federal officials opted to conduct relations and keep order on reservations through Indian police, courts, and councils with limited powers and responsibilities. For example, to replace traditional tribal justice practices, the Interior Department in 1884 created Courts of Indian Offenses, which tried Indians accused of offenses such as assault or theft but also enforced regulations defining indigenous social and religious customs as crimes. Although US agents initially sat as judges, that role soon went to Indians who served at agents' will.[20] Indians' reasons for taking these and other colonial government offices ranged from economic need to hopes of exploiting weaknesses in US power or salvaging some leverage in negotiations with federal overseers.[21]

The necessity and potential benefits of knowing the colonizers' legal-political culture had been apparent to Indians since colonization began. While some Indian children learned about American government in schools, their elders gained that knowledge in other ways.[22] They learned as they dealt with American officials, became ensnared in colonial criminal justice systems, or heeded whites' advice to lay their complaints before non-Indian court judges.[23] One historian's study of Indians in Washington Territory showed that they "became increasingly aware of American law as a mechanism for redressing grievances, and they learned what was required to activate it. . . . This law-mindedness showed up . . . particularly in the Puget Sound region, [where] contact between whites and Indians was more intimate and intense." Thus, between 1884 and the 1920s, Indians of the Pacific Northwest were involved in at least four federal court lawsuits filed on their behalf by US officials after the Indians complained of interference with rights guaranteed to them by treaty.[24]

As of 1924, Indians no longer had to "earn" US citizenship by accepting an allotment of land and renouncing tribal affiliations. That year, Congress bestowed citizenship on all Indians born within the United States. By then, however, the Supreme Court had decided that American citizenship, tribal membership, and federal wardship were not incompatible.[25] Indians' unique "wardship" status under federal law would thus endure, but so would widespread puzzlement and controversy about the extent of their citizenship rights and their tribes' separate sovereignty.[26]

Four years after the Indian Citizenship Act passed, apparently confirming the assimilation program's success, a government-commissioned study exposed its failures. The most damning consequences were Indians' loss of vast lands and their descent into poverty. The ensuing Great

Depression finally spurred a different approach to Indian affairs. In 1934, Congress halted further allotment of reservation land, agreed to recognize specified constitutional tribal governments, and empowered the reorganized tribes to prevent the disposition of tribal land. That so-called Indian New Deal was the first of three policy shifts in five decades—swings between the goals of absorbing Indians into the general American populace or accommodating their desire for land-based survival as distinct peoples. By 1953, lawmakers favoring absorption again controlled Congress. They resolved to end federal administration of Indian lands and relieve the government of other responsibilities it had assumed for Indians by treaty or legislation. Two decades later, however, Congress committed the United States instead to dealing with Indian tribes as polities entitled to self-determination. These twentieth-century developments, recounted with more detail and analysis in chapters 2 through 7, produced conditions conducive to a surge of tribal government assertiveness.

Neither the Supreme Court rulings from the turn of the nineteenth century nor laws enacted by twentieth-century Congresses reversed all earlier rulings and legislation concerning Indians. As of 1978, US law contained vestiges from all eras of federal Indian policy. Among them were treaties that promised tribes continuing access to vital resources, treaties and executive orders that created exclusive reservations, regulations and trusts maintaining the federal administration of tribal and allotted Indian lands, statutes and administrative measures acknowledging the legitimacy of tribal governments, laws allowing non-Indians to acquire and lease Indian reservation land, and a 1968 statute specifying the rights that tribal governments must afford to all persons within their jurisdiction. Among the legacies of the past, too, were Supreme Court declarations across a fourteen-decade time span that the relationship between the United States and Indian tribes was a relationship between sovereign nations.

When the Supreme Court decreed that Indian tribes could not prosecute non-Indians, it resolved two specific habeas corpus cases that arose from a few local facts, which are summarized in this book's first chapter. However, court members knew when they took the case that their decision would turn on additional facts from the two-century history of US-Indian relations. Chapter 1 promises that the book will likewise consider a broad history of the issue before the court, including history the justices did not take into account.

The story of tribal governments' determination to expand the powers they exercised begins in chapter 2 with Indian opposition to unilateral federal authorization in the 1950s of state law enforcement on reservations. That opposition reflected expectations arising from Indian experiences since the 1920s: US-endorsed opportunities for self-government after 1934, tastes of life with reduced bureaucratic oversight during World War II, and increased access to lawyers and legal redress in postwar years.

Quinault objections to the imposition of state law also reflected their longer, local experience of gradually losing the power they expected to have over conditions in the territory reserved for them by treaty. Chapter 3 describes the Quinault Reservation's initial isolation, eventual allotment to hundreds of outsiders, and ecological degradation under federal management. Then in the 1960s, as recounted in chapter 4, Quinaults were one of many tribes that strengthened their governments when they received unprecedented direct federal funding to plan and implement community development programs during the War on Poverty. Chapter 5 considers two concomitant phenomena that further encouraged tribe leaders' visions of Indian-managed reservations: lawyers working full time for tribal governments and a surge of pan-Indian and intertribal prosovereignty activism.

Meanwhile, Suquamish Indians had contended with early, pervasive non-Indian impacts on their original territory and their treaty-reserved lands, but they were slower than Quinaults to organize a government capable of countering colonial controls. Their story, told in chapter 6, carries into the seventh chapter, which shows that the initial success of the Suquamish Tribe's jurisdiction claims encouraged other tribes to exercise more of their sovereign powers. Chapter 7 details additional events and circumstances of the 1970s that raised Indian expectations of US government support for inclusive tribal jurisdiction on reservations.

Chapter 8's analysis of the Supreme Court ruling against the Suquamish compares the accounts of history told by the parties and their allies, by the court majority, and by legal scholars critical of the decision. It concludes with a reflection on political and practical factors that may explain why other, arguably pertinent history, such as this book explores, did not figure in the court's deliberations.

Chapter 9—a survey of legal and political developments that followed the court's decision—is an epilogue, but it also offers evidence that the central story of this book has not ended. American Indian history will indefinitely be a struggle to negotiate terms of relations with other Americans that can ensure Indian societies' survival. The chapter samples diverse Indian efforts since 1978 to secure control or meaningful influence over factors that determine the viability of tribal community life. One successful effort even enabled tribes to prosecute some non-Indians for domestic violence against Indians.

During the nineteenth century, US Army commander Nelson A. Miles made a name for himself in wars to subjugate indigenous peoples. Setting his gun aside briefly in 1879, he took up a pen to address a dilemma that had bedeviled "the European races" for four hundred years—"the Indian problem." His recommendations appeared in the *North American Review.* "The white race," he wrote, having recently gained "complete control" everywhere in the country, now needed to "devise some practical and judicious system" for governing Indians.[27] Over the following decade, US lawmakers and officials did devise a system for governing Indians much as Miles recommended. Their plan to civilize and assimilate Indians, they predicted, especially by allotting and privatizing tribal lands, would at last solve "the Indian problem." But for tribal communities, one consequence of the program could fairly be dubbed a "non-Indian problem" because allotment and privatization eventually opened Indian reservation lands to non-Indians who did not expect to live there by Indian or by federal rules. *Reclaiming the Reservation* is a story of Indian efforts to solve that non-Indian problem.

1. Facts Are Tough

WHENEVER JUSTICE HARRY BLACKMUN SAT DOWN TO ANALYZE A new case on the Supreme Court docket, he took pen in hand and made a page or two of pithy notes. His cramped cursive and idiosyncratic abbreviations can frustrate an effort to read much of what he wrote, but the first line of notes on case number 76-5729 is unmistakably legible. Under the heading "Suquamish," it says simply, "Indians again."[1]

Did that oddly gratuitous remark express displeasure? Was Blackmun tired of considering disputes involving American Indians? One scholar suggested as much when he wrote that Chief Justice Warren Burger widened a rift with a longtime friend by making Blackmun write "more than his share" of the court's opinions in Indian cases. At least two other justices reportedly did resent Indian cases. According to journalist Bob Woodward, William Rehnquist "had nothing but contempt" for them, and William Brennan "seethed" at having to write the opinion in one that he regarded as "chickenshit."[2]

Perhaps case 76-5729 struck Blackmun as trivial and annoying in some respects. The parties involved were obscure and far from influential. On one side were two young working-class men apparently given to reckless behavior. On the other side was a tiny Indian tribe in Washington State, all but unknown in the nation's capital. The incidents that triggered court proceedings—arrests for alleged misdemeanors—were commonplace. Petitioners Mark Oliphant and Daniel Belgarde sought a ruling that their detention and prosecutions were illegal, but they did not personally have a great deal at stake in case 76-5729. The Suquamish court had long since released them from custody and postponed their trials indefinitely. If the justices disagreed with two lower court rulings and allowed the prosecutions to proceed, the penalties for convictions would at most be modest fines or short-term incarceration.[3] In such circumstances, the Supreme Court could reasonably have declined to hear the case, as it does in all but a few cases that reach it each year.

Nevertheless, influential advocates persuaded a majority of court members that the case presented issues significant and urgent enough to warrant their consideration. Along with the lawyer for Oliphant and Belgarde, Washington State's attorney general asked the justices for a decision. The justices in turn asked the solicitor general, the federal government's top trial lawyer, whether review was desirable, and the answer was a qualified yes.

By the time Harry Blackmun was collecting his thoughts about case 76-5729, the file contained eleven briefs on behalf of twenty-nine amici curiae (friends of the court) who professed to have vital interests in the litigation's outcome. A brief from South Dakota and seven other states asserted that the lower court decisions broke "new ground in the area of tribal criminal jurisdiction" and had "profound implications." Justices may have seen a *Washington Post* article describing the case as one with "enormous" possibilities and "a staggering array" of potential repercussions. A city official in Washington State predicted consequences "so far reaching that you don't even want to contemplate it." An Indian police officer told the *Post* reporter, "Every Indian in the United States is sitting on the edge of his chair," and the Suquamish Tribe's chairman said, "This is it man. This is the biggest shot. This is the whole ballgame."[4]

Thus, on January 9, 1978, Blackmun and seven fellow jurists took their places in the high-back chairs behind the Supreme Court's imposing bench and directed their attention to four lawyers who took turns presenting arguments about the case titled *Mark David Oliphant and Daniel B. Belgarde v. The Suquamish Indian Tribe, et al.*[5] One of the few legible phrases in Blackmun's notes from that hearing reads, "This is a hard argmt & a hard case."

The next day, court members met to air their thoughts and preliminary inclinations regarding the decision to be made. As usual, Blackmun brought a two-sided sheet of paper on which lines marked out a square for each of the other justices. There he noted concerns or views suggested by his colleagues' questions and comments. In the space for Justice Lewis Powell, he scribbled, "This case a farce factually" and "a non-case." Although he did not record an explanation of Powell's opinion or his own reaction to that opinion, Blackmun also took a dim view of the facts reported to the court. In other notes on the case he wrote, "Fax here r tough."[6]

Which facts bothered Blackmun and Powell? Neither man left a clear indication. If by "tough" Blackmun meant confusing or uncertain, he was not referring to the few basic facts that triggered the litigation in 1973; they were undisputed. On separate occasions fourteen months apart, officers deputized by the Suquamish Tribe arrested first Mark Oliphant and then Daniel Belgarde, accusing them of conduct prohibited by the tribe's code of criminal offenses. Judges appointed by the Suquamish governing council arraigned each man on two charges and set trial dates. Soon after their respective arrests, Oliphant and Belgarde petitioned the US district court in Seattle to review the legality of Suquamish authorities' actions, and the tribal court voluntarily suspended its process pending the federal judge's decision. Two other accepted facts were essential elements of the dispute. First, the alleged crimes and arrests occurred within the boundaries of the Suquamish Tribe's reservation. Second, neither accused man was Suquamish. Rather, Oliphant and Belgarde were non-Indians.[7]

Other allegations in the court record complicated this bare-bones narrative and possibly prompted Blackmun's cryptic comment about the facts. Contrary to accepted practice, the opposing parties stated as fact in the Supreme Court some things they had not mentioned in the lower courts. They differed on some details and on the relevance of some circumstances. For example, the petitioners included disparaging descriptions of the tribe's procedures even though they did not ask the court to judge the propriety of those procedures. They also cast doubt on the authenticity of the Suquamish Tribe itself, but rather than offer a direct rebuttal, the tribe's attorney wrote about the tribe as if its bona fides were unquestionable.

The parties agreed that the first arrest came in the wee morning hours of August 19, 1973, when a festival known as Chief Seattle Days was in progress on land belonging to the Suquamish Tribe. According to the report of a "special deputy" employed by the tribe, officers patrolling the festival grounds responded to another deputy's call for help at a camping area where a fight was under way. When help arrived, "the guy who was fighting the people turn on the deputys and hit one of them and knock him down and when the other deputys try to arrest the guy he started to run away but ran into a fence."[8] Mark Oliphant never denied he was the combative "guy." He later told a journalist that the fight was a minor altercation fueled by the abundant liquor "around."[9]

Once the police cornered Oliphant, two of them walked him a short distance to the tribe's office in the town of Suquamish. There, he complained, they shut him in a tiny room without food, heat, or a toilet.[10] After six hours or more, two judges of the tribal court reviewed the deputy's report, signed an order of commitment on charges of assault and battery and resisting arrest, scheduled trial for August 27, and set bail at $100 on each charge. The police then delivered Oliphant to the Bremerton city jail, which had contracted with the Bureau of Indian Affairs to hold the tribe's prisoners.

Perhaps to suggest that the tribe's procedures were irregular, Oliphant alleged that a Suquamish administrator and a policeman called on his wife at home, then came to him with a proposal that he post bail by delivering his automobile and its title to the tribe.[11] Meanwhile, the prisoner contacted a local lawyer, Philip Malone, who arranged with an attorney in Seattle to initiate a federal habeas corpus action for which Malone would ultimately take responsibility. On August 24, after Oliphant promised to appear for trial on September 25, Suquamish judge Cecilia Hawk signed an order for his release.

Daniel Belgarde also engaged Phil Malone's services after Suquamish police jailed him on October 12, 1974. Malone's description of events implied that tribal officers had no business pursuing Belgarde's allegedly speeding pickup truck "on non-Indian land"—a state highway through the reservation—let alone arresting him. According to Malone, the chase ended when a Suquamish vehicle pulled in front of the truck, causing an "unavoidable" collision. The officer who emerged from the car discharged a gun in the pickup's direction. Although a state patrolman and a county sheriff came to the scene, the tribal cops prevented them from enforcing state law.

Suquamish accounts of that night contradicted Malone's on several points. In the district court, the tribe claimed that police chief Carl Big

Man and two deputies began their pursuit of a truck racing recklessly through town streets only after reporting the problem to the county sheriff and waiting nearly two hours for action in response. The tribal officers finally managed to block the truck when it slowed, but just as Big Man opened his door to step out, the pickup accelerated, ramming the police car and injuring Big Man. The truck driver backed up, trying to flee, but stopped after an officer fired a warning shot into the air. Of the three men in the vehicle—driver Belgarde and passengers Mark Oliphant and Brad Bay—Big Man placed only Belgarde under arrest. He then phoned the sheriff again. The deputy who eventually came called in a state patrolman, and the two of them made out an accident report. When they declined to take Belgarde into custody, tribal police did.[12]

Attorney Malone deemed it important to mention that the officers drove Belgarde to a jail sixty miles away, where he remained until posting bail that afternoon. He learned his trial date at a subsequent tribal court arraignment on charges of endangering another person's life and destroying public property. The judge, whom Malone "believed to have little knowledge, training or practice in the law," presided at the back of a barbershop in an eight-by-ten-foot space "not physically capable of handling a fair, free and open public trial or arraignment." "The remaining part of the room," Malone recounted, "was occupied by tribal police officers and persons prejudiced and openly hostile to the Petitioner and non-Indians opposed to the police authority of the Suquamish Indian Tribe over non-Indians."[13]

Justice Blackmun may have frowned at some specifics in this description of Suquamish law enforcement, such as the makeshift court facilities or the solicitation of a car as bail. But "facts r tough" could have pertained instead to circumstances that suggested why antagonistic non-Indians attended Belgarde's arraignment, particularly the fact that the population of the Port Madison Indian Reservation was overwhelmingly non-Indian. Oliphant's original habeas corpus petition supplied the following data.

> Port Madison Indian Reservation consists of approximately 7276 acres of which approximately 63% thereof is owned in fee simple absolute by non-Indians and the remaining 37% is Indian-owned lands subject to the trust status of the United States, consisting mostly of unimproved acreage upon which no persons reside. Residing on the reservation is an

> estimated population of approximately 292
> dwelling units. There lives [*sic*] on the reserva
> members of the Suquamish Indian Tribe. With
> numerous public highways of the State of Washi
> public utilities and other facilities in which neithe
> Tribes nor the United States has any ownership or in

The petition and Supreme Court brief included t ... im that only one tract of reservation land, forty-one acres la ... commu-nity" land. The tribe had never occupied that land, Malone alleged, and in 1969 leased most of it to non-Indian developers for fifty years. (He did not disclose that he was the lessee.) The five remaining acres held a baseball park, a graveyard, and a lot leased for the American Legion hall.[15]

This landownership data drew no specific comment from the tribe's lawyer, Barry Ernstoff. In his brief for the Supreme Court, Ernstoff adopted the statement of facts in the United States' amicus brief, which effectively conceded that Malone's numbers were accurate enough. The reservation was "more than 7,000 acres, of which approximately 36 percent [were] allotments held in trust for individual Indians" and forty-one additional acres were "tribal lands."

Ernstoff did contradict Malone's Indian population figures. Citing a tribal employee's affidavit, he told the Supreme Court, "There were 550 members of the Suquamish Tribe at the time of the events in issue. Approximately 150 of those members lived on the Port Madison Reservation. The remaining members lived in nearby communities, which afforded better employment opportunities. In addition, 50 Indians with other tribal affiliations lived on the Reservation."[16] Otherwise, Ernstoff did not make an issue of population statistics. He could not dispute what they showed: a great majority of reservation residents and landowners were not Indians. Nor did he deny a fact that Justice Blackmun highlighted more than once: because the non-Indians were not tribe members, they could not participate as voters in Suquamish Tribe decision-making.

Population and landownership statistics were apparently of little or no importance to the district court judge. He cited a Supreme Court decision from 1909 for the principle that all tracts within Indian reservation boundaries remain part of a reservation "until separated therefrom by Congress," and he noted that Congress never acted to diminish the Port Madison r boundaries were set in 1874. Did Blackmun, in contrast, non-Indian ownership figures worthy of consideration? That be the significance of another puzzling note in his papers—"thinness [of the] reservation."

The case record contained possibly disconcerting claims on another subject: the recent history and origin of the Suquamish tribal government. On one hand, attorney Ernstoff—seemingly unconcerned that the tribe's small size and limited land holdings might undercut his claim—wrote in a brief for the district court, "The Suquamish Indian Tribe . . . has retained full control over the tribal administration of justice on the Reservation. An extensive and comprehensive Law and Order Code was adopted by the tribe at a meeting of the full membership of the tribe."[17] On the other hand, petitioners Oliphant and Belgarde asserted in the Supreme Court that Kitsap County provided law enforcement for the reservation's non-Indian residents—a claim the county backed with its own brief.

In one memorandum Malone declared flatly, "The Suquamish Indians have not had a tribal community at Port Madison for quite some time." He alleged further that the tribe and its members "ceased to occupy any of the lands as a tribal community and ceased to maintain any customs, government, culture, regulations and/or authority over those lands and persons therein" until 1965, "at which time it received recognization [*sic*] from the United States Government" and adopted a constitution.[18] Ernstoff—faced with insinuations that the tribe and its government institutions were recent creations of dubious legitimacy—put on record an alternative political history. Since American officials and Suquamish leaders signed a treaty in 1855, he wrote, the United States had never not recognized a distinct Suquamish Tribe. Tribe members acted in 1916 to establish a formal governing structure, as specified in a document attached to the district court brief. "The fact that the governmental organization of the Indians . . . was in disarray prior to the adoption of their 1965 Constitution is neither surprising nor relevant," Ernstoff maintained. "The Government's policy of allotting land to individual Indians had discouraged tribal government," but that policy had since been reversed, encouraging the recent reorganization of a tribal community that had never passed out of existence. Briefs for the United States largely corroborated this claim of tribal continuity and federal support for a modern Suquamish government.[19]

Even so, no one claimed that the Suquamish government had a long record of reservation-wide law enforcement. In fact, policing was a brand-new venture for the tribe when its cops clapped handcuffs on Mark Oliphant. The "extensive" law and order code mentioned in a Suquamish brief had taken effect less than three weeks earlier, on July 29, 1973. The court that would enforce the code came into existence the following day when tribe members Grace Duggan and Cecilia Hawk accepted appointments as chief judge and associate judge respectively. In federal court records, the word "provisional" was part of the tribal court's name. No pleading, brief, or exhibit explained why.[20]

Without suggesting that his clients doubted their authority or ability to enforce the new code, Barry Ernstoff stated that Suquamish officials pragmatically sought assistance as needed from the other governments that claimed some jurisdiction on the reservation—the county and United States. His account of circumstances that left tribal police to cope alone with intoxicated brawlers was quoted as fact in the ruling of the Ninth Circuit Court of Appeals.

> When the Suquamish Indian Tribe planned their annual Chief Seattle Days celebration, the Tribe knew that thousands of people would be congregating in a small area near the tribal traditional encampment grounds. . . . A request was made of Kitsap County to provide law enforcement assistance. One deputy was available for approximately one 8-hour period during the entire weekend. The tribe also requested law enforcement assistance from the Bureau of Indian Affairs, Western Washington Agency. They were told that they would have to provide their own law enforcement out of tribal funds and with tribal personnel. . . . The only law enforcement officers available to deal with the situation were tribal deputies. Without the exercise of jurisdiction by the Tribe and its courts, there could have been no law enforcement whatsoever on the Reservation during this major gathering which clearly created a potentially dangerous situation with regard to law enforcement. Public safety is an underpinning of a political entity. If tribal members cannot protect themselves from offenders, there will be powerful motivation for such tribal members to leave the Reservation. . . . Minor offenses committed by non-Indians within Indian reservations frequently go unpunished.[21]

"Tough" as such facts of contemporary Suquamish circumstances may have seemed to Justice Blackmun, they concerned him less than facts from earlier decades. Yet indisputable, pertinent facts about more distant history were also scarce in case 76-5729. For instance, the 1855 treaty between Suquamish Indians and the United States—the legal basis for the reservation where the tribe claimed jurisdiction—was a settled, essential fact, but the treaty was opaque on the issue before the court in 1978. No language there explicitly addressed Suquamish authority to govern non-Indians, either acknowledging such authority or forbidding the tribe to assert it. Less ambiguous landownership records documented numerous transfers of reservation land to non-Indians, but nothing in the case file explained how or why those conveyances occurred. Justices were thus free to make a variety of inferences about Suquamish conceptions of their reservation and the depth of their current belief in the tribe's broad jurisdiction there.

Nonetheless, Blackmun expected facts from long-term history to reveal the correct resolution of *Oliphant v. Suquamish Indian Tribe.* One of his notes on the case reads, "This gets down to a basic [philosophy] (and [history]) of [Indian] govt." By "this" he meant more than the legality of the Suquamish Tribe's arrests and prosecution of Oliphant and Belgarde. The justices had agreed to decide whether any tribe in the United States ever had jurisdiction to prosecute a non-Indian lawbreaker. Blackmun's papers show that his thinking about this task was consonant with that of a law clerk who wrote, "I find the weight of history heavy in this case." But Blackmun did not let history's great weight paralyze him; he felt equipped to examine it and determine which way the scales tipped. Midway through his recorded thoughts on case 76-5729 was this declaration: "I am [satisfied that history] . . . [does not] support [the Indians]."

That is a firm declaration, but it is by no means unambiguous. After all, the word "history" has several meanings. Dictionaries commonly list three connotations: all events in the past, accounts of the past, and the study of the past. Either of the first two meanings could have been on Blackmun's mind when he jotted, "Modern 'thought' has [changed], but [that does not change the history]." Nor is it clear what he meant by "history" when dictating the following sentence of a memorandum: "History would seem to suggest that the tribes possessed no jurisdiction over non-Indians."

Did Blackmun consider the many kinds of information "history" can encompass or the many possible ways to select, present, and interpret information about the past? As British historian Eric Hobsbawm observed, "In theory, the past—all the past, anything and everything that has happened to date—constitutes history." However, the concept of history has practical utility only if we select and order knowledge about that infinity of past occurrences; and so we do. Our selections are unavoidably influenced by "where we stand in regard to the past, what the relations are between past, present and future."[22] Hence the *New Oxford American Dictionary*'s definition of history as "the whole series of past events connected to someone or something." Blackmun's notes reflected this relational conception of history. Connection to "something" was implicit in his conviction that "history" would determine whether an Indian tribe's prosecution of non-Indians in the 1970s was permissible. The events of interest would be those with a connection to the present and future of the Suquamish Tribe, other tribes, and the tribes' relations with non-Indians.

Blackmun's view of events necessarily depended on where he stood "in regard to the past." They were the consequence of what he looked for and could see from his perch in the United States Supreme Court. As a jurist, he expected to answer the central question in case 76-5729 by examining particular kinds of past events. From a vast array of information about decades of human activity and experience, he would identify as apropos a limited record. In one note, he mentioned a time span he considered relevant. Regarding the tribe's belief in its jurisdiction, he jotted, "The [assumption] 1850–1950 [was] just [the] other way." Other notes and a dictated memorandum indicate the kind of occurrences Blackmun deemed salient. He wanted "history" to tell him whether certain people in the designated period—particularly US government officials—assumed that Indian tribes were within their rights to take actions like those the Suquamish had taken against Mark Oliphant and Daniel Belgarde.

Using information about the past as a guide to resolving present conflict is not unusual for Supreme Court justices. Indeed, that is arguably the essence of appellate judges' role in American legal culture. They are expected to ascertain and apply principles established or articulated in previous cases involving similar issues. Other legal history is often germane too—not only laws and regulations of government bodies with recognized authority but also the intentions of legislators who enacted laws or the understanding of administrators who applied them. This deference to judicial precedent and government practice, Hobsbawm wrote, makes law an aspect of human affairs in which "the past retains its authority." Conversely, constitutional law scholar Charles Miller noted, it makes judges authorities on the past. Because the Supreme Court is an accepted interpreter of "products of the past" such as treaties and laws, the court has "become a public interpreter of American political history."[23]

However, as Miller and Canadian historian D. G. Bell have explained, what judges do is not history in the sense that historians generally conceive of it. Unlike history scholars, judges do not consider historical records with the aim of understanding the past in all its complexity. For jurists and other legal professionals engaged in litigation, history has a restricted, utilitarian meaning. They consult it simply to resolve present-day legal problems. They also "sit as passive receptors of information" presented by advocates and rarely concern themselves with the contexts of those facts.[24]

Thus, to Justice Blackmun in 1978, another case about Indians meant that he and his colleagues had to determine the significance of past court opinions and other government records concerning the nature and powers of Indian tribes. Since the creation of the republic, the terms of Indians' relations to non-Indians, and tribes' relations to non-Indian governments, had been at issue in numerous acts and decisions of United States legislators, judges, and executive officers. To Supreme Court members' way of thinking—that is, in the culture or discipline of American law—those acts and decisions were essential context for deliberations in the Suquamish jurisdiction dispute. Indeed, that context would likely furnish the grounds for the ruling they ultimately issued.

For judges and justices, the primary sources of historical information germane to Indian law cases have been previous court rulings, lawyers' briefs, and law clerks' memoranda. Those may even have provided Harry Blackman's entire education on Indians' history. Granted, that was not a trifling amount of reading. Since joining the Supreme Court in 1970, Blackmun had considered at least twenty-three cases concerning Indians.[25] (That alone could account for his "Indians again" note.) By the time the Suquamish case reached his desk, he had certainly read a substantial number of judicial opinions or opinion summaries that told him how his predecessors on the court conceived of Indian tribes' status and power. He was familiar with a body of jurist-authored history that acknowledged aboriginal Indian societies' autonomy and self-governance. He knew about later court opinions approving the federal government contention that the US Constitution and Indians' "dependency" permitted nearly unlimited congressional control of Indians, but he was also aware that the government had never renounced all Indian treaties or purported to abolish all tribes. In fact, Blackmun had authored an opinion in 1974 that affirmed the United States' continuing "special relationship" with Indian tribes as "quasi-sovereign" political entities.[26]

If the high court—sometime before 1978—had issued an opinion that clearly identified the contemporary components of tribal sovereignty, or if Congress had turned out legislation explicitly delineating the acceptable scope of tribal jurisdiction, the justices' survey of legal history bearing on case number 76-5729 could have been brief, confined to little more than a summary of the pertinent recent ruling or statute and its general background. The lower court judges who denied Oliphant's petition had already done something similar, even though no such clear directive had issued from the Supreme Court or Congress. They explained their decisions with tidy historical synopses. The court of appeals opinion, for instance, mentioned two Supreme Court decisions in the 1830s, two more in the late 1800s, and a handful of rulings since the 1950s.

Philip Malone thought a much more extensive survey of legal history was necessary. In his petition for Supreme Court review, he signaled his intent to recount a history spanning two hundred years, during which numerous treaties, statutes, court opinions, and government officials had things to say about tribal powers. By granting Malone's petition, the justices effectively consented to consider that long historical record. Their consequent reading would consist in large part of lawyers' memoranda that highlighted arguably relevant parts of the record and analyzed their significance for the issue of tribal jurisdiction. It was a record of so much change and contradictory action over time that advocates and opponents of expansive tribal power alike could find precedents for their positions.

Thus, as Harry Blackmun foresaw, the Supreme Court's decision in *Oliphant v. Suquamish Tribe* would ultimately turn on an account of the past that a majority of justices endorsed. It would be history that reflected their distinctive way as judges of acquiring, selecting, and using information about the past. But beyond the courtroom—in homes and meeting rooms on Indian reservations, on reservation rivers and beaches and highways, in federal and state government legislatures and offices, in law firms, and in hotels where leaders of tribes gathered for conferences—there was much more to the history of the tribal jurisdiction issue than the justices would consider. As historian Fred Hoxie wrote, "If we open the door of the Supreme Court building and begin asking the people waiting on the steps how they got there, the historical questions begin multiplying like white rabbits."[27]

Among the people waiting on those steps, at least figuratively, were Indians and their lawyers from the Quinault Reservation. What brought them there, wondering how the court would rule on a dispute from the Suquamish reservation, is a story worth telling for several reasons. Although Quinault leaders were not alone or certifiably first in the modern era to assert jurisdiction over non-Indians, and although their influence on other tribes is hard to determine with confidence, they as well as allies from other Northwest tribes moved into national Indian leadership during the period when Indians elsewhere in the United States were also thinking that they could and should govern non-Indians on their reservations. Tracing how the Quinault, Suquamish, and other tribal governments came to believe that, then following their subsequent activities, enables us to see how a national movement for tribal control in reservation homelands developed.

Also waiting for the Supreme Court's ruling were non-Indians likely to find themselves on reservations where tribes would assert control. Many feared that control and considered it unfair. Their concerns are a necessary part of the story, but the account that follows focuses primarily on Indians and a story the Supreme Court did not hear or acknowledge—history that explains why and how Indians in the 1970s proposed a significant change in the terms of their subordination to the United States.

2. Promises of Power

For four days in 1965, a US Senate subcommittee took comments on a set of legislative proposals concerning Indian tribal governments and court operations. The first Indian witness spoke the second day. Dispensing with opening formalities, James Jackson launched right into a grievance against Washington State. Two years earlier, he said, the state had taken jurisdiction away from tribes despite their objections and "the very strong protest of the Quinault Tribe." Quinaults now wanted Jackson, their president, to voice support for Senate Bill 966 because it would preclude such a preemption of tribal authority. Tribes would then be free to request or reject state jurisdiction on their reservations. Given the choice, Jackson added, Quinaults would certainly vote "no" because their experience with state officials had been "poor." Besides, the state "never did provide adequate law enforcement."[1]

Nearly every Indian tribe and organization the senators heard from, in oral testimony or written comments, took a position on SB 966, and they all echoed Jackson's reasons for favoring it. Unlike Public Law 280, in force since 1953, the new legislation would require tribes' consent before states could exercise jurisdiction over Indians on reservations. By also letting states relinquish jurisdiction, SB 966 would give Quinaults and other tribes a chance to reverse PL 280's effects.

An attorney for six Northern Plains tribes said the proposed changes were long overdue. "Of all Indian legislation on the books," he stated, "none is better known to Indians, or more generally despised, than Public Law 280." The reason: it authorized state rule without giving tribes a vote. That disregard of Indian desires drew criticism in 1953, not only from tribes but also from President Dwight Eisenhower, who deemed PL 280 "un-Christianlike" and contrary to principles of democracy. Ever since Eisenhower signed the act anyway, Indians had proposed an amendment similar to SB 966 during each session of Congress.[2]

Tribal representatives' unanimity on SB 966 did not reflect general Indian solidarity or agreement on every issue the senators were considering. More than one Indian speaker stressed the distinctiveness of his tribe's political history and traditions. Others urged the lawmakers to legislate with the great diversity of tribal cultures, experiences, and situations in mind. Consensus on the need for tribal consent was not even paired with a consensus that state jurisdiction was undesirable. Although several Indians proclaimed their people's long-standing aversion to state law enforcement, a few spoke for tribes that welcomed it. In contrast to Sioux who boasted of defeating successive South Dakota bids for jurisdiction, including one pertaining just to highways, Lester Oliver described "excellent" White Mountain Apache relations with the Arizona highway patrol. Overall, Indians' testimony revealed that their views on federal, state, and tribal authority varied with local history and circumstances.[3]

Yet underlying Indians' quarrel with PL 280 was a shared conception of their tribes. Vine Deloria, Jr., executive director of the National Congress of American Indians (NCAI), put it plainly when a subcommittee lawyer asked why Indians would be more fearful than immigrants of absorption into "melting pot society." Because, Deloria replied, "we were here as independent nations, and treaties were made with us." Indian tribes understood themselves as historically self-governing peoples whose negotiated pacts with the United States confirmed their nationhood. To change the terms of those pacts, the United States should renegotiate with the tribes. Contemporary tribal groups were "in transition to new forms," Deloria conceded, but their external relations still reflected their political autonomy. He said, "The organization I run is kind of a miniature United Nations."[4]

A few Indian spokesmen used a weighty term for their people's political essence: sovereignty. Written comments from Pojoaque Pueblo stated, "The status of sovereignty which we have always enjoyed has made us dedicated to the task of preserving it." Crow Tribe chairman Edison Real Bird opposed a proposed requirement that tribal governments adopt a specified bill of rights because that would "subject the tribal sovereignty of self-government to the Federal Government." The Yakima Tribe's submission declared, "The powers of an Indian tribe in the administration of justice derive from the substantive powers of self-government which are legally recognized to fall within the domain of tribal sovereignty."[5]

Although "sovereignty" was an old term for Indians' historical autonomy, it did not trip frequently from tribe leaders' tongues in 1965. That was about to change. Within the next few years, Indians across the United States would use the word more and more often to denote both their conception of their original nationhood and their modern political aspirations. They would take part in a movement to rescue the notion of Indian sovereignty from threatened irrelevance and give it meaning suited to contemporary circumstances. A key stimulus of the movement was anger at the US government's decision in 1953 to abandon the responsibilities it had assumed for Indian tribes, dismantle reservations, and engineer Indians' absorption into a political system that housed only two kinds of sovereigns—federal and state governments.

Tracing the transmission of an idea involves considerable guesswork, especially transmission among people like Indians with their limited influence on the dominant institutions of power and information diffusion. An account of the increase in Indian assertions of sovereignty must therefore be more suggestive than conclusive, but contributing developments are apparent if we examine Indian reactions to Public Law 280 and its parent policy, known as termination, then view those reactions in the light of hopes and expectations engendered by Indian experiences during the 1930s and World War II.[6]

Key federal government policies of the 1930s—the so-called Indian New Deal—endorsed a conception of indigenous North American peoples as autonomous nations. Early US treaties had acknowledged that nationhood and autonomy, and American jurists and some Indians had recognized "sovereign" as an apt English term for it. Through subsequent generations, even as the United States overpowered indigenous peoples coast to coast, the notion of Indian sovereignty endured both in tribal communities and in US law. It took on renewed, inspirational meaning in the mid-twentieth century as colonized peoples elsewhere in the world gained independence while the United States proposed to deny its indigenous peoples the same opportunity for self-determination.

TRIBALISM UNDER THREAT

In the winter of 1954–55, the prospect of subjection to state authority troubled many Indians on reservations. Harold Fey heard this repeatedly from tribe members he met during a tour of the West. Fey, a white clergyman and writer-editor for the nondenominational journal *Christian Century*, "found Indian leaders full of foreboding" about the recently announced federal plan to cede responsibility for Indian affairs to the states. State governments, they assumed, would be more hostile toward Indians than federal policy makers because states were in direct competition with tribes for land, tax dollars, and services.[7]

The apprehensive Indians were aware and thankful that American law had historically prohibited states from governing Indians on reservations. As the Supreme Court explained in *Worcester v. Georgia*, "The whole intercourse between the United States and [Indian nations] was, by our Constitution and laws, vested in the Government of the United States." Therefore, state laws could "have no force" in tribal territory except with the tribes' consent or "in conformity with treaties and with the acts of Congress."[8] For more than a century after that decision in 1832, Congress largely maintained barriers to state jurisdiction.

At the end of World War II, however, lawmakers began considering legislation that would remove the barriers. They did not doubt their right to take that step; the Supreme Court had declared in 1903 that congressional power to govern Indian affairs was nearly unlimited.[9] On August 1, 1953, Congress invoked that broad power in order to relinquish it. With the goal of ending federal supervision and protection of Indians entirely, legislators resolved to dismantle the laws and administrative apparatus that set Indians apart from other Americans, preventing their complete political emancipation and integration. The passage of Public Law 280 two weeks later kicked that dismantling process into gear. PL 280 directly delegated Indian country jurisdiction to six specific states and permitted any other state to assume jurisdiction as well. Federal government withdrawal from the management of Indian affairs was under way.

Congressional supporters of the new policy had objectives that included shrinking the federal bureaucracy and removing impediments to the development and taxation of tribal lands.[10] By also pitching the federal withdrawal plan as the liberation of Indians from oppressive US guardianship, proponents appealed to some tribe members who resented Bureau of Indian Affairs (BIA) domination of tribal life. Casting the plan as Indians' opportunity for self-determination had even broader appeal. Beyond Indian country, "self-determination" was a popular term for the aspirations of conquered and colonized peoples—aspirations the United States had endorsed. To some Indians, including several founders of the National Congress of American Indians, self-determination meant the right to choose full assimilation into US civic life.[11] But when members of Congress suggested that state jurisdiction over Indian communities would be a nonnegotiable condition of phasing out the federal guardianship, most advocates for Indian rights were taken aback. A unilateral alteration of tribes' relationship to the United States did not comport with their concept of self-determination.

Alarms sounded in the NCAI when legislation authorizing state jurisdiction on reservations passed the House of Representatives in 1948. A "special bulletin" went out to member tribes, bringing news that HR 4725 would not give tribes a choice between state law enforcement and other means of suppressing crime. "In prior bills of this sort," the bulletin noted, "this choice has always been given to the affected tribes, and the bills . . . have all been passed at the request or with the approval of the tribes involved." The latest House proposal "would not even take into consideration the extent to which many tribes who have adopted their own codes and established their own courts . . . are handling their own law and order problems in exemplary fashion."[12]

Meanwhile, the Senate was considering bills to impose state jurisdiction on reservations in New York. Rather than include a clause giving tribes a choice in the matter, lawmakers merely invited comments on the legislation. During three days of hearings, they got an earful from indignant Indians. The bills "by their very nature would violate every provision of our treaty for self-government," declared Alice Lee Jemison, a Seneca. Tuscarora chief Harry Patterson protested that the legislation would replicate a wrong done in 1924 when Congress unilaterally conferred "blanket citizenship" on Indians. "There has been a violation of the treaty," he said, "on account of not asking the Indian people." Speaking for the Six Nations Iroquois Confederacy, William Smith said, "The Six Nation [*sic*] people being an independent people are desirous of retaining their own sovereignty."[13]

Advocates of a tribe-by-tribe opportunity to refuse state jurisdiction could feel validated the next year when President Harry Truman vetoed the initial version of an act authorizing aid programs on the Navajo and Hopi reservations because its provision for state jurisdiction would "conflict with one of the fundamental principles of Indian law . . . , namely, the principle of respect for tribal self-determination in matters of local government." The president's stand cheered the multitude of Americans, non-Indian and Indian, who had urged a veto. Their letters referred to treaty promises, to tribes as "nations," to Indian expectations of home rule or self-government, and—in at least one instance—to tribal sovereignty.[14]

US officials and lawmakers also heard from some Indians who favored a general transfer of jurisdiction to the states, but the far more numerous objections to a unilateral transfer gave Congress fair notice that protests would greet the passage of PL 280. It was the legislators and president who served up a surprise instead. Congress approved the bill with minimal notice to concerned Indians, and Eisenhower signed it despite his qualms about its inconsistency with American political and moral principles.[15]

Adding to Indians' sense of betrayal was the language of House Concurrent Resolution 108, approved two weeks before PL 280. It declared flatly that federal responsibility and services for Indian tribes should be terminated, and it mandated administrative steps toward that end.[16] A few months later, at a convention with the theme "Crisis in Indian Affairs," NCAI leadership rallied members to fight the plan, which they interpreted as a means of compelling tribes to disband and members to assimilate into the American populace. While continuing to denounce handovers of jurisdiction without their consent, the tribes would also try to prevent US abdication of other treaty and statutory pledges to Indians.[17]

In the ensuing campaign against the federal termination policy, NCAI representatives and allies appealed to the ideals of self-determination and consent of the governed. They emphasized that moral obligations came with the United States' superior power and its historic promises to Indians. Some spoke of their reservations' vital functions as tribal homelands and as tangible foundations for the right to be Indian.[18] At the heart of these arguments was the idea Vine Deloria expressed in his 1965 Senate testimony: Indian populations had originally been independent nations with dominion over territory. The United States made treaties that acknowledged as much and brought Indians under federal protection as nations. Most of those treaties remained US law.

During his 1955 western tour, Harold Fey saw that this view of history, together with other stories from the past, strongly influenced Indians' gloomy views of the latest turn in federal policy. Indians "have long memories," he observed. "They recall other periods like this one and remember what happened then." Still, they could not believe the United States would abolish the Bureau of Indian Affairs and thus "finally and irrevocably violate what [the Indian] regards as a sacred and perpetual trust."[19]

The memories shaping Indian reactions to the federal termination policy were not solely about old "sacred" pledges to sovereign tribes and US betrayal of those pledges. Many Indians also recalled relatively recent federal rhetoric and policies supporting tribal autonomy. Paul Rosier is one of several historians who have explained Indian resistance to the termination policy as an effort to salvage such favorable legacies of the past. In Rosier's words, "Native people . . . understood that the coercive behavior of the federal government not only rolled back gains of sovereignty from the Indian New Deal era but also represented a form of total war against Native Americans' right, embedded in instruments of international law called treaties, to preserve their Indianness and their 'reserved homelands.'"[20]

NEW DEAL PROMISES

New Deal programs did promote gains in tribal power, and they led Indians to expect more. The detribalization policy of the 1950s therefore struck many Indians as dishonorable backsliding. Take the reaction to HR 4725 in 1948. NCAI argued that a vote to impose New York state law without tribes' consent would not only violate US treaties with tribes; it would "mark the first major retreat in 30 years from an established policy of giving the Indians control of their local reservation problems." It would break the promise of the Indian Reorganization Act "that if the tribes would do thus and such they should have the rights of self-government."[21]

Although the Indian Reorganization Act of 1934 (IRA) did not explicitly promise tribes general sovereignty, it sanctioned their establishment of governments with all powers "vested by existing law," including the power to prevent alienation of tribal assets and negotiate with other governments. The act's sponsor, newly appointed Indian affairs commissioner John Collier, hoped for open-ended congressional consent to Indian self-government. Telling tribal leaders that he foresaw a time when Indian communities would have "complete supervision over internal affairs," he initially proposed a bill with an extensive list of tribal powers, such as administering justice and managing land reserved for tribes by the United States. Years later, Collier claimed that his agency had "tried to extend to the tribes a self-governing self-determination without any limit."[22]

In Congress, however, Collier faced lawmakers who saw his reform plan as an unacceptably radical change from the long-standing policy of discouraging Indians' tribal ties. Adjusting his pitch to that reality, Collier said he envisioned Indian government on a modest scale, conducted by United States permission. Combing through his testimony, Russel Barsh and James Youngblood Henderson found him likening the proposed tribal governments variously to "'municipal government,' 'town government,' and 'little colonies,' with powers limited to 'matters of local concern.'"[23]

The act that Congress ultimately approved signaled that Indian self-governance would be restricted in scope, and supreme power would remain with the US government. For example, it required Interior Department approval of the tribes' constitutions. In fact, simply by enacting the legislation, Congress asserted tribes' subservience to federal power.[24] Nevertheless, the IRA's endorsement of tribal self-government also represented a substantial change in official expectations for Indian tribes—expectations that Collier encouraged in numerous descriptions of the new law and his agency's mission.

When informing BIA employees and tribe leaders by newsletter that the president had signed the act on June 18, 1934, Collier wrote, "Whether that date shall be known hereafter as the Independence Day of Indian history will be determined by the Indians themselves." The act "frees them to do what they want to do and need to do."[25] He predicted meaningful increases in the power tribes would exercise. His 1934 annual report pledged that implementing the IRA would give tribes "limited but real power, and authority over their own affairs." "In the past," he wrote, "they managed their own affairs effectively whenever there was no white interference for selfish ends. They can learn to do it again under present conditions with the aid of modern organization methods, once they realize that these organizations will be permanent and will not be subject to the whims of changing administrations." Collier anticipated that tribes organized under the IRA would ultimately become capable of functioning with "a minimum of governmental interference."[26]

Two other architects of the Indian New Deal share responsibility for raising Indian hopes of empowerment. Interior Department solicitor Nathan Margold and assistant-then-associate solicitor Felix Cohen concluded from their study of legal doctrine and history that Indians did not need the United States to tell them they had a right to self-government. The right was inherent in the autonomy Indians had enjoyed as North America's indigenous peoples. US courts and executive officials in the early republic, like Spanish legal scholars and English officials before them, acknowledged Indians' independent nationhood, occasionally referring to it specifically as sovereignty. Relations with colonizing nations had diminished the range of Indians' original sovereign powers, Margold and Cohen conceded, but in principle if not in fact, tribes retained any attribute of sovereignty they had not relinquished. Sovereignty was not an all-or-nothing state or quality; in modern law, it could be less than absolute.[27]

This reasoning informed Cohen's work as he helped draft Collier's initial bill. When objections from lawmakers forced Collier to accept legislation that set stricter limits on independent tribal action, Cohen and Margold looked to legal doctrine for work-arounds. Margold identified one opening in a memorandum titled "The Powers of an Indian Tribe." Every tribe originally had numerous powers besides those specified in the IRA, Margold wrote. Unless any of those powers had since been renounced or nullified, the tribe still had them all. Congress tacitly conceded this in the Reorganization Act by providing that three listed powers were in addition to those "vested . . . by existing law." Thus, in Margold's analysis, US domination had restricted tribes' sovereignty in some respects but not extinguished it. Margold's memorandum, which struck some old-guard administrators as dangerously radical, remained an internal document, out of the public eye, but it was available to bureau personnel who helped Indians write constitutions, some of whom were Indians. Felix Cohen laid out the same argument for readers of *The American Indian*, an Indian-published magazine with national circulation.[28]

One IRA provision was a ground-breaking concession to Indians' desire for self-determination. The act would "not apply to any reservation wherein a majority of the adult Indians" voted "against its application" at a "special election duly called by the Secretary of the Interior."[29] Furthermore, a vote for application did not obligate a tribe to establish a government. Ironically, Collier did not leave tribes to ponder on their own whether they should organize IRA governments. Maintaining that corporate-style constitutional self-rule was essential for Indians' welfare and perhaps for their continued existence, he orchestrated an intensive BIA effort to win tribes' acceptance of the act and then to spur their adoption of constitutions. The law that Collier celebrated as freeing Indians to do what they wanted he described elsewhere as "a *command* to the various tribes to assert their right to run their own affairs."[30]

Felix Cohen's assignments included preparing BIA field agents for their role in the tribes' constitution-writing efforts—a role he also assumed at times. In a memorandum intended for those agents, Cohen emphasized that a constitution should state the governing body's powers clearly and comprehensively. "In effect," he added, "this statement will be a declaration of independence for the Indian tribe. . . . Complete freedom from Indian Office supervision may be secured by a tribe which demonstrates its capacity to care for its own affairs." Cohen's memorandum went to the commissioner and not much farther, but his generous conception of tribal sovereignty gained visibility later by means of a substantial published work—his *Handbook of Federal Indian Law*.[31] That historic digest of legal history and doctrine became available to BIA employees and tribal governments in 1941. Until the bureau replaced Cohen's opus in 1958 with a volume that discounted the tribes' autonomy, the *Handbook* informed readers that "each Indian tribe begins its relationship with the Federal Government as a sovereign power."[32]

The Margold/Cohen argument about inherent, continuing tribal sovereignty encountered nonbelievers in Congress and the BIA, but it rang true in Indian country, where people knew that their indigenous ancestors had governed themselves in autonomous nations or communities. Many tribe members had kept alive memories or orally transmitted traditions concerning those days. As Cohen recognized in several publications, elements of ancient political institutions and practices persisted in some Indian communities, from Iroquois longhouses to New Mexico pueblos.[33] A few tribes even openly refused to acknowledge the supremacy claimed by the federal government. Among the undaunted holdouts were traditionalists of the Six Nations Iroquois Confederacy or League, the Haudenosaunee. Drawing on history related by generations of forebears, they maintained that eighteenth-century treaties with the United States explicitly recognized their sovereignty, which they had yet to surrender.[34]

Yet for many other tribe members in 1934, the days of largely unfettered self-government were gone—the subject of stories passed down from parents or grandparents. During five or six decades of US domination, numerous ancestral Indian governance systems had collapsed. Where tribes were left without an effective political culture, BIA functionaries ruled. By Collier's count, that was the situation on more than half the reservations.[35] Although he and top deputies expressed hope that tribes could draw on aboriginal traditions when organizing under the IRA, Collier also believed that political modernization was essential for Indian prosperity. The Reorganization Act enabled tribal communities to form the kind of corporate governments he thought they needed to hold their own against powerful twentieth-century, non-Indian-controlled institutions.

Although Collier sometimes implied that the New Deal opening for Indian self-government was unprecedented and a complete reversal of federal policy, some reservations already had BIA-sanctioned Indian governments.[36] American efforts to undermine traditional tribal leadership had always coexisted with a federal need for some tribal decision-making and self-policing. For example, US treaties, laws, or desires to appear honorable usually required a show of Indian consent to a transaction involving tribal land and resources. Convening general Indian councils for that purpose was cumbersome and could backfire. Therefore, as proposals for such transactions multiplied in the early 1900s, the Indian Office pressured tribes to install smaller governing councils. In some places, it was Indians who wanted those new forms of governance.[37] A 1947 BIA assessment of the Collier years stated, "The first suggestion for the incorporation of tribes was advanced in 1927 by the Klamath Indian tribe of Oregon," with input from other Indians.[38]

At the Rosebud and Pine Ridge Sioux reservations, among others, BIA-initiated councils proved to have minds of their own. They launched efforts to establish governments with more autonomy and more purposes than federal officials advocated. According to historian Richmond Clow, the Sioux wrote and adopted seven constitutions between 1916 and 1933.[39] That did not make them exceptional. Political scientist David Wilkins discovered that approximately sixty tribes had constitutions or comparable documents on file with the Interior Department when the Indian Reorganization Act passed, and at least forty predated the act by many years. In the case of two Sioux tribes, and presumably in other cases, the Indian bureau accepted the Indian-produced charters as tribal law.[40]

Some Indians therefore reacted to the IRA with their ongoing self-governance in mind. At a gathering where delegates from Northwest tribes heard BIA officials describe Collier's initial bill, Tulalip representative Wilfred Steve commented, "Self-government is not new to us, we have been working on it for over twenty years." Harry Shale said Quinaults had decided to reject Collier's grant of self-government because they were already self-governing. Joseph Hillaire, secretary of the Lummi Tribe, congratulated Collier by letter for recognizing that some Indians, like him, were well prepared for modernized self-government.[41]

Whether Indians wanted to salvage traditional governments, modernize their governing practices, or maintain political structures approved by federal overseers, Collier promised Interior Department respect for their decisions. Throughout his twelve years in office, he said that tribes could eventually assume all the responsibilities of other local governments. In 1944, he even described Indian tribes as dynamic "sovereign nations."[42] If BIA practices had been consistent with such rhetoric, Indian disappointment with Collier's administration would have been rarer than it ultimately was, but Indian New Deal realities seldom matched the high expectations he encouraged. In practice, significant federal restraints on tribal government power persisted.

The constitution-drafting process was partly responsible for continuing restrictions. To help Indians write constitutions that would meet with the required BIA approval, Collier assigned his staff a leading role in the process. Special agents left the national office for the reservations carrying a prototype constitution prepared by Interior Department lawyers. Although Felix Cohen had announced that a primary function of tribal constitutions was to "reassert and reestablish the ancient powers of the tribe," he and his colleagues chose contemporary non-Indian municipalities as the model. BIA advisers invited Indians to suggest alternatives or modifications that reflected tribal traditions, but they deemed many

By the time of this appearance before the Senate Indian Affairs Subcommittee in 1940, Indian commissioner John Collier had overseen much less progress toward tribal self-government under the Indian Reorganization Act than he had promised. Impediments included Indian objections to BIA-prescribed models of tribal government as well as opposition in Congress. Courtesy of the Library of Congress, LC-DIG-hec-28781.

suggestions unworkable or impermissible, from governance by traditional chiefs to tribal jurisdiction over criminal non-Indian conduct.[43]

Given the preceding half century of US-enforced Indian political weakness and BIA claims of expertise, it is not surprising that many a new tribal constitution conformed to the bureau's prototype. In most small western Washington tribes, for instance, constitution-drafting councils or committees accepted federal agents' word about what was possible. They copied the short list of government powers listed in the IRA, and if they added to that list, they provided for Interior Department review of all tribal legislation.[44] On the Sioux reservations that Clow studied, constitutions requiring secretarial approval of ordinances replaced constitutions containing no such provision. Apparently, Clow concluded, "Indian service personnel considered the new tribal governments . . . as mere advisory bodies to the Office of Indian Affairs."[45]

Then again, no constitution would have been proof against BIA power. At the Pine Ridge and Rosebud Sioux reservations, as anthropologist Thomas Biolsi found, "the OIA deployed several technologies of power . . . for retaining control over reservation affairs in the face of demands from the councils for expanded authority and for an attendant reduction of agency authority." Based on a broad survey of tribes, historian Donald Parman made a similar observation with more specificity: "Strong [BIA] superintendents used job patronage, credit and budget decisions, and a host of informal pressures to dominate tribal councils."[46]

Internal BIA resistance to Collier's agenda accounted for some of the continuing agency control. As a legal adviser to the bureau observed in 1947, Collier took over an agency with a history of "institutional opposition to tribal government." After years of administering authoritarian policy, some of his staff "did not believe in Indian self-government." Some dragged their feet because they remembered and resented Collier's scathing attacks on the Indian service before he became commissioner. Yet "Collier removed remarkably few personnel." Although Parman found that many BIA employees "genuinely respected tribal self-government and cooperated whenever possible," institutional and legal impediments to tribal empowerment persisted. For example, "Washington sometimes intervened in council operations to insure conformity with federal statutes, to protect against infringements of religious or civil rights, or to preserve the authority of agency officials."[47]

Collier himself did not set an example of consistent respect for Indian decision-making. Some of his mandates, such as the notorious disregard of Navajo opposition to a drastic cull of their sheep, reflected a conviction that federal expertise should prevail over tribe members' judgment in land use and natural resource development. BIA doubt about Indians' economic proficiency also kept key fiscal decisions out of tribal councils' hands. As historian Graham Taylor observed, Collier and his top advisers "were reluctant to relinquish the power of the purse to communities whose members had little or no experience with modern business practices." In its role as trustee of Indian assets, the bureau also kept control of contracting, the selection of lawyers for tribes, and probates of deceased Indians' property.[48]

By the mid-1940s, resentment of such restrictions made some Indians impatient for an end to the federal guardianship. Ironically, contrasting experiences could inspire the same sentiment. During the 1930s and the war years, many Indians had agreeable tastes of comparative freedom from BIA control; others at least had opportunities to take initiative and make decisions in matters that were formerly the domain of reservation superintendents. Were it not for those experiences and the expectations they engendered, the Indians who campaigned against federal policy in the 1950s might have been less inclined to mount a challenge and less equipped to back it with effective organization.

IRA governments, despite their limitations, were not utterly powerless, and self-governance on IRA terms was not invariably a demoralizing experience. The organized tribes' new legitimacy boosted their leverage in Washington, DC. If nothing else, it enabled them to block the alienation of tribal lands and assets. In some communities, such as the Swinomish and Tulalip tribes, the IRA afforded access to seed funds for successful tribal economic ventures. Minnesota Chippewas declared themselves happy with the IRA, apparently for just such reasons. Their spokesmen opposed a proposal in 1944 to repeal the act, saying that the people of their five reservations, after organizing under one constitution in 1936, had acquired property and begun largely managing affairs on their own.[49]

The New Deal also made it possible to imagine life without BIA rule by breaking the bureau's monopoly on federal power in Indian country. The Roosevelt administration spawned new agencies that counted Indians among their beneficiaries—the Social Security, Works Progress, Farm Security, and Civil Works administrations, to name a few. A simultaneous shift of BIA education and medical services to the states sapped the bureau's power too. In the estimation of anthropologist Henry Dobyns, these changes "afforded emergent tribal governments considerable room in which to maneuver."[50]

At the very least, the Indian New Deal aroused "a remarkable degree of Indian political activism," Graham Taylor astutely observed, thus injecting "an important new element" into Indian affairs.[51] To muster Indian support for his reform proposal, Collier gathered hundreds of them at regional congresses where they had first-ever opportunities to question and address top administrators regarding policy. Many tribe members answered the commissioner's call to lobby for his bill in Congress. Furthermore, as provided in the eventual Reorganization Act, Indians on 258 reservations voted in referenda on the new law, often following intense campaigns and controversy. The process of establishing and operating an IRA government drew many Indians into additional heated controversies. Thus, even if Indians' experiences during the New Deal did not include all hoped-for gains in operational sovereignty, they provided significant political education, including the revelation that influential non-Indians could sometimes be disposed or persuaded to support Indian aspirations for self-government.[52]

POSTWAR POSSIBILITIES

World War II gave Indians new opportunities to experience life free from colonial controls. Wartime exigencies, spending cuts, and military conscription weakened the BIA, draining its workforce and curtailing its services. More importantly, thousands of tribe members traded BIA supervision for army or navy discipline, gaining new perspectives on their subjection to federal paternalism. Serving in integrated military units alongside whites, Indians saw thought-provoking aspects of the world outside their tribal communities. As a Coast Guard recruit, for instance, Suquamish tribe member James Forsman traveled to the East Coast, Cuba, Panama, Mexico, India, and the Mediterranean. Such exposure to other people and countries made many Indians aware of possible new personal aspirations and of other subjugated peoples longing for independence.

Thousands of Indians also left reservations to fill defense industry jobs or jobs vacated by employees sent to war. Martha George worked alongside non-Indian women at an ammunition depot not far from her Suquamish reservation home. Experiences like hers and James Forsman's led Indians to expect more freedom, opportunities, and respect in the country that wanted their service and labor. Some realized that their ability to exploit new opportunities would depend on having the education that equipped white comrades-in-arms and coworkers for life in the society beyond the reservation.[53]

Back home at war's end, Indian veterans and laid-off workers faced conditions that were often worse than when they left. Historian Alison

Bernstein found that many of them, having "learned to take care of themselves in the white world without the Indian Bureau or the tribal governments to interfere," wanted to leave the reservations again. In numerous instances, they requested full control of land held in trust for them, often selling it and heading for cities where veterans' benefits could make home purchases or higher education feasible. Of those who stayed on reservations, a significant number, especially veterans, moved into tribal leadership. In many of their communities, pride in tribal identity had surged with the patriotic sentiment of wartime and public praise for Indian contributions to victory.[54] But whether Indians interpreted their experiences during the war as encouragement to enter the American mainstream or as confirmation that they could manage their own tribal affairs, historian Kenneth Townsend's insight applies: "World War II heightened the Indians' expectations for self-direction."[55]

Those expectations were evident in a slogan of the newly created National Congress of American Indians: "Let Indians speak for themselves." The NCAI owed its establishment in 1944 largely to ambitions inspired by the Indian New Deal and wartime experience. Many founders of the organization were already speaking on behalf of fellow Indians. More than half of the four score people at the inaugural conference held positions in IRA governments. Another fourth, roughly, were current or former BIA employees—likely beneficiaries of the Indian Reorganization Act mandate for Indian preference in bureau hiring.[56] The NCAI constitution reflected drafters' familiarity with the constitutions of IRA tribes.

Influences of the war years were evident in the NCAI's first plans. Members resolved to press for increased veterans' benefits and for repeal of laws that discriminated against Indians. A 1947 resolution favored the gradual "liquidation" of the BIA. But because the National Congress was a loose organization of tribes in diverse circumstances, members had varied opinions on what "liquidation" should mean for US-tribal relations. There was no consensus that taking control of their lives would end the federal guardianship.

Virtually everyone agreed, however, that greater control meant Indians speaking for themselves at the tribal level. Not long before, tribes had voted on whether a major act of Congress would apply to them. Why not let them also decide how much freedom or federal oversight they wanted in the postwar era? Why should federal withdrawal, state jurisdiction, and assimilation be their only option? Within four years of the NCAI's creation, members united around a demand that "any withdrawal of services to Indians proceed locally on a case-by-case basis."[57]

NCAI members also shared a desire for adjudication of Indian claims against the United States. Every tribe in the country seemed to have at least one grievance, be it a treaty violation, an uncompensated appropriation of land, or a breach of fiscal trust. Yet under existing US law, a tribe wishing to sue for redress had first to secure an authorizing act of Congress, and few tribes had the means to muster legislators' support.[58] The NCAI therefore established a legal division from the start, tasking it with seeking legislation to establish a general claims resolution process. Over the long run, that investment in legal advocacy would significantly enhance tribes' ability to assert sovereign powers.

The idea of a special Indian claims process was not new. Since early in the century, members of Congress had periodically considered and declined to pass bills that would either open US courts to all tribes or create a new tribunal to hear their cases. Proponents' aims ranged from upholding American ideals to increasing congressional efficiency. Hoping for justice and for monetary awards that could jump-start tribal economies, John Collier vainly included an Indian claims court in his first draft of the IRA. When the conditions for passage of such legislation finally ripened a decade later, Collier's other initiatives were facing stiff political headwinds. His critics had gained the upper hand in Congress. In 1945 they forced him to resign, but they knew that unresolved tribal claims were an impediment to ending federal Indian guardianship. The Indian Claims Commission Act ratified in 1946 therefore had backing from an uneasy alliance of termination and Indian rights advocates.[59] In the end, however, the act's consequences did not fulfill the desires of either faction.

The procedures and decisions of the new Indian Claims Commission (ICC) frustrated many Indians. Contrary to expectations that a commission would forgo the formalities and technicalities of federal court litigation, a tribal petition to the ICC triggered a three-step process requiring extensive evidence preparation and written memoranda about complex questions of history, land rights, and economics. Cases took years, even decades, to reach conclusion. Many awards to tribes—limited by law to money—were in amounts that Indians found insulting. The Suquamish took offense at an ICC determination that the United States owed them only the 1859 value of 75,000 acres on which cities, suburbs, farms, and industry had since sprouted and thrived. They refused the award. The tribe's attorney said his clients' dissatisfaction was greater than if there had been no Indian Claims Commission Act.[60]

The ICC thus dashed American officials' hopes for a final resolution of Indian grievances—a precondition to shedding federal guardianship responsibilities honorably. Instead, unintended effects of the claims process furthered Indian tribes' political revitalization. By the time the commission adjourned in 1978, Indians' desire for observance of their treaties had intensified, tribes had developed new relationships with lawyers, more lawyers were aware of tribes' need for legal counsel on a range of concerns, and tribes were increasingly inclined to assert their interests in American courts.[61]

While tribal claims lingered on the ICC docket from the early 1950s through the 1960s and beyond, Indians of two or more generations had occasion to collect, hear, tell, and ponder stories of unfulfilled US promises. Although memories of treaties and treaty violations would surely have endured without the claims commission, the experience of deciding to file petitions, identifying the wrongs done, and preparing necessary evidence enhanced Indians' consciousness of their history as autonomous peoples who had enforceable agreements with the United States. In a history of the ICC, H. D. Rosenthal drew a direct connection between those years of preoccupation with old promises and a demand that Indians made in 1972 during a protest at BIA national headquarters. Organizers of that Trail of Broken Treaties campaign called for "a thorough review of Indian treaty commitments and violations, and . . . the elimination of the system that had resulted in unending and expensive legal battles for Indian rights which produced indecisive results."[62]

Other repercussions of the Indian Claims Commission Act followed from attorneys' role in the ICC process. Not that Indians needed lawyers to identify the US misdeeds for which they wanted compensation. Rosenthal found "ample evidence" that Indians were aware of their injuries; many had agitated for redress "unaided by attorneys."[63] Indeed, most tribes lacked legal help before 1946. Few had previously retained steady counsel. More commonly, though not often, they had hired lawyers for short-term work in emergencies or other specific circumstances. That usually meant choosing from a handful of specialized law firms in Washington, DC.

With the advent of the ICC, tribes needed attorneys to represent them for extended periods in proceedings that eventually numbered in the hundreds. Before long, the demand for claims counsel outstripped the supply of known practitioners.[64] Some tribes turned then to local lawyers who lacked the specialists' experience but were more familiar with conditions the tribes faced and more readily available for meetings on the Indians' home ground. In 2003, Billy Frank remembered that his Nisqually Tribe joined with other small ones in western Washington to engage the firm that pressed their claims against the United States. "Into the sixties," Frank said, "we had the constant play of the claims attorneys" that "kept us moving in the I-5 [Hwy 99] corridor" and traveling to meetings in Seattle.[65] During a field study of "emergent tribal governments," Henry Dobyns learned that one "Northwest Coast tribe" in the 1950s "decided good representation was important enough to hire an attorney fresh out of law school. The tribe was willing to suffer some losses while he learned the specialty of Indian law, because the tribe had in mind the long-term goal of obtaining capable, sympathetic counsel." Whether they came from near or far, the lawyers also learned about their clients' numerous unmet needs for legal assistance, and they could tell tribal leaders how lawyers might help. As a result, more tribes hired attorneys to advise them on various ongoing concerns. According to Dobyns, many of those attorneys, "impelled" by "personal value systems . . . to champion the subordinate ethnic groups," committed themselves to the Indians' causes.[66]

The recollections of two lawyers corroborate Dobyns's findings. Norman Littell began providing general counsel services for the Navajo Tribe not long after agreeing to handle the tribe's ICC claims. He saw "vital and volatile developments in Navajoland." Tribe members increasingly participated in councils, and council officers were assuming more management of Navajo affairs. Because the tribe had not previously had an attorney, its leaders needed some basic legal education. In an undated memoir, Littell described the inaugural meeting of the Advisory Committee: "I pointed out that in addition to their general proprietary powers, pursuant to Article 2 of Treaty of 1868, no person other than government employees 'shall ever be permitted to pass over, settle upon or reside in' the Navajo Reservation. It was difficult for them to believe me." Littell's first assignment for the tribe was to "find relief" from the "debacle" of Collier-era grazing regulations for the reservation, which had shattered the Navajo economy and embittered the people. Thanks to his efforts, federal officials suspended the regulations. That success, in Littell's view, exemplified the "sharp impact" of bringing "independent, non-governmental, legal opinion . . . to bear on . . . the conduct of Indian affairs."[67]

Z. Simpson Cox's advocacy for tribes began with his unexpected exposure to US disregard for their rights. As Cox recalled it, he arrived at his Phoenix office one day in 1948 to find five Pima Indians and a "lady lawyer" waiting for him. They wanted his help fighting the Interior Department's rejection of the tribe's proposal to hire that "lady." Wondering how federal permission could even be required, Cox set aside his reluctance to get involved and began asking questions. He learned that the secretary vetoed the Indians' choice of an attorney because she had advised them to defy an unauthorized federal assessment of irrigation costs. US officials had responded to the Pimas' defiance by turning off their irrigation water, killing their crops. After the tribe obtained permission to hire Cox, another reprehensible federal action came to his attention. The War Relocation Authority, without the tribe's knowledge, had paid just $2,000 to lease reservation land worth an estimated $2 million on the open market. A petition for the difference was among the Pima claims that Cox filed with the ICC.[68]

Like Cox, other attorneys were dismayed by the tight federal control of tribes' legal representation. As lawyers are wont to do, they questioned administrators' authority and seemingly arbitrary actions. When a widely supported, high-visibility challenge to that authority partially succeeded, it gave Indian leaders additional evidence of independent attorneys' value as allies and strategists in the quest for true tribal self-government.

The contested federal oversight dated from at least 1874. Early regulations—supposedly needed to protect naive Indians from unscrupulous lawyers and prevent excessive fees in claims cases—required Interior Department authorization for contracts to represent Indians or settle their cases. The Indian Reorganization Act perpetuated that supervision. It provided for tribal government power to employ lawyers but added a qualification: "The choice of counsel and fixing of fees to be subject to the approval of the Secretary of the Interior." The ICC Act allowed tribes to select the lawyers who would represent them, but it incorporated the qualifying phrase from the IRA and limited counsel fees to 10 percent of any award.[69]

In 1950, the commissioner's liberal interpretation of his authority over tribes' relations with lawyers, together with long waits for approval of proposed contracts, drew fire from several directions. One provocation was Commissioner Dillon Myer's promulgation of detailed new regulations giving him complete control of fees and contract terms, allowing him to terminate contracts, and requiring periodic reports from the lawyers. When Indians, their legal advisers, and assorted Indian rights organizations condemned the regulations as "illegally restrictive," Interior Secretary Oscar Chapman suspended them and scheduled public hearings on the issue. Myer applied some of the new rules anyway. His allies in the Senate, suspecting that lawyers "in the Indian business" were selfishly exploiting unsophisticated Indians and engaging in multiple unethical practices, named as an example a former BIA employee who had served for several years as general counsel to the National Congress of American Indians.[70]

The NCAI objected that Commissioner Myer was "attempting to dictate to the Indian people what attorneys they may hire with their own money, or whether they shall be permitted to have any attorney at all." The American Bar Association added influential voices to the chorus of critics, charging that the new regulations, "by impeding the discretion of the tribes to choose their own lawyers . . . , would reverse substantially the march of Indians toward self-rule." A few months later, "in the face of universal opposition from the legal profession," the Interior secretary withdrew the offending regulations.[71]

Unchastened, Myer kept tight reins on lawyers who represented tribes, in many cases denying tribes attorneys of their choice. While continuing to object, Indians drew encouraging lessons from the Interior Department's retreat when faced with a determined alliance of tribes and influential non-Indians.[72] In a newsletter titled "Indian Progress," Association on American Indian Affairs (AAIA) president Oliver La Farge wrote, "For the first time the tribes united in common action before their government, and from this gained an entirely new understanding of their strength. Also for the first time, the Indians discovered the strength of public opinion that will rally to their support when there is a real issue."[73]

In 1959, a tribe's use of lawyers for matters other than suing the United States yielded results that La Farge and AAIA could chalk up as another advance in Indian rights. At the urging of the Navajo Tribe's general counsel, the US Supreme Court ruled that nineteenth-century treaties and court opinions still served to protect tribal affairs from state government interference. The litigation had begun seven years earlier when Hugh Lee, a non-Indian, sued Indian residents of the Navajo Reservation in an Arizona court, seeking to collect a debt incurred at Lee's reservation trading post. Lawyers for the defendants, Paul and Lorena Williams, argued that only the tribal court had jurisdiction to hear Lee's claim. The Supreme Court based its unanimous agreement on the 1868 treaty that created the Navajo Reservation. It also relied on the 1832 ruling in *Worcester v. Georgia*, which affirmed that state laws had no force within US-protected tribal territory unless the Indian government or the United States consented.[74] The opinion in *Williams v. Lee* explained why that principle was applicable to twentieth-century Navajos:

> Today the Navajo Courts of Indian Offenses exercise broad criminal and civil jurisdiction which covers suits by outsiders against Indian defendants. No Federal Act has given state courts jurisdiction over such controversies. In a general statute Congress did express its willingness to have any State assume jurisdiction over reservation Indians. . . . To date, Arizona has not accepted jurisdiction. . . . The exercise of state jurisdiction here would undermine the authority of the tribal courts over Reservation affairs and hence would infringe on the right of the Indians to govern themselves. It is immaterial that respondent is not an Indian. He was on the Reservation and the transaction with an Indian took place there. . . . The cases in this Court have consistently guarded the authority of Indian governments over their reservations. Congress recognized this authority in the Navajos in the Treaty of 1868, and has done so ever since.[75]

The *Williams* opinion stated that Indian tribes were originally "separate nations" and cited Cohen's *Handbook of Federal Indian Law* as a source for relevant legal doctrine. Although it did not use the word "sovereignty" to denote the "right of the Indians to govern themselves," it cited two lower court opinions that referred explicitly to tribes' sovereignty.

One was an Arizona Supreme Court decision quoting Cohen; the other was a US appeals court ruling that the Oglala Sioux Tribe could collect taxes on a non-Indian's lease of Indian-owned reservation land.[76]

The Sioux levied and defended their tax, and Navajos fought Hugh Lee's lawsuit, out of concern for their right of self-government. Fortunately for them, Cohen-influenced attorneys were available to help claim that right. Although the Navajo government was not a party to the suit against the Williamses, it arranged for and paid the couple's first lawyers. Tribal attorney Littell then urged the Navajo council to support an appeal of the Arizona court judgment, and he represented the Williamses in the US Supreme Court.[77] Littell also rejected federal lawyers' advice to argue that US authority precluded state court jurisdiction; he successfully staked his case instead on the contention that tribal sovereignty itself precluded state interference.[78]

In the Oglala Sioux tax case, the tribe's advocates were Richard Schifter and Arthur Lazarus, young lawyers who took over Felix Cohen's private practice after Cohen died in 1953.[79] During the 1950s, Lazarus and Schifter also served as counsel for the AAIA and helped to establish a Federal Bar Association Committee on Indian Law.[80] These men and a few others in Washington, DC—particularly Ernest Wilkinson, his partner John Cragun, and solo practitioner Marvin Sonosky—were the lawyers from whom tribe leaders and intertribal organizations were most likely to seek help in that period. They were also positioned to hear and tell Indians about disputes, legislation, or administrative measures that could have general impacts on tribes' efforts to govern themselves and their reservations.[81]

LOSING PATIENCE

During its first decade, the NCAI tried to protect Indian interests tribe by tribe as threats arose. Then the federal plan to withdraw from Indian affairs jolted the organization into concentrating its resources on a fight for the tribes' continuing existence in the United States as autonomous polities. By 1954, NCAI had assumed leadership of a campaign to preserve the US trust relationship with tribes and clarify the government's attendant responsibilities. San Carlos Apache leader Clarence Wesley forcefully articulated NCAI concerns at an emergency conference that year. Tribes wanted continuing protection for their lands and treaty rights, Wesley said. They wanted their "day in court" on outstanding claims, federal assistance for development, an "end to bureaucratic dictatorship," and a government that dealt honorably "with conquered peoples."[82] Meeting-goers were intent on defeating legislation that presented grave threats to Indian rights and property.

One specific goal was a provision in Public Law 280 requiring tribes' consent to state jurisdiction on reservations.[83] When NCAI representatives sought Interior Department support for that demand, officials were unmoved. Tribes could expect nothing more than "consultation" regarding proposed state control, they said. An assistant secretary advised a senator that a bill allowing tribal consent would set an unwelcome precedent at a time when the government aimed to phase out Indian enclaves. By withholding consent, a minority of Indians might "impose a condition of lawlessness." Tribal jurisdiction was not an acceptable alternative because a permanent "third system of law operating outside the Federal-State system [was] undesirable." Besides, the tribes' criminal law systems—"borrowed largely from State or Federal codes"—were "elementary and inadequate."[84]

In the meantime, evidence mounted that state jurisdiction—touted as a remedy for lawlessness on reservations—was no guarantee of improved law enforcement. In numerous instances, Indians complained that services deteriorated instead. At a Senate hearing in 1961, Edwin Jackson, Jr., of the Quechan Tribe described the bewildering consequences on his reservation in California, a state to which Congress had delegated jurisdiction outright.

> Now here we were a tribe organized under the Indian Reorganization Act; we had our constitution and bylaws and law and order code approved and adopted. When that Public Law 280 went into effect, it knocked our code out completely. . . . We went along with the code set up by the California State and the county. Well, when this took effect, it left us in the middle of three governing bodies. . . . The [federal] Government told us that they had no control over us on our law and order. . . . But the county comes back and says, "Well, we don't know whether we have the right on the reservation or not, because . . . the land is under Federal status. We don't know whether we have the right to get in there and make arrests or not."

Federal officials "were taking a 'wait-and-see' attitude," Jackson added. The district attorney would not say whether the tribe could legally fill the enforcement vacuum; he found the question of jurisdiction too confusing.[85]

In Washington State, which initially declined to take jurisdiction on a reservation without the tribe's request, the law enforcement question confused and divided Indians. After cuts in federal funding for Indian police, a "law and order struggle" reportedly split Lummi Tribe members. To those who argued that state jurisdiction was the only practical response, a "chief" replied that the state—barred from taxing reservation land—was unlikely to fund enforcement adequately. Other Lummis, like many Indians in Washington, worried that the state would impose its fishing laws on them.[86] That fear prompted Nisqually Indians in 1959 to petition the BIA to "abolish" an earlier petition for state jurisdiction, signed under pressure from a bureau employee.[87] That same year, in contrast, Tulalip leaders announced their satisfaction with state law enforcement, which they had requested because BIA and tribal law enforcement were both inadequate. Curiously, state prosecutors were even then reportedly refusing cases from reservations because a county court had ruled in a case from Tulalip that Washington's assumption of jurisdiction contravened the state constitution.[88]

Tulalips' satisfaction was apparently unusual for a Northwest reservation where the state had responsibility for keeping order. Complaints predominated when Indians from twenty-six area tribes gathered at the University of Washington in 1960 for a "workshop" on jurisdiction issues cohosted by the Association on American Indian Affairs. According to the moderator, anthropology professor Erna Gunther, the discussions helped the Indians see "that the confusing question of who has legal jurisdiction over what on a reservation is a common problem that needs united effort to find a solution." Gunther told the *Christian Science Monitor* that tribes under state jurisdiction "find they have even less law enforcement because they are so far away from even a deputy sheriff that it takes a long time before any help can be had." In addition, she said, state jurisdiction could be "an opening wedge for other restrictions and losses of rights. On the Quinault reservation on the seacoast, for instance, traditional fishing practices guaranteed by treaty have been interfered with by state fisheries employees. . . . Every Indian present was earnestly concerned with finding ways to improve law and order on his or her reservation." The workshop ended "with the delegates clamoring for another session."[89]

Two years later, Indians who journeyed from Washington State to North Carolina for the annual NCAI convention learned that dissatisfaction with state law enforcement was rife outside the Northwest as well. US senator Sam Ervin told the assembly that a Senate investigation confirmed what many Indians alleged: where states had assumed jurisdiction in Indian country, they often failed to provide equal protection of the law, failed to "bring the criminals to justice," and exhibited hostility toward Indians. The Omaha Tribe's secretary supplied specifics for the *New York Times*: Nebraska police did not station officers near the reservation until pressured to do so, and when officers were finally available, numerous Indians endured severe beatings at their hands.[90]

On several reservations, meanwhile, tribes tried to make state jurisdiction unnecessary by undertaking law enforcement and related government functions themselves. That strategy influenced the Supreme Court ruling that the Navajo court had exclusive jurisdiction over Hugh Lee's lawsuit. In the previous decade, the Navajo Tribe had constructed a substantial justice system of its own, modeled largely on non-Indian examples. Navajos had not lost confidence in their customary law or come to prefer Anglo-American law; but to improve their chances of preempting state jurisdiction, they emulated institutions that non-Indian federal judges were likely to respect.[91]

Several Sioux tribes were flexing their governing muscles for similar reasons. Lakota scholar Edward Charles Valandra wrote, "The Lakota decided, without much fanfare, to invoke the principle of self-determination as a viable alternative" to the federal withdrawal and termination policy. Around 1950, the tribes signaled to non-Indians in Lakota territory that "Lakota governance had arrived, was proactive, and could not be dismissed." Valandra's primary example was the Oglala tax on grazing leases that provoked the *Iron Crow* litigation. When the federal court approved the tax, it galvanized a non-Indian campaign for state jurisdiction on reservations. The prospect of state law enforcement dismayed Lakotas, who had long traded stories about the discrimination and injustices they suffered outside the reservations. All but one South Dakota Sioux community therefore voted against state jurisdiction when given the chance in 1957. The state then announced its unilateral assumption of jurisdiction over reservation highways, but that move did not pass muster in the state supreme court. Undeterred, the South Dakota legislature in 1963 approved a bill imposing general state jurisdiction in Indian country, only to see that decision reversed the next year in a Lakota-initiated statewide referendum.[92] Across the United States, Indian leaders and their lawyers took note, as did major news media.[93]

A bold Quechan Tribe move against non-Indian trespassers made national news as well. In 1960, Quechans decided not to wait for authoritative clarification of their right to control activity on land "in federal status." As the *New York Times* reported it, members of the tribe, "upset by squatters" on the reservation, went on an "off-beat warpath . . . using the white man's weapon of the toll gate." The tribal council deputized more than two dozen Indians to blockade four private roads and demand payment from every motorist seeking access. In short order, county authorities agreed to an alternative way of meeting the need for reservation law enforcement. According to the *Los Angeles Times*, by May 1961 ten Quechan Indians were patrolling the reservation as officers of a new tribal police force—the only Indian police force in California. Because Quechan cops were also deputized as Imperial County sheriffs, non-Indian lawbreakers could find themselves in Indian custody.[94]

Such attention-getting Indian actions both stimulated and exploited an increase in mainstream press attention to Indians. By 1956, journalists in rising numbers, responding partly to Indian public statements, were giving the new national Indian policy and Indians' resulting circumstances a close look. Newspapers, magazines, and television networks eventually reported that coercion and Indian property loss were sullying the supposedly liberating termination process. At the same time, Indians from a handful of tribes, welcoming and nurturing the media interest, expressed their critiques of federal policy dramatically, and voiced bold ideas about their legal status as tribes.[95]

In November 1958, the *New York Times* reported that Miccosukee Seminoles had visited the embassies of Great Britain, France, and Spain in Washington, DC, requesting support for their contention that those countries had eighteenth-century treaties with Miccosukees promising them land in Florida. "They say the treaties still are effective," the *Times* article elaborated, "because the Miccosukes [*sic*] form a sovereign nation, which has never been conquered." Early the following spring, the paper publicized the Miccosukee claim again when the tribe hosted a gathering of "thirty-six spokesmen for eight Indian nations" who took "steps to form a united Indian nation." Noting that the Indians did not want to be US citizens, the *Times* concluded without condescending commentary, "Each tribe will have to vote in favor before the nation is formally organized and an application is made for membership in the United Nations."[96]

Like the *Times* correspondent, historians Laurence Hauptman and Harry Kersey named Wallace Mad Bear Anderson, a Tuscarora, as instigator of the parley in Florida. Anderson had already garnered national notice by staging protests against the construction of a dam on the Tuscarora Reservation. Although he was neither a title holder nor a person of high status in the Iroquois Confederacy, Indians from five of the six Iroquois nations joined Anderson at the Miccosukee-hosted meeting.[97] Around the same time, confederacy members—angered by New York state tax policy and federal government appropriation of Seneca lands for a flood control project—handed power in the Six Nations council to a faction described by historian Larry Burt as "very traditional and anti-BIA." They adopted "sensational" resistance tactics such as a march on the White House and an attempted citizen's arrest of the Indian commissioner.[98]

Some Iroquois and at least two other tribes decided also to seek acknowledgment of their sovereignty from nations outside the United States. In early 1957, Clinton Rickard led a delegation of Iroquois in a publicized ceremonial appearance at the United Nations, which he compared to his people's venerable confederation of indigenous nations. In July 1960, taking past United States recognition of their sovereignty to the logical next step, the Chippewa Tribe petitioned for United Nations membership.[99]

By then, Miccosukees had threatened to present their case for a reservation to the United Nations or another international body. Miccosukees wrote their claims on a buckskin and sent it to Cuba's new president, Fidel Castro, with congratulations for liberating his country from dictatorship. When the Castro government subsequently invited Indian leaders to Havana for ceremonies in July 1959 commemorating the revolution, Miccosukees sent an eleven-member delegation bearing a letter signed "the Sovereign Miccosukee Seminole Nation." They received in return a Cuban ministry letter acknowledging the sovereignty of the Miccosukee government. US officials hastened to drop the curtain on this daring foreign relations theater, which was getting coverage in Miami newspapers, albeit coverage that ridiculed the Indians' gambit. Miccosukee spokesman Buffalo Tiger later said he received a call from Washington, DC, conveying a promise that appropriate federal officials would work with the tribe and Florida authorities to create a reservation if Tiger would end Miccosukees' diplomatic relations with Cuba.[100]

A few months later, an "action" anthropologist at the University of Chicago responded in a different way to Indians' publicized frustration with a federal policy that denied them self-determination. Professor Sol Tax proposed to host a conference at which Indians from all parts of the United States could "review the record of everything that [had] happened in the field of Indian affairs" since 1928 and make policy recommendations. The NCAI endorsed this idea in late 1960. An announcement to "Tribal Officials, Indian organization officers, [and] Indian community leaders" billed the conference as "the first time in history that Indians, themselves, have had the opportunity and the necessary assistance to report their experiences and to say what they would like to see done on their reservations." The invitation to participate promised that Indians would lead at every step; the university would simply provide logistical and technical support. It was a chance "to go 'on the offensive'—take initiative—as Indians working together all over the nation." The result—ultimately known as the American Indian Chicago Conference of 1961 (AICC)—was a weeklong assembly of several hundred Native people who produced and disseminated a Declaration of Indian Purpose.[101]

Nancy Lurie, a coordinator of the conference, described it years later as a "direct response to the all-out federal threat during the 1950s to what is now commonly referred to as tribal sovereignty." But at the time, Lurie recalled, the term "sovereignty" "had little currency in Indian discourse," except in some small "pan-Indian" organizations that sent few people to Chicago. One advocate of proclaiming Indians' sovereignty—William Rickard, a Tuscarora—had a seat on the conference steering committee, but he could not muster support for his position. Lurie attributed Rickard's ineffectiveness partly to his stridency and humorlessness, which "put people off." More importantly, she thought, a large majority of conference participants regarded any talk of enduring tribal sovereignty as foolish, pointless, even dangerous. In their view, the realistic alternative for

Indians in 1961 was to accept the US legal framework of federal/tribal relations and strive for significant federal policy change.

Accordingly, the Declaration of Indian Purpose adopted the language of reformers rather than radicals. The word "sovereignty" appeared only in a quotation from the 1832 Supreme Court opinion in *Worcester v. Georgia*, where Justice John Marshall recounted the history of colonial nations' recognition that indigenous tribes had some attributes of sovereign nations. In two other places, the AICC declaration referenced tribal sovereignty obliquely. A section on treaties read, "The right of self-government, a right which the Indians possessed before the coming of the white man, has never been extinguished; indeed, it has been repeatedly sustained by the courts of the United States." A critique of federal policies proposed "that recommendations be adopted to strengthen the principles of the Indian Reorganization Act . . . , which recognized the inherent powers of Indian Tribes."[102]

When Clinton Rickard denounced the Declaration of Indian Purpose as uselessly timid, the assembly voted to strike his speech from the conference record. Nevertheless, the idea of continuing tribal sovereignty was not as unfamiliar or troubling to Indians in 1961 as Rickard's cool reception in Chicago suggested. Other allusions to the concept circulated during preparations for the conference, which included nine regional meetings as well as correspondence between the organizers and people in Indian country.[103] At a Northeast regional meeting, a Sioux man invoked "our sovereign rights," and the group considered a possible appeal to the United Nations or the World Court. A meeting on the Yakima Reservation generated the following statement.

> Our concern is, to refer our Indian people back to their original status of "tribal self-government" in the absence of dominance from another, in the SPIRIT and manner the ETERNAL CREATOR provided for all mankind. . . . American Indians are citizens, only in the sense, by virtue of their original occupancy and the treaties which provided the status of "sovereignty," hence, qualified for self-government. . . . The Constitution of the United States never intended to presume to legislate over the affairs of the Indians no more than it would presume to legislate over the affairs of a foreign power.[104]

The Chicago conference also inspired or provoked some young Indian observers to demand respect for tribal rights in ways that "radicals" such as the Rickard brothers had already done. Two months after leaving the conference, a group of college students, impatient with the reform strategy and mild wording favored by their elders, formed the National Indian Youth Council (NIYC) and announced their intent "to carry forward the policy of making their inherent sovereign rights known to all people." Years later, Shirley Witt recalled that she and other NIYC founders conceived of the council primarily as a service and leadership training organization; they did not consider themselves radicals. Yet their desire for rapid change in the status quo fostered militancy. NIYC would soon adapt civil disobedience tactics from the black civil rights movement to the struggle of Indians against Washington State's suppression of treaty-secured fishing rights.[105]

Furthermore, an influential facilitator of the Chicago meeting regarded tribal sovereignty both as a historical reality and as a continuing basis for Indians' essential right of self-government. D'Arcy McNickle chaired the committee that produced the first draft of a charter for the conference. He guided discussions in Chicago and crafted the wording of the declaration that meeting-goers finally approved.[106] A scholar and member of the Salish-Kootenai Tribes, McNickle had worked closely with John Collier to implement the Indian New Deal and helped found the NCAI. He was thoroughly familiar with the history and doctrine of Indian tribal sovereignty that Cohen and Margold explicated. He wrote a proposal in 1960 for a tribal leader training program that asserted, "The Indian tribes retain a residual sovereignty, the heritage of their pre-Columbian occupation of the western hemisphere. They are asked to yield the last fragments of this birthright, as the price for acceptance in the American economy. They feel strongly that the choice is a false one."[107] At a Senate committee hearing one year after the AICC, McNickle said many non-Indians seemed to think that Indians' admission to US citizenship had "some effect on the legal doctrine of the sovereignty of the tribes"—that it was impossible or wrong to have a sovereign nation within another nation. But Indians, he countered, "see no reason why they should cease to be Indians . . . in their relations with non-Indians."[108]

Founders of the National Indian Youth Council—some of them future tribal officials—knew D'Arcy McNickle. Many also knew or would soon know what McNickle knew about the history and legal basis of tribal sovereignty, because he created an opportunity for them to learn it. Beginning in the late 1950s, he sponsored and oversaw annual summer workshops for Indian college students at which he and other scholars, including Sol Tax and Cherokee anthropologist Robert Thomas, exposed the young people to literature and discussions regarding their tribes' political character. Among their readings was a Cohen article about Indian affairs titled "Colonialism, U.S. Style." By all accounts Thomas, who explicitly aimed to train the leaders of a nationalist Indian movement, was a particularly influential member of the workshop faculty.[109] Bruce Wilkie, an early NIYC member who would soon become an official of the Makah Tribe, found the thinking of McNickle and Thomas persuasive. In reaction to an assigned reading that argued for Indians' assimilation, Wilkie wrote, "Much Indian land was secured by treaties of one sovereign nation with another. In order not to appear hypocritical in the international situation, Americans must look upon the abrogation of treaties in terms of aggressive acts, not as a beneficial sacrifice made by the Indians to better society."[110]

When Wilkie penned those objections to federal assimilation policy in 1962, the movement for black civil rights was using strategy and tactics that would inspire both the NIYC and a new generation of lawyers for tribes, calls for Indian rights were reaching the ears of many sympathetic Americans, and Indians in growing numbers were living in cities or going to colleges where encounters with non-Indians and Indians of other tribes heightened their consciousness of Indians' distinctive shared history and desire for self-determination. Meanwhile, on reservations, federal programs to prepare Indians for the end of their unique legal status and promote non-Indian access to tribal resources also encouraged the emergence of new tribal leaders.[111] All those developments would nourish the seeds of Indian hope and agitation for renewed sovereignty that had been germinating during the previous three decades.

3. Colonial Controls in Quinault Territory

By 1973, talk of sovereignty was common at American Indian leadership meetings, and it thrilled Richard Belmont, Jr. As the recently elected chairman of the Suquamish tribal council, Belmont was eager to make sovereignty a practical reality for his small tribe. He knew that would require written laws and the means to enforce them, so he called a "buddy" whose tribe had just enacted a law and order code. Quinault president Joe DeLaCruz set aside some initial concern about sharing the code and agreed to send Belmont a copy.

Thanks to that favor, the fiscally strapped Suquamish government soon had its own ordinance defining criminal offenses, setting penalties, establishing a court, and detailing court procedures. Years later, Belmont recalled that he deleted portions of the borrowed code pertaining to a "coastal reservation," substituted "Suquamish" for "Quinault," and easily persuaded fellow councilors to make the document Suquamish law.[1]

The new ordinance, like the Quinault original, would apply to everyone within the boundaries of the tribe's reservation. For the Suquamish government, that was an unprecedented claim of power. For Quinaults, in contrast, an assertion of all-inclusive jurisdiction was a statement of fact. They had regulated land use and other activities throughout the reservation for several years before Richard Belmont called Joe DeLaCruz.

Non-Indians as well as Indians had come before the tribe's court to answer charges of violating Quinault law. To Quinault political leaders, adopting a comprehensive criminal code was the next commonsense step toward effective management of their homeland, which represented Quinault hopes for survival as a people.

In 1980, Joe DeLaCruz told a US Senate committee that jurisdiction on reservations was an issue he had lived with most of his life.[2] His consciousness of the issue probably dated from his teen years in the 1950s, when the federal government encouraged states to take jurisdiction over Indian country. The Quinault Business Committee's subsequent consent to state jurisdiction ignited a firestorm of protest from tribe members. Reservation law enforcement all but ceased as a result, and practical considerations frustrated Quinault plans to fill the void. Nonetheless, DeLaCruz came to believe that his tribe had the ability and "a sovereign right" to police everyone in its reserved territory and to regulate their use of resources ranging from land, timber, and fishing grounds to ocean vistas and Indian children.

At the time of that Senate testimony, Joseph Burton DeLaCruz was well known in congressional offices and tribal governments across the country. Smart, articulate, forceful, and politically savvy, he had been president of the Quinault Nation since 1972 and president of the National Tribal Chairman's Association since 1977. In 1981, the National Congress of American Indians would make him its president. His expansive view of Native American concerns was evident in a recent speech to a conference of Indian chiefs in Canada. "No longer can Tribal leaders deal only with the internal affairs of our own Bands and Tribes and hope to protect the interests of our Peoples," he exhorted. "We must become increasingly aware of and actively involved in the external political processes which will affect our lives and resources. Our leaders must go among our Peoples and to outside communities to advocate the needs and interests of our Peoples."[3]

DeLaCruz's call for Indian engagement in "external political processes" had deep-rooted local origins and motivations. He first ventured out to intertribal meetings and congressional hearing rooms as a promoter and defender of his own community's interests. The initial and ultimate aim of his insistence on Indian tribes' sovereignty was to secure Quinault control over the rain-drenched earth, forested hills, clam-rich beaches, and salmon-nurturing waters of his isolated tribal homeland at the northwestern edge of the United States.

In the mid-twentieth century, Quinault history, evolving local circumstances, and national developments interacted to make the Quinault Reservation a place where Indians could imagine achieving such control. When DeLaCruz returned there in 1967 after more than a decade away for military service, college, and work, he joined a cohort of Quinaults intent on building a tribal government that could protect and manage all of their reserved territory and resources for the Indian community. Some of the factors inspiring that ambition were motivating Indians elsewhere too, fostering parallel developments in tribes across the United States, but Quinaults' unique historical experiences also contributed significantly to their belief in their tribe's ample sovereignty.

An 1855 treaty with the United States, followed by a half century of relative isolation for Quinault territory, instilled an expectation among Quinaults that their homeland resources would remain theirs to use as they wished. Successful early lawsuits to block state and US meddling in reservation fisheries reinforced that belief and encouraged Quinaults to defend their autonomy in American legal forums when new threats arose. Some threats followed from the US government's allotment of reservation land to hundreds of outsiders. By the 1960s, non-Indian acquisition of allotted land, unwanted state jurisdiction, and inadequate law enforcement intensified tribe members' sense of diminishing power and humiliation in their own land, but some Quinaults resolved to reverse that trend and maintain their tradition of resisting domination by employing tactics and expertise borrowed from non-Indian society.

MAKING A RESERVATION

On twentieth-century maps of Washington State, the designated Quinault homeland appeared as a triangular tract with roughly equal sides about twenty-five miles in length. The Pacific Coast side bulged slightly; the other two borderlines met on the east where Lake Quinault lay at the base of the Olympic Mountains. The space thus delineated bore the name Quinault Indian Reservation because the United States government, in return for a cession of Quinault and Quileute tribal territory in 1855, promised to leave the Indians land enough for their "use and occupation."

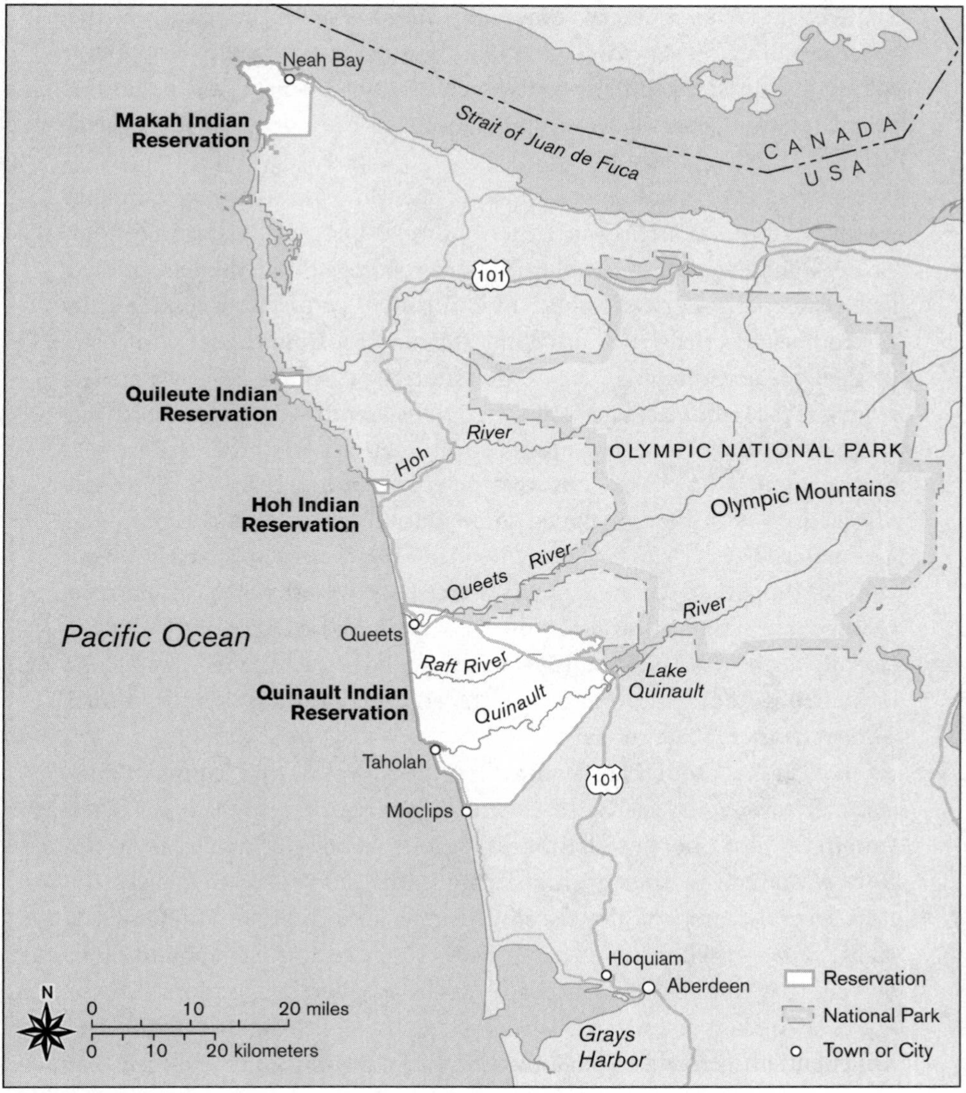

Quinault Reservation in relation to towns and other Indian reservations west of the Olympic Mountains.

The area that federal officials eventually did reserve for the tribes was the heart of Quinaults' ancestral domain. By 1900, it was home to approximately five hundred Indians concentrated in two towns—Taholah, at the mouth of the Quinault River, and Queets to the north on the Queets River.[4]

American colonization of Quinaults' then-known world began in 1845 when five families settled near the south end of the saltwater inlet they called Puget Sound. According to anthropologist Ronald Olson, that locale was the eastern periphery of Quinaults' "cultural horizon." Olson traced horizons that ran south along the seacoast from the Strait of Juan de Fuca to the Columbia River and east up the Chehalis River watershed from Grays Harbor to Puget Sound's southern reaches. In that unbordered realm lived other indigenous peoples with distinct territories, languages, and customs but a shared culture of intercommunity relations. Quinault associations with them included some marital ties as well as ceremonial and material exchanges between extended kin groups. Comparatively foreign as the American newcomers were, they would not have alarmed Quinaults. For half a century by then, adventuresome Quinaults had occasionally dealt with Britons and Americans who visited the region in ships or staffed distant forts where they traded their exotic goods for animal pelts and other local products.[5]

In 1846, without Native inhabitants' approval, the United States claimed sovereignty in the so-called Oregon Territory, which stretched from latitude 42 north to latitude 49 and from the Pacific Ocean to the Rocky Mountains, thus encompassing Quinaults' homeland. Over the next several years, additional colonists appeared closer to Quinault villages. Some settled south of Grays Harbor, drawn to a bay abounding in oysters that Indians harvested and traded to merchant sailors. United States lawmakers encouraged more immigration with an 1850 statute permitting citizens to claim land anywhere in Oregon—up to 320 acres per married couple.[6]

Four years later, after creating Washington Territory from Oregon's northern and eastern expanses, US officials moved belatedly to quiet indigenous peoples' claims on the land. By then, treaties were the standard means of securing rights to Indian-occupied country. In this instance, Americans planned to acquire the tribes' entire terrestrial domains by promising payments in cash or equivalent goods, services such as schools and medical care, a continuing right to fish at their usual places, and reserved enclaves where the Indians would locate homes.

The first such attempt to acquire Quinault territory was futile. It ended on March 2, 1855, when territorial governor Isaac Stevens angrily aborted treaty negotiations because Chehalis, Satsop, Cowlitz, and Chinook peoples would not agree to move north onto an unspecified tract in Quinault country. Four months later the governor's deputy, expecting to deal separately in the future with the recalcitrant tribes, brought Quinaults together with Indians to their north and clinched a US purchase of the western Olympic Peninsula below Makah tribal territory. The written record of that transaction, signed by the governor in January 1856 and ratified by Congress in 1859, pledged to reserve "for the use and occupation of tribes and bands" identified as the Qui-nai-elt and Quil-leh-ute "a tract or tracts of land sufficient for their wants within the Territory of Washington, to be selected by the President of the United States."[7]

It was 1861 before the president's proxies made the selection of land. The 10,000 acres they chose were miles from Quileute homes and did not encompass Queets, a village of Quinaults' linguistic, cultural, and familial relatives. In 1873, finding that the tract had insufficient farmland, federal officials decided to enlarge it, both "for a hunting and fishing area" and to accommodate the Quileute and Hoh Indians, who had thus far declined to move south. Because the tribes that previously defied Governor Stevens still lacked reservations, officials added "Indians from the Columbia River northward" to the reserve's expected residents. An ensuing executive order delineated a reservation of 189,621 acres "for the use of the Quinaielt, Quillehute, Hoh, Quit, and other tribes of fish-eating Indians on the Pacific coast."[8]

The Americans aimed to restrict Indian land use and limit interracial relations without rendering Indians dependent on government support. By those standards, the executive order apparently provided an ideal reservation. The area's natural environment could serve the Indians' essential needs well. Through the demarcated tract ran four glacier-fed rivers, which had furnished indigenous people with abundant salmon—their important dietary staple—for countless generations. The ocean shore, forests, and nearby mountain meadows offered a rich buffet of other foods, including clams, smelt, herring, oysters, mussels, crabs, seals, deer, elk, bears, smaller mammals, waterfowl, starchy roots, and berries. From ubiquitous cedar trees, the people obtained materials for substantial dwellings and waterproof clothing. So bountiful was nature around Taholah and Queets that two early ethnographers thought aboriginal Quinaults had no need to work hard and were therefore unambitious. Ronald Olson wrote that "an overwhelming supply of toothsome razor clams" and a "never-failing year-round supply of salmon made life . . . easy and secure." In 1902 Livingston Ferrand claimed, "'In consequence of these conditions the majority of the people are indolent, but peaceable and comparatively prosperous.'"[9]

The reservation also seemed well situated for separating Indians from non-Indians who might find them offensive, antagonize them, or introduce them to vices prevalent on the American frontier. The Quinault and Queets valleys were isolated by distance and transportation hazards from the places where non-Indians were building towns and conducting commerce but also imbibing liquor and patronizing prostitutes. Oliver Wood, a US agent on the reservation in 1878, considered Quinault "the most inaccessible and isolated agency under the government." Wood's predecessor repeatedly lamented the difficulty of getting basic provisions into Taholah: it was 150 miles from a railroad terminal, there was no coastal steamboat service, the wagon road from Puget Sound to Grays Harbor was impassible in winter storms, and no roads connected Taholah to Grays Harbor. The agency packed in supplies via the beach at low tide. None of those conditions had changed by 1886, when another agent vented his frustration. The beach route passed "through soft sand and shingle. A dangerous and high bluff [had] to be crossed at some 4 miles from the agency. . . . The top of the bluff, some three-quarter mile across, [was] swampy, [and] extreme high tides invariably [filled] in the roadway at the foot of the ascent on either side."[10]

Few early American settlers were eager to bridge the distance separating their "civilization" from Quinault country. In 1869, the US agent at Taholah reported a "feeling of jealousy" among the Indians "towards white hunters who trespass upon the hunting grounds of their reservation," but for most non-Indians, the west side of the Olympic range otherwise had little allure. Its dense cover of enormous trees, scarce open spaces, prodigious rainfall, and exposure to storms rolling off the ocean were potent deterrents. Oliver Wood, who deemed the reservation "a paradise for these Indians," pronounced it "worthless for white settlements" and elaborated:

> It is not possible to make self-supporting farmers of these coast Indians. . . . The farming lands are only to be had in isolated patches along the streams that flow into the sea, and the expense of clearing and preparing these lands in a manner suitable for farming would be more than enterprising white people would pay, and I feel safe in saying that if this reserve was thrown open to white settlers it would be many years before respectable people would undertake to make homes on it. The situation is very discouraging to an agent that desires to make progress in industrial pursuits.[11]

Men in Wood's role at Taholah—preoccupied with the logistical challenges of maintaining a federal outpost at the edge of a vast rain forest—made little headway for years on their chief assignment: converting their charges to a "civilized," agrarian way of life. Indians on the reservation embraced new practices selectively, and their overseers could not keep them under close supervision or prevent their exposure to disapproved practices. Remote as the reserve was from non-Indian settlements, it was not prison or quarantine. Most Quileute, Hoh, and Chinook Indians continued to live somewhere else, and Indians on the reservation periodically left, going off to spend weeks or months fishing, hunting, visiting kin, and working at times for whites.[12]

The Indians' economic relations with settlers attested to their appreciation of the wealth they could acquire that way but not necessarily to their admiration for all aspects of the newcomers' culture. More than one American official noted ruefully that Indians at Taholah—while exhibiting a desire for "ordinary dwellings," dresses, and other tangible markers of "civilized" life—held stubbornly to "heathen" customs and beliefs. In 1897, agent Frank Terry called Quinaults "the least civilized of all the tribes under this agency."[13]

Quinaults may have preferred to live much as their forebears did, but they could read the signs of American power to make that increasingly difficult. Even so, leading Indians showed that they expected their American counterparts to show them respect. Stories told by elders who remembered the treaty instilled a belief that US officials had a continuing obligation to consider Quinault concerns about the relationship established at that council in 1855. Thus, several times in the first years of the twentieth century, eminent Quinault men made the long trip east to the seat of American power. In May 1902, the *Seattle Republican* reported that "Chief Tahola III," a treaty

With spears and nets, ca. 1895, Indians fished for their dietary staple of salmon at the mouth of the Quinault River, steps from their homes in the village of Taholah, where Sarah Willoughby, wife of US Indian agent Charles Willoughby, watched and sketched them. University of Washington Libraries Special Collections, NA 4042.

signer's prominent grandson also known as Billy Mason, had recently returned from Washington, DC, "where he attended a council of 24 tribes of Indians." Five years later, according to a San Francisco newspaper, three Quinaults headed for the US capital to protest the American president's plan to include their reservation in a federal forest reserve.[14]

MEDDLING AND MISMANAGEMENT

By the new century, non-Indians had identified something in Quinault country that would draw enterprising investors. The attraction was neither farmland nor clams, salmon, and game; it was timber. Whites in noteworthy numbers began scouting the neighborhood for timber-producing real estate during the 1880s. Most hoped to exploit a lumber industry boom that would surely accompany surging immigration to Washington Territory and attendant railway construction. Harbingers of the boom had reached Grays Harbor, some forty miles south of the reservation. Settlers with their eyes on the area's lush forests built sawmills in the towns of Hoquiam and Aberdeen and lobbied Northern Pacific Railroad Company to make the harbor its western terminus.[15]

Indians were among the men who felled trees for the mills. Their participation in wage labor calls into question Ronald Olson's allegation that "ambition was hardly one of the vices of a Quinault." Indeed, his own description of leadership in Quinault society contradicted that claim. He noted that the ability to produce, acquire, and distribute wealth brought a Quinault respect. The two Quinault words for someone that Americans would consider a chief roughly meant "rich man." When British and American traders had offered new forms of wealth, Quinaults adept at obtaining it had enjoyed increasing prestige.[16] Subsequent American settlement and commercial logging gave Quinaults additional ways to prosper, particularly laboring for non-Indians in fields, homes, and businesses.[17]

A century later, Quinault historians viewed the late nineteenth-century influx of timber seekers as an unfortunate turning point in tribe members' relations with non-Indians. According to *Land of the Quinault*, a history of the reservation published by the Quinault Nation in 1990, the "vigorous, imaginative, literate, social-minded, and strongly individualistic . . . pioneers" who staked claims around Grays Harbor in the 1850s and 1860s not only "accepted the Indians' presence without question"; they welcomed Indians' help and "struck up friendships that would last a lifetime." Lumber tycoons, however, were prepared to "wrest a fortune from the forests, on the backs, if necessary, of the less fortunate. The pioneers would be quite over-whelmed by these people."[18]

At the time, agents of the US government were of two minds about the Indians' economic relations with non-Indians. One reported in 1880 that some Indians "employed by farmers" were "considered quite useful laborers," but other agents complained about settlers who regarded Indians primarily as surefire customers for contraband liquor. Charles Willoughby did not worry that many young Quinault men in 1887 spent their days at logging camps and mills; they might be exhibiting an industriousness not usually attributed to Indians. Two years later, Edwin Eells lamented the lumber industry's effects on Quinaults, claiming, "Strong drink and disease have been very destructive with those who have lived near these mills." In his next report, Eells postulated instead that enterprising non-Indian neighbors could set motivating examples for Indians. "During the year a large number of white settlers have taken up claims bordering on three sides of the reservation," he wrote, "and they have been brought into contact with the white man as never before. This has stimulated them very considerably. There is a development of ideas and energy which is very pleasing to note."[19]

As it happened, the whites who staked those claims had years to wait before circumstances in the area matched their hopes. They had come more than a decade ahead of the railways that would bring commercial logging to the Quinault forest. Northern Pacific tracks did not reach Hoquiam until 1899, and six more years passed before the company completed a line to Moclips, near the reservation's south boundary. Shortly after that, however, giant firs, hemlocks, and cedars within sight of the reservation were falling to crosscut saws and riding railcars bound for Grays Harbor mills. By 1920, some logs went no farther than an Aloha Lumber Company mill on the reservation line.[20]

In the meantime, lumber industry captains, coveting timber touted as the region's finest, maneuvered for access to forests on the reservation.[21] They expected to benefit from federal legislation that seemed to suit their purpose. The General Allotment Act of 1887 authorized the division of tribal land into private parcels for individual Indians, ostensibly to make them self-supporting property owners and thus give them a stake in American legal culture. Once all Indians belonging on a reservation had received family-farm-size plots, the government could sell any remaining acreage to non-Indians. Between 1887 and the 1920s, amendments to the act, additional acts of Congress, and administrative practices also enabled non-Indians to purchase, lease, and inherit Indian allotments.

The first step in opening the Quinault Reservation to non-Indian use and ownership—a specific law mandating allotment there—came in 1892, but Indian objections to subdividing the land and questions about eligibility for lots delayed further action for more than a decade. Eventually, while rumors circulated in Hoquiam that government agents were arranging for local whites to get the best tracts, an agent informed the commissioner of Indian affairs that lawyers had turned Indian sentiment in favor of allotment by offering to arrange lucrative logging and right-of-way contracts.[22] Another indication that potential timber income induced Quinaults to accept allotment was a report in the *San Francisco Call* that Chief Billy Mason spent two months of 1913 in Washington, DC, seeking permission for tribe members to cut and sell their trees.[23]

The Indians consenting to allotment included Quileutes. A belief that private lots would yield income or entitle them to other reservation resources may have made allotment even more attractive to Quileutes than to Quinaults, who already had unquestioned rights to fish the Quinault River and reportedly enjoyed "quite an income" from selling their catch.[24] In any event, federal officials reported that they secured the necessary assents from Indians "belonging on the reservation," and allotment began in 1907.

Even if the Indians did think of their lots as a source of cash, few would have expected the new landownership scheme to change their personal habits or subsistence options substantially. They would continue living in their villages, taking fish from area rivers and clams from familiar beaches, hunting in the woods, and working occasionally for whites.[25]

Reservation acreage was many times greater than that needed to give every Indian on the reservation an eighty-acre parcel. Even so, non-Indians who expected surplus land to go on sale were destined for disappointment. US agents first marked out lots for Indians totaling just over 55,000 acres—the maximum conceivable arable land on the reservation. Then they suspended the subdivision process because federal law prohibited the allotment of reservation forests. A lawsuit on behalf of a Quileute man successfully challenged the suspension in 1924, and allotment resumed. By the time a clerk recorded the last allotment of Quinault Reservation land in 1933, the entire 190,000-acre reserve was meted out in 2,340 parcels to people identified as Indians. However, most allottees were not Quinaults; they were outsiders—people with ancestors in other tribes.[26]

Initially, local officials and Indians were not sure who qualified for a Quinault Reservation lot—just resident Quinaults and affiliated Quileutes, as indicated in the treaty, or also Indians of other tribes mentioned in the executive order? The ambiguity of relevant records necessitated a special act of Congress, and legislators produced one in 1911 that opened Quinault Reservation land to "all members of the Hoh, Quileute, Ozette, or other tribes of Indians in Washington."[27]

The authors of *Land of the Quinault* inferred from Indian bureau correspondence that some officials favored a narrow range of eligibility for allotments, so there would be excess acreage for non-Indians. Agent W. B. Sams seemed to think whites were "far more deserving of the resource rich lands than the Indian people." But Sams's superior, regional superintendent H. H. Johnson, opined that allocating land to additional Indians was better for the Indians than throwing most of the reservation open to whites, and Quinaults apparently agreed.[28] In councils to consider requests for allotments, Indian residents voted on scores of applications from people claiming ties to Quinaults' broad social network, and most votes were affirmative. By 1911, according to *Land of the Quinault*, "there were 748 allottees, most of them adopted [into the Quinault Tribe]. . . . All the new adoptees were blood relations. Whole families at a time, led by their elders, returned to the reservation."[29]

The councils apparently approved so many adoptions for a strategic reason. Quinaults "expressed themselves as desiring to always remain the predominant tribe of the reservation," agent Sams reported, "and recognizing that the applicants for adoption would probably be included" in a government order declaring them eligible for land, "they desired to admit these people as Quinaielts in order that they might outnumber any other tribe that might be admitted to allotment in the future on the reservation."[30]

In the view of higher federal personnel, the adoption process was haphazard and at times corrupt. After a council in 1912, they lamented that the Indians had "passed upon the cases *en masse* and without giving any reasons whatever for their action in 'adopting' nearly all of the persons who applied." Many applicants made no showing that they were poor, homeless, or members of the region's "fish eating tribes." The Indian Office remanded the applications for a case-by-case review and another council vote. When a special enrolling agent submitted the results in 1918, the successful applicants were allegedly people with ancestors in one of the tribes specified by Congress and a credible story of personal affiliation with a Quinault-Quileute community.[31]

Still, questions about eligibility persisted. At a meeting after the Supreme Court allowed allotment to resume, Quinaults declined to grant tribal membership to numerous petitioners from across Washington State.[32] Once again, unsuccessful applicants sought help from the Supreme

Court, which settled the issue in 1931. Any Indians designated in the 1873 executive order were entitled to reservation land. Neither adoption nor kinship with Quinaults was necessary. Thereafter, nearly two thousand people with varying degrees of Indian ancestry and social connection to other tribes of "fish eating" Indians received allotments even if they did not intend to reside on their land or take part in tribal affairs.[33]

Indian agency records do not document Quinault reactions to this development at the time. They do mention opposition, both before and after 1924, to "tribal rights" for allottees who were not community members.[34] In any event, troublesome consequences of giving so much land to outsiders soon became apparent, coloring subsequent Quinault views of the allotment process and non-Quinault allottees. Gary Morishima identified the problems when he worked as natural resource manager for the Quinault Nation in the 1970s. Federal personnel, he alleged, issued allotments "to individuals who claimed to belong to tribes which did not exist and which had no reliable membership roles [*sic*]." Furthermore, "because official policy had precluded selection of [the forested] lands by the first allottees," it was "the non-resident Indians" who received the heavily timbered tracts and thus "could reap the greatest economic benefit from the reservation." One source for the latter claim was J. P. Kinney, a former chief forester in the Office of Indian Affairs, writing in 1930: "'The shrewder, non-resident individuals, having tribal affiliations, but with only a small amount of Indian blood, have secured selections ten or twenty times as valuable as those taken at an earlier period by full blood Indians who had always made their home on the reservation.'"[35]

The 1887 General Allotment Act provided that the federal government would hold Indians' lots in trust for twenty-five years, protecting them from imprudent alienation, taxation, and seizure for debts. Subsequent legislation authorized transfers of trust allotments to non-Indians in some circumstances, and a handful of Quinault Reservation allottees did convert their new property to cash by sales to whites. For most allottees, however, the best or only way to make money from their land was selling timber. Terrain, soil quality, climate, and thick stands of immense trees precluded other income-generating uses. The consequence of that incentive to log the land, and of federal administrators' inability or unwillingness to bar unwise logging practices, was severe environmental degradation, which Quinaults would eventually seek to reverse by taking full charge of the reservation.

The damaging practices occurred despite the desire of some government employees to prevent them. Although the United States treated Indian forests as a public domain resource—an undeniable example of colonial exploitation—federal foresters took their mission of resource conservation seriously. The division of the Quinault forest into a multitude of private holdings disregarded a warning from the Indian bureau's chief forester that it would frustrate wise management of the trees, compromising their long-term economic potential, but other personnel in the bureau had an opposing mandate to manage Indian trust property so that it yielded income and promoted the owners' engagement with the market economy.[36]

Lumber companies typically wanted contracts for stands of trees that spanned multiple Indian allotments. For such a contract, bureaucrats needed either the consent of each Indian owner or authorization to act on the owner's behalf. The superintendent could streamline the work of obtaining consents by prevailing on owners to give him durable power of attorney or by finding individual Indians "noncompetent" to manage financial affairs. Aside from a story of one woman who tried in vain to block logging, unwilling allottees do not appear in existing records. Rather, allottees by the score requested speedy approval of contracts to cut their trees, usually citing their urgent need for cash.[37]

That many nonresident allottees would choose cash over standing trees is not surprising, but reservation residents also sought permission to sell. Gary Morishima attributed their pleas to poverty resulting in part from a merchant-trader's crass exploitation of his government-authorized monopoly on purchases of Indians' fish. According to Morishima, the trader priced his goods "about 30% higher than those off the reservation," gave the Indians liberal credit allowances, then cut the prices he paid for their fish so sharply that he bankrupted "the entire village of Taholah." Unable to reverse their descent into debt, Quinault families turned to selling timber or land, and once they decided to sell trees, they usually wanted maximum removal. "Within a few short years of allotment," Morishima found, the "clamoring of allottees for money from the sale of timber" convinced federal officials "that responsible management of reservation forest resources was not possible." Some proposed that the agency buy allotted land so it could manage tree harvests properly, but they did not get approval from Congress, "largely due to opposition by Quinaults who feared loss of their reservation."[38]

Aloha Lumber Company bought the first reservation logging rights in 1920 and began felling trees two years later on the southern Moclips unit. In 1929, federal officials accepted bids on all timber north of the Quinault River. Within ten years, the four companies with long-term contracts had logged 26,748 acres, most by clear-cutting.[39] Inspectors from the Department of Agriculture soil conservation division lamented the effects on the land. They found debris "so dense that it [was] almost a hopeless task for an individual" to clean up an allotment "for cultivation." The property sat idle, susceptible to fires that were far too common "because of campers, berry pickers, woods workers and highway travelers." In subsequent litigation regarding Quinault allottees' liability for taxes on timber income, the Supreme Court observed that an allotment with its timber removed "no longer [served] the purpose for which it was by treaty set aside." It was inadequate for the Indian's needs.[40]

Absentee allotment owners would not live with the damage done by clear-cuts, but even residents with deep local roots "clamored" at times for wholesale tree removal. Perhaps to their shame later, when logging's adverse effects on fishing streams became apparent, some Quinaults berated federal personnel who appeared to hinder timber harvests. At the 1937 annual meeting of tribe members, for example, "Harry Shale said he thot the timber belongs to the Indians and shouls [*sic*] be logged off clean so the allottees could get all the money coming to them. The only solution was to stand together and show the white people that the Indians are the owners of the timber and do all they can to keep the timber for themselves." Such records are the basis for Morishima's comment that tribe leaders of the 1930s added to allotment's harmful consequences by refusing to let the Bureau of Indian Affairs "employ . . . forest management policies which were consistent with the then state of the art." The ironic result, another analyst observed, was that the bureau for several decades "consistently acquiesced to the demands of the timber companies."[41]

In a 1970 study of Quinault forest management history, University of Washington law student Robert Beaty suggested that the forests' relative unimportance to Quinault traditional life could partially account for the Indians' unwise advocacy of clear-cutting. In a 1973 interview, Joe

DeLaCruz made a similar conjecture. The forests "were just something to look at" while fish were still abundant, he said.[42] But a few tribe members, early on, looked at the forests and saw wealth or influence to be gained from cutting and milling logs. "Functioning among the indifference of fellow Quinaults and the impotence of the non-Quinault allottees," Beaty suggested, they "found it personally profitable to encourage" policies that facilitated aggressive logging.[43]

Shortly after Beaty's study, Quinaults and other allottees were in court seeking redress for US government mismanagement of their forest resources. The lawsuit—ultimately successful—charged the federal trustee with failure to manage timber on a sustained-yield basis, failure to get fair market value for timber, and malpractice that siphoned off allottees' returns.[44] Later in the 1970s, the Quinault Nation published an account of reservation logging that emphasized BIA disregard of its obligation to prevent adverse ecological consequences. *Portrait of Our Land: A Quinault Tribal Forest Perspective* declared, "For more than 50 years, our lands have been managed to meet the demand for short-term profit with no thought to the future," leaving "mountainous accumulations of logging residue and fields of brush" on thousands of acres and "streams which once supported large runs of salmon . . . clogged with silt and debris."[45]

In one respect, these accusations indicate a change over fifty years in Quinaults' relationship to their reservation forests—a shift from accepting deforestation for individual gain to insisting that timberlands be managed sustainably for multiple community needs. In another respect, there is continuity in Quinault views on the issue of forest management—a consistent belief in Quinaults' right to control what was theirs. Tribe leaders of the 1970s were intent on controlling all the resources reserved to them by treaty, but so were Harry Shale and other tribe members who spoke in 1937 of reservation resources as theirs alone to manage and use. Since the beginning of the century, federal government agents had increasingly acted contrary to that notion, not only by assuming control of reservation land and forests but also by a holier-than-thou attempt to govern another realm of tribal life: fishing. By the time Shale urged Indians to stand together against whites on logging issues, Quinaults had already compelled federal officials to back off from controlling fishing opportunities.

RESISTING CONTROL

Superintendent Johnson provoked possibly the first concerted Quinault resistance to US controls on their fishing. In 1913, he ordered the Indians to halt fish harvests until they completed a road under construction since 1908. More than forty fishers promptly endorsed a protest to the Indian commissioner. Declaring the road "unnecessary," they insisted, "We must have voice in all common affairs in this reservation, and such a step must not go too far as to deprive us of our rights and privileges to make honest living." The commissioner replied that the road was for the fishers' benefit, a route for hauling their catch to market. Johnson's decree was therefore a reasonable exercise of his authority as the official in charge at the reservation. (That year a group of Quinaults also confronted a visiting congressional committee, demanding that Johnson be charged with illegal use of the reservation for oil drilling.)[46]

When and why US agents began meddling in Quinaults' reservation fishing is hard to determine. Researchers in the 1970s found several inconclusive records on the subject. A Quinault employee discovered a 1915 bureau report of a cannery operator's recollection that the Indians adopted the first conservation regulations in 1908 and submitted them to the Office of Indian Affairs the next year. An Interior Department lawyer, gathering evidence for a lawsuit to confirm the tribes' treaty fishing rights, credited federal employees with drafting the first regulations in 1917, after tribe members saw whites fishing with "modern" methods on the Columbia River and requested an assessment of the potential for similar fisheries on the Quinault. Gary Morishima concluded instead that government men encouraged the Indians to assign fishing sites on the river and adopt other rules in response to white encroachment, which followed the sale of some riverside allotments. *Land of the Quinault* authors stated simply, "Between 1910 and 1925, the [Quinault] Nation refined its philosophy of fisheries management and developed fishery regulations and a formal pattern of harvesting fish in reservation rivers."[47]

Rather than clarifying whether Indians or federal employees initiated formal regulation, Taholah agency records tell yet another story. The earliest document—a set of rules dated May 22, 1909—concerned fishing stations for individual tribe members. Among other things, it limited the area each station could encompass and the number of sites a person could use. It also stipulated, "Any person, holding a fishing location, who does not use the revenues derived therefrom for the support of himself and his family, the improvement of his home or allotment, or for other good and legitimate purposes [*sic*], shall be deprived of the use thereof and such location will be given to those more deserving." That language was surely supplied by the agency employee who signed the document and submitted it to the superintendent. Johnson forwarded it with his approval to the acting commissioner, who returned it with his signature and a letter saying, "You report that the fishing since May 22, 1909, has been carried on under these regulations with great satisfaction, and that the Indians are hearty in their commendation of the plan."[48]

Over the next decade and a half, federal officials periodically received Quinault petitions for changes to annual fishing regulations. Those appeals do not mean that government personnel imposed the regulations without Indian input; indeed, Indian input is indicated by a petition regarding the time by which fishers had to pull nets. It stated, "We made a badly mistake" in the choice of a time. Still, the Indians likely saw the regulatory regime that began in 1908 or 1909 as a concession to US agents.[49] Through countless generations, Quinaults had fished at stations along the river without external supervisors and without exhausting fish stocks, but any rules they observed were unwritten. US officials, who considered law a requisite of civilized life and did not recognize unwritten norms as law, deemed Quinaults' customary rule making inadequate.

Even if officials demanded or suggested a formal regulatory system, they were reacting to new circumstances that some Indians also wanted to address. By 1908, non-Indians in the region had created an unprecedented, lucrative commercial market for Quinault salmon and steelhead. One result was sometimes nasty competition for fish and places to catch fish. As migrating salmon headed into Quinault rivers, the owners of the first nets they encountered had a significant advantage over fishers stationed upstream. Federal personnel maintained that the unfair competition incited wanton fishing, which could annihilate salmon stocks. When Indians also complained about the allocation of fishing sites, fishers who overharvested, or non-Indians and other outsiders who conned their way into sites meant for Quinaults, the government men thought it was time for written regulations.

Thus, some Quinaults saw reasons for formalized regulation, and federal agents learned about those reasons from Indians. That Indians would also want or expect US officials to mediate the competition for fish is not surprising, but neither is the fact that the officials—true to the role of colonial overseers—would claim authority to formulate and enforce regulations as they saw fit. Employing a common means of keeping order on other reservations, they also appointed Indian men to patrol Quinault waters and Indian judges to adjudicate alleged rule violations.[50]

Nonetheless, Indians did not take kindly to rules that imposed significant curbs on their fishing. For example, over Indian objections, federal fisheries managers installed a salmon hatchery at Lake Quinault in 1914. When they insisted that Indians limit their harvest of fish bound for the lake so that enough spawners could reach the hatchery, Quinaults protested that the escapement goal was unnecessarily high.[51] At least one man expressed his displeasure with the new regulatory regime in a memorable way. As *Land of the Quinault* recounted it, "In the 1920's . . . , the five foot high, featherweight boxer 'Indian Pete' Pickernell . . . forcedly [*sic*] removed the BIA agent from the Quinault River, when he tried to divest the tribal government of its authority on that river."[52]

About the same time, new rules drove chief Billy Mason and eight other Quinault fishers to contest the agent's authority peaceably but more decisively than Pickernell. They sued Superintendent Sams in US district court, seeking to prevent him from enforcing two provisions he had added to that year's fishing regulations. One allowed him to designate the only authorized buyers for Quinault-caught fish; the other levied a tax on fish sale receipts and "placed" the revenue "to the credit of the tribe as a royalty . . . to be used for the care of the aged and destitute members of the tribe . . . or for other general agency purposes."

Judge Edward Cushman granted the plaintiffs' petition on April 9, 1925. After studying the Supreme Court's interpretation of other Indian treaties, he construed the words of the Quinaults' treaty with the United States "as giving [an] exclusive right of fishing upon the reservation to these Indians." On the question of individual fishers' tax liability, Cushman reasoned, "The treaty was with the tribe; but the right of taking fish at all places within the reservation . . . was plainly a right common to the members of the tribe," making it "the right of an individual of the community." In the treaty, "no intention is shown, nor implication warranted, that the Indian who fished should pay, from his fishing, the Indian who did not care to fish but chose, rather, to hunt, pick berries, gather roots, or run his ponies upon the public domain." In sum, the tax was unjustified. The judge did not rule on the Indian commissioner's authority to license fish buyers.[53]

By letter on October 9, 1928, the commissioner informed Sams that the Justice Department had opted not to appeal from Cushman's order, and the case "should be considered as closed." He was apparently responding to a report from Sams that the Indians' victory on the tax issue had assuaged their resentment; they were content to abide by the rest of the regulations. For his part, Sams said he "allowed them to use the police force to keep the channel open, see that they remove their nets, etc."[54]

Years later, a regional Interior Department solicitor wrote that the lawsuit titled *Mason v. Sams* had more immediate results than Sams's letter indicated. Not only were the objectionable regulations redrafted, but the tribe also assumed "exclusive responsibility" for their enforcement.[55] The suit also had longer-term effects on Quinaults. The success of their legal venture meant more than exemption from a BIA-imposed fish tax. It confirmed to their satisfaction that Quinaults had an exclusive right to exploit and manage reservation river fisheries. Just as importantly, the experience of appealing to an American judge for affirmation of a tribal right and getting the desired results was a memorable achievement. *Mason v. Sams* set a precedent that would influence the strategies of Quinault political leaders for generations to come.

Taking to heart Judge Cushman's declaration that "the fish in the waters of this stream do not belong to the state, nor to the United States, but to the Indians of this reservation," Quinaults exerted their power as owners. Early in 1927, the *Seattle Times* newspaper learned that "the Quinault Tribe" had prohibited "white men" from fishing on Lake Quinault or any stream in the reservation. The Indians reportedly complained that they had "given up the entire Grays Harbor Country to the white people, reserving only that portion now embraced in the Quinaielt Reservation," that white people wanted "to take that from them" too and were "destroying fish by taking out large numbers of them." An unspecified reaction from Grays Harbor County game commissioners prompted Washington's senators to request an Indian Office investigation of the tribe's move.[56] Perhaps to the disappointment of county officials, not only did US officials indicate in reply that they accepted the ruling in *Mason v. Sams*, but the Washington Supreme Court soon arrived at the same understanding of the Indians' rights.

The new case was *Pioneer Packing Company v. Winslow*, decided in 1930. The company claimed that a state law prohibiting interstate shipments of steelhead trout could not rightfully be enforced when Quinaults caught and sold the fish on the reservation. Lawyers for the tribe submitted a supporting brief that referenced the tribe's treaty with the United States and *Mason v. Sams*. Like Judge Cushman, the state justices concluded that Quinaults were the sole owners of fish in reservation waters and therefore entitled to sell the steelhead without regulation or interference by Washington authorities.[57]

SUPERVISED TRIBAL GOVERNMENT

The Indian community at the mouth of the Quinault River harbored some determined and daring people in the 1920s, but by metrics that federal supervisors considered meaningful, it was a sleepy, rustic village. In 1921, responding to an inquiry from those supervisors, a Taholah resident reported a population of 275. Two percent of the people were "white" (and probably agency employees). Twenty-five of the sixty-four family homes had just a single room, ten had gardens, and all had "privies." Forty of the residents over age ten could neither read nor write, but all could speak English. The occupations of the Indians—"all of them"—were "fishing and clam digging."[58]

The next year, hopes of fending off interference from federal supervisors and outsiders may have motivated another Quinault adaptation to American ways of regulating human affairs: the establishment of a government with written bylaws. In Quinault history before that, as Joe DeLaCruz heard it, community leaders were always "hereditary chiefs." The bylaws that tribe members approved in 1922 rested authority in a general council composed of all adult Quinaults, who would elect four officers and seven other individuals each year to serve on a Business Committee. This new method of choosing leaders did not immediately shake up social ranks in the tribe, DeLaCruz said. For many years following, the people elected were "more or less the chiefs of the different families."[59] However, formalizing their leadership structure and decision-making process enabled Quinaults to assert their right of self-government in terms favored by US officials.

The institutionalization of community leadership extended to educational affairs. In 1920, as related in *Land of the Quinault*, "the tribe assumed command" of a state-created school district for children in Taholah. Thereafter, Quinault Indians filled all three school board seats. To *Land of the Quinault* authors, this move exemplified "the revolutionary thinking of tribal leaders." It showed an "ability to approach problems logically and rationally, and to seek outside advice"—something the tribe also did during the early fishing controversy and "in organizing its government."[60] The writers did not reveal where Quinault leaders went for "outside" advice, nor did the records I found in US archives.

Unsurprisingly, a chartered Quinault government with elected leaders was not a panacea for problems confronting the tribe by then. Federal law and other circumstances presented stubborn impediments to Quinault management of conditions on the reservation. As a result of allotment, a multiplicity of private owners now decided individually what use to make of their land. A few were non-Indians who did not expect tribal policies and plans to affect them or their property. Many more were nonresident Indian allottees or their heirs, who were apt to balk at Quinault government or federal actions that might limit income from their reservation property. Timber harvests therefore proceeded under US-approved contracts even as it became apparent that the consequences were incompatible in the long run with the reservation's original purpose of sustaining its Indian residents.[61]

Incongruously, clear-cutting continued in the 1930s under a new commissioner of Indian affairs who advocated sustainable resource management by tribal governments. John Collier aimed to reverse the ruinous economic and social effects of allotting reservation land and undermining traditional tribal decision-making. In 1933, he wrote, "If we can relieve the Indian of the unrealistic and fatal allotment system . . . [and] if, through group organization and tribal incorporation, we can give him a real share in the management of his own affairs, he can develop normally in his own natural environment."[62] One year later, Congress gave Collier a green light in the Indian Reorganization Act (IRA), which provided that a tribe or tribes "residing on the same reservation" would have "the right to organize for its common welfare, and . . . adopt an appropriate constitution and bylaws." The prescribed procedure for adopting a constitution was a majority vote for ratification by "the adult members of the tribe, or of the adult Indians residing on such reservation." The new law would not apply "to any reservation wherein a majority of the adult Indians, in a special election duly called by the Secretary of the Interior," voted "against its application."[63] Within months, the Bureau of Indian Affairs (BIA) was overseeing referenda on reservations across the country, including western Washington.

The Taholah agency reported the results of the Quinault referendum on April 23, 1935. Ballots went out to 784 people, and 360 returned valid responses—184 in favor of accepting the IRA, 176 opposed. Despite the law's provision for voting by residents, nonresident voters outnumbered reservation residents, 217 to 143.[64] The BIA construed the tally as Quinault approval of the IRA. Historians and leaders of the tribe subsequently disputed that conclusion. Charles Hobbs suggested why in a 1965 letter to an assistant commissioner. An attorney who was advising Quinaults on a related matter, Hobbs wrote, "Your records show that the election was close, and that the nearby Indians . . . voted to reject the IRA, while the far-away Indians voted to accept it. We question whether it was proper to count the votes of the non-Quinault allottees living far away, who had no tribal relations at Quinault."[65]

Even if the BIA count was proper, Quinaults were not required to organize an IRA-authorized government, and they declined to do so. Field agent George LaVatta told the commissioner, without further explanation, that the "obstacles" to forming an IRA government at Taholah included "three or four individuals . . . trying to keep the Indians from organizing due to selfish interests and desires." Another official reported "a fear on the part of those Indians . . . residing on the reservation and possessing good fishing locations that going further into the matter of reorganization [could] afford some opening through which Indians not . . . residing on the Indian reservation [would] acquire possession and control of these fishing grounds."[66] In later years, Quinault representatives preferred to state simply that there was no need at the time for a new governing document. The bylaws of 1922, slightly revised in 1935, were equivalent to a constitution, and a satisfactory one.[67]

Records of tribal affairs from the late 1930s through the 1950s suggest that Quinaults were satisfied not only with their government as structured in 1922 but also with the man they elected to lead it. Cleveland Jackson served continuously as president from 1938 or 1939 until his death at age sixty-nine in 1960. Scattered accounts of his activities during that long tenure evoke an enterprising man who cultivated relations with non-Indians in government and business, especially people who could protect Quinault resources or direct new resources to the tribe while offering Jackson opportunities to enhance his own prosperity.

When Jackson reported in 1939 that the US government was proposing to buy half the reservation and Lake Quinault for inclusion in Olympic National Park, he warned tribe members not to trust a promise that they would retain their hunting and fishing rights in the purchased area. Already, Jackson said, he had contacted chambers of commerce, influential clubs, and most labor unions in the Grays Harbor area, persuading them all to oppose the sale, "as it would affect the Harbor industries too if the Reservation timber was put into the Park and logging stopped." Not coincidentally, Jackson's personal fortunes rested on logging, and probably his political fortunes as well. Early in his years as Quinault president, general council members proposed that he go to Washington, DC, for discussions with the BIA about logging contracts. Cleve, they explained, was the community's most knowledgeable person on that subject. At a meeting in 1943, Harry Shale said of Jackson, "He has worked all along the Coast and knows more about timber than any other member of the Tribe."[68]

A striking indicator of Jackson's economic ambitions is a joint venture he arranged in 1951. His partner was a non-Indian, F. A. Polson of Hoquiam. Jackson pledged his best efforts to locate stands of marketable reservation timber for Polson, who would acquire them in Jackson's name. Polson would advance the necessary funds, and Jackson would execute a promissory note for half the cost and carrying charges. From time to time, the parties would sell the tracts with proceeds going to Polson, who would apply half to Jackson's note and divide profits equally. During the second year of the venture, the *New York Times* carried a photograph of "Chief" Cleve Jackson signing a thirty-four-year lease that opened 35,000 reservation acres to Rayonier Corporation logging.[69]

When Robert Beaty referred with implicit disapproval to Quinaults who profited personally from ill-advised logging policies, he may have had

Cleve Jackson in mind. But in the eyes of Indians who associated with Jackson or worked for him, his enterprise may not have seemed selfish. In 2016, a Quinault elder remembered Jackson as a man who kept his hold on the presidency by favoring tribe members with jobs in his logging business. Those favors and the loyalty they engendered may have seemed analogous to the traditional roles of a family headman or chief and to the respect of the kin who recognized his organizational abilities and shared in the resulting wealth.[70]

Throughout Cleve Jackson's years as president, logging contracts were common items on Quinault Business Committee agendas. For example, in 1949, the BIA superintendent advised the commissioner that committee members had refused to approve a sale of timber from lands still in tribal ownership because "they believed the few tracts of tribal land should be reserved for possible use by the Indians themselves." They agreed to reconsider, however, as logging progressed toward the tracts in question.[71]

Law enforcement was another persistent Business Committee concern, one that predated Jackson's presidency. Ever since Indian officers had begun patrolling the rivers and violators of fishing regulations had answered to Indian judges, filling those enforcement roles had been a shared issue for Quinault and BIA officials. Finding and retaining judges could be difficult, not least because they were subject to BIA control. The court was a federal government creation—one of many Courts of Indian Offenses tasked with suppressing "uncivilized" Indian behavior—and judges served at the pleasure of federal supervisors. Quinault leaders identified potential appointees, but the superintendent made the appointments and expected Business Committee approval of his choices.[72] At least one superintendent was not shy about telling judges how to do their jobs or performing judicial functions himself. N. O. Nicholson, who presided over the agency responsible for the Quinault Reservation through much of the 1930s, occasionally issued search warrants and orders to seize contraband. He also instructed judges how to handle specific cases and passed judgments of his own on their rulings, as when he chastised a judge for failing to penalize a couple living in unmarried "sin."[73]

Meeting the need for police was likewise a recurring challenge, addressed in ways that varied over time. In 1932, the superintendent commissioned sheriffs in several counties as deputy special officers for the reservations under his charge, explaining to the Indian commissioner, "The lack of jurisdiction over these areas by county officers has operated to the disadvantage of the Indians and the enforcement of the laws thereon." When Cleve Jackson informed the superintendent that Horton Capoeman had been "elected by a majority vote of the Tribe to enforce fishing regulations for the 1940 blueback season," he added, "It has been the custom in the past that he be sworn in as Special Police by your office, although he will be paid from the Quinaielt fish tax fund." In 1948, Superintendent Marvin Helander notified the Business Committee that he was dismissing the current officer and appointing a temporary one until the committee identified its choice of candidates for the position. Four months later, mentioning "the Business Committee's keen interest in the past on the matter of providing adequate law and order services for the Quinaielt Reservation," Helander wrote to Jackson that agency funds for law enforcement that year were not enough "to pay the salary of even one policeman. . . . It appears that for the most part, law and order activities must be supported from tribal funds." Furthermore, unless federal funding increased in 1950, Jackson could expect to "be placed in a position of not having any law and order services one year hence."[74]

During the 1940s, elected leaders and other Quinaults did indeed show keen interest in law enforcement, as when Business Committee secretary Anna Jackson, unhappy that community children were "getting out of hand," asked the BIA for a model curfew resolution.[75] More frequently, the objective was to control outsiders who took fish from reservation waters without the tribe's permission. Tribal officials seemed certain of Quinaults' right to impose such bans, even if the means to enforce them were limited. At a general council in 1943, for instance, "Simon Charley thought something should be done about white people getting clams and crabs on the Reservation beach. [In response] C. Jackson said every allottee was an officer in that case, and if they found white people poaching, it is their duty to stop them." In 1946, members of an unspecified "tribal committee" approved a resolution "that we allow onely resident-alotte's [*sic*] to dig on our clam beach."[76]

This belief in Quinault authority had a basis in tribe members' knowledge that reservation police and judges had previously exercised jurisdiction over misbehaving non-Indians. In 1932, for example, Superintendent Nicholson received a letter from Taholah reporting, "Mr. Bagley and Jack Mason arrested a white man by the name of Harvey Locke for drunkenness. . . . He was put in jail and kept till the ball games were over and then released to Mr. McGee who is manager of the Copalis Beach ball team." (Bagley was a Quinault police officer.) In 1936, an allegedly drunk "White man" stood trial in the Indian court for "misconducting." Judge Simon Charley ordered him to leave the reservation or pay a fifty-dollar fine. Two years later, a "White" man described as "drinking, gambler, undesirable" pled guilty as charged. Given the choice of ninety days in jail or leaving town, he "preferred the latter." BIA records mention no instances in which the superintendent overruled a decision affecting a white person. Indeed, in the case of one probable non-Indian defendant, he told the Indian judge that his action "was quite proper," adding, "The presence of such persons in Taholah at any time, particularly during the fishing season, is highly undesirable, and we are, accordingly, better off without him."[77]

By the 1950s, judging from scanty BIA records, Quinault power or confidence in their power over outsiders had waned. Economic constraints were clearly a contributing factor. Federal funding for reservation police had ended as Superintendent Helander predicted in 1948, even as non-Indians' presence on the reservation was growing. A 1954 Business Committee communication to the superintendent bemoaned the dual challenge of dwindling funds and numerous visitors who were loath to respect Indian authority.

> We must do something drastic to enforce our Reservation rules regarding fishing on Lake Quinault, which has been neglected for several years, until we are faced with a condition that must be remedied this year. We have fishing permits costing one dollar which are required for trout fishing on the lake and permits for rowboats and outboard motors, but one or two if [*sic*] the resort owners claim they will not pay any boat tax, nor do they think fishing permits are necessary. A number of white sports fishermen are 'snagging' blueback salmon, which is against our regulations, and are encouraged by these resort owners to defy our reservation rules. In the past we received one half of the proceeds of the sale of fishing permits to help defray our share of this patrol, but for some years this has not been paid into our local fund. The tribe feels that if nothing can be done to bring the resort owners into line and force them to obey our Reservation laws, then the only thing we can do is to close the

> lake to sport fishing, as we did once in the past when outside interests interfered with out [*sic*] Reservation rules.[78]

The arrangements for reservation law enforcement were undeniably inadequate.

ALLIES

The Business Committee was appealing in 1954 to a US government that had recently disavowed John Collier's policy of fostering tribal self-rule and development. The plan instead was to eliminate laws, administrative practices, and jurisdictional enclaves exclusive to Indians. Congress had announced a goal of terminating the United States' self-styled guardianship of tribes as soon as practicable and had taken a step toward that end by approving Public Law 280, the act that required some states and permitted others to assume jurisdiction on reservations.[79]

Six decades later, some Quinault elders remembered the 1950s not as a time of federal withdrawal from the reservation but as a time of BIA domination. Justine James, Sr.—still a teenager then—"got involved with the general council." "We just kind of floated along at that time," he said in 2012. "The bureau pretty much had control of us. Pretty much made all the decisions for us." Harold Patterson also recalled a lopsided power relationship. A non-Indian motivated by Christian beliefs to work among Indians, Patterson took a custodial job at the Taholah school when his wife began teaching there. He was soon drawn into Quinault affairs. In 2012, he reminisced, "At that time—1955, '56—the tribe had no office, no telephone, no administration. . . . They could make decisions regarding the local situation, but the Bureau of Indian Affairs controlled everything else and were not very kind. I can remember going into the Bureau of Indian Affairs office when some Indians came in with some kind of request, and he treated them like animals. It was insulting."[80]

Of the many things under bureau control, real estate and trees mattered most in the long run. As observed in *Land of the Quinault*, the Eisenhower administration "assaulted federally held timber bearing lands." Although a new Congress "stopped this raid on public resources" outside of Indian country, "Indian people were not so well served [due to] the termination policy." The BIA stepped up the pace of moving Indian property out of the federal trust, increasing the likelihood that it would pass into non-Indian hands. Consequently, "in a few brief years, a large portion of the Quinault Reservation was alienated."[81] In 1955 alone, the bureau issued fee patents for 7,066 acres, and 1,164 acres were sold.[82] As of 1960, about 540 allotments had lost federal protection. By the 1970s, non-Indians would own nearly one-third of Quinault Reservation land and half of the prized coastline acreage.[83]

In the face of BIA power and condescension, Quinaults were hard pressed to maintain self-respect or self-confidence, let alone meaningful self-rule. Investing time and energy in an oppressed, precarious tribal government could yield more frustration than rewards. If the Quinault Business Committee and general council did "float along," taking few consequential actions, they can perhaps be forgiven. Yet the record suggests that Quinault officials were not resigned to passivity even then. Some determined individuals not only requested or demanded respect and responsiveness from federal administrators; they actively sought to promote or protect Quinault interests by taking their concerns to American courts and joining multitribal advocacy organizations.

Horton Capoeman was one vigilant and frank advocate of Quinault rights as he saw them. In 1955, he evidently wanted state officials to restrain outsiders who violated the rights of what he termed "a bona fide Quinault treaty indian." Identifying himself as the elected "River Judge for the protection of our salmon & all game and a member of the Quinault Council," he complained by letter to the Washington fisheries director that "non-treaty Indians" were engaged in "commercial digging" on the "clam beach with in [*sic*] the Quinault Reservation." The following year, Aloha Lumber Company received a blunt notice from Capoeman that their removal of riverbed gravel was contrary to their contract, state law, and the Quinault tribe's property rights.[84]

Capoeman was particularly jealous of rights to Lake Quinault. At a general council meeting in 1956, he proposed that the tribe take control of the lake, "as it belongs to we Indians."[85] Four years later Capoeman was vice chairman of the council, exhorting the BIA superintendent by letter to support tribal management of fishing on the lake, where non-Indians violated the terms of their trout fishing permits from the tribe. "My contention is that a man subject to the laws of the state should not be voided because he has entered a reservation if in violation," he wrote.[86] It was probably Capoeman who proposed a council resolution in early 1961 that barred "White fishermen" from the lake. Tribe leaders said members approved it "in the interests of conservation," because "sportsmen" were snagging salmon with hooks, contrary to the tribe's ordinance, and "power boats were running close to shore, grinding up little fish with the propellors."[87]

Witnessing that vote to eject non-Indian fishers, and perhaps providing advice on its legality, was John Cragun, a lawyer from Washington, DC. Cragun's firm—Wilkinson, Cragun, Barker, and Hawkins—had represented the tribe for several years in the Indian Claims Commission (ICC), seeking fair compensation for land the United States had appropriated in the 1850s. Cragun also had some responsibility for an ongoing lawsuit contesting federal taxation of Indians' income from sales of allotment timber. The plaintiffs were Horton and Emma Capoeman, who evidently sued with tribal government approval or at its behest. When the Supreme Court ruled in 1956 that Indian timber proceeds were indeed tax exempt, Cleve Jackson sent an exultant letter to the National Congress of American Indians, which relied on the same firm for legal counsel. "We have been fourteen years on this case," Jackson wrote, "and four different attornies have handled the case for us—they all died on the job but 'The Cragun' seems to get fat and sassy on it. What a Guy!!!!!"[88]

Jackson's breezy letter exhibits a familiarity with lawyers and lawsuits that might seem unlikely for an Indian logger from a small tribe on an isolated reservation, particularly in the demoralizing 1950s, but that familiarity reflected a Quinault history of litigation much longer than the protracted tax case. According to oral history relayed in *Land of the Quinault*, tribe members consulted lawyers in Hoquiam as early as 1916 or 1917 in their effort to foil federal interference with Indian fishing.[89] After the success in *Mason v. Sams*, the tribe's litigation experience included an appearance as amicus curiae in *Pioneer Packing Company v. Winslow* and a monetary award from the US Court of Claims in 1945 for tribal land that the government had effectively appropriated by surveying the reservation boundary inaccurately.[90]

The general council's central role in Quinault self-government ensured that many tribe members would know this legal history. Reports about ongoing litigation, voting on attorney contracts, and discussion of legal issues were common at council meetings. For instance, the boundary litigation was on the agenda in June 1943. Ninety-seven people heard President Jackson say, "The Lake was part of the Reservation now and always would be. This suit will explain just what we are suing for and what we must be paid for; that we could never get the land back, all the tribe could hope for was its value." Simon Charley responded that "the Tribe would have to stand behind their Council members and give them all the help needed if this suit was to be won, that it would take lots of work and money to get the suit lined up." At the same gathering, Jackson mentioned an earlier lawsuit that had yielded a lasting benefit for tribe members. "In 1927," he said, "we got a judgement against Grays Harbor county to stop their taxing automobiles belonging to Quinaielt Indians. You have never paid taxes on your automobiles."[91]

Fred Saux, the council secretary in 1956, touted the tribe's successful appeals to American courts in a letter to the Association on American Indian Affairs: "Throughout the past thirty (30) years we have instituted several lawsuits against the federal and state governments to protect our commercial fishing industry . . . ; also our timber interests, income tax questions, boundary line disputes, encroachment of state authority within our reservation boundaries, in all events the courts ruled in our favor."[92]

In Saux's time, the tribe also looked to a local woman, Gladys Phillips, for legal services. Data on Phillips and other early Quinault counsel indicate why tribal officials would know and hire them. Phillips not only worked and lived in nearby Aberdeen; she was Indian, reportedly Menominee. Her husband, J. M. Phillips—identified by agent Sams in 1923 as a respected Cherokee lawyer—had resided in Aberdeen for many years and served as the town's mayor. Sams called him "the best friend the Indians of this country have." Many Indians apparently agreed. The Quinault council voted unanimously to make him an adopted tribe member.[93]

W. H. Smiley, a lawyer who contracted to represent Quinaults in the 1930s, was three hundred miles away in Spokane, Washington, but had previously worked at the BIA's Taholah agency. Ralph Case, who handled the Quinault boundary lawsuit, was based in Washington, DC, and well known to Indian organizations for his long-running effort on behalf of the Sioux to win compensation for the US government's confiscation of the Black Hills.[94] As an Indian claims specialist, Case worked on a contingent fee basis; any pay he received for his services came out of the awards he won for clients.[95] Quinaults were also able to cover some lawyer fees and litigation expenses with fish tax revenues or funds from previous court awards.[96]

Quinault dealings with lawyers were symbiotically related to tribe leaders' participation in intertribal affairs, but the reciprocal influences are hard to trace precisely. Did Quinaults' acquaintance with Cragun encourage them to join the National Congress of American Indians, or did NCAI membership lead them to Cragun's firm? The firm periodically notified client tribes and the NCAI of legislation and court actions that could affect Indians in general. Those bulletins may have motivated Quinaults to get active in national and intertribal affairs, or conversely, intertribal relations may have made Quinaults aware of Cragun in the first place.[97]

In any event, by 1956 the Quinault tribe was participating in Affiliated Tribes of Northwest Indians, a three-year-old regional organization that monitored a variety of legal affairs. Through Affiliated Tribes, if not otherwise, Quinault leaders knew that a Coeur d'Alene Indian was contesting federal taxes on her trust land rental income just as the Capoemans were challenging taxes on their timber money. Perhaps Quinault delegates were among those who voted in 1956 to create an Affiliated Tribes fund for expenses in the Coeur d'Alene case—a step that proved unnecessary when the litigation was suspended while courts considered the Capoeman case.[98]

Meanwhile, representatives of the NCAI and an older Indian advocacy organization—the Association on American Indian Affairs (AAIA)—had made appearances in Washington State Indian country, describing their programs to protect tribal rights. NCAI president Joe Garry, a Coeur d'Alene tribe member from Idaho, circulated through Northwest tribes in the mid-1950s, warning that the new federal termination policy threatened tribes with oblivion. In 1955, Garry wrote to Fred Saux, the Quinault council secretary, that bills pending in Congress all "had the same purpose, to liquidate all Indian lands and assets and then to disintegrate the Indian people."[99] Saux identified the AAIA as a likely ally for Quinaults who opposed state jurisdiction on the reservation. By articulating homegrown reasons for their opposition, Indians such as Saux in turn provided NCAI and AAIA leadership with ammunition for their national campaigns to defeat the US government plan.[100]

JURISDICTION CONTROVERSY

A Lummi Indian, Joseph Hillaire, initiated connections between Indians in western Washington and the Association on American Indian Affairs. A newspaper article about the organization inspired Hillaire to send letters seeking AAIA help in 1951 and 1953.[101] He wrote about his people's need for training and for help with home purchases. In 1955, an AAIA bulletin named Hillaire as one of eight tribal representatives who testified at a state legislative hearing against a bill that would repeal Washington's constitutional disclaimer of jurisdiction over Indian lands.

That reference appeared in an article denouncing the federal government's planned "destruction of trusteeship status" for Indians. "Indian tribes everywhere are standing at the crossroads of their tribal existence," the AAIA warned. "Never before have we had a greater need for Indian leaders of vision and determined courage to continue the vast resources of American Indians, both natural and human." Whether the Indians who addressed state lawmakers were exemplary leaders, the bulletin did not say. Nor did it indicate whether the AAIA had arranged their state senate testimony, which "solidly opposed" legislation that would enable the state to enforce its laws on Indian reservations. Unlike the NCAI, which was campaigning to amend Public Law 280 by adding a tribal consent requirement, the AAIA wanted all tribes to reject state jurisdiction outright, and it sometimes agitated on its own for that option.[102]

The eight named speakers did not include a Quinault, but the mobility, intertribal kinship ties, and intertribal gatherings characteristic of Indian life in western Washington virtually ensured that Quinault officials would know about the bill in the state legislature and about the Indians' appearance at the hearing.[103] Even if they did not have prior knowledge, Quinaults were not unaware for long. Information about emerging Indian opposition to state control soon cycled through the AAIA to Taholah, where it reached approving eyes and ears.

In the spring of 1956, AAIA president Oliver La Farge received a letter from Fred Saux rejoicing that his tribe had "a champion" in the AAIA, which promoted "the very same concept in relation to Indian questions that most of us here on the West coast of Washington have been advocating these many years." Government officials had turned "deaf ears" to those Indian voices, Saux charged. His current frustration was with BIA functionaries who were issuing fee patents to allotments so that Indians could quickly, on their own, sell timber or the land itself. In effect, that was "throwing the doors open to eventual liquidation of the supervision of federal jurisdiction over our reservation, the very thing we are opposed to." Saux added that Quinaults had actively opposed all legislation contrary to their wishes and "instituted several lawsuits against the federal and state governments" to protect economic interests and prevent "encroachment of state authority within our reservation boundaries."

The AAIA response to Saux was a letter from director La Verne Madigan announcing that the association had commissioned Erna Gunther, a University of Washington professor, to investigate "Indian problems in the State of Washington." Taholah was "one of the areas" she would study.[104] However, four years passed before the AAIA received a report on problems at Taholah, and that document was not a product of the promised Gunther inquiry. Because the association failed to raise sufficient funds for a broad investigation, Gunther focused only on the Makah reservation.[105] Meanwhile, a "Quinault fact-finding committee" of obscure origins prepared a report for the AAIA. Committee members were Fred Saux, his mother Hannah Bowechop, and Jennie Boome. They gathered facts, they said, by attending tribal government meetings and taking "a poll of the Quinault people . . . in the form of a questionnaire."[106]

Between Saux's correspondence with AAIA officials in 1956 and his submission of the fact-finding report in 1960, national Indian criticism of the termination policy and PL 280 gained coherence. In Washington State, however, lawmakers complicated the issue for tribes by deciding to extend jurisdiction to Indians reservation by reservation, only at tribal government request. Contradictory Quinault responses to that state law triggered confusion, acrimony, and eventual litigation, but in the end, the controversy strengthened the resolve and influence of tribe members who wanted to maintain what they saw as a long Quinault tradition of independence and self-government.

In November 1958, the Affiliated Tribes of Northwest Indians executive council, meeting at the Makah reservation, adopted two resolutions concerning the direction of US Indian policy. The first resolution denounced the congressional declaration in 1953 that the federal government's aim thenceforth was to end Indians' "status as wards of the United States" and, "as rapidly as possible, to make the Indians . . . subject to the same laws and entitled to the same privileges and responsibilities as are applicable to other citizens of the United States." The second resolution took issue with the 1957 Washington legislation that authorized the state to extend full civil and criminal jurisdiction over a reservation and Indian occupants if the governor received certification that a majority of the tribe or tribal council desired state jurisdiction. That provision for tribal consent did not satisfy the Affiliated Tribes executive council. Their resolution insisted on a vote for state jurisdiction by at least two-thirds of adult tribe members.[107]

The AAIA did not report whether Quinaults attended the executive council meeting, but Quinaults would have been on the minds of meeting participants in any case. In fact, the second Affiliated Tribes resolution was likely a reaction to events at Taholah. A well-publicized dispute about state jurisdiction was under way there. Five members of the Business Committee had requested state law enforcement by resolution on April 22, 1958, and Washington's governor duly issued a formal proclamation of jurisdiction, effective July 14.[108] A week later, the *Seattle Times* reported a Quinault "family feud . . . brewing" in the wake of this development. Two petitions protesting the Business Committee's action, each signed by dozens of tribe members, had landed on the governor's desk. For an explanation of that protest, the *Times* relied on Fred Saux, who said the Business Committee—contrary to tribal law—did not get tribe members' consent. Furthermore, members would not give their consent because they preferred federal jurisdiction. At general meetings, they had repeatedly voted against proposals to accept state jurisdiction.[109]

The stated impetus for the April 22 Business Committee request was a perception that laws of the United States and the tribe were inadequate to protect Quinaults on the reservation. A BIA official reportedly furnished the wording of the resolution and pressed for its approval at three successive meetings. The governing bodies of nine other tribes had also done as the BIA urged. Dismayed AAIA personnel pondered how to counter the bureau's influence. La Verne Madigan wrote to a correspondent in Seattle:

> I have the impression that the state of Washington has no interest in getting tribes to accept state law and order, but that the Bureau does and pressures the tribes. . . . The Bureau is probably aided by special industrial

interests which would benefit from Indian loss of jurisdiction in Indian land. . . . What on earth are we to do in Washington where the tribal governments vote away their own rights . . . ? I know instinctively that the Washington Indian people do not simply want to vote themselves out of existence.

To prove that the BIA was pressuring demoralized Indians to vote against their own interests, Madigan recommended a Washington field study—"a project of some kind, on the reservations, to get rank and file Indian people active in tribal affairs" and "to come to grips with the western Washington tragedy."[110] The 1960 Quinault "fact-finding" report may have been a response to her recommendation.

On the subject of federal guardianship termination, the Quinault fact finders' language was fierce: "To a people accustomed to living in quasi-sovereignty, termination is a vile word—a denunciation of our culture, a relinquishment of what little tribal and individual possessions we own today, a sad omen to our coming generations." Termination would nullify the tribes' treaty-guaranteed rights to fish and hunt, which they had defended valiantly for decades. The prospect of state jurisdiction was equally unacceptable. "The Quinault and Queets tribes' opposition to extending state civil and criminal jurisdiction into the Quinault reservation does not stem from the two tribes' defiance to law and order," the report insisted, "but rather the tribe desired to retain their own law and order code under the U.S. Code of Federal Regulations, Sec. 161, with their own court of Indian offenses, and with their own reservation Indian law officers."[111]

According to the fact finders, the Business Committee's request for state jurisdiction came about as follows. At two separate meetings, the officers declined to approve the BIA-prepared resolution and maintained that the question should be posed instead to the entire tribal membership. Consequently, at a special general council on February 1, 1958, Quinault voters considered arguments for and against state jurisdiction, including the arguments of BIA superintendent C. W. Ringey. After prolonged debate, the people voted against the proposed jurisdictional change. A second show of hands at the regular March meeting went the same way. Less than a week later, five members of the Business Committee sent the BIA a plan to designate themselves policemen until the tribe's annual budget could be approved and a police officer selected. "Then like a bombshell," the fact finders wrote, the same five men signed the resolution asking for state law on the reservation. "The tribe was totally unaware of what took place" on that April day until the Aberdeen *Daily World* ran an article about it.[112]

The fact finders ventured no explanation for that surprising move, and other pertinent records are nearly as uninformative. In a subsequent state court trial, Business Committee member Horton Capoeman reportedly said that the general council referred the jurisdiction issue to the committee, and the five committeemen approved the resolution after realizing the impracticality of acting as policemen themselves. Cross-examination revealed that Capoeman signed a letter twelve days later acknowledging that the general council had rejected state jurisdiction. Other court testimony convinced a county judge that BIA pressure was a significant factor in the Business Committee's decision. Contrary to their usual practice of meeting in Taholah, committee members were in Hoquiam with BIA officials when they gave their consent to state law enforcement. Francis Rosander, who "always went to the meetings," thought that the lack of effective law enforcement could also explain some committee members' decision. "The law and order got to the point where people were actually afraid to live in their houses," Rosander recalled in 2012. "And they kinda sweetened the pie by sayin' that we needed money for schools, and so they accepted that public law."[113]

President Cleve Jackson's role in the affair was not in doubt; he urged acceptance of state jurisdiction. He had support in that effort from his wife, Anna. On April 12, 1958, she wrote Superintendent Ringey (marking her letter "personal and confidential") to complain that a meddling non-Indian had turned tribe members against state jurisdiction. "Ever since we started talking about the State law enforcement program Harold Patterson, the principal in the school here, and his wife have preached against it," she alleged.

> He really did a job of stumping against the program, telling the meeting [March 19] they would lost [*sic*] the control of the reservation, the river, their hunting and everything on the reservation. He told them the State would step in and take over everything, that the Indians would have no rights left. . . . I was able to answer most of his contentions, but I tired

after a while and left the meeting. . . . We feel that we have been doing all right for ourselves and resent this high-handed interference.

Jackson pleaded with the superintendent to stop Patterson if he could and added, "As it is, we have no law of any kind." Years later, Harold Patterson recollected the council meeting differently: "I just attended as an observer. But Sully Pope said to me, he said, 'Mr. Patterson, what do you think [about accepting state jurisdiction]?' And I said, 'Well, I'd like to see you keep what you have.'"[114]

Anna Jackson's letter indicates that personal antagonisms or loyalties played a part in tribe members' alignment on the state jurisdiction question. Other records say little about such frictions, but Cleve Jackson and Fred Saux did leave evidence that their views of the issue were colored by their dislike or distrust of each other. At a meeting with BIA officials and the tribe's lawyer in 1960, Cleve Jackson seemed to characterize the opposition to state jurisdiction as a personal crusade of Saux's mother, Hannah, allegedly motivated by the fact that her three sons were "McNeil Graduates"—that is, former inmates of a federal prison presumably hoping for minimal law enforcement.[115] Meanwhile Saux, complaining that Jackson habitually withheld information from other elected Quinault officers, was inclined to believe a report from an "outside source" that Jackson and Ringey were secretly working out a termination program for the Quinault tribe.[116] Hannah Bowechop's disapproval of Quinaults who converted trust allotments to fee holdings may also have been a factor. Cleve Jackson had done that.[117]

By the time Saux's fact-finding group was compiling its report, their version of events was the basis for a federal court lawsuit contending that the Business Committee exceeded its authority when requesting state jurisdiction. Bowechop was one of two plaintiffs. Although the judge dismissed her case for lack of court jurisdiction, she and other challengers of the Business Committee action had an opportunity to make their arguments in a concurrent state court case. In August 1959, the state charged tribe member George Bertrand with a felony committed on the Quinault Reservation. Bertrand's attorney, Gladys Phillips, contended that county sheriffs had no right to arrest him because the proclamation extending state jurisdiction to the reservation was invalid; the governor had not received a request from the general council, the sole body with power to make it. The testimony of Bowechop and her son persuaded Judge Warner Poyhonen that Phillips was correct: the Business Committee lacked authority to approve state jurisdiction. Poyhonen therefore dismissed the charges against Bertrand on December 17, 1959.[118]

The state appealed Poyhonen's judgment, and the higher court ordered the case reopened for additional testimony. In preparing for the new hearing, the county prosecutor had help from state attorneys, BIA officials, US attorneys, and regional solicitors for the Interior Department. His witnesses included Superintendent Ringey, who recollected that only twenty-seven people had voted against state jurisdiction at the February 1 general council meeting. Although fewer than that signaled their desire for state law, Cleve Jackson had assured Ringey that others would have done so if Bowechop's group had not intimidated them. On the issue of Business Committee authority, the BIA produced minutes of a 1925 general council that directed the committee to "carry on the affairs of the tribe." The prosecutor urged the judge to construe that mandate liberally.[119] Nevertheless, Judge Mitchell Kalin came to the same conclusion as Judge Poyhonen: the five officers' request for state jurisdiction was invalid under Quinault law.

Ultimately, the Washington Supreme Court disagreed with the county judges. For one thing, the justices reasoned, Washington courts had no jurisdiction to resolve the Quinault tribe's internal disputes, including the question of Business Committee power. Doing so would constitute unauthorized interference with the tribe's sovereignty. Additionally, the governor's proclamation of jurisdiction was a political act and an authorized exercise of his discretion, which courts were obliged to respect. Accordingly, on January 31, 1963, the justices restored the charges against George Bertrand and affirmed state jurisdiction over the Quinault Reservation.[120] By then, however, Cleve Jackson had been dead for more than two years, and Quinault leaders, faced with new developments that threatened further erosion of Quinaults' power in their homeland, had united in opposing state jurisdiction. Elected Quinault officials were determined to defend and exercise more actively their rights to self-government and reservation resources.[121]

For five decades following Quinaults' treaty with the United States, Indian families on the reservation had had near-exclusive use of local resources. The twentieth century had brought enterprises, neighbors, and federal government management practices that compromised Quinaults' ability to benefit from those resources. With their accustomed self-sufficiency and US treaty promises in mind, Quinaults had protested some of the infringements on the autonomy they expected. In key instances, they raised their objections in courts of law with satisfactory results. Then the 1950s ushered in challenges that called for more elaborate strategy. Quinaults' ultimate decision to resist state jurisdiction and assume more functions typical of non-Indian governments was a response to those distinctive local experiences and conditions, but it had counterparts elsewhere in Indian country. During the 1960s, shared experiences, shared information, and a conducive national context would prompt Indians across the United States to take increasing interest in developing their capacity for comprehensive self-government.

4. "Arising" in the Sixties

In 1963, the Bureau of Indian Affairs produced an "acculturation report" on Indians of the Quinault Reservation—an assessment of whether they had embraced "white culture." The impetus for the study was the decade-old plan to terminate federal government responsibility for Indians, beginning with those who could hold their own in the competitive modern world. At the time of the Quinault assessment, the BIA was trying to prepare tribes for self-reliance by providing more aid rather than less, particularly in economic development.

What bureau investigators saw at Taholah did not please them. Quinaults seemed vexingly indifferent to economic advancement. The great majority of adults were "unskilled" and getting by without "regular, permanent-type employment." Most Quinaults appeared "content to live at a level . . . considered substandard." Furthermore, the study authors detected "strong hostility toward outside organizations" and overtly moderate but covertly intense animosity toward non-Indians in general. They concluded:

> For future progress and guided acculturation there needs to be a great deal of work done to improve the effectiveness of the tribal organization and especially the attitudes of the tribal members towards progress and

acceptance of the white culture. The Quinault Reservation has one of the better basis [*sic*] for development, both as to timber and lumber operations, and also tourist attractions. At this point, however, the Tribe is antagonistic to any infiltration by outside elements on the reservation, development of a tourist industry or utilization by members of adjacent work opportunities. . . . [I]t will be necessary to break down the individualism and strive towards united tribal effort for the general tribal good.[1]

Such BIA characterizations of Indian attitudes deserve skepticism. In this case, there is corroborating evidence of Quinault hostility to certain "outside elements," but that is hardly the whole truth. Investigators either did not see or neglected to mention that tribe members directed their animosity primarily at people they regarded as threats to Quinault control of reservation resources. Quinaults who were active in self-government appreciated non-Indians who showed them respect, and they valued "white culture" that could help them keep or gain resources. While BIA personnel apparently met with a cool reception, tribe leaders were cultivating non-Indian allies at local and national levels. Moreover, Quinaults would soon intensify their efforts to develop and manage a "progressive" reservation economy, as the BIA advocated.

Unlike the bureau evaluators, reporters from area newspapers saw signs of Quinault desire for economic progress. In 1961, Marshall Wilson of the *Seattle Times* found that some of the Indians wished to be "left alone," but most had "learned enough to know that to advance they need money—not among the individual families that have won and lost big timber fortunes, but money in the Tribal Council where it can be used for the advancement of the tribe." Two years later, under the headline "Quinault Plans 'Working Out,'" Wilson relayed a tribal councilman's claim that his government had recently overseen the creation of eighty-four jobs for Indians. Tribe members were employed in stream improvement, road construction, and timber thinning. Indian fishers sold their catch to the new Quinault Tribal Enterprises, which had an ice house, trucks, and $5,000 in annual profit. Additionally, the tribe had budgeted $25,000 for a new tourist facility on the Quinault River's south bank.[2]

In June 1964, the *Seattle Post-Intelligencer* predicted that Quinaults' get-up-and-go would soon end Taholah's status as "one of the state's last remaining, true Indian villages." Ron Fowler wrote: "Although a majority of the families residing in Taholah are in the lower income bracket, mostly derived from fishing and logging, their standard of living is among the highest of Washington Indian tribes and they probably are enjoying better economic conditions at present than at any time in the past. With vigorous, determined leadership from progressive-minded members of the governing tribal council, headed by chairman James Jackson, the Quinaults are attempting to 'pull themselves up by their own bootstraps.'"[3] Over the following decade, while pulling forcefully on community bootstraps, "determined" Quinault leaders also demanded respect for an increasingly expansive interpretation of their right to self-government.

A year after the acculturation report, James Jackson made that demand in a written communication to the BIA's Western Washington Agency. His cover letter read simply, "This is the position of the Quinault Tribe. We would like you to take note of it." The enclosed document was equally blunt. In matters affecting "their inherent rights as Indians," it announced, Quinaults based their position on a treaty with the United States that "guarantees the right of self-government to this tribe under the jurisdiction of the Federal Government," whose Constitution "places the Quinault Treaty above State law. . . . The legal sanctions which protect the Quinault Tribal rights are quite strong, and we feel secure in resting our case on them. . . . Any differences which might arise in the interpretation of their rights can be resolved at the conference table or through legal processes."[4]

Two years later, Quinaults notified the commissioner of Indian affairs that they intended to fashion a tribal government capable of preserving their homeland and resources for the tribal community: "We do not resist change, but we will resist being deprived of our rights of self-determination to the last man. Quinaults governed themselves on this land before anyone else reached its shores. We will change our methods, but we will maintain our identity and traditional control of our land as long as we are a people. . . . [W]e are now trying to put modern education, modern economics, and modern governmental procedure behind our great human and natural resources."[5]

In their drive for control of land and resources, Quinaults led by James Jackson and a cadre of protégés would make the most of conducive federal government programs, especially the one known as the War on Poverty. They would deepen their engagement with the political-legal system that had originally limited their self-government but now seemed to offer the means to cast off those restrictions.

ON THE DEFENSIVE

Early in the 1960s, Quinault political activity focused less on the potential of federal programs to enhance tribal power than on threats to the reservation community and tribal autonomy. The threats stemmed primarily from the federal policy of terminating protection for tribes and ceding jurisdiction over Indian country to states and state subdivisions.

Implementation of the termination policy had caused the Quinault Business Committee to request state law enforcement services in 1958. When county judge Walter Poyhonen declared that request invalid, he described it as a well-intentioned reaction to a serious predicament: the tribe no longer had money for a police force or court. The result was a dismal law and order situation on the reservation. Poyhonen did not mention the reason for the fiscal crisis—that the federal government, expecting to devolve law enforcement responsibility to the state, had cut off funding.[6]

Ironically, Poyhonen's ruling in December 1959 exacerbated the law enforcement problem on the reservation. Grays Harbor County suspended the minimal policing it had provided since July 1958, and offenders reportedly went free. In 1962, a federal officer investigated complaints of rampant crime on the reservation—four larcenies, two trespasses, a threat of bodily harm, assault with a deadly weapon, breaking and entering, assault and battery, and attempted rape. "Due to the jurisdictional problem," he found, "no action has been taken on any of these cases. The Sheriff's office has indicated that they will only enter the reservation on a matter of life and death. The Quinault Reservation remains completely devoid of Law and Order enforcement."[7]

Quinault representatives pleaded for help with the situation during a call on high-level BIA officials in November 1960. They had heard "active talk" of establishing a vigilante committee if federal police or another agency did not assume responsibility for law enforcement. A state attorney subsequently agreed to research whether the governor could rescind his proclamation of state jurisdiction "if he were advised by the Quinault Tribe and the Department of the Interior that . . . the earlier resolution of the business committee did not correctly reflect the desires of the tribe."

BIA officials pledged to supervise a tribal vote on the issue, but they subsequently rebuffed a formal Quinault request for that referendum. They chose to await the Washington Supreme Court's ruling on the legality of state jurisdiction.[8]

The court's affirmation of state jurisdiction in January 1963 displeased Quinault officials and their constituents. Three months later they approved a resolution declaring, "The Quinaielt Tribe disavows, repudiates and annuls any action purporting to have been taken on behalf of the tribe which would accept state jurisdiction; and . . . wishes to be and remain for the indefinite future under the traditional tribal and federal jurisdiction over civil and criminal matters."[9]

In a memorandum for BIA personnel, the tribe's lawyer attributed their stance to a conviction that the state would do little to keep order on the reservation. John Cragun also implied that anger at recent state legislation influenced Quinault voters' "nearly unanimous" rejection of state jurisdiction. Washington lawmakers had acted a second time on the opening created by Public Law 280. They extended state jurisdiction to Indians on all reservation land not in federal trust and to Indians on trust land in eight subject areas: school attendance, public assistance, domestic relations, mental illness, juvenile delinquency, adoption proceedings, dependent children, and motor vehicle operation. This time they did not provide for tribal consent. Cragun communicated Quinaults' resentment forcefully: "The tribe feels the legislation was imposed upon it, over its repeated protests and pleas, without even a gesture at consulting the tribe to ascertain its wishes. An unworkable jurisdiction was imposed, since police officers will have to carry plat books and be title experts to distinguish fee from trust lands to enforce the most elementary laws relating to public safety."[10]

Many Quinaults opposed state jurisdiction for fear of laws forbidding them to fish and hunt as their treaty allowed. Events in the early 1960s reinforced a mounting, widespread Indian perception that their access to fish and game was under attack in Washington.[11] State and federal records complement what tribe members told legal scholar Charles Wilkinson in 2001: "State game officials began arresting tribal fishermen for violating state license requirements and other laws. . . . At Quinault, non-Indian fishermen provoked ugly confrontations at off-reservation sites. At least one Quinault fisherman was shot at."[12]

According to Quinault spokesmen, that disregard for their treaty rights prompted the 1961 council vote to bar outsiders from Lake Quinault. Tribal officials simultaneously requested enforcement of a federal statute making it a crime to trespass on Indian lands for hunting or fishing. Their entreaty reached an Interior Department lawyer who informed his superiors, "The Quinault tribal authorities feel that many white people in the area either are unaware of the relatively new law or do not believe that it will be enforced. The Council is troubled by repeated instances of violation of the law."[13] A journalist claimed to know that "vigilant" individual Indians often took it upon themselves to turn back "motorists and hunters" on reservation logging roads, accusing them of trespass.[14]

State officials thought the tribe had closed the lake in reaction to a different reason for resenting non-Indians. The tribe, they said, was retaliating for state legislation making it illegal to transport steelhead in common or commercial carriers. That law did indeed anger Indians throughout Washington. Quinaults' conservation supervisor estimated that enforcement would reduce Indian fishers' income by thousands of dollars. Already alarmed at state regulations that shifted the burden of conservation to Indian fishers, tribes joined in establishing a commission to advocate for their treaty-protected fishing rights and chose Horton Capoeman to lead it. When the state game department director claimed in early 1962 that off-reservation Indian fishing was depleting salmon and trout stocks, Capoeman and two other Quinaults went to the press with a plea that Indians "be given a chance to enforce fish-conservation practices before steps . . . to change their treaties with the United States."[15]

Quinaults garnered additional press attention by withholding consent to a proposed state highway bridging the river at Taholah. Some observers wondered whether the veto was not a show of fierce desire for independence or isolation but a ploy to extract more compensation for the right-of-way. Quinault leaders at the time and tribal historians later denied any monetary motive. They explained opposition to the bridge as a reasonable reaction to unregulated non-Indian activity on the reservation. The misconduct of non-Indians at the lake, they maintained, was symptomatic of a general disrespect for Quinault rights, also evident in the inadequate federal law enforcement and escalating development of non-Indian-owned reservation properties.

Horton Capoeman, speaking as the new tribal council president in May 1961, told the *Seattle Post-Intelligencer*, "The tribe has nothing to gain by a bridge and road." Pointing out that the BIA withdrew police protection on the reservation, and the county court invalidated state jurisdiction, Capoeman asked rhetorically, "If timber thefts and shooting of our game occur, which it does, what would happen if we allowed the reservation to open up?" Quinaults also took offense at not being consulted about the bridge plans, he said. "There could have been a right approach to the Indian. If it had been done right—for us, too,—then arrangement [*sic*] might have been made, but we don't agree to letting others run roughshod over us."[16]

By 1963, when the tribal council formally repudiated the 1958 Business Committee request for state jurisdiction, Quinault government leaders were more determined than ever to prevent state agents or their non-Indian constituents from running roughshod in Quinault country. They urged the federal government to restore tribal responsibility not only for criminal law enforcement but also for civil regulation. They especially wanted to regulate land use.

In March 1963, they took a bold step toward that end. Without waiting for a formal federal pronouncement on the extent of their authority, the general council approved an Ordinance Subjecting Motels and other Businesses on the Quinault Reservation to Tribal Regulation.[17] They expected non-Indian owners of land within reservation boundaries to dispute that assertion of tribal power and did not expect the local BIA to help them foil those challenges. Quinault officials and an AAIA representative had heard the agency superintendent say, in effect, that the tribal government had "limited authority over tribal lands and practically none over individuals or allotted land."[18] So Quinaults bypassed the BIA in western Washington and went to national headquarters with their request for support.

Two Quinaults and a lawyer from John Cragun's firm met with bureau officials in June 1963. As the BIA director of tribal operations reported the conversation, "The delegation was quite concerned over the use of fee-patented land along the coast by non-Indians. The tribe is seeking ways to prevent non-Indian development of this land. . . . The basic question was whether tribal 'zoning laws' applied to this area, particularly subsequent to Public Law 280. They were advised that the Bureau could not come to the defense of the tribe until the relationship Public Law 280 had with tribal sovereignty . . . was clarified." The official in charge also advised Quinaults to seek a federal solicitor's opinion. Afterward he told the associate commissioner, "Involved . . . are the provisions of Article II of the Quinault Treaty which in effect holds that no white person shall live on the Quinault land without the consent of the Quinault Tribe. In that the right of the tribe to act when fee-patented land is involved has apparently never been litigated, the group may seek an injunction . . . until the tribe's rights and the applicability of the treaty have been determined by the courts."[19] By October, a regional solicitor was researching the subject of tribal control over three non-Indian activities on reservation fee land: house construction, logging, and other business operations.[20]

With their regulatory authority still in question, Quinault leaders watched unhappily as more reservation acreage passed to non-Indians, some of whom planned to create and sell smaller lots for vacation homes and recreational uses. For the time being, it seemed, the tribe's only sure way to control development was to acquire the land. That was a tall order for a tribal government with minimal cash reserves or revenue and few possible sources of assistance besides the federal government. Nonetheless, in a 1961 resolution addressed to a new secretary of the Interior, Quinaults announced a strategy of restoring alienated reservation land to federal trust status. Declaring the issuance of fee patents "a grave threat to the future" of the reservation, they requested help getting federal loans, "not gifts," for tribal government land purchases. They asked the BIA to give the tribe priority as a purchaser. The next year, when it seemed that some allotments would soon go out of trust unless the tribe bought them, council secretary Fred Saux alerted southwest Washington's congressional representative. Needed immediately, he wrote, was a suspension of all reservation land sales "pending a workable solution for the tribe to buy lands that are up for sale."[21]

RISING HOPES

Quinaults' opposition to highway construction, to non-Indian activity on the lake, and to non-Indian landownership fed perceptions that the tribe wanted isolation. Other Quinault actions, such as organizing a multitribal defense of fishing rights and soliciting a congresswoman's support, invited more nuanced analysis of the tribe's aims. Instead of hiding from outsiders, the supposedly isolationist Quinaults were attracting attention, often deliberately. In April 1961, Marshall Wilson reported in the *Seattle Times* that Indians in many tribes were "talking of new means to protect their reservations and their fish—by following the examples of the Quinaults." His series of articles about Quinaults illustrated and ensured that "even the white man [was] becoming aware that something [was] going on out on the Olympic Peninsula."[22]

Quinaults who spoke to Wilson said they were engaged in "an arising rather than an uprising." Their aims, as he summarized them, were "to build new industry, to educate their children, to regain lost arts and to preserve the reservation as a 'place to come home to.'" "The new Tribal Council," Wilson wrote, "is concerned with the poor use which has been made of their natural riches and is concerned with the future, or lack of future, for their children." Their closure of Lake Quinault and opposition to road building "are part and parcel of the Indians' fight for survival."[23]

It was indeed new leadership that charted the Quinaults' course of action in the early 1960s. Horton Capoeman served as interim president after Cleve Jackson's death, then won the post in a March 1961 vote. He was not new to the Business Committee, but the elections of two women and of a man who resided off the reservation—Wilfred Petit—were unprecedented.[24] Cleve Jackson's son James, known as Jim or Jug, became vice president and succeeded Capoeman as president two years later. The tribe now had officers who had come of age during World War II, some of them while serving in the US military alongside non-Indians, gaining exposure to the national context in which Quinaults would have to wage their struggle for survival and prosperity.[25]

The man who headed that struggle throughout the 1960s was a chief's grandson but not the most sophisticated person on the Business Committee. As a young adult, Jim Jackson had labored in Quinault forests and fishing grounds with fellow tribe members. An attorney employed by the tribe in the 1970s saw Jackson as a "big, gruff logger, fisherman [and] hard, tough character."[26] Yet several political colleagues described him as a far-sighted leader. His revolutionary influence included mobilizing Quinaults to sue the federal government for mismanaging reservation timber, pushing young tribe members to train for professions of use to their community, and envisioning a modern tribal government that would regulate non-Indian activities.[27]

Their roles in Quinault tribal leadership earned these three men—Horton Capoeman, Joe DeLaCruz, and Jim Jackson (left to right)—a place in the 1975 Taholah Days parade, which commemorated the Quinaults' treaty with the United States in 1855. Photograph by Larry Workman, Quinault Indian Nation.

Justine James, Sr., recalled, "When Jim Jackson got in, he started our regular meetings. He conducted business as it pretty much supposed to've been." In Harold Patterson's view, relying on Jackson and Wilfred Petit for leadership was a game changer. As a politician, Jug "was a complete opposite" of his father. "He was very strong on Indian identity and Indian rights . . . , self-control and self-government. And he was successful in that because he turned things around completely." About Petit, Patterson said, "He was a good man. . . . He'd been a military man. . . . Being as sophisticated as he was, he helped Jim get into . . . the political scene. And they made good friends with our congresswoman, Julia Butler Hansen."[28]

Hansen's records confirm the evolution of that valuable "friendship" and document Quinault leaders' increasing visibility on "the political scene." In a 1962 letter describing herself to a Yakima tribal councilman as a staunch defender of Washington Indians, Hansen mentioned that she had just met with three Quinaults who came to the nation's capital "to present, as they did very ably, the Indian side of the fisheries question." Those able spokesmen were Wilfred Petit, Jim Jackson, and Horton Capoeman.[29]

The effects of new Quinault leadership seemed dramatic and hope-inspiring to *Seattle Post-Intelligencer* reporter Ron Fowler. When he checked on conditions at Taholah in June of 1964, he found that the state highway bridge had at last been constructed, and outdoor recreation opportunities were drawing visitors to the reservation. The tribe was clearing a spot for a public park that would include picnic, camping, and trailer facilities. Fowler called the park project "a shining example of the Quinaults' desire to maintain 'peaceful co-existence with their non-Indian neighbors.'"[30]

The Quinault "arising" was both a response and a contributor to developments that galvanized activism on many Indian reservations in the 1960s—some encouraging developments, some frustrating. A signal event was John F. Kennedy's election as US president following a campaign that promised aid programs for populations stuck in poverty despite the postwar expansion of the American economy. As historian Larry Burt observed, Kennedy took office at "a time of ferment among indigenous, traditional, ethnic, and colonized peoples throughout the world. . . . Political independence and economic growth became prominent themes in nationalist movements." Kennedy's avowed sympathy for the cause of colonial liberation and his pledge to promote economic improvement for Native Americans fostered an "atmosphere of rising expectations" in tribal communities.[31]

To head the Interior Department, Kennedy appointed Arizona senator Stewart Udall, who quipped that his familiarity with Indians and Indian policy might induce him to serve as his own Indian commissioner. Mindful of Indians' economic straits and widespread demoralization, Udall created a task force on Indian issues, which recommended more federal aid for industry and agriculture on reservations and applauded lawmakers' decision to make tribal governments eligible for assistance under a new Area Redevelopment Act.

The Redevelopment Act primarily funded infrastructure improvement, feasibility studies, and incentives for manufacturers to locate in impoverished communities.[32] Not surprisingly, it did not inspire Quinault visions of factories at Taholah. The tribe chose instead to fund infrastructure that would attract short-term visitors; hence their $25,000 investment in a tourist facility near the new Quinault River bridge. Another infrastructure grant financed a water and sewer system.[33] Ultimately, Quinault development plans during the Kennedy administration were modest by comparison to the tribe's surge of ambition under Kennedy's successor, Lyndon Baines Johnson. Johnson's far-reaching antipoverty program opened the door to that surge. Like Indians across the country, Quinaults saw it as an opportunity to advance their quest for meaningful control in their homeland.

On January 8, 1964, barely two months after the assassination that made him the president, Johnson declared "unconditional war" on poverty in America. The campaign would be waged on many fronts, primarily by people personally familiar with the foe's cruel effects on their communities. In his first State of the Union address, Johnson told Congress, "Poverty is a national problem, requiring improved national organization and support. But this attack, to be effective, must also be organized at the State and local level. For the war against poverty . . . must be won in the field, in every private home, in every public office, from the courthouse to the White House."[34] Within the year, Congress produced implementing legislation. The Economic Opportunity Act (EOA) authorized direct federal aid to local governments and nonprofit organizations in impoverished areas. The recipients, dubbed Community Action Agencies, would plan and carry out antipoverty programs suited to their constituencies' specific needs and resources. As a condition of that privilege, they were to strive for "maximum feasible participation" of the poor.[35]

Johnson and the strategists of his nonviolent war expected from the outset to take the fight to Indian country, but they were unprepared for tribes' determination to set and carry out strategy themselves. Only after a large delegation of indignant tribe leaders paid the president a visit did he revoke plans to funnel funds for Indian programs through the BIA. A new directive permitted tribal governments to constitute themselves Community Action Agencies and receive grants directly from the new Office of Economic Opportunity (OEO), the first federal agency to fund programs that tribal governments designed and managed. For Indians who viewed the BIA as an obstacle to self-determination, Johnson's concession was a reason to rejoice.[36]

On the Quinault Reservation, Jim Jackson and tribal government associates needed no coaxing to enlist in the crusade against poverty. Even before the implementing legislation passed, Quinaults agitated for action on at least one front of the war—the drive for decent housing. In January 1964, they dispatched a delegation to Washington, DC, for discussions about the dilapidated homes on their reservation. When Congress approved housing aid bills that year and the next, establishing the Department of Housing and Urban Development (HUD) and making tribes eligible for house construction and rehabilitation funds, Quinaults were ready with a newly established housing authority that could administer the federal bounty.[37] Harold Patterson was then principal of the Taholah school. In 2012, he recalled the dismal state of reservation housing. "There're maybe a hundred houses, and in one house there were twenty people living in a house not a whole lot bigger than this room. It was a terrible situation. And people were having to leave the reservation because of inadequate housing, and that was against my interest as a school administrator. So at a general council meeting, Francis McCrory nominated me to be the first chairman of the housing authority, and I accepted."[38]

In November 1964, less than three months after Johnson signed the Economic Opportunity Act, the OEO received Quinaults' proposal for a Community Action Program (CAP).[39] Almost five decades later, Patterson had vivid memories of the proposal's origins. "School board chairman Dave Purdy and James Jackson came to me one day . . . and James Jackson said to me, 'We need to make an application for a Community Action Program, and we don't have anyone capable of doing it. So if you're willing to do it, we'll pay you.' And . . . I said, 'Well, I'll do it whether you pay me or not.'" Purdy and Patterson called a series of meetings at which reservation residents listed improvements they wanted for the community. Patterson assembled the application by drawing "from that list all of the things that might qualify for funding." After the tribe submitted what he wrote, it "just sat in limbo" until Jackson called congresswoman Julia Butler Hansen. Patterson thought her intervention largely explained why Quinaults had "the first Indian action program funded in the state."[40]

As revised and resubmitted in April 1965, the Quinaults' application sought $92,502.25 for educational counseling, educational research, a preschool, adult education, Neighborhood Youth Corps training and employment, a youth recreation program, and health services. Did the emphasis on education indicate Patterson's dominance of the planning process? He denied that he unduly influenced the choice of activities to fund. According to the application, adult education and a preschool were on the list because of unyielding "pressure" from community members, which reflected Indians' increasing awareness "that education is a necessity for survival" but not Indian desire to join the American mainstream. The application narrative declared, "The American Indian has successfully resisted assimilation. He has retained a degree of cultural integrity which is embarrassing to those who would promote the 'melting pot' theory of cultural genocide." Accordingly, Quinaults wanted "to facilitate academic success of Indian students" by adapting education programs to their cherished Quinault culture. The research component of their action plan was included for that purpose.

Less obvious in the CAP proposal, but significant nonetheless, were indications that Quinaults would also use OEO funds for land and natural resource management. The program applicant was the Quinault Tribal Council—"the governing body of the Quinault Indian Reservation"—which had responsibility for "the enforcement of all tribal laws and regulations, including civil, criminal, and conservation laws." Of the total funding requested, $16,556.08 would cover program development and coordination. Among the activities to coordinate were forest, soil, and fish conservation work, including the operation of a federal-tribal hatchery scheduled to open in 1965. Neighborhood Youth Corps participants would be assigned fishery and stream management tasks.[41]

The plan to manage natural resources prompted a subsequent bid for a business development adviser's salary. The Community Services Administration received an application dated December 8, 1965, declaring, "Almost unlimited resources representing extensive potential for relief of poverty exist on the Quinault Indian Reservation," but with fish runs "depleted" and forests "rapidly disappearing in the absence of proper methods of conservation . . . , the resources which are the birthright of the people of the Reservation will remain dormant or slip into other hands skilled in their exploitation unless knowledgeable leadership can be developed to secure their utilization." Previous attempts to establish "business concerns" that would realize the economic potential of reservation resources had failed, the application explained, "not due to any lack of effort or will on the part of the people, but to the absence of a knowledge of good business practice, public relations and proper business management and skills."[42]

Not quite a year after the Office of Economic Opportunity approved the Quinault CAP, a consultant for OEO extolled the results: "Entire program seems to be functioning extremely well—very impressive reports. *This could well be an excellent success story for CAP publicity.*" Within the next two years, according to another OEO report, the Lummi, Swinomish, Makah, and Tulalip reservations in western Washington also had "ongoing funded CAP's." The region's "lesser-developed" tribes could look to those five "sophisticated" ones for models and assistance as they prepared to follow suit.[43]

Researchers at the University of Montana in 1977 deemed the antipoverty program a "terrific breakthrough" for tribes in that it sapped BIA power over them and afforded an education in "the non-Indian system."[44] Historians and Indian witnesses to OEO-funded efforts have generally agreed. Where tribal governments doubled as Community Action Agencies, Indians had experiences that whetted their appetite and equipped them for self-governance. Sherwin Broadhead applauded another OEO program for a similar reason. He worked in the OEO office that oversaw Volunteers in Service to America who were stationed on Indian reservations. Those outsiders working under a tribe's direction represented "a new kind of relationship with the white man," Broadhead observed. Previously, few non-Indians except missionaries, government officials, and lessees of allotted land had spent time in Indian country. As tribal governments gained control over people who brought new skills or energy to the reservation, they might make mistakes, but they were at least "allowed to fail and thus learn a hard lesson."[45]

Sobering realities eventually tempered the sense of empowerment that Indian CAPs aroused. For one thing, Indian country battles against poverty were not waged solely with CAPs; the BIA still controlled other forces. More importantly, funding cuts, legislative restrictions, and increasing red tape stalled the offensives by 1971. As economic data eventually showed, the CAPs and other development programs of the 1960s fell far short of banishing Indian poverty.[46] Years later, in conversation with historian Daniel Cobb, the former director of the OEO's Indian division lamented that a congressional "stranglehold" undermined frontline efforts. Still, he maintained that the federal government did right by Indians in one important respect: it funded the tribal organizations directly. Direct funding, he said, was "'the most helpful thing we could do to support tribal rights and sovereignty.'"[47]

For federal help of that sort, Quinaults were eager and felt ready. The same was true of Indians on many other reservations. Henry Hough, research director for the National Congress of American Indians Fund, recognized the tribes' preparedness in a CAP manual for tribe leaders and committee members. As the OEO geared up, Hough wrote, Indian reservations "were found to have ready-made organizations with experienced leadership endeavoring to cope with community needs through democratically elected tribal councils." Before 1966 was half over, more than sixty Community Action Agencies had formed in Indian country across the United States.[48]

Hough's statement did not describe all reservations in western Washington. Of the eighteen then in existence, most had considerably less Indian-owned land and less abundant natural resources than the Quinault reservation. They housed tribes that an OEO adviser labeled "lesser-developed," with governments not as active as the one Jim Jackson led. Even so, thanks to the regional network of intertribal relations, word of what CAPs could do reached all tribes. As OEO officials hoped, that motivated the smaller, less organized communities also to take advantage of the new federal support for Indian self-government.

Tribes in western Washington, big and small, also shared a history of organizing jointly to claim or defend rights under US law. Before World War I, they had established the Northwestern Federation of American Indians (NFAI), which orchestrated a lawsuit that accused the United States of failing to fulfill treaty promises. Tribes had since conducted other legal and political business through a succession of similar organizations—the Inter-Tribal Council of Western Washington Indians, the short-lived Indian fish commission that Horton Capoeman led, and Affiliated Tribes of Northwest Indians.[49] During the 1950s, the Inter-Tribal Council was a forum for discussing responses to federal termination policy and state jurisdiction. Once OEO funds became available, the council—describing itself as a multipurpose organization with a long-standing focus on poverty—applied for a grant to assist small tribes with the new development programs. Member tribes included the Quinaults.[50]

Intertribal political relations and Indians' desire for respect as self-governing treaty makers found expression in a 1964 protest demonstration at the state capitol. The grievances, as reported to the *Seattle Times*, included "the violation of treaties and other agreements with the United States," Washington's "assumption of jurisdiction over Indian tribes and reservations, without consent," and state failure to protect fisheries from pollution, improper logging, watershed degradation, dams, and irresponsible fishing. Those concerns aroused righteous anger in the National Indian Youth Council (NIYC), which took a central role in planning the demonstration and articulating its purposes. However, Bruce Wilkie was the only NIYC representative identified in the *Seattle Times* as a demonstration organizer; the other four were elected officials of local tribes—two Makahs and two Quinaults, Jim Jackson and Philip Martin. According to local NIYC member Hank Adams, when founder Clyde Warrior addressed the massive crowd on March 3, he said, "We did not come here to Olympia as militants. We came in protest, as sovereign nations to a sovereign State."[51]

By the time of the protest, a federal biologist was actively supporting the notion that sovereign Indian nations could manage fisheries better than the state government did. James Heckman had recently opened a tiny US Fish and Wildlife bureau office in Olympia and begun working with tribe members on projects to benefit their fisheries. In short order, Jim Jackson presented Heckman and the BIA with a Quinault fisheries rehabilitation program.[52] Years later, Nisqually activist Billy Frank, reflecting on decades of fighting for treaty rights and fish conservation, described Heckman as a man with a "winning personality" and a genuine appreciation of Indians as fishers and fisheries managers.

> Without condescension, Jim argued that doctorates and master's degrees in fisheries sciences already existed among the Indian tribes, who had managed the resources properly and without undue harm for centuries. . . . Heckman quickly moved with Coastal and Puget Sound tribes, and those on Hood's Canal, to enhance their resources management postures and to initiate their own recovery and production activities. . . . By early 1963, major stream clearance projects were underway on the Quinault Reservation. First reports about unconscionably destructive forestry practices were soon prepared by Heckman at Jim

> Jackson's request. As well, with paid workers and volunteers, the first re-seeding of Quinault razor clam beds and beaches was undertaken.[53]

Thus, even before the OEO vote of confidence in tribal governments, a federal agency had shown admiration for Northwest tribes' resource management.

Meanwhile, the US Senate signaled that respect for tribal government was also budding there. After hearings in nine states and Washington, DC, the Judiciary Subcommittee on Constitutional Rights published findings from its first-ever study of Indian rights. Language in the report rewarded witnesses who had emphasized the right of self-government: "Tribal government is the result of the Indians' original sovereign power to govern their affairs. . . . Before the early settlers came, each tribe was a sovereign, independent nation managing its own affairs and directing its activities with other tribes." Notwithstanding the limits on tribal power that followed from colonization and conquest, the report continued, "the tribe retains quasi-sovereign authority." Regrettably, however, a broad interpretation of the federal guardianship power had "been used to thwart the development of meaningful tribal self-government."[54]

PREPARING FOR POWER

As restraints on tribal governments loosened somewhat and their functions seemed likely to increase, both BIA and Indian officials saw a need for leadership training. Although the federal government had yet to renounce the termination policy, bureau personnel tried to meet the training need as they construed it. In 1963, the Portland Area BIA office began planning a workshop for current and potential tribe leaders, to be held in Pullman, Washington.

Through his lawyer, an official of the Spokane Tribe made bold to suggest topics for the workshop. "Speaking techniques, parliamentary procedures or . . . methods of communication" were not essential. Most Indian leaders had had years of practice in those aspects of their work. To develop as a leader, an Indian needed "detailed knowledge of the legal framework and policies within which he must operate." Useful discussions would be the ones that addressed "the Indian and the Federal Government," "aboriginal sovereignty and its present significance," "tribal rights and duties," "the Indian and the State," and the "growing influence and power of state and government over Indians."[55]

The thrust of the workshop ran instead to subjects such as group decision-making processes. Even so, the BIA subsequently received "numerous requests for a repeat of the Pullman Conference from tribal leaders west of the mountains." The bureau obliged the next year, and fifty Indians came to the conference from western and eastern Washington reservations. Again the stated purpose was to identify leadership qualities and develop individual skills. Nevertheless, in one conversation about problem solving, the discussion facilitator—a local college instructor—encouraged the participants' obvious interest in economic and policy issues. They would want to determine what resources their tribes had, he said, and why they had not used them in the past. "Particularly here, one of the big problems would be State or Federal regulations. We have to check the law first of all to find out what resources are available." They might "set up" their own regulations, he added, but not "so only a few people control it. You want the whole tribe to control it. Maybe the reservation would become self-sustaining."[56]

BIA-sponsored leadership seminars were annual events in western Washington for several following years. Although they maintained a focus on skills and processes, they provided more opportunities to discuss governance issues. For one session about "problem-solving through Tribal Councils," break-out groups could choose topics from a list that included "What can be done to develop united action among Indian Tribes," "What are the goals an Indian tribe should have," "What can be done to improve law enforcement on reservations," and "What can be done to prevent trespass and legal infringement on Tribal sovereignty."[57]

BIA records do not disclose the criteria or procedures for choosing seminar participants. At least two Quinaults attended: Marian Holloway, the Quinault secretary-treasurer, and Elizabeth Cole, who served the tribe in several capacities. Helen Mitchell's presence in 1965 deserves mention. A Quinault allotment owner, she resided on the Chehalis Reservation but took active interest in some Quinault resource management issues. According to Justine James, Sr., who described himself as "one of the first ones" Jim Jackson "picked out to be a so-called quality leadership," Mitchell was "one smart lady" who had "a lot of input" with Jackson, and taught Jug things a tribal leader should know. She was "on the national level for years. She was secretary of National Congress of American Indians for some time. . . . She had a lot of contact with lawyers, but Helen was also teachin' Jug the ropes, pushin' him."[58]

Perhaps Jackson's association with Helen Mitchell accounts for his increasing activity "on the national level" in the 1960s. Or perhaps, as Harold Patterson believed, former military officer Wilfred Petit coached Jackson to get involved in national politics. Regardless, Jackson's inclination and ability to deal with national lawmakers and bureaucrats probably reflected also his innate assertiveness, his experience and relative wealth as a business owner, and the example of a mother who was not shy about communicating with government officials in well-written letters.[59] A Quinault staff attorney who met Jackson in 1971 thought that "Jug presented well, and he presented as a modern Indian."[60]

Accordingly, Jim Jackson gained visibility beyond Quinault as a strong-minded tribe leader with well-defined goals. In 1965—thanks to the relations he nurtured with Representative Hansen—he received an invitation to Lyndon Johnson's inauguration. In conversation with the *Seattle Times* reporter who covered that "historic call," Jackson divulged his plan to stay a week in the capital and visit various federal offices, "seeking solutions to tribal problems in fisheries, education and housing."[61] In subsequent years, such visits were commonplace for Jackson and other Quinault officers.

NCAI headquarters was one of Jackson's regular stops in the capital, much to the satisfaction of that organization's new executive director, Vine Deloria, Jr. Hoping to counter the conservative influence of officials from some large tribes, Deloria reached out to young activists and leaders of smaller tribes, including several in the Pacific Northwest.[62] He told Jackson that a sustained Quinault connection with the NCAI could be mutually beneficial. They had the same lawyer, Charles Hobbs, with whom Deloria was "in constant contact" and from whom he could learn Quinault positions "on various things." Deloria also had "a fine working relationship" with Julia Butler Hansen, who kept him informed about legislation that might affect Quinaults.[63]

Within a year, the tenor of NCAI leadership shifted decisively in a direction that Deloria and Jackson welcomed. The new president, Mescalero Apache Wendell Chino, was a vigorous advocate of tribal sovereignty.[64]

By then, Jackson and other Quinault officers were prominent at regional intertribal gatherings, which afforded leadership training at least as valuable as BIA seminars. In the mid-1960s, Jackson chaired the Washington State Indian Conference, where the theme was full utilization and development of natural and human resources. At the 1966 conference, he was a featured speaker on fisheries and shellfish projects. There, too, Wilfred Petit shared the stage with Yakima, Makah, Colville, and Spokane panelists for a session on forest resources; Alice Chenois, administrator of the Quinault CAP, sat on a panel about income-generating projects; and Philip Martin appeared on one concerning law and order.[65] The following year, at the Western Inter-Tribal Coordinating Council Convention, Jim Jackson and Helen Mitchell joined a lawyer and state lawmaker in a presentation titled "Effective Legislative Approach." Jackson's topic at a separate discussion of "Major Indian Problems" was jurisdiction. In 1967, when NCAI members met in Portland, Mitchell was the recording secretary, and Jackson was a panelist for the session on treaty rights.[66]

Discourse at those meetings of tribal politicians increasingly reflected and encouraged bold conceptions of Indian tribes' political status and rights under federal law. Records of the 1966 Northwest Affiliated Tribes conference exemplify that trend. The cover of the conference program proclaimed, "The Sovereignty of Indian Rights and Prerogatives shall not be extinguished." The subject of one panel discussion was "Treaty Rights, Fishing and Hunting Rights, issues arising from conflict of understanding between Indian Tribes and political sub-divisions of state governments and state agencies, and the issue of state jurisdiction in civil and criminal causes of action in Indian country." Conference Resolution 6 indicated delegates' desire for limits on federal power in Indian country. It protested that Interior Department plans for wildlife reserves on reservations totally disregarded "the exclusive rights of the Indian people to manage their hunting on their reservations."[67]

Seven weeks later in Spokane, representatives of Affiliated Tribes had an opportunity to hand that resolution directly to the new US Indian commissioner. Robert Bennett was on a swing through the West to meet with Indian leaders. An Oneida from Wisconsin, Bennett was only the second Indian to head the BIA and the first one since the 1870s. At his swearing-in on April 27, 1966, Lyndon Johnson told him, "Your President thinks the time has come to put the first Americans first on our agenda . . .

so we can remove the blush of shame that comes to our cheeks when we look at what we have done" to them. In closing, Johnson exhorted Bennett, "Do anything you have to do."[68]

By his examples of reasons for shame, Johnson implied that the commissioner's to-do list would consist primarily, if not entirely, of efforts to alleviate Indian poverty. Bennett knew that tribe leaders had additional priorities in mind. Many were hoping he would ease their lingering fear of forcible detribalization, perhaps even reverse some effects of the termination policy. At the regional conferences he convened, Bennett seemingly endorsed this aspiration when he advised the assembled Indians to strengthen their governments. He said he wanted more opportunities for Indians to take responsibility. Speaking to Northern Plains tribes about constitutions they had adopted in the New Deal years, he said, "You may want to take a look at these and see if there are any provisions in these Constitutions and By-laws which might be holding you back or restricting you from taking advantage of the opportunities that exist."[69]

During three days of meetings with Indians from twenty-four Northwest tribes, Bennett received their written statements and heard many of them speak about issues they wanted him to address. Quinaults, whose seven-person delegation was one of the largest, submitted forty-one pages containing numerous recommendations for action. Jim Jackson's introduction was characteristically forceful: "Governing bodies and leaders of Indian tribes should have a stronger voice in the planning of their own destinies. The Quinault Tribe is ready to put this proposition to a test . . . because we know that it is *our* heritage, *our* resources, and the future of *our* children that are at stake."[70] Attached were several memoranda on subjects ranging from fisheries and land to education.

A memorandum titled "Tribal Jurisdiction" had a prominent place in that compilation. It began with a foundational declaration: "All treaty rights, including the economically vital rights of hunting and fishing, the right to regulate the activities of non-Indians on its lands, and the right to develop and regulate the development of the reserve-lands [*sic*] all hinge upon the sovereignty of the Quinault tribe over its lands." The ensuing text protested the state's assumption of jurisdiction and BIA promotion of that change. It branded the Washington State scheme of partial jurisdiction unworkable. Where reservation lands were a patchwork of fee simple and Indian trust ownership, imposing state law on the fee lands was sure to cause "utter confusion." The memorandum concluded with four specific proposals. Three urged BIA action consistent with the tribe's objection to state law; the other one recommended reservation law enforcement solely by tribal officers. Indian police would enforce tribal law under a tribal contract with the United States. A separate contract with the county would enable the tribe's police to enforce local and state law applicable to non-Indians. A final sentence elaborated, "Since tribal laws do not apply to all activities of non-Indians, and since we do not wish to exclude them from the reservation, we feel that this method would provide for the maintenance of law and order without abrogating tribal jurisdiction."[71]

Among the tribes' submissions to Bennett, the Quinault statement on jurisdiction was notable for its prominence, specificity, and concern with non-Indian activities on reservation. Some tribes did not address jurisdiction at all. A briefer Spokane Tribe statement on the subject objected primarily to state and federal assumptions that state jurisdiction precluded simultaneous tribal jurisdiction. Only a memorandum from the Shoshone-Bannock Tribes in Idaho devoted as much attention as Quinaults to problems arising from non-Indians' presence on reservation. Those problems included trespasses and game violations, uncertainty whether state and Indian courts had concurrent jurisdiction, and lack of clarity about the tribes' authority over "licensing and taxing of uses, businesses and utilities." Shoshone-Bannocks suggested a solution that rested on their belief in uncompromised tribal sovereignty. "Expand [the tribe's] law and order code . . . to accomplish the following," they urged: "Arrest or citation of non-Indians, when the same are within the territorial jurisdiction of the Indian reservation and are committing a misdemeanor against Indian property or rights therein." A wrap-up section restated the problem: "lack of jurisdiction to punish non-Indians for petty offenses occurring on Indian reservations specifically regarding offenses to land, game and livestock, of Indians." It recommended that a non-Indian offender "be cited or arrested and taken before a Tribal Magistrate and fined, or his weapons taken, or both."[72]

In the AAIA file containing the Quinault and Shoshone-Bannock memoranda, there is no response from Commissioner Bennett, but it is safe to say he did not encourage such far-reaching conceptions of tribes' powers. Bennett, who had been a BIA employee throughout the heyday of the termination policy, ultimately disappointed advocates of maximum tribal autonomy. According to writer Stan Steiner, a sympathetic observer of Indians' new assertiveness, Bennett advised an NCAI audience in 1967 that "tribalism would have to be homogenized and modernized. The tribes had to accept 'goals of economic and social compatibility with the other peoples of the country.'" A local journalist heard Bennett say later that the government should legislate an end to tribalism.[73]

Federal agencies in western Washington also tried to cool the growing Indian zeal for tribal power. In July 1967, when representatives of nineteen tribes and the state congressional delegation met with personnel from the BIA, Indian Health Service, and OEO, an unidentified witness jotted down points the agencies made: "Indians must learn to accept the tools offered by the government and learn to make those tools work, rather than demanding special tools for themselves"; "Indians must assimilate themselves into the American Culture"; "Self-determination might be a desirable objective but it must be considered in the light of cold, hard facts"; and "Congress is the ultimate authority on what the Indians will get."[74]

The agencies' advice fell mostly on ears that were closed to such assimilationist messages. Community Action Programs had fanned and added fuel to a smoldering Indian desire for consistent recognition of their legal rights, for freedom from forced assimilation, and for the chance to weigh "hard facts" themselves as they decided how much autonomy they wanted.

ASSUMING POWER

At Taholah, the Community Action Program launch coincided with increasing efforts to wield Quinault government power over activities on the reservation, particularly activities affecting natural resources and the ecosystem. Some efforts were under way when Harold Patterson put the final touches on the first CAP application in November 1964. Quinault officials and voters had resolved to challenge state power within reservation borders and to assert tribal authority over objectionable non-Indian activity, even without an assurance of BIA support.

To Quinaults jealous of their reserved territory and historic autonomy, one alarming infringement was Washington's decision in 1963 to regulate eight kinds of Indian activity on all reservation land. That move came on the heels of the state supreme court's refusal to invalidate the governor's proclamation of state criminal law jurisdiction. Quinault officials therefore decided to seek federal intervention. In June 1964, attorneys from the Wilkinson, Cragun and Barker firm, assisted by a former US attorney and local counsel Gladys Phillips, asked a federal judge to enjoin all state law enforcement on the Quinault Reservation. They contended that Washington's constitution barred state jurisdiction over reservation lands.[75] Nine months later, the judge dismissed the suit for failure to meet a prerequisite of federal court jurisdiction: a claim of harm to the tribe valued at more than $10,000. While preparing to appeal, the attorneys petitioned Congress to eliminate that financial harm requirement.[76]

In the meantime, Quinault leaders asked their federal guardians to confirm that the tribe could limit or prohibit non-Indian use of reservation beaches. Specific Quinault complaints about non-Indian clam diggers prodded the Western Washington Agency to undertake an investigation that reportedly lasted "many hours" and produced curiously brief findings in July 1963: "The alleged offenders have purchased lands, within the reservation, from a real estate development company. These purchasers, as well as the real estate company, feel that they have beach rights. Extensive research by the Branch of Realty has now shown that subject beaches are not tribally owned."[77]

Quinault officials were unconvinced. Aware that the executive order of 1873 set the reservation's coast boundary at the low water mark, they opted to proceed as if they did own the beaches.[78] At a meeting one year later, BIA staff and state and federal law officers learned from tribal representatives that "during the month 17 Warning Trespass Citations were issued by the Deputy Special Officers on the Quinault Reservation. All of these were against non-Quinault persons for clam digging on Tribal Beaches . . . , and the Business Committee desire [*sic*] to make a point of the fact that the Committee can control clam digging on the Tribal Beaches." The committee made its point with an announcement that non-Quinault residents of Taholah would receive "special privilege" clam-digging passes.[79] Knowing that a pass system would not resolve the issue of rights on beaches adjoining non-Indian-owned property, Jim Jackson told the general council, "The Business Committee should have authority to close the beach to all non-Indians when we feel our rights are endangered, so that we will let them know who owns the beach."[80]

An immediate concern at that council meeting was construction debris on the beach, allegedly dumped there by a non-Indian. The conversation also turned to a tribal ordinance that prohibited construction of motels or other businesses without permission from the tribe and BIA. The effectiveness of that two-year-old regulation was at stake because Northwest Realty and Appraisal, a Seattle company, was reportedly planning a substantial commercial tourist development on the so-called Taholah Ocean Tract. BIA superintendent George Felshaw had responded to this news with a letter informing the company that "the Quinault Tribal Business Committee passed an ordinance on March 30, 1963, entitled 'Ordinance subjecting Motels and other Businesses on the Quinault Reservation to Tribal Regulation,' enclosure 1. This ordinance was published in the local newspapers and also recorded in the appropriate county offices." Felshaw enclosed the Quinault treaty and executive order as well.[81]

Northwest Realty and Appraisal announced that it would proceed with its project anyway. Spokesman Dewey Whittaker told a journalist, "The Indians can't stop us. We bought the land from them and we are not part of the reservation. . . . Jackson is standing in the way of progress and if he keeps fighting everything that comes along he will just bring the reservation closer to its end. In fact, I predict that in another 20 years there will be no Indian reservation. Actually, there are only four or five of the leaders out there who are making it bad for the rest of the tribe. Ninety-nine percent of them are nice people."[82]

Quinault officials did not pin their hopes of deterring the development solely on local BIA intervention. They took their concerns to the Grays Harbor County government and to higher BIA personnel. The county response in August 1965 was notably respectful. Upon learning from Jim Jackson that the developer had not requested a tribal building permit, the commissioners voided county permits for the Taholah Ocean Tract.[83] The next year Jackson and a fellow councilman asked the commission to deny all proposed beachfront plats within reservation boundaries until the tribe could complete "a comprehensive reservation plan." According to a local newspaper article, the commissioners pledged to continue a county policy of permitting "only those plats on the reservation" approved by the tribal council. They also offered to help the tribe prepare its comprehensive plan.[84]

BIA officials, in contrast, thought the tribe was out of bounds. At a July 1966 meeting with Associate Commissioner James Officer, Jim Jackson and Helen Mitchell emphasized Quinaults' desire to prevent "junky" development of the beachfront strip where non-Indians were purchasing lots. The seashore was a "scenic asset," they said, and they were loath to lose it "forever." As noted in bureau files, "Mr. Officer felt the tribe was overly optimistic in believing that it could exclude private developers completely from the Quinault beach." Although Jackson had flatly rejected BIA advice to invoke state law, Officer put that advice in a letter. Consider "some kind of State Court action against the individual who presently is developing beachfront property," he urged, "in view of the fact that he has created a nuisance by pushing debris on to the beach." Someone else in the bureau determined that the secretary did not have power to adopt regulations restraining the development; that was a matter for the state or county to accomplish by a zoning ordinance. Yet another functionary suggested that the tribe ask the National Park Service to "determine the scenic importance of the ocean beaches" and seek an extension of the Olympic Park beach area southward through the reservation.[85]

Jim Jackson knew as well as developer Whittaker that access to scenic seashores not only attracted visitors but drew buyers for oceanfront land. He also knew that Northwest Realty's potential customers read newspapers; so when opportunities for press publicity arose, he made statements calculated to reduce the appeal of the waterfront lots. In August 1966, Jackson told a *Seattle Times* reporter, "Real-estate men from Seattle are selling lots and are implying the beach frontage and the beach itself go along with the lots." That was a falsehood, Jackson said; the beaches were not open to the public.[86]

By then, the actions of waterfront developers had gone from worrisome to alarming for the Quinault Business Committee. Minutes from a July 18 meeting described "heavy equipment on beach, scooping sand from below the rocks and from the low water line up onto fills" on the shore. Quinault officials decided to petition Interior Secretary Udall directly for "a regulation temporarily suspending commercial development of the beach area." They requested a halt to all Quinault Reservation real estate development within a mile of the coastline for a year, during which the tribe would conduct a "massive survey" and draft a zoning plan to protect reservation resources "for the use and benefit of the Indian people."[87] The survey and planning process culminated in March 1967 with tribal council adoption of an interim ordinance that zoned all land inside reservation boundaries.

Meanwhile, Quinaults also prepared a law and order code and constructed a tribal jail.[88]

Neither of those legislative actions was part of the Quinault Community Action Program, but CAP projects and the extension of tribal government power were mutually reinforcing elements of the drive for a homeland under Quinault control. Their synergy and structural footing were evident in *Nugguam*, a reservation newsletter launched in September 1966. Editor Alice Chenois was also the tribal council secretary, the CAP secretary, and eventually the CAP administrator. The lead article in *Nugguam*'s first issue announced:

> Important things are happening at Taholah and Queets—things which may affect the lives of everyone living here, both in spite of us and because of us. They cannot be prevented because the whole world is changing. James Jackson and the Business Committee are working hard to turn these changes into advantages for Indians, to protect the Reservation from the kind of development that makes us angry, and to keep our resources for the people who rightfully own them. . . . [Therefore,] this little news bulletin is being written by your Community Action Program.[89]

Because the reservation population was small, and a council of all adult tribe members decided matters of common interest, many residents were involved to some degree in both kinds of happenings: in CAP projects and in other exertions of government power.[90] Presiding over all those Quinault endeavors and enlisting people to lead them was the "tough" but "modern Indian," Jug Jackson.

In 2012, three men who worked with Jackson gave him much of the credit for making the 1960s a period of remarkable Quinault progress in self-governance. Justine James, Sr., was one of Jackson's many protégés, recruited first to serve as conservation officer and later as tribal manager.[91] Jackson "had his vision how this tribe should be," even "kind of handpicked the council for us," James said. He "had the personality that 'I am the one in charge.'" James thought people went along with plans that Jackson worked out, often "behind the scene," because "he was a sharp man in a lot of ways." Off-handedly, James remarked that Jug also "held a big hammer"—perhaps an allusion to Jackson's influence as the owner of a shingle mill where a majority of Taholah's wage earners worked.[92]

Francis Rosander described Jackson's leadership in similar terms: "When you'd go to a meeting with Jim, he usually had everything figured out before he got there, and instead of saying, 'Well, you know, let's talk about this,' . . . a lot of times he'd just say, 'Well, now this is what we're gonna do.' . . . He was a kind of an opportunist, you know, in a lot of ways, but then that's what they had to be back then. . . . He did hire mostly Indians. Anybody'd work, he'd put 'em to work." Asked whether he meant that Jackson engaged in political patronage, Rosander replied, "That's what I thought. He was kind of like the godfather. If he liked you, you were all right."[93]

By his own account, Harold Patterson "got completely involved with James Jackson," listening to him "to the point where I could get into his mind, I could learn to think as he did" and therefore write letters over Jackson's name. Patterson thought his faithful channeling of Jackson's views explained why Jug "never changed a word in any letter." It was "silly," he said, to ask whether Jackson let Patterson or other associates determine the positions he took. As an example of Jug's strong will, Patterson mentioned a "very cooperative" BIA response to the tribe's request for help with a zoning ordinance. "They were threatened by James Jackson," he explained. "One time the assistant superintendent came to me and he said, 'Will you tell James Jackson to call Washington sometime when he's not angry?' I just laughed at him."[94]

The recollections of Patterson, Rosander, and James complement views that Jackson's contemporaries voiced at the 1967 general council meeting. Speaker after speaker applauded the changes under way in the tribe and attributed them to Jackson's leadership. Business Committee members Dave Purdy and John Shale praised Jackson as the best president "to serve yet." Herbert Capoeman expressed gratitude for the tribe's elected officers, attorneys, "and their efforts in consulting with us and passing information on to us that is important to our tribe." "The last few years," he noted, "the business on this reservation has been more than ever. All development and business has been our peoples' business." Ralph Capoeman chimed in that the tribe could be proud of Jackson's regional and national visibility. "It gave me a good feeling to be traveling with a man recognized everywhere we went," he said. "Everyone respects our president and looks up to him wherever we are. We are fortunate to have such a man leading us." Jim Jackson's response to such fulsome acclaim was a politic offer to share the credit for recent improvements: "We have taken a big step forward on development of the reservation."[95]

The agenda for that meeting included updates on some of the accomplishments that inspired all the self-congratulation. Following a report on housing construction, it was the CAP director's turn. Blanche Pennick said the two-year-old program now had fourteen regular employees. With Neighborhood Youth Corps money, it had given almost three hundred young people temporary paid work. Pennick, a non-Indian and retired county schools director, intimated that she did her job with two contrasting values in mind: tribal tradition and progress. "On one hand we must keep our interest in the salmon berries," she said, "yet on the other hand we must recognize we are living in the age of jet planes and the future."[96]

In the future that Jackson and his allies envisioned, managing reservation resources and land use would be the Quinault government's responsibility alone. The tribe could not afford to wait for reluctant federal bureaucrats to affirm that responsibility. By the mid-1960s, the reservation was experiencing several undesirable effects of a US economic expansion. Logging was at an all-time high, but timber prices were consequently low; increases in state-licensed commercial salmon fishing and industrial damage to fish habitat were rapidly depleting salmon stocks; middle-class northwesterners were cruising an expanding highway system in search of scenic vacation spots and recreational property; and a lively real estate market was inducing more sales of reservation land to outsiders.[97]

Two events of the 1960s highlighted the deleterious effects of logging on reservation fisheries. First, when the tribe and US Fish and Wildlife Service installed a hatchery on the Moclips River, it took days of back-breaking Indian labor to clear the stream of logging debris that would impede fish passage. Then in 1967, fire roared across five thousand reservation acres, fueled by the copious slash that loggers left behind. The many tribe members who still depended on fishing for income and food could no longer tolerate logging's threat to their livelihood and traditional subsistence. Allotment owners' dissatisfaction with stumpage rates and tribal officials' unhappiness with BIA-approved logging contracts also fed Quinault desires for tribe-controlled forest management premised on "the essential unity of the natural resources"—fish, wildlife, plants, and timber.[98]

At times, Quinault officials and planners wrote and spoke about management of the reservation's natural resources as if development were the

Clear-cutting left much of the Quinault Reservation covered in vast piles of slash like this one in the Camp Creek drainage, surveyed in 1972 by Corky Perry, salvage forester for the Quinault Indian Nation. Photograph by Larry Workman, Quinault Indian Nation.

problem. Jim Jackson complained to Julia Butler Hansen that the BIA had not helped the tribe solve two long-standing, "related problems"—"accelerated land sales and . . . irresponsible development of reservation lands and resource [*sic*]."[99] In another letter to Hansen, Harold Patterson identified a "disappearing land base" as the Quinaults' greatest problem and proposed two solutions, including "curtail commercial developments . . . as much as possible." He continued, "The non-Indians who have bought land on the Reservation do not understand the feelings of the Indian people about their reservations. To the newcomers, it is merely an investment, a scenic retreat, or an opportunity for development and, in some cases, exploitation. . . . Indians cannot compete with non-Indian commercialism because they have too much reverence for their land and for their fellow man." With other members of the Quinault Planning Commission,

Patterson had written the new zoning ordinance. Its designation of all undeveloped land as wilderness "meant that they couldn't do anything on it without the permission of the tribe, no matter who owned it." In an issue of *Nugguam*, the Planning Commission argued for preserving some undeveloped land, saying, "It is attractive because it is undeveloped! It has not occurred to some people that the Indians might have a good reason for leaving much of their land in a natural state. They do not realize that the highest value of some land is to use it as it is, without changing it, or slicing it up into little private back yards."[100]

At other times, the tribal government sought money and assistance enabling them to exploit reservation resources. In a 1966 meeting with BIA staff, Quinault spokesmen emphasized their eagerness for economic initiatives. Patterson said the need for development "sprang into the minds of the people when they saw that private interests were beginning to divide and plat subdivisions on the reservation which had heretofore been considered to be tribal assets."[101] The tribe's earlier application for an OEO-funded business adviser had identified several potential targets of development: recreation areas along the ocean beaches, the Native fishing industry, forests managed for "perpetual yield," human resources, "general community improvement," and "numerous small business concerns."[102]

Taken together, the words and actions of Quinault government officials and advisers showed their desire not to block economic enterprise but to regulate it according to priorities that reflected Quinault traditions. Patterson, who sometimes romanticized those traditions, probably expressed the tribe's contemporary goals accurately when he wrote, "They seek, through the use and development of their resources, to live in harmony with nature and in tune with the times."[103]

While suffering the ill effects of BIA practices and facing resistance from non-Quinault allottees as well as non-Indians, Quinault leaders tried to build a government capable of serving those goals.[104] Their approach was pragmatic. They cultivated supporters. They considered familiar American examples of local governance and emulated what seemed feasible as well as obligatory. After more than a century of exposure to their colonizers' legal culture, Quinaults knew that lawmaking and enforcement were essential to government in the United States; they assumed the same was true for the tribe.

Of those two functions, lawmaking was primary; it was also more affordable. Thus, in January 1967, BIA personnel noted that Quinaults had composed a "very comprehensive" law and order code, which could "provide residents of the Reservation with a more complete framework of Tribal Government." Records suggest that the code writers adapted a sample furnished by the law firm in Washington, DC. In a May 1 letter informing Representative Hansen that code enforcement was stalled for lack of BIA approval, Harold Patterson wrote, "Many people mistakenly believe that the Quinault do not want to be governed by law. Nothing could be further from the truth." In fact, the tribe's new code was stricter than state law.[105]

The code did not provide for Quinault prosecution of non-Indians. The drafters probably assumed the tribe would turn non-Indian offenders over to county authorities. Even so, by enacting the code, the tribe signaled its aversion to state law on the reservation and its readiness to serve as the principal reservation police agency. In November, Jim Jackson conveyed that message in writing to a congressional subcommittee. Authorizing state criminal jurisdiction on reservations is "impractical and unjust," he asserted. It violates vital Indian rights because state officers "neither understand nor recognize the fact that the Quinault Tribe must have a jurisdiction which is capable of protection [*sic*] hunting, fishing, and land use rights guaranteed to Indians by their treaty." Accordingly, four full-time tribal officers currently patrolled his reservation.[106]

Quinault lawmakers did claim authority to regulate non-Indians' use of reservation land and natural resources. The lawyers in Washington, DC, had sent them a memorandum setting out a federal law argument for the tribe's right to zone the entire area within reservation boundaries. By then, the Quinault Planning Commission was well into the process of developing an ordinance that would do exactly that. According to commission chairman Patterson, the drafters worked with minimal legal advice; their principal advisers were BIA "specialists" and the Grays Harbor County planner. By spring of 1967, the Business Committee had in hand three pieces of legislation—a zoning ordinance and two permitting ordinances—which unambiguously applied to development on all reservation land, even land in non-Indian fee ownership.[107]

The most common justification for this assertion of power was the tribe's treaty with the United States. Some records indicate that the argument originated with people in Taholah, not their distant lawyers. Consider a letter to the law firm that Jim Jackson signed in May 1967. It read, "I would like for you to develop a case that the Quinault Treaty constitutes a limitation upon the title of all land within the Quinault Indian Reservation including patent-in-fee land. I don't believe there is anything in the general allottment [*sic*] act to destroy this concept." Treaty language justified the conclusion that the tribe had a right to set the conditions on which "white men" could enter or live there. Jackson's letter concluded, "In summary, perhaps it is time to spell out what an Indian Reservation is."[108]

Even if Patterson—the college graduate—wrote such law-inflected correspondence for Jackson, it is very unlikely that he introduced Jackson to treaty language and federal statutes. It is more probable that Jackson or other Indians initiated Patterson's education in applicable law. When questioned about how he or Jackson acquired knowledge of federal Indian law, Patterson mentioned the *Handbook* by Felix Cohen but did not say how those writings came to his attention. Joe DeLaCruz, a Jackson protégé, emphasized that his mentor knew how important and potentially useful US laws were for Indians.[109]

No matter how Jackson arrived at his convictions about Quinault tribal rights and powers, he held to them in the face of BIA skepticism and stonewalling. Anticipating that non-Indians would defy the new land use regulations and the tribe might appeal in vain for bureau backup, he and Patterson sought to bring Julia Butler Hansen into the debate on their side. Patterson wrote: "The Tribe feels that they have the express right to do this under the terms of the treaty. The attorneys for the Tribe advise them that they are on sound legal ground. The Grays Harbor County Commissioners and the Regional and County Planning Commissions, likewise, give full recognition to the tribal right. . . . In spite of this, the Tribe has doubts as to the position that the high-level Bureau people will take. Jim is convinced that they are still adhering to a policy of termination."[110]

Hansen, expressing pride in the tribe's progress, obligingly directed an inquiry to Commissioner Bennett. The response would not have surprised Jug Jackson. Bennett reminded Hansen of a previous letter from Secretary Udall pointing out "legal problems" associated with the Quinault tribe's attempt "to regulate non-Indian property and activities." Declaring himself "in full accord" with the tribe's aims, Bennett nonetheless equivocated: "Before the ordinances can be approved, we must be satisfied that they do not exceed the Tribe's jurisdiction limitations." Bennett was similarly unhelpful when Jackson questioned state authority to regulate non-Indian fishing on the reservation. There was no legal basis to prevent it, he wrote.[111]

In 1965, Harold Patterson drew a state senator's attention to the Quinault tribe's history of resorting to prescribed legal procedures when aggrieved. "The efforts of our people to preserve what is theirs has [*sic*] frequently brought them into conflict with other interests," he wrote. "May I point out that they have not sought to gain their point by using cheap publicity or by participating in mass demonstrations of a negative and unsavory nature. They have consistently used the resources of the courts and the conference table to resolve their differences, and have frequently succeeded."[112] As 1967 drew to a close, however, the resolution of Indian and non-Indian differences on the jurisdiction question was clearly not imminent.

To no one's surprise, some people were not intimidated by ordinances asserting Quinault tribal authority on private land and reservation beaches. *Nugguam*'s editor noted that "non-Indian land owners" seemed surprised to learn they had "responsibilities to the Indian nation," and they were "strongly resisting." She urged Quinaults to unite for the impending battle.[113] Jim Jackson made sure that the tribe's friend in Congress heard the story from him. "On May 10, 1968," he told Hansen, "the Santiago Realty Co. again dumped several truckloads of brush and debris on the beach. They also removed 1000 yards of sand from the beach for fill purposes. Both actions tend to damage the clam beds, which are an important tribal resource. You can also appreciate that these activities destroy the beauty of our coastline."[114]

Meanwhile, the tribe had lost a battle in US courts. First a court of appeals and then the Supreme Court declined to countermand the state's assumption of jurisdiction on the reservation.[115] Not long afterward, it seemed that Quinaults had succeeded in ridding themselves of state jurisdiction by other means. In January 1965, Governor Albert Rosellini granted the tribe's long-standing petition for repeal of the 1958 decree extending state law to the reservation. However, Justice Department lawyers—claiming that they could find no federal authority for the governor's action—maintained that Rosellini's action was ineffective. Finally, in 1968, Congress authorized state governments to rescind their proclamations of jurisdiction over reservations, and Quinaults promptly prevailed on Governor Daniel Evans to do that for them.[116]

At Taholah, Jim Jackson must have celebrated Evans's good turn with the tribe's new business manager, Joe DeLaCruz. Jackson had recently persuaded DeLaCruz to come home from Oregon and help his native community with ongoing battles and those yet to come. As Harold Patterson remembered it, the tribe's Community Action Program was off to a good start when Jackson called one day and said, "I want you to put a program in there for a tribal business manager. . . . I'm going to hire Joe DeLaCruz." To Patterson's comment, "He's kinda young, isn't he?" Jackson replied, "Well, how's he going to learn?" "And that's when things began to take off," Patterson recalled, "because the tribe began to assume responsibility for tribal programs and things like that. And the Bureau became very

Joe DeLaCruz led the Quinault Indian Nation as council president for twenty-two years, but he and many other Quinaults credited the preceding president, James Jackson, with inspiring their commitment to take control of conditions on the reservation. Photograph by Larry Workman, Quinault Indian Nation.

threatened by that. . . . They didn't like it, but there wasn't anything they could do about it."[117]

Five years after he was hired, Joe DeLaCruz told a congressional subcommittee, "Since the tribe got its first OEO grant and it was able to establish a tribal office which they never had before, we have moved really fast." In later decades, DeLaCruz was often credited for inspiring and orchestrating that rapid movement. But when Jim Jackson died in 1999, DeLaCruz revealed that his own inspiration was the simple exhortation of the man who had called him home to Taholah. "I remember very clearly Jim telling us that, 'It's time people know who owns the Quinault Reservation.'"[118]

5. Lawyers on the Scene

When Michael Taylor finished law school in 1969, he left California for western Washington, where he would fulfill a two-year commitment to Volunteers in Service for America (VISTA). That year, as Richard Nixon assumed the presidency and Warren Burger became chief justice of the Supreme Court, many Americans seemed inclined to defy the laws and institutions that Nixon and Burger pledged to uphold. By October, "race riots" had scarred Connecticut's capital, "homosexuals" had rioted in New York City, and eight men were on trial in Chicago for inciting mayhem outside the recent Democratic Party convention. Even among American Indians, described in the *New York Times* as "traditionally . . . conservative," a "swing to harsh militancy" was under way. Angry, impatient young tribe members were promising to "raise some hell."[1]

In Seattle, where Indian disobedience of state fishing regulations was frequent news and Vine Deloria's "Indian manifesto" *Custer Died for Your Sins* was a best seller, Mike Taylor joined nine other VISTA recruits assigned to Seattle Legal Services Center (SLSC), a recently established base of operations in the War on Poverty.[2] When the VISTA recruiter named three Indian reservations as possible placement locations for them, Taylor expressed interest. Consequently, his long career in Indian law began on the small Muckleshoot Reservation, which bordered Seattle's southeast suburbs.[3]

The impoverished Muckleshoot Tribe had no headquarters, no office space for an attorney. Taylor interviewed clients behind a portable partition in an Indian Shaker church. The Indians' economic desperation appalled him, as did the bigotry they faced from non-Indians. He heard anguished accounts of children removed from families by state social workers who deemed Indians' child-raising practices and material environment deficient. Death was also taking children. In 2012 Taylor recalled,

> A visiting nurse out there . . . did some statistics on their infant mortality rate, and it was fairly clear that they would not survive. With a 25 percent infant mortality rate, you can't sustain a population. And there was no health care at all. There was a retired former BIA or IHS [Indian Health Service] contracting doctor . . . [who] would take Indian patients, but he didn't have an office anymore. The physicians in [the adjacent town of] Auburn didn't want to have Indian patients in their office, not because they couldn't pay but because of the racism there. The other patients objected to having Indians around them.[4]

VISTA recruiter Seth Armstrong, who "had some connections" with local Indians, gave Taylor and two other volunteers the names of several individuals, saying, "Go meet these people." So the novice lawyers made the acquaintance of Indians from the Canada border to Oregon. They listened to Lummi Tribe members worried about non-Indian development on their reservation, landless Stillaguamish who received no federal services for Indians, salmon fishers embroiled in conflict with state regulators, and other Indians with issues of governance and policy on their minds.

Taylor and his colleagues learned that Indians' lives played out in a unique legal context. They were subject to laws, court decrees, government policies, and jurisdictional rules that law school classes had not covered. To understand those special circumstances and identify legal remedies for the problems of indigent Indians, the VISTAs needed supplemental education. Armstrong found them a *Handbook of Federal Indian Law*—not Cohen's original work but the "bowdlerized" Interior Department publication of 1958. Then they heard that University of Washington (UW) professor Ralph Johnson "was trying to teach a course in Indian law."

Armstrong and Johnson approved their request to spend on-the-job time auditing the class.[5]

In 1970, Johnson asked Taylor and another VISTA lawyer to speak with Quinault Tribe member Guy McMinds about his recent withdrawal from the UW School of Fisheries graduate program. Johnson thought the circumstances smacked of politically motivated mistreatment. Officials in the state fisheries department—a major funder of the university program—had reportedly complained to faculty that McMinds was persuading tribes to oppose state regulation. When the school threatened to revoke McMinds's fellowship, he quit and returned to the reservation.

Taylor and McMinds later told similar stories of their first encounter at McMinds's home. The unsmiling, husky young Indian scrutinized the two white strangers, growled that they looked more like hippies than lawyers, rebuffed their offer to help him challenge the university's stance, and said, "I'm going to use what happened to me to build . . . a fisheries structure here at Taholah. I'm going to use my connections at the U to do that." Maybe those were not his exact words, Taylor added, "but he did do this." Within a couple of years, two fisheries biologists with graduate degrees, two with undergraduate degrees, and a forestry graduate student were working for Quinaults at Taholah.[6]

McMinds, also known as Butch, envisioned a Quinault "fisheries structure" that included a lawyer. One day in 1972, after a meeting in Seattle about state harassment of Indian fishers, he told Taylor he needed an attorney on the reservation. He was in touch with a sympathetic foundation director, he said, and requested Taylor's help with a grant application. When the application paid off, McMinds offered the new position to a young man he had once dismissed as a hippie, and Taylor accepted.[7]

A condition of Taylor's appointment was to reside as well as work on the reservation. The move to Quinault country distanced him from professional colleagues. Seattle Legal Services and the university were a three-hour drive away. Communication by letter took several days, and telephone calls were not cost-free. Taylor's status as Quinault staff also distinguished him from most lawyers he knew. As a tribe's legal adviser, he did have cohorts, however. By early 1973, ten or twelve attorneys in the region served Indian governments, at least part time. In Indian country elsewhere, other lawyers funded by governments and foundations were expanding the ranks of advocates for tribes.

The importance of those lawyers to the tribes' twentieth-century resurgence cannot be overstated, so long as an account of their roles and influence acknowledges the tribal clients' reciprocal influence on their attorneys. Mike Taylor's exposure to Indians' unique legal issues, his recognition of their need for power, and his ready commitment to that cause composed a story that numerous contemporary counterparts could tell about themselves, including me.

During the 1970s, American Indians' relations with lawyers changed rapidly in extent, focus, and effect. Across the United States, individual Indians and tribes with little or no means to pay private counsel gained regular access to attorneys for the first time. In a process of mutual education, a new generation of lawyers and tribal clients equipped themselves to argue for Indians' empowerment by invoking historic promises, past injustices, judicial pronouncements, government policies, and legal logic. As a result, the untidy accumulation of treaties, statutes, court opinions, and administrative measures that defined Indians' unique legal status increased in volume and visibility. So-called federal Indian law became the subject not only of lawyers' briefs and many new court decisions but also of law school courses, national conferences, scholarly publications, and news media attention.

To the growing cadre of Indian law practitioners and to tribal leaders, the American legal system seemed an increasingly promising arena in which tribes and their members, armed with the principles of tribal sovereignty and federal responsibility to Indians, could challenge their subordination to non-Indian governments. At the tribal level—on the Quinault Reservation and others—local history, local aims, and local power relations strongly influenced how Indians and their advocates interpreted law, legal issues, and prevailing allocations of power.

NEW LAWYERS FOR TRIBES

Until the 1960s, attorneys with knowledge and experience of use to Indian tribes were as scarce as money to pay for such services.[8] Even for the National Congress of American Indians, legal representation was catch-as-catch-can. In 1954, when NCAI executive director Helen Peterson was preparing testimony for a legislative hearing, she wrote to the Yakima Tribe's chairman, "Since we do not have the funds for our own legal counsel, I must necessarily ask the help of lawyers who are willing to give this service without charge. . . . So far the several lawyers representing the different tribes have been willing to give me help, but we cannot depend on this forever."[9]

To retain general counsel or pay fees and expenses for specific cases, an organization such as the NCAI or Affiliated Tribes of Northwest Indians had to elicit contributions from member tribes. In all but the handful of tribes with natural resources to sell, money for such discretionary outlays could only come from taxes on their members or Indian Claims Commission (ICC) awards. Tax revenue was trifling, if available at all, and ICC awards—many barely reaching five figures—were in trust accounts that required federal approval for expenditures.[10]

Quinaults' arrangements in 1961 show how a small tribe, neither rich nor penniless, tried to meet needs for legal assistance. To pay attorney fees, tribal officials could tap a little tax income and some court judgment funds, but they had to limit what they asked of lawyers.[11] Tribe members told Claude Heyer, an Association on American Indian Affairs representative, that they hired John Cragun "because he was 'cheap and available' and was their claims attorney." A problem with the tribe's choice, in Heyer's opinion, was that Cragun had a conflict of interest. Contrary to the express desire of "a good many" Quinaults, even tribal officers, he was seeking dismissal of the tribe's suit to invalidate the 1958 Business Committee request for state jurisdiction.[12]

NCAI director Peterson's education included two quarters of law school, and she studied Indian legal issues on her own. With occasional help from attorneys, she spoke and wrote capably about law. She knew other politically active Indians who could do the same, but she also knew that Indians needed more than lay advocates and part-time lawyers. During her decade-long tenure at NCAI, Peterson brooded about tribes' unmet need for reliable, affordable legal assistance. To a lawyer in New York she wrote, "American Indians, *unlike any other citizens*, must deal with a body of law that applies to no other citizens. The volume and complexity is incredible. There are some 350 treaties, almost 5,000 Federal statutes, and almost 10,000 regulations which must be taken into account in working in the broad general total field of Indian affairs." Despite Indians' exceptional need for "good legal advice," lawyers who tried to help endured unwarranted criticism from government officials and "people in high places."

Media coverage unfairly implied that Indian claims attorneys were "collecting fortunes from poor Indians." In fact, Peterson explained, they carried cases for years or decades, usually bearing all expenses, received pay only if they won compensation for their clients, and then received just 10 percent of the award.[13]

To make matters worse, Peterson continued, other lawyers were often "deeply involved . . . in representing the interests of those groups that want[ed] Indian land or other resources." Even if a tribe could find one who was not, officials authorized to approve attorney contracts might raise "picayunish" objections. Tribes waited long periods for decisions. The tribe "is fortunate indeed," Peterson declared, "that finds a local attorney who takes a deep and enthusiastic interest in the problems of the tribe which often times include a demand for him to serve as public relations and economic counselor as well as legal counselor." The government should help those lawyers, not discourage them.[14]

The man who succeeded Peterson at the NCAI in 1964 was acutely aware of law's special impacts on Indians. Decades later, Vine Deloria, Jr., told historian Daniel Cobb that he "spent much of his first year immersing himself in Indian law."[15] Around the country, many new lawyers and law students would soon have reasons and opportunities to do the same. During Deloria's four years as NCAI director, while he pondered whether to earn a law degree, more law school graduates were choosing to advocate for Indians. A new federal program paid many of them to advise and represent the nation's poorest Indians. Some were Indians themselves.

Shortly before the NCAI hired Deloria, the Makah Tribe lured two partners from a new Seattle law firm into the Indian law arena. Tribe member Bruce Wilkie, home from several years of college and agitating for Indian rights elsewhere, was the Makah government's new executive director. The tribal council was dissatisfied with their attorney and seeking a replacement. Wilkie thought of Alvin Ziontz, who had handled some matters for the Wilkie family and helped Bruce resolve a consumer complaint. He phoned Ziontz, who re-created the surprising conversation in a 2009 memoir. Wilkie, railing about Washington State's disrespect for Indian treaties and deploring tribal councils that were "afraid to stand up to the white man," said it was time to "kick ass." He had heard of Ziontz's work with the American Civil Liberties Union. Could he nominate Ziontz as the tribe's new general counsel? Ziontz's response as he remembered it: "Of course I was interested."

So, on a rainy November evening in 1963, Al Ziontz found himself in the Makah Reservation town of Neah Bay, admitting to tribal council members that he had never done legal work for a tribe. However, when he assisted the Wilkies, he had "studied the law pertaining to Indians" and "discovered something important—under the law Indian tribes are sovereign." As luck would have it, sovereignty was a subject he had explored thoroughly before and during law school. "If I were representing the Makah Tribe," Ziontz remembered saying, "the principle of tribal sovereignty would be the way I would go about defending your rights." Three days later, the Makahs asked him to be their attorney.[16] Ziontz's partner was Robert Pirtle. In a self-published account of his career, Pirtle identified an early 1964 office visit by "the entire Makah Indian Tribal Council" as the event that pulled the firm into representing tribes—something they soon did exclusively and would then do continuously for almost three decades.[17]

The ink was barely dry on the firm's contract with the Makahs when, in Pirtle's words, "Bruce Wilkie, working with the National Indian Youth Council, of which he was a leading member, conceived a brilliant scheme to launch a counterattack on the relentless State erosion of tribal fishing rights." Movie star Marlon Brando had called the Makah Tribe's office to offer support for Indian treaty rights. Wilkie responded that Brando could draw public attention to the cause by joining Indians who deliberately disobeyed the state's net fishing ban. When Brando assented, people from nine tribes—Makah, Lummi, Puyallup, Sammamish, Swinomish, Quinault, Suquamish, Quileute, and Hoh—converged at his hotel to plan a "fish-in." Also present were the Makahs' new lawyers.[18]

A few years later, the Lummi tribal government turned to Ziontz and Pirtle for general counsel services. In 1971, the firm added Colville Confederated Tribes to their clientele. Eventually, their practice expanded to a nine-lawyer partnership with five associates and client tribes as far away as Montana and Alaska. "We became known and respected in the national community of Indian lawyers and Indian leaders," Ziontz believed, while earning the respect of government officials "for our ability and our integrity." In a foreword to Ziontz's memoir, Charles Wilkinson, a legal scholar and former attorney for tribes, endorsed this claim. Praising Ziontz as "idealistic and public spirited," Wilkinson counted him among "the very first private practitioners to come forward and represent tribes, which had compelling causes but little ability to pay other than minimal attorneys' fees."[19]

Having "come forward" to advise tribes, Ziontz and Pirtle needed to develop Indian law expertise rapidly, but federal Indian law also had developing of its own to do. As of 1964, Ziontz found, it was "such a little-known branch of American law that few American lawyers had heard of it." Pirtle described it as "almost totally inchoate." Although legal historians might quibble with that description, the two partners understandably thought they had entered largely unmapped legal territory. By the time they retired, they could justifiably claim to have taken prominent part in making federal Indian law "an established field, a subject taught in many law schools in America." One mark of their firm's contribution to that progression, Ziontz suggested, was the "exceptional" number of cases they "brought before the U.S. Supreme Court: seven."[20]

When they entered the Indian law field, Ziontz and Pirtle had scattered company—a handful of contemporaries who also assisted tribes with matters besides claims against the United States. At least two were in Washington State.[21] Robert Dellwo, identifying himself as an attorney for the Spokane, Coeur d'Alene, and Kalispel tribes, said in 1975 that he had practiced Indian law for thirty years. Born on the Flathead Reservation in Montana, raised there by a father "active in Indian law," Dellwo felt he had always "lived in an environment of Indian law and Indian problems and Indian needs." In south-central Washington, general practice attorney James Hovis took on a new kind of client in 1958—the Yakima Tribe (known after 1993 as the Yakama Nation). Over three succeeding decades, Hovis made several appearances before the Supreme Court to argue principles of federal Indian law.[22] Of necessity, these lawyers got acquainted and took an interest in each other's work on matters with possible repercussions for multiple tribes. They understood, as Pirtle emphasized, that "any single sovereign tribal governmental power damaged in a lawsuit for one tribe has effect on every other tribe."[23]

Representing Indian tribes proved as interesting as Ziontz expected and gratifying in many respects, but the financial rewards were modest. "Like every Indian reservation in America," Pirtle learned, "the Makah Tribe had a huge backlog of legal work . . . long neglected for want of either competent Indian tribal lawyers or money with which to pay legal fees." Because a BIA-approved contract set a flat annual fee for the firm's services—Pirtle remembered the figure $3,000—the lawyers had to choose between making little headway on the backlog or working for much less per hour than most attorneys charged. According to Ziontz, they did the latter. They adopted a principle of "undivided loyalty to the tribes" and "never took any share of money . . . recovered for . . . tribal clients." Lawyers in the firm accepted "lower incomes than their counterparts in general law practice." Pirtle's comment on this subject reflected the strain on and between the lawyers that eventually contributed to the partnership's break-up. "Throughout our entire legal practice we were on the bottom economic rung of the legal profession. . . . Again and again we found tribes willing to retain fresh young lawyers just out of law school to handle complex Indian legal issues which demanded the very highest degree of proficiency in the field of Indian law because their hourly rate was dirt cheap. The end result was that our hourly rate had to be routinely set at less than half the going rate for lawyers of our skill and experience."[24]

In retrospect if not in 1964, Ziontz saw that his Indian practice "rested on an insecure foundation—the ability of tribes to pay a private law firm." Those that could not generate the necessary funds "found it more practical to replace us with lawyers from the Legal Services program." The program lawyers he knew were "a highly competent and dedicated group," Ziontz conceded, but because their services were free and they were willing to live on reservations, they represented a challenge to his firm's relationships with tribes.[25] Contrary to Ziontz's belief, Seattle Legal Services did not provide on-reservation attorneys to tribes free of charge. However, those attorneys worked on terms that differed significantly from contracts with private firms, and some tribes appreciated the practical benefits of that difference.

In western Washington, alternatives to private counsel took several years to evolve, beginning with services sponsored by the federal Office of Economic Opportunity (OEO). Recognizing legal problems as common causes and effects of poverty, the OEO funded a few Community Action Programs dedicated to legal aid during its first year of operation. In 1965, Congress created a separate OEO division for law programs, and two years later, a Navajo program became the first recipient of OEO funding for legal services on an Indian reservation.[26] By 1971, the number of Indian programs had reached eleven. Additionally, at least four general urban programs, four statewide ones, and two regional ones provided specialized assistance to Indian populations in their service areas.[27]

If a group of tribal representatives and Seattle lawyers had had their way, the states with statewide programs would have included Washington. In 1967, the group requested OEO funding for an entity dubbed Indian Legal Services Incorporated, which would station fifteen attorneys at offices around Washington, near high-poverty Indian populations. Asserting that law affects Indians "as it does no one else," the applicants described an unmet need for free attorneys who understood the tribes' "peculiar" relationship with the US government, the legal status of reservation land, and the "mixture" of federal, state, and local jurisdiction on reservations. No such services were then available. County legal aid bureaus provided only volunteer attorneys who had "little awareness of the Indian or his problems."[28]

Generally, the proposed program would serve "the individual Indian" and not "the tribal unit able to afford a tribal attorney to handle tribal affairs." In the latter category was the Yakima Tribe, whose officers often sat at intertribal conferences with attorneys at their elbows. But the application continued, "There are a large number of small tribes and reservations so poor that even the tribe as a unit cannot afford an attorney. In these cases, our staff attorneys can act as tribal attorneys." Among the letters supporting this request for funds was one from Quinault chairman Jim Jackson, who wrote, "As our people are now more and more concerned with land development, modern planning, and are ever more involved with affairs outside the Reservation, there is increasing need for establishment of legal aid services." Jackson and the others made their pitch in vain. OEO Legal Services sent word that it had no money for another program in Washington; existing local programs would have to address the needs of the state's Indians.[29]

Seattle Legal Services Center's first effort on that front was sending VISTA volunteers Mike Taylor, David Allen, and John Sennhauser to reservations in 1969. Until then, SLSC lawyers had been mostly at city neighborhood offices, where more walk-in clients wanted help with personal problems than with systemic causes or consequences of poverty such as unsafe housing, racial discrimination, and predatory commercial practices. Hoping for maximal per-lawyer impact on poor people's problems, the OEO allowed local programs to represent groups and organizations as well as individuals, but demand for assistance outstripped the programs' capacity to meet it. In response, and in keeping with OEO Community Action's mandate to attack the roots of poverty, Legal Services policy makers authorized proactive advocacy, such as proposals for remedial legislation and administrative practice reforms. Finally, in 1967, declaring "law reform" the chief goal of OEO Legal Services, a new national director required local programs to set explicit priorities for allocating resources.[30]

Managers of the Seattle program embraced this strategic approach to their mission, but formulating a plan to meet Indian needs took time. Assistance with one issue of concern to many Indians—state obstruction of their fishing—was clearly appropriate. Securing fishing opportunities would benefit low-income Indian families. The VISTA lawyers therefore advised Indian fishers on civil law matters arising from the treaty rights dispute, such as state confiscation of their nets. Then in 1970, the US Justice Department, acting on behalf of the Nisqually and Puyallup tribes, filed suit in federal court for affirmation and clarification of their treaty-reserved right to take fish. Several more tribes intervened in the case, titled *United States v. Washington*. Al Ziontz represented the Makah and Lummi Tribes, James Hovis appeared for the Yakimas, and the initial counsel for five other intervenors—tribes poor enough to qualify for federally funded legal services—were the VISTAs Taylor, Sennhauser, and Allen.

When Taylor accepted the position on the Quinault Reservation three years later, his employer would be the tribal government, the source of his salary a small foundation grant. However, the director of Seattle Legal Services and Taylor shared a concern that he would lose some benefits and opportunities afforded by his recent transition from VISTA to SLSC staff attorney: health care insurance, a retirement savings plan, specialized training programs, and access to legal publications. The solution they devised was a unique arrangement with the Quinault Tribe. While Taylor technically remained an SLSC employee, the tribe would contract for his services and take control of his assignments and work conditions. The cost to the tribe—an amount that covered Taylor's modest salary and benefits—was substantially lower than a private law firm would charge for equivalent work. In following years, other tribes adopted this model for employing legal counsel until, as of 1980, nearly a dozen men and women worked as staff attorneys for tribal governments and an intertribal organization in western Washington—all of them linked on the same basis as Taylor to the program in Seattle, eventually renamed Evergreen Legal Services. (In early 1980, I began a four-year stint as "coordinator" of that so-called Native American Project.)

Meanwhile, the context of Indian law practice had changed significantly since Ziontz and Pirtle began representing the Makah Tribe. For one thing, a tribe could now ask a federal court to resolve an issue of US law even if nothing of monetary value was at stake. Before 1966, the US code allowed only tribal suits that sought awards of at least $10,000. Judges cited that requirement in 1964 when they dismissed the Quinault challenge to state jurisdiction on the reservation. An act of Congress two years later gave district courts "original jurisdiction of all civil actions brought by any Indian tribe or band with a governing body duly recognized by the Secretary of the Interior, wherein the matter in controversy arises under the Constitution, laws, or treaties of the United States." It made no mention of monetary value.[31] The Supreme Court eventually agreed with several lower courts that lawmakers intended by the new act to exempt tribes from the $10,000 requirement. With freer access to federal court, tribes had more use for lawyers. A consequent wave of litigation resulted in more judicial opinions about the extent of Indians' rights or other governments' power over Indians, thus enlarging the body of doctrine known as Indian law.[32]

A second piece of federal legislation—the Indian Civil Rights Act (ICRA) of 1968—signaled clearly that tribes' elimination as legal political entities was not imminent; it was no longer even a US government priority. Instead, two provisions of the ICRA indicated that lawmakers expected tribes to continue governing themselves indefinitely. One allowed tribes to reject state jurisdiction over their reservations, the other required tribal governments to observe restrictions on their power much like those specified in the Constitution's Bill of Rights. For tribes, legal advice was thus more essential than ever. Tribal police and judges would need to know American legal doctrine concerning subjects such as due process, unreasonable searches, and cruel punishment. Indeed, all tribal officials—encouraged to sustain their governments but told to govern in ways that non-Indians expected—would have increasing reasons to consult and employ attorneys.[33]

INDIAN ATTORNEYS

Around the time that federal courts opened wider to tribes, some recently minted lawyers in California learned by chance about Indians' unique legal status, saw the need for specialized legal services, and acted with alacrity to meet it. In short order, they helped establish a nonprofit law firm "dedicated to asserting and defending the rights of Indian tribes, organizations and individuals nationwide." That firm, the Native American Rights Fund (NARF), rapidly became a significant force in the emerging movement for clarification and expansion of Indians' rights under US law.[34] NARF also promoted a vital aspect of the movement by employing and taking leadership from lawyers who were Indians themselves.

As he recounted in a 1971 interview, Monroe Price played a crucial role in events that led to NARF's creation. Price came to Los Angeles in 1965 with a Yale law degree. Before joining the faculty at the University of California, he helped a University of Southern California professor prepare a brief arguing that the city of Palm Springs lacked jurisdiction to zone land belonging to Agua Caliente Indians. Meanwhile, the California Rural Legal Assistance program (CRLA), created primarily to serve Mexican Americans, found that its Santa Rosa office had a surprising number of American Indian clients. Recognizing that legal work for Indians required "expertise different from the expertise they were normally developing," CRLA management asked Price and a staff attorney "to concentrate on Indian legal problems." The two men worked up a proposal for OEO-supported services to "the rural California Indian." The OEO responded first by funding an expansion of CRLA's program. Shortly thereafter, it authorized a separate California Indian Legal Services (CILS).[35]

David Getches—three years out of law school and seeking to move from private to public practice—agreed to open a CILS office in Escondido. "From there," he confessed in 2006, "we started doing some cases outside California, which we really weren't supposed to do . . . , because there was a dearth of people who had any knowledge of Indian law. . . . We were only one tiny step ahead of the people we were helping, but there was clearly a demand outside California for this kind of work." Soon the Ford Foundation approached them, Getches recalled, signaling possible interest in funding "a national program" with Monroe Price.[36] In 1970, the foundation tendered $40,000 of seed money. The following year, thanks to a larger Ford grant and contributions from other foundations, the newly constituted Native American Rights Fund separated from CILS and moved to Boulder, Colorado. The OEO then contracted with NARF to function as a backup center for programs serving Indians. Legal aid lawyers across the country could call on NARF for research, strategy advice, and—in select cases—litigation counsel.[37]

The ranks of NARF attorneys grew to twelve by 1972. Among the hires was Charles Wilkinson, a 1966 Stanford Law School graduate who had suffered a self-described "crisis of consciousness" while working "for corporations that were just going to get a lot of money." A hoped-for move to the Sierra Club was not an option; they were not hiring, but a staffer there advised Wilkinson to inquire at a new public interest "Indian firm" reportedly doing some "environmental work." In 1983 Wilkinson said, "As soon as I met David Getches and John Echohawk at the nascent Native American Rights Fund, I knew there was something special going on." During his five subsequent years as a NARF attorney, Wilkinson found it "tremendously exciting" to be litigating and "winning so many cases"—"big cases"—for legal services programs. Sometimes, though, the contests seemed almost unfair because lawyers in the rural areas where Indians lived were seldom prepared to battle well-funded, sophisticated opposing counsel.[38]

In 1972, David Getches's second year as NARF director, he published reflections on the "difficult beginnings for Indian Legal Services." Indians' access to lawyers had improved since 1966, when legal representation was "virtually unavailable," he wrote, but the shortage of free services for Indians remained "greater than for most groups of poor people." The scarcity was due in part to the difficulty of luring qualified attorneys to "remote" reservations. Even so, the Navajo program had recruited impressive graduates of premier law schools who were staying longer than new hires in many urban legal aid programs. Getches attributed that longevity to the attorneys' "intense involvement in the communities," where the need was enormous. Community involvement was desirable, if not necessary for lawyers on reservations, Getches believed, but it gave rise to new problems. By drawing the lawyers into tribal politics, it could present them with decisions that non-Indian newcomers were ill equipped to make—for example, whether to pursue cases for individual tribe members when the result might be "infringement of the tribe's governmental prerogatives."[39]

In view of such tricky issues and the distinctiveness of Indian communities, Getches considered it "vital" that Indian legal services programs employ lawyers who were Indians themselves. "Most Indians," he observed, "are well-acquainted with the strange relationship between Indians and the federal government." Having experienced "the intrusion of law into nearly every aspect of their lives gives them a feel for Indian legal problems which no one but an Indian could have." Charles Wilkinson was of the same opinion. Yet seven of eight original CILS and NARF attorneys were non-Indians. All had attended prestigious schools that prepared them for careers among the non-Indian elite, not impoverished Indians.[40] Getches estimated in 1972 that fewer than three dozen attorneys in the United States were Indians. However, processes then under way would soon boost that number significantly.

The Native American Rights Fund would not have materialized without Indian participation in its establishment.[41] Years later, executive director John Echohawk identified NARF's organizers as "a number of Indian law students and tribal leaders." Their inspiration, he said, was the "new generation of lawyers": non-Indians who had gone to reservations during the War on Poverty and "done wonders . . . on behalf of enforcing Indian law."[42] Some Indians were eager to follow that example. By 1972, six of America's few practicing Indian attorneys were in legal services programs, four of those at NARF. Two years later, NARF's board of directors deemed it time for Indian leadership in all key roles. They asked Getches to cede his position as director to Echohawk. In retrospect, Wilkinson saw that as an "excellent move."[43]

John Echohawk had been with NARF since graduating from law school in 1970. His story exemplifies a third factor that fueled and reflected the surge in federal Indian law activity after 1964: a sharp increase in the number of Indians who earned law degrees and put that training to use in the cause of Indian empowerment. A Pawnee, Echohawk grew up in New Mexico where his father, a land surveyor, worked on reservations. Taking to heart his parents' admonition to get more education than they did, he gratefully accepted an undergraduate scholarship to the University of New Mexico (UNM). Going on to law school there was an attractive possibility because, in his words, he "happened to be in the right place at the right time." UNM faculty had "put together one of the first courses in

When John Echohawk and David Getches helped to establish the Native American Rights Fund in 1971, their mission was to meet Indians' acute need for legal representation on issues of federal Indian law, many of which affected Indians across the United States. Photograph courtesy of Native American Rights Fund.

Indian law" just as the federal government began offering Indians money for graduate school.[44]

Dean Tom Christopher and visiting professor Fred Hart made a case for federal money to train Indian lawyers by documenting the dearth of Indian attorneys in the United States. They calculated that nearly one thousand more Indians needed law degrees before the Indian population would have the same percentage of attorneys as the non-Indian population. The OEO responded by financing a pilot law school preparation program at UNM in 1967 and thereafter supporting an annual pre-law summer institute for twenty or thirty Indian college students. Those who did well at the institute could enroll, with financial aid, at one of several law schools where faculty with appropriate expertise would mentor them. In 1971, Monroe Price, a co-creator of the summer program, knew of former participants studying law at Stanford, Yale, Arizona State, three University of California campuses, and the universities of Minnesota, Washington, Colorado, Oregon, Utah, Montana, and Arizona.[45]

John Echohawk found the course on Indian law "a real eye-opener." It exposed him and other Native American students to the legal and political history of their tribes. "We learned that sovereign nations negotiated treaties," he wrote later, "which means that the law says an Indian tribe is a sovereign nation. My fellow law students and I wondered about the gap between all those things in the law books and the reality back on the reservations where we grew up."[46]

Fresh from a bracing law school experience, Echohawk arrived at California Indian Legal Services just as Ford Foundation money for the Native American Rights Fund came through. He made the move to Boulder with the new organization, which soon hired other alumni of the New Mexico summer institute. One was Tom Fredericks, a former director of the Standing Rock Sioux Community Action Program. Fredericks followed Vine Deloria's example when he enrolled at University of Colorado Law School. As of 1986, Philip S. (Sam) Deloria, who took charge of the New Mexico scholarship program in its fifth year, counted 150 alumni with law degrees. Nearly all of them, including Echohawk and Fredericks, were "working in Indian affairs."[47]

The reminiscences of Alan Parker and Rodney Lewis illustrate the far-ranging impact of this early effort to produce Indian lawyers, particularly its contribution to a growing network of tribal sovereignty advocates. Both men attended the 1969 pre-law summer institute. To Parker, a Chippewa-Cree from Rocky Boy's Reservation in Montana, that experience was important for the friendships it engendered. At UNM he met and hit it off with Richard (Dick) Trudell, a Santee Sioux. Trudell went on to Catholic University Law School and a long career as director of the American Indian Lawyer Training Program, which he founded with Parker's help.[48] Parker declined an offer of admission to Harvard Law School in favor of UCLA so that he could study Indian law under Price and Reid Chambers, another professor with ties to California Indian Legal Services. Price found Parker a summer internship with Alaska Legal Services just as historic Native claims settlement negotiations there were bearing fruit. A second highlight of Parker's law school years was a conference where he heard NCAI president Wendell Chino deliver a powerful address replete with references to Indians' sovereignty. Immediately after graduating in 1972, Parker worked in the Interior Department solicitor's national office, primarily doing research for a task force created by the 1968 Indian Civil Rights Act to produce a revised version of Felix Cohen's *Handbook of Federal Indian Law*.[49]

Parker remembered two other Indians in his entering law school class. Muckleshoot Tribe member Leo LaClair left UCLA after a year to finish his studies at the University of Washington. Rodney Lewis, a Pima from the Gila River Tribal Community in Arizona, graduated with Parker. Lewis traced his interest in law to the example and encouragement of his tribe's general counsel, Simpson Cox—a "good guy" who was "always around" the reservation during Rod's youth. Information from fellow participants in the New Mexico institute inspired Lewis to head for Los Angeles next. At UCLA, they told him, law students could work at nearby California Indian Legal Services and hear staff lawyers describe ongoing cases. Once Lewis had his law degree, he returned to Gila River, initially for a job in the new legal services program there. He subsequently performed various functions in the community, including tribal prosecutor, before assuming the tribal counsel position formerly held by Cox—a position Lewis would keep for thirty-three years.[50]

During his stint with Indian legal services, Lewis attended periodic regional and national meetings where he and lawyers from other such programs discussed issues arising in their work. Because talks with reservation-based attorneys were especially useful, Lewis valued his acquaintance with Mike Taylor. Despite stark differences between Southwest and Northwest reservations, tribes in the two regions faced some similar issues; so Taylor likewise appreciated chances to compare notes and brainstorm with Lewis. "Rod Lewis and I are the same age," he said in 2012, "and we had some of the same notions about . . . strategy. . . . We spent a good deal of time either meeting at various places or talking on the phone about what to do about all kinds of stuff."[51]

The widely dispersed lawyers who pondered what to do for Indian clients devised additional ways to pool ideas and give each other support. Their desire for information sharing and collaboration prompted the creation of new organizations and new committees in existing professional organizations. The American Bar Association established a committee on Indian legal problems in 1969. Over the following four years, a national Indian law student association, American Indian Lawyers Association, and the short-lived Puget Sound Indian Law Society also organized.[52] Some attorneys found it useful to attend the meetings of intertribal political organizations. Beginning in 1969, when it "dawned on" Robert Pirtle and his partners "that progress in the fight for tribal sovereignty must be a national, concerted effort," Pirtle rarely missed an annual NCAI conference. "Little by little," it seemed to him, "tribal lawyers from around the country began to play a very important role" there.[53]

Simultaneously, assorted individuals and institutions acted to meet a perceived need for publications and educational programs on Indian law. Monroe Price was the first to develop instructional materials on "Indian legal problems"—the basis for an eventual law school textbook. Faculty at additional universities followed Price's and Ralph Johnson's example by offering courses on the subject. The American Indian Law Center at the University of New Mexico expanded its programs to include training for tribal court personnel and services in support of tribal governance. NARF established a National Indian Law Library in 1972. The next year, the University of Oklahoma initiated the *American Indian Law Review*, aiming both to fill a "void" in scholarly writing about Indian law and "to assist in the alleviation of the numerous problems that confront American Indians because of their unique relationship with the federal and state governments and their different social and cultural backgrounds." In 1974, at the American Indian Lawyer Training Program in California, Dick Trudell oversaw the launch and distribution of the *Indian Law Reporter*, a compilation of administrative decisions and federal, state, and tribal court rulings on questions of law pertaining to Indians.[54]

Founders of the Institute for the Development of Indian Law (IDIL) saw a need not only to educate affected people about existing law but also to imagine the law as it could be and then work to make such visions reality. Vine Deloria, a law school graduate by 1971, explained the nascent organization's purpose in a letter inviting Sherwin Broadhead to serve on a "legal advisory council." IDIL would "act as a center in which innovations in Indian law can be developed which will be of benefit to Indian people everywhere." Believing that Indians are "the 'losers' when a monocultural legal standard is applied to a bicultural situation," IDIL organizers aimed to articulate "a philosophy of Indian law" and alternatives to "existing theories and policies."[55]

RADICAL INFLUENCES

In an understated way, John Echohawk passed on a lesson from law school that was hard to overstate: United States Indian policy, he observed in 2010, has been shaped "by what is happening in the larger society." Although Echohawk did not explicitly invoke that lesson when accounting for his personal "Indian policy," he did mention his awareness of important "happenings" outside Indian country. One "brilliant event" that strongly influenced him and his associates was the civil rights movement—the campaign to secure for black Americans the same legal and political rights that white Americans expected. "For us," Echohawk explained, the notable aspect of "that movement concerned law and advocacy for poor people who didn't have lawyers." The Legal Defense Fund of the National Association for the Advancement of Colored People inspired Indians to dream of their own defense fund, but with a crucial difference: "We weren't advocating equal justice and equal treatment. We were after enforcement of the treaties and our rights as sovereign Indian nations."[56]

Vine Deloria, too, considered black Americans' example as he pondered how to frame Indian demands for greater freedom. It had to be something other than "this big push for integration that civil rights was doing," lest Indians seem to condone the termination of the United States' special obligations to tribes.[57] Nonetheless, civil rights movement victories gave many an activist Indian reason to believe that lawyers could help them challenge long-standing, unjust limits on Indians' opportunities and power.[58]

For some Indians, it was the tactics of insurgent African Americans that merited emulation, particularly the deliberate lawbreaking that dramatized the injustice of Jim Crow regimes.[59] By organizing mass defiance of state laws that violated constitutional mandates or basic human rights, black people won media attention, sympathizers, federal government help, and legal change. Why not Indians? Bruce Wilkie and members of the National Indian Youth Council were game to try.[60] In the Pacific Northwest, state laws and regulations were preventing Indians from freely exercising fishing rights guaranteed by federal law. If sit-in protests by young blacks could delegitimize whites' humiliating domination of public spaces, perhaps Indian fish-ins could discredit non-Indians' domination of state waters.[61]

Fish-in participants were not the first Indians to stage such extralegal protests, but their timing, broad exposure, and support from celebrities gave their example staying power.[62] Thus, even as some Indians increasingly pinned their hopes for justice on appeals to judges, lawmakers, and principles of federal Indian law, a less law-abiding, more confrontational Indian resistance movement also gained momentum. The same year that California Indian Legal Services lawyers and an Indian advisory group laid plans for the Native American Rights Fund, several dozen Indian city dwellers and college students launched a nineteen-month illegal occupation of the former Alcatraz prison in San Francisco Bay. The occupiers issued a proclamation reclaiming the island for Indians of all tribes. In 1972, the year that John Echohawk became director of NARF, several hundred Indians descended on Washington, DC, calling for renewed US treaty relations with tribes. Some in that crowd reacted to federal officials' apparent brush-off by commandeering and vandalizing the Bureau of Indian Affairs building. In early 1973, the year the *Indian Law Review* made its debut, Oglala Sioux and armed activists of the American Indian Movement (AIM) took over the hamlet of Wounded Knee on the Pine Ridge Reservation, disputing the legitimacy of the tribal government and demanding redress for a century or more of Indian grievances against the United States.

As news media gave the Alcatraz, BIA, and Wounded Knee takeovers abundant coverage, opinion polls documented widespread sympathy for the Indians' complaints of historical betrayal, deprivation, and powerlessness.[63] In part because of that plentiful coverage, historians have paid more attention to brash Indian activists and their protests in the 1970s than to tribal officials and lawyers who simultaneously tried to reclaim Indian land and government powers more conventionally. Studies of both phenomena should acknowledge not only their concurrence but also their influence on each other. Organizers of the protest demonstrations and occupations adopted language drawn from law and treaties, while many of the lawyers representing tribes conceived of their work as supporting a national movement for Indian self-determination or sovereignty. The extralegal actions made that movement visible to the lawyers along with other Americans, and the movement popularized legal terms such as "Indian sovereignty" and "treaty rights."

Indian demonstrations that flouted laws and Indian tribes' appeals to law proceeded independently for the most part, but in hard-to-pinpoint relationship to each other. Many Alcatraz and Wounded Knee occupiers, members of AIM, and other Indian rights activists were living outside reservation communities, some of them isolated or alienated from political affairs in their tribes, yet they demanded respect for a capacious conception of Indian sovereignty. They knowingly violated state and federal law, and some openly disputed US authority over tribes, yet they sought lawyers' help.[64] Their provocative tactics, militant rhetoric, and often disdainful characterization of existing tribal governments angered or alarmed many older and conservative tribal officials.[65] Even so, more than a few individuals moved between the two camps of Indian rights advocates. Some tribal officials of the 1970s had participated in the Alcatraz occupation, and some Indian activists brought the call for militant rebellion and uncompromising Red Power to NCAI conventions.[66] In public statements, some tribe leaders took exception to tactics such as occupations or rowdy demonstrations, but they endorsed the demonstrators' stated aims. From the late 1960s to the mid-1970s, bold assertions of Indian sovereignty became increasingly common in NCAI resolutions and tribal attorneys' briefs as well as manifestos of the American Indian Movement.[67]

In western Washington, the interplay of legal and extralegal Indian strategies for empowerment had several facets, including disagreements about the wisdom of relying on law and lawyers. A young Assiniboine man stirred such debate when he came to mistrust tribal governments and their attorneys. Hank Adams grew up in his mother's Quinault community. A standout high school student and athlete, he dropped out of the University of Washington to agitate full time for Indian rights.[68] Letters he sent to Washington's governor in 1963—the year he became special projects director for the National Indian Youth Council—displayed Adams's self-taught command of law and talent for writing legal arguments. He was angry then about state efforts, under color of law, to limit the powers of a recognized tribal government. One letter declared, "The state's assumption of civil and criminal jurisdiction on the Quinault Indian Reservation is the most despicable case of discrimination in recent Washington history. . . . The local self-government becomes a farce when [Quinaults] lose the right to enforce their own ordinances, as they can do under federal Indian law, or tribal law." Compromising tribal government "or internal sovereignty" was bad enough; worse was requiring Quinaults to expend resources on prolonged court proceedings when "they should, and could, be spending this energy, time, and money in the development of the natural and human resources, and to seek the goals and aspirations of their peoples."[69]

As a key organizer of the 1964 demonstration protesting state disregard for treaty fishing rights, Adams worked with tribal officials, but his relations with them soured not long afterward. During a short tenure as Community Action director on the Quileute Reservation, he concluded that such federally funded programs did not empower tribes; instead they "strengthened the established institutions that Indian people did not recognize as their own." Believing that Indians could not depend on compromised tribal officials to represent their true interests, Adams decided to fight for treaty rights outside tribal structures, as leader of a new organization. That Survival of American Indians Association (SAIA) would clash with Indian governments for which Adams had previously demanded state and federal respect.[70]

For their part, tribal officials took issue with Adams's confrontational tactics as well as his disdain for their governments. Leaders of several tribes, including Quinaults, publicly condemned SAIA support for the 1968 black-led Poor People's demonstration in Washington, DC. Historian Daniel Cobb learned later that NCAI leaders and tribal councils were especially incensed by Adams's provocative role in a march on the Supreme

Court during that weeks-long assembly in the capital. He confronted police, demanding "that a delegation be allowed to enter the building and present Indian grievances directly to the justices."[71]

Adams's distrust of the federal government, tribal officials, and lawyers caused him to question the tribes' participation in *U.S. v. Washington*, the suit to clarify their treaty fishing rights. He had heard some Indians express fear that the tribes did not know what their attorneys were doing. As the trial date neared, he concluded, "That has indeed proven to be the case." On the margins of a transcribed speech in which Al Ziontz assured tribal representatives that a favorable judgment was likely, Adams wrote with evident disgust that Ziontz seemed to expect settlement negotiations resulting in further restrictions of Indian fishing. "One of the difficult questions," he mused, "is whether the Indian can ever be truly represented by a non-Indian." Adams signaled his answer: Ziontz might share basic values with Indians, but neither he nor the other attorneys in the case had "a basic means of survival at stake," as Indians did.[72]

Political scientist Linda Medcalf also wondered whether lawyers for Indians shared and served their clients' interests. Therefore, in 1974, she interviewed sixteen individuals in the Seattle area who seemed to exemplify the "new breed" of attorneys working on Native Americans' behalf. Her research revealed lawyers who believed they were allied with Indians in historic public discourse about tribal sovereignty—discourse not limited to lawyers, judges, and tribal officials or even to Americans. All of Medcalf's unnamed subjects spoke of having a mission to reverse the loss of power that had left Indians poverty-stricken, culturally adrift, and demoralized. Several depicted themselves as ardent recruits for a far-reaching, multifaceted Indian empowerment campaign. One told Medcalf, "The movement for tribal sovereignty is the biggest movement right now." Another viewed Indians as "part of a world wide [*sic*] system of minority assertiveness" and egalitarian movements.[73]

LOCAL ISSUES

For the lawyers who met with Linda Medcalf, the idea of contributing to a broad tribal sovereignty movement was inspiring but largely an abstraction. What their clients wanted from them, day to day, was help attaining specific, often limited objectives. A tribe's need for lawyers arose from place-based history, conflicts, and aspirations. Attorneys' role was finding legal remedies for community problems, legal means to prevent infringement of community interests, and legal tools for community improvements. Even at NARF, where the ideal case could result in benefits for Indians beyond a particular client, the initial issue was usually a localized grievance. That was true in several early NARF cases that Charles Wilkinson cited as broadly significant—one for Pyramid Lake Paiutes who needed an adequate reservation water supply, another for Menominees seeking to reverse their reservation's termination, and one for tribes in Maine hoping to void eighteenth-century state purchases of their lands.[74]

A specific regional grievance also led to the litigation that Wilkinson deemed the most important of NARF's first decade. *United States v. Washington* was a suit to determine the contemporary effect of one clause found in each of several US treaties with Northwest tribes. NARF joined local legal services lawyers in representing five of the plaintiff tribes, who contended that Washington State's regulation of their off-reservation fishing violated the treaties. The provision at issue promised simply that "the right of taking fish at [their] usual and accustomed grounds and stations" would be "secured to said Indians in common with all citizens of [Washington] Territory." Yet the lawyers rightly expected that a victory for Washington tribes would have precedential value for other tribes in other places. Four years after the Supreme Court upheld the trial court judgment for the tribes, Wilkinson said, "It stands for fishing rights and hunting rights all along the country."[75]

Counsel in *U.S. v. Washington* inherited a conflict that other lawyers, over many decades, had asked courts to resolve, yet essential questions about the meaning of the treaty promise remained unanswered. As the state's discriminatory regulation fell ever harder on Indian fishers in the 1960s, settling those questions in their favor became an urgent concern for tribes. At the same time, the tribes had other important problems to tackle, most of which had localized causes and effects. When did tribe leaders seek lawyers' help with those problems and to what end? With limited time and resources, how did lawyers determine what they could most usefully do for their client tribes? These were among the questions Linda Medcalf posed. The answers she got suggested that lawyers and Indian clients in western Washington were moving together, in a process of mutual education, toward a strategy that prioritized tribal government development.

Medcalf left little doubt that private attorneys participated in her study, probably including members of the Ziontz Pirtle firm. Of her other subjects, one was "publicly funded," another was "tribally employed," and at least three had "come through" legal services. If any were Indians, Medcalf withheld that information. All the interviewees said, one way or another, that advising Indians required special sensitivity. To determine "the needs of the people," more than usual "involvement" with the clients was necessary. One person, noting the successes of certain locally prominent Indian law specialists, said, "They think like Indians." Several interviewees declared their intention of avoiding faults ascribed to an earlier generation of lawyers, especially acting for Indian clients without telling them all their options. Based on what she heard, Medcalf concluded, "The newer attorney respects the Native American as a person and recognizes the tribe as a government."[76]

To Medcalf, the attorneys seemed certain that they had discerned their clients' needs and defined their own roles correctly. First, they should be educators, acquainting the Indians with their rights and likelihood of success in legal matters. "Secondly, since 'self determination is the road to salvation' [*sic*] for Native American groups," they must help "strengthen the tribal community." One person said tribal council members were more confident when legal services attorneys attended their meetings and added that just "the fact of legal representation contributes to a feeling of power." Other interviewees maintained that strength grows with action, "but before tribes act, they must want to do so. They must become ready and willing to take control of their own destiny. In the lawyers' words, Native Americans' political consciousness must be raised." Tribal officials who felt ready and willing to act could then set goals, but they would need lawyers' advice about implementation.

Another of the lawyers suggested that "consciousness raising" was a two-way process. Since Indians' legal representation was improving with their intensifying insistence on their rights, "it could be . . . a kind of reciprocal thing."[77] That sensible supposition pointed toward questions Medcalf did not fully explore. Did the parties to that consciousness-raising process have equal influence on its purposes, topics for discussion, and vocabulary? Was that "reciprocal thing" at work as lawyers and Indians increasingly used the word "sovereignty" to designate what tribes wanted and believed to be their right? Medcalf's analysis implied as much, perhaps unintentionally. To the lawyers, she wrote, the concept of tribal sovereignty "appears . . . to be made to order as a tool or weapon for breaking Indians' cycle of powerlessness. Though the concept is 'fundamentally of Western origin,' the tribes have been dealt with in such terms by Anglo society for many years." It is unclear whether Medcalf thought that lawyers prompted Indians to claim sovereignty or—hearing Indians speak of their sovereignty—agreed that it was an appropriate term for the tribes' historical self-governance.

If Medcalf had interviewed Mike Taylor or Daniel Raas, they could have shed additional light on the give-and-take between tribe leaders and lawyers. For example, when Taylor joined the Quinault Tribe's staff, the draft of a possible criminal code was circulating there, likely furnished by the firm in Washington, DC. It was "one of the things they gave me to work on," Taylor recalled in 2012, "and so I did some writing on it," trying to make it reflect "this notion of tribes actually becoming governments of their territory." Not that anyone in the tribe had articulated the notion for him in precisely those words. He gleaned that objective from "the whole atmosphere" at Quinault. The Indians were "felling trees across a logging road, closing the beaches," requiring Quinault fishers to sell their catch to the tribe's "fish house," and taking other actions consistent with intent to govern the reservation comprehensively.[78] Dan Raas saw the same determination. A 1972 law school graduate who became the tribe's second staff attorney after a year at Seattle Legal Services, Raas understood that Quinaults were asserting a political status for which "sovereign" was an appropriate word. "That sovereignty language was there when I arrived at Quinault," Raas recalled in 2012, although "it was not as refined in terms of what lawyers might take it or in terms of what it really meant."[79]

"That sovereignty language" had reached Quinault ears and eyes in multiple ways over many decades. When and how it moved into common Quinault usage is a matter for speculation. Indians in national leadership employed it in rhetoric with increasing frequency during the 1960s. An NCAI bulletin in 1968 exhorted, "The fundamental right of sovereignty which Indian tribes have . . . must be protected at all costs in the days to come."[80] Neither tribal officials nor their lawyers were sure then how extensive that "fundamental right" could be in practice. Yet at Quinault, even before lawyers were on staff, "sovereignty" had become a license as well as a name for the tribe's assertion of comprehensive, reservation-wide governing power. From at least the early 1960s, some Quinaults publicly expressed belief in their right to govern their entire reserved territory, and before the decade ended, they took action reflecting that belief. As Mike Taylor testified to a federal Indian policy task force in 1976, Quinaults had known "for a long time" that principles of Indian law assured them of all "normal kinds of governmental authority," and by the time they hired him, they had been "asserting their authority right along."[81] In that respect, however, Quinaults differed from Indians he had met on other reservations.

Quinault officials also knew from experience that assertions of authority rang hollow without effective enforcement. After the tribe enacted ordinances in 1963 and 1967 to regulate land use on non-Indian and Indian property alike, some non-Indians made clear their intent to defy the tribe's laws. Quinault leaders saw a need for bold, perhaps unconventional reactions. They pulled Mike Taylor into discussions about their options, as he told a *Los Angeles Times* reporter in 1986: "We sat in dark little offices on the beach. . . . McMinds would walk around asking, 'What's our strategy? What's our strategy?' Gradually, we began thinking about how we could get people to fight us or how we could attack them, so we could go to court and establish tribal authority over life on the reservation. We were making a conscious effort to develop specific issues."[82]

By Joe DeLaCruz's account in 1973, Taylor was a latecomer to such strategizing, which had produced the first provocative move in 1969, when Jim Jackson announced to major news media that he had ordered the Indian police to eject nonmembers of the tribe from beaches along the reservation coastline.[83] *Nugguam* reported that the closure decision was by voice vote of the general council, citing the Quinault treaty with the United States as recognition that the tribe was a self-governing entity. More specifically, the treaty provided, "No white man shall be permitted to reside [in the reserved area] without permission of the tribe and of the superintendent of Indian affairs or Indian agent." Also, according to *Nugguam*, the US attorney general had ruled that "the legal right to purchase land within an Indian nation gives to the purchasers no right of exemption from the laws of such nation. These nations are fully authorized to absolutely exclude outsiders or to permit their residence on business upon such terms as they may choose to impose."[84]

DeLaCruz told an interviewer the beach closure was his idea, the first step of a multistep plan to regain Quinault dominion over the lands reserved by the treaty of 1855. After accepting appointment as business manager in 1969, he said, "I laid out a strategy to close up the reservation—first the beaches, then logging, then the lake. And the highway." Within a year, DeLaCruz and the tribe were doing what he recommended. They arrested four non-Indians for illegal fishing, "killed" the projected state highway from Taholah to Queets by insisting that it be a limited access route, and barricaded reservation roads to logging trucks until two companies agreed to raise timber prices and adjust practices that damaged fisheries.[85]

Quinaults employed those rough-and-ready tactics in service to a sophisticated vision of tribal economic progress. When regional Indian Community Action staff visited in November 1969, DeLaCruz first mentioned the publicized reason for the beach closure: non-Indian conduct that fouled the shoreline and "stripped" it of its "natural beauty." Then he said: "The more meaningful reasons for closing the beach were to increase the clam production for commercial use and lower the property value of beach frontage property. . . . Local speculators are purchasing the individual allotments and sub-dividing them for beach cabins. If people know they will not have access to the beach it should lower the sales, lower the value of the land and perhaps the council then can purchase some of this land as a tribal investment."[86]

DeLaCruz, who had left a federal agency job to take the business manager position on his home reservation, approached relations with the press strategically too. In September 1971, when the *Seattle Times* printed a long article under the headline "Quinault Indians Now Run Reservation with Firm Hand," it was DeLaCruz whom the reporter quoted most, giving him the last word on behalf of the tribal government. "We have 1,412 Indians living on the reservation," DeLaCruz said. "If we don't protect what we have, their own and their children's futures are at stake."[87]

When Jim Jackson suffered a heart attack that year, DeLaCruz moved into leadership not only as the tribe's top administrator but also as president of the general council, an office he would hold for twenty-two years.[88] A 1971 tribal planning report described the community's circumstances and aspirations at that time. Because of the reservation's "isolated location" and a dearth of jobs in the surrounding area, economic development was a top priority. The goal was "adequate Quinault employment." The means would be a program of public works primarily promoting productive management of resources such as fish and logging by-products. The tribal government was "continually searching for possible sources of financial support with the realization that once an adequate economic base is established, the Tribe can become independent."[89]

By the time Mike Taylor came on board in early 1973, DeLaCruz presided over a tribal staff that included the Community Action Program director and assistant director, a nurse, education counselor, Neighborhood Youth Corps supervisor, forester, Tribal Enterprises director, and housing program manager. Additional Quinault government initiatives were the responsibility of the Resources Development Project (RDP) funded by the federal Economic Development Administration. RDP director Guy McMinds oversaw biologists and technicians who managed

Guy McMinds's determination to include a staff lawyer in the Quinault Natural Resources Development Project, which he headed from 1970 to 1984, led to the Quinault Nation's employment of reservation-based attorneys at modest salaries—a means of obtaining legal services that other Northwest tribes soon adopted. Photograph by Larry Workman, Quinault Indian Nation.

the tribe's salmon hatchery and pen rearing operation while also studying ways to improve wild fish runs.[90]

McMinds had impressive human resources at his disposal because he had realized his plan to exploit his connections with University of Washington fisheries faculty. By 1971, an employee of the university's Center for Quantitative Science in Forestry, Fisheries and Wildlife was coordinating a team of faculty advisers who offered their expertise in support of the Quinault "dream of self-determination." Their role, they knew, was "not to decide what is best for the Quinaults, but to help Quinaults define the alternatives available to them." Team members received an anonymous writer's account of Quinault history that summarized the tribe's aspirations.

> Progressive tribal leadership has created a tribal goal of reestablishing the tribe as the authority over the reservation. The Quinault see their goal of self-determination depending upon a collective effort toward the acquisition of a tribal land base and an integrated natural resources management plan. Support for tribal management has increased as the Indians have witnessed the dissipation of their lands to real estate developers and outside interests, and the destruction of fish runs and forests by irresponsible logging practices. The concept of tribal ownership and control of the reservation is not a retrogression into the past, but a means to insure use of reservation resources to the benefit of the tribe, to return to the land, to return to the tribe, to gain an identity, to find a meaningful life, to provide a more hopeful future.[91]

When McMinds and DeLaCruz added Taylor to the tribal staff, attorney services were already a significant aspect of Quinault self-government, albeit not in-house. Professor Johnson was the RDP's designated legal adviser. For representation in court and other legal help, the tribe still depended on private attorneys, particularly the Indian claims firm of Wilkinson Cragun and Barker. In 1971, the firm had filed a set of four lawsuits seeking accountability for United States mismanagement of timber resources on the reservation.[92] According to Jim Jackson's obituary, he and DeLaCruz rallied tribe members to support the suits, and "to pay the lawyers, 620 individuals signed a contract to have money withheld from their timber receipts."[93] A 1971 decision to blockade logging roads embroiled Quinaults in other litigation, necessitating the employment of a Seattle attorney.[94] By then the tribe, with Charles Hobbs as counsel, was also a plaintiff-intervenor in *U.S. v. Washington*, seeking affirmation of Quinaults' treaty right to fish off the reservation without state interference.

Taylor found that the tribe had work for more than one staff attorney, even without litigation, so he moved quickly to bring Dan Raas on board. As Raas remembered it, there were tax questions to answer, codes to draft and revise, contracts to negotiate with logging companies, and logging contracts the tribe wanted to scuttle. One big question, Raas said, was whether Quinaults who caught salmon in the river or the lake were subject to state tax on sales to campers, tourists, and Lake Quinault Lodge. By finding legal precedent for claiming that the lake was within the reservation to the high-water mark, Raas could help Indian fishers maximize their income. The financial benefits to tribe members were even greater when he "negotiated an agreement with Aloha Timber Company to give all of their salvage contracts through the Quinault Natural Resources." Raas estimated the value of the next year's contracts with Indians at half a million dollars—money that otherwise would have continued going to "non-Indian shake rats, as they were called, who were by and large sketchy characters. . . . Then Rayonier [the other logging company] just fell into place because they said, 'Well, if it works for Aloha, it works for us.'"[95]

"I got all the internal issues," Raas explained—"timber stuff . . . , land use, and taxation"—while Taylor was "busy with the fishing case and . . . state and national issues." Taylor assumed responsibility for the fishing case only after a memorable turn of events. "When I got to Quinault in '73," Taylor said, "Quinault was withdrawing from *U.S. v. Washington* . . . , and the reason I was given was that Charlie Hobbs had told the tribe that this was a weak case." Then Taylor received a state official's written testimony for the case, which "was of course extremely derogatory with regard to Indian fishing and net fishing on the rivers. . . . And a long section of that direct testimony just disrespected Quinault in the most pejorative terms." Taylor showed the transcript to McMinds, who "exploded" out of his office, demanding to know what Quinaults could do about such a slur. Taylor told him, "We can't do anything about it. You're withdrawing from the case." Unwilling to accept that answer, McMinds took the issue to a general council meeting. Prompted in part by Taylor's opinion that the tribes' case was strong, the council reversed the decision to withdraw and appointed Taylor to represent them in *U.S. v. Washington*.[96]

Taylor's status as a modestly salaried employee removed the prospect of steep attorney fees as a factor in that decision. In later conversation with Taylor and Raas, Charles Hobbs alluded to that advantage of in-house counsel. When recommending legal action, his private firm necessarily had to consider whether it would require more lawyers' time than the tribe could afford. Raas had seen another undesirable effect of that need to ration the private lawyers' time on Quinault business. The proposed zoning ordinance that Hobbs's firm provided was one "they'd done for somebody else and sold to Quinault. . . . It was not based on research."[97]

When DeLaCruz asked the two staff lawyers to review the draft ordinances that Hobbs supplied, one on zoning and one on criminal law, he posed a question that lay at the heart of Quinaults' quest to govern their reserved territory: could the tribe successfully assert jurisdiction over non-Indians? It was a question Quinaults had asked well before Taylor and Raas arrived. In 1972, they had received a cautiously positive answer from one lawyer. Five months later, with Mike Taylor's help, they were ready to act accordingly—to authorize tribal court prosecutions of non-Indians for criminal violations of Quinault law. Shortly after that, the Suquamish Tribe would follow suit, contributing to an Indian country trend that built rapidly in the next few years.

6. Colonial Controls in Suquamish Territory

The headline declared, "They greeted whites: and lost Their Way of Life," but the article told a less tragic story about Indians of the Suquamish Tribe. Although *Seattle Times* reporter Bruce Johansen wrote that the Suquamish in 1976 could do little "to prevent urbanization of the reservation," he focused much of his article on eighty-three-year-old tribe member Martha George, who was "[sitting] on about 200 acres of land," refusing to sell it to developers while "bedroom communities" sprouted around her. Johansen described George as one of many Suquamish who still shared "much with the existence their ancestors led centuries before white men and women saw Puget Sound."[1]

Without Johansen's knowledge, the Suquamish Tribe was taking bold steps to counter urbanization's threat to Indian life on the reservation. In 1972, at the urging of George's husband, Ben, and with federal government approval, the tribal council adopted a zoning ordinance prohibiting garbage dumps on the reservation. Two years later, the tribe's claim of reservation-wide jurisdiction induced the county to modify a sewer system construction plan. The summer after Johansen's glum prediction, the Suquamish announced an eighteen-month moratorium on new construction. Tribal chairman Richard Belmont expressed sympathy for the concerns of affected non-Indian reservation landowners, one of whom told the *Seattle Times* he was ready to battle the "dictatorship . . . invading my private rights." Nevertheless, the tribe saw an urgent need to correct the "irresponsible" county zoning of reservation land, which allowed clear-cutting, housing on tiny crowded lots, and a sewage drain field adjacent to a tribe member's property.[2]

The back story of the Suquamish Tribe's efforts to regulate non-Indians differs from the Quinault story in crucial respects. Americans in Washington Territory located their first towns within easy reach of Suquamish homelands, where they helped themselves to timber and home sites much earlier than settlers in Quinault country. Although the acreage reserved for Suquamish by treaty and executive order included an important village site, it was not as well suited to US government purposes or Indian needs as the Quinault Reservation. A significant number of Suquamish families opted to maintain or locate homes elsewhere, often near American activity that afforded economic opportunities. Moreover, exclusive Indian use of the reserved land was short lived. Early in the twentieth century, speculators from the burgeoning city of Seattle, nine nautical miles to the east, purchased reservation lots and subdivided them for sale to fellow whites. By the 1960s, unlike the Quinault situation, far more non-Indians than Indians lived on the Suquamish reservation.

The Quinault and Suquamish tribes had contrasting political histories as well. While a formalized Quinault government functioned continuously at least from 1922 on, the widely distributed Suquamish conducted political relations less systematically and more sporadically until the 1960s. Nor did the Suquamish have the Quinaults' record of successfully blocking non-Indian interference with tribal resources by appealing to American courts. Before the 1970s, the tribe ventured into colonial legal forums only twice, each time with congressional permission, seeking monetary compensation for wrongs of the US government. The results were disappointing: no award in one case and a paltry one in the other.

Thus, it was a relatively new, largely untried Suquamish government that charged a non-Indian man in 1973 with violating tribal law and then defended that action in the US Supreme Court. The immediate inspiration for the tribe's decision to exercise comprehensive jurisdiction on the reservation was the example of other tribal governments expanding the powers they wielded, but specific Suquamish experiences generated the motivation to follow that example. Particularly galvanizing, in the mid-twentieth century, were actions by county officials and non-Indian neighbors that indicated disrespect for tribe members and doubts about the tribe's and reservation's continuing existence. In sum, for the Suquamish more than the Quinaults, the history of the non-Indian problem on the reservation was a long, ambiguous one. That local history was an essential context of latter-day Suquamish desire for meaningful self-government in the area once reserved for their exclusive use.

AN IMPERFECT RESERVATION

Even before US treaty negotiators arranged to purchase Suquamish lands in 1855, non-Indians were cutting down trees there. They delivered many of the logs to a narrow inlet of the Puget Sound on the north end of Bainbridge Island, just across Port Madison Bay from a major Suquamish village. Ships from California, Hawaii, and elsewhere dropped anchor at the cove to take on lumber from a mill that George Meigs installed in 1854. Meigs invited "pioneer" families to settle around his operation and soon presided not only over steam-powered saws, which ran night and day, but also over a town with fifty dwellings, shops, and a schoolhouse. The mill office doubled as the seat of a new Washington Territory county named for Suquamish war leader Kitsap.[3]

Sam Wilson, a Suquamish man whose father lived on the bay's west side, testified in a US court in 1927 that Indian buildings on the east side were destroyed when the mill came.[4] However, the activities of lumber-hungry Americans attracted as well as displaced Suquamish families. White crew bosses recruited Indian men to cut trees and boom logs that went to mills at several places in Suquamish territory. Rather than beat a retreat from mill sites, many Indians stayed or moved near them to trade with and work for non-Indians.[5]

Knowing that Indians expected compensation for Americans' use of land and that potential settlers wanted assurance of the Indians' pacification, Washington Territory's first governor was anxious for formal Indian consent to American colonization and resource appropriation. In late December 1854, Isaac Stevens therefore launched a series of treaty councils with tribes in his jurisdiction, beginning at the south end of Puget Sound. Suquamish and Duwamish were on a list of tribes that Stevens summoned to the second council—a huge assembly at a place on the sound's east shore called Mukilteo or Point Elliott. There on January 22, by touching an inked quill to a document that Stevens and his advisers had prepared, ten leading Suquamish and Duwamish men ostensibly ceded all interest in the lands their people could claim to own. In return, they and seventy-two signers from twenty other "tribes and bands" received pledges that their people would have exclusive use of much smaller specified areas, a continuing right to fish at their usual places outside those reservations, and access to customary foods available in "open and unclaimed" areas. Additionally, the Americans promised medical care, a school, other services, and a total of $150,000 dollars, to be paid in cash or goods over twenty years.[6]

The provision for one reservation to house Suquamish and Duwamish Indians was more wishful thinking than realistic plan. Those two names denoted populations distributed across extensive territories both east and west of Puget Sound. The area to be reserved—described in the treaty simply as 1,280 acres "surrounding the small bight at the head of Port Madison"—encompassed only one of many Suquamish and Duwamish house groups. To be sure, that village at a site known as d'suq'wub (Place of the Clear Waters) was a prestigious one in the heart of Suquamish territory. Contemporary reports and early ethnographic research identified it as "a great place of concourse." Suquamish histories refer to it as the home of Chief See-athl, the two tribes' principal, US-designated representative at the treaty.[7] As of 1855, however, See-athl reportedly stayed most of the time with Duwamish kin near the little colonial settlement that took the name Seattle, allegedly in his honor. Although he apparently approved of a reservation at Port Madison, the Americans were naive to expect that he would lead all Duwamish across the sound to live alongside the Suquamish.[8]

The treaty obliged the Indians "to settle upon the reservation" within a year after US Senate ratification "or sooner if the means [were] furnished them." Senators did not act promptly, and the reserve's precise location was still unidentified by late fall, when territorial officials tried to gather the Duwamish and Suquamish at Port Madison, hoping to isolate them from armed hostilities under way between Americans and tribes in the Cascade Mountain foothills. Settler D. C. Maynard, charged with overseeing Duwamish removal from Seattle's environs, reported that many were loath to go because the Port Madison area lacked adequate fishing grounds.

Seattle businessmen who employed Indians also opposed their removal.[9] By year's end, Maynard had assembled just 250 of the estimated 900 Suquamish and Duwamish at a camp near d'suq'wub. Citing a shortage of government-furnished supplies, he let twenty-two Indians stay at Meigs's mill, where they could earn their own support.[10]

Neither the treaty's ratification in 1859 nor the enlargement and demarcation of the reservation five years later induced more than a few Duwamish to make their homes there. US Indian agent G. A. Paige offered another explanation for that recalcitrance. His 1859 report to superiors repeated a request from the previous year "that the Suquamish and Dwamish Indians be allowed separate reservations, as the feud which has long existed between these tribes, instead of becoming less, is daily growing greater."[11]

The Duwamish were not the only Indians in the region who declined to settle on a reservation as expected. At some reservations, essential subsistence resources, including land, were insufficient. At most of them, supplemental US government support was all but nonexistent. In many cases, options and opportunities outside the reservations seemed worth the risk of trouble with American officials or non-Indian neighbors.[12] On the reserves, once an infrastructure of US government supervision was in place, the repression of indigenous customs and eventually a policy of sending Indian children away to boarding schools were potent deterrents for many people.[13]

All these factors influenced some Suquamish families to keep or locate homes at off-reservation sites. Four mills were turning out lumber in Suquamish ancestral territory by 1857; a fifth began operation in 1863. They made it possible for Indians to earn money not only as mill workers but also as suppliers of food, dogfish oil to grease log skids, and knitted socks to cushion loggers' feet. Some Suquamish therefore clustered around mills farther from d'suq'wub than Port Madison. Small Indian communities formed and persisted for generations about thirty miles southwest of the reservation along Dyes Inlet, where several non-Indian men established homesteads, employed Indians in logging ventures, married Native women, fathered numerous children, and left some or all their land to their Indian wives or offspring.[14]

By 1880, an influx of non-Indians—many white, some black, some Hawaiian—had swelled Kitsap County's population to nearly two thousand.

Spotty head counts of Indians showed them greatly outnumbered and almost evenly divided into reservation and off-reservation residents. Census takers found 118 Indians outside the reserve, probably including Klallams living across from the Port Gamble mill ten miles north of Port Madison. Reservation population tallies between the 1870s and the early 1900s were in the 130 to 160 range, but those numbers suggest unlikely rootedness. Most Indians who maintained a base on the reservation left there regularly for extended periods at logging camps, mill towns, fishing grounds, hop ranches, and homes of kinfolk. Neither geographical nor social boundaries separated on-reservation from off-reservation Indians.[15]

US government minders were ambivalent about the opportunities for Indians outside the reserve. On one hand, because of settler demand for Indian labor, Indians' industriousness, and Indians' access to off-reservation sources of food, local agents could report that their charges were self-supporting—something national officials wanted to hear. On the other hand, Indians off the reservation were not present for government-prescribed instruction in "civilized" practices. They were exposed instead to the supposedly corrupting influence of liquor sellers, gamblers, lustful loggers, and unsupervised Indians who clung to "heathen" ways. Officially, it was preferable to keep Indians on reservations, where federal agents would model and coach them to adopt an approved way of life, particularly farming on private plots of land.[16]

A catch in the Suquamish situation was that the 1,280-acre tract promised in the treaty had room for very few farmsteads. Therefore, in 1864, shortly after a Suquamish delegation petitioned the territorial superintendent of Indian affairs for additional land, federal officials drew the boundaries for a reservation six times that large. An order of the Interior secretary delineated two noncontiguous areas separated by a small inlet and some land already claimed by non-Indians. Together, the tracts encompassed just under 7,300 acres with roughly eleven miles of saltwater coastline where Suquamish obtained shellfish and other essential foods on extensive tidelands. Behind the shore was mostly forest—dense stands of fir, cedar, hemlock, spruce, and alder. For their dietary staple of salmon, the Indians would have to leave the reservation; no river ran through it.[17]

In 1878, a petition bearing the names of thirty-three Indian men asked the American president to divide the Port Madison reserve into lots for

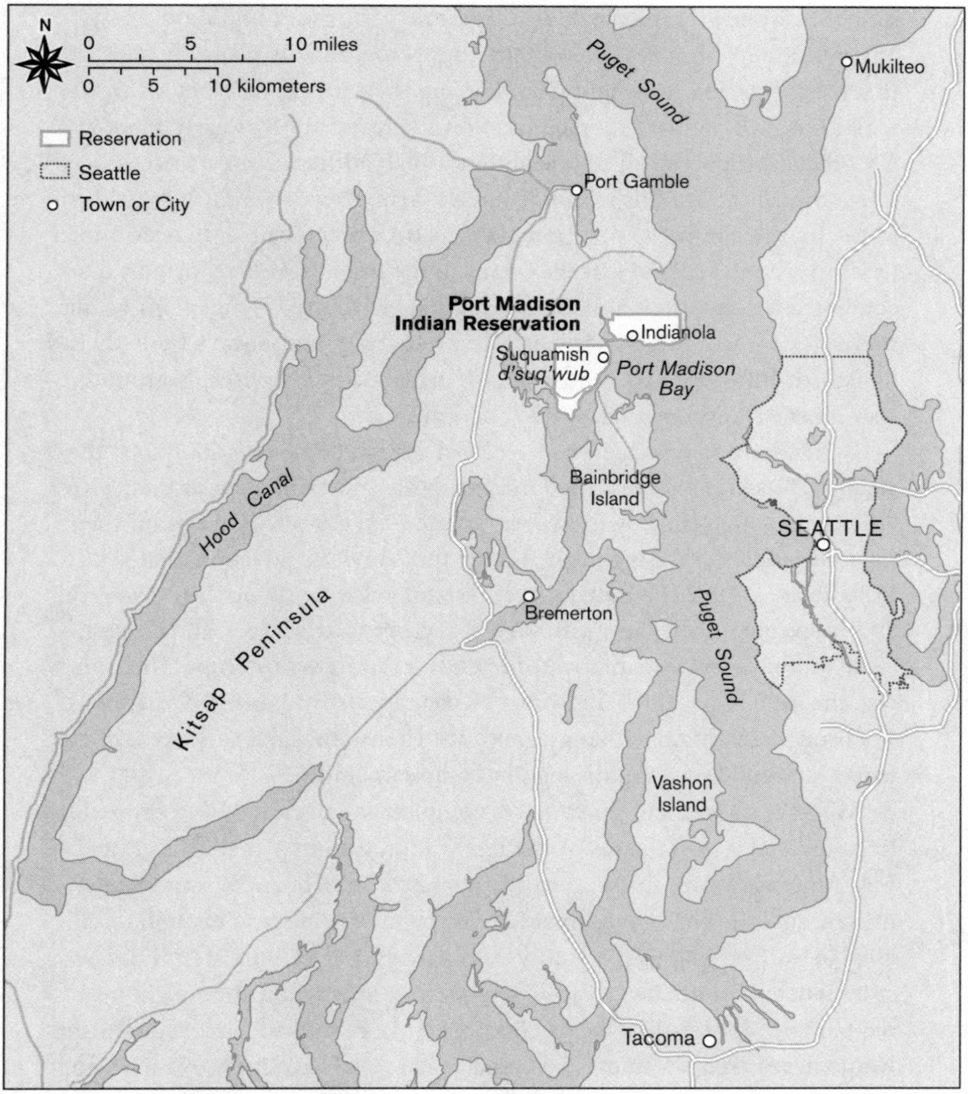

Port Madison (Suquamish) Indian Reservation as of 2000 in relation to the aboriginal Suquamish heartland.

individuals and give them patents, as permitted by the Point Elliott treaty.[18] The petitioners' motives are obscure, but some records plausibly suggest that they expected to benefit from logging their properties. Indian crews with axes and saws had toppled trees on the reservation as early as 1867.[19] US officials approved of deforestation and land allotment as necessary steps toward the establishment of Indian farms, but Suquamish reactions to the first assignments of separate tracts do not indicate enthusiasm for tending crops on inland acreage. Many of the Indians were reportedly discontented because they could not have what "all desired"—"a lot or two on the water front." The waterfront was where they had always built their houses; it afforded access to shellfish beds, seine-net fishing grounds, waterborne transportation, and log booming areas.[20]

By 1886, thirty-five men had received patents to reservation plots; the smallest was eighty acres, the largest slightly more than twice that. Five years later, US agent Edwin Miller reported twenty-one families on their separate lands, cultivating them, but the space under cultivation totaled just forty acres.[21] While the Indians were generally willing to log their property and supplement their diets with vegetable gardens, fruit trees, and domesticated animals, few were motivated to clear large areas of stumps. Throughout the late 1800s, men in Miller's role repeatedly lamented that Port Madison Reservation Indians would not choose to farm so long as they could earn good wages in the logging camps and mills.

When the allotment process was complete in the early 1900s, property lines divided 7,201.54 acres of the reservation into fifty-one private holdings ranging in size from 40 to 178.5 acres.[22] Subsequently, some Suquamish accused the US government of failing to provide land enough for all eligible Indians who wanted individual parcels. For a Court of Claims lawsuit on behalf of nineteen tribes in western Washington, sixty-eight-year-old Sam Snyder testified in 1927 that many more of his fellow Suquamish would have taken allotments had land been available. Witness Nancy Sigo, age eighty, implied that insufficient acreage was the reason for several persistent clusters of off-reservation Indian homes.[23] In a 1982 oral history interview, eighty-three-year-old tribe member Lawrence Webster recited a lengthy list of Suquamish families and individuals who did not receive allotments as they expected.[24]

Indians who felt cheated of their right to a lot on the reserve likely had no more interest in farming than most allottees. The meager results of cultivating reservation land confirmed the wisdom of the economic strategy that most tribe members adopted: eschewing agriculture and relying instead on a flexible combination of fishing, wage labor, gardening, trade, and timber sales. In an 1896 report to the commissioner of Indian affairs, the supervisor of the four Point Elliott treaty reservations declared, "Port Madison Reservation is the poorest of all under my care, but a small portion being at all fertile or adapted to agricultural purposes. The Indians make little or no pretense at farming but depend almost entirely upon fishing and clam digging for a living, upon which they chiefly subsist." Twelve years later, the subagent at Port Madison likewise made no pretense of discouraging his charges' dependence on such resources. Cyrus Pickrell wrote, "No Indian of this reservation ever has been, or is now, regularly engaged in agricultural work. The land is heavily timbered and very hard to clear."[25]

American officials still expected nuclear families and single adults to establish homes and make improvements on their allotted land, but the persistence of a waterfront village at d'suq'wub demonstrated that the homestead model of "civilized" life held no charm for most of the Indians. Lawrence Webster, born in 1899, spent his childhood in that village. He told an interviewer in 1980 that his neighbors built just enough on their scattered allotments to "hold" them but "barely lived" there because they "wanted to go live down by [the] water to live next to each other."[26]

Perhaps if US agents had resided and worked full time on the reservation before 1900, they would have seen more progress toward their goal of depopulating the shoreline village and getting families to develop their allotments. Instead, responsibility for overseeing affairs at Port Madison rested on personnel of the Tulalip Indian Agency, twenty-six miles across the sound. The government men asserted their authority, with varying effectiveness, by visiting Port Madison periodically or deputizing local settlers to report and discourage undesirable Indian behavior. Until the turn of the century, when Allen Bartow became the first resident subagent, the only on-site, institutionalized, non-Indian effort to promote acceptable Indian habits was St. Peter's Catholic Mission, which claimed most of the Suquamish as parishioners and supported a small school at d'suq'wub.[27] The belated subagency lasted just two decades, during which higher officials had little direct involvement in reservation affairs. As far as Lawrence Webster knew, Charles Buchanan, superintendent at Tulalip from 1901 to 1920, never came to the reservation.[28]

Although the Indians finally abandoned their houses at d'suq'wub a few years after Bartow arrived, neither he nor Cyrus Pickrell, his successor in 1906, could claim credit for persuading them to move. That dubious achievement belonged to a negotiator for the United States War Department, who browbeat the Suquamish in 1905 into selling seventy acres of waterfront land, complete with the aboriginal village, church, dock, US agency building, and schoolhouse.[29] Lawrence Webster, six years old at the time, recalled sixty-five years later that once the American officials had Suquamish signatures on a sales agreement, they "gave the Indians $23.00 a piece—men, women, and child. And told them to move onto their allotments. . . . We had to move everyone ourselves." Still, subagent Pickrell could detect "no genuine desire on the part of the indian [*sic*]" to comply and settle on private land. Most village residents did not disperse until "force of circumstances" left them no choice. "Last winter," Pickrell related in 1908, "a number of families living on the Military strip were removed by the War Department and they were thus compelled to build new homes, others were led to build on their allotments through fear of losing them."[30] In old age, Webster lamented that the dispersal of village residents frayed and snapped many threads of the tribal community fabric, as his grandfather predicted when opposing the site's sale to the federal government.[31]

Military brass did not hurry to install the defenses for which they claimed to require the village site. In fact, the War Department never used the land it acquired; nor did the United States fulfill the Indians' expectation that it would return the unused tract to the tribe. Years later, elected Suquamish leaders referred to the transaction that needlessly uprooted the village as a "sore spot" and a cause of "ill feeling with the Indians for a long time." They told the commissioner of Indian affairs in 1956 that a housing development for non-Indians had taken the place of Chief Seattle's old village. The development's new residents expressly prohibited the sale of a lot or house to anyone with "Indian blood," and Indians who went on the beach to dig clams were often threatened with arrest and chased away.[32]

NON-INDIAN LANDOWNERS

Perhaps the Suquamish resistance to farming and consent to US acquisition of the village tract helped federal officials rationalize a course of action they adopted as a new century dawned. They began selling off land that they had just allotted to individual Indians. The buyers were non-Indians. Agency personnel arranged some sales even before the process of surveying and assigning allotments was complete. Thus, for Indians who preferred the exclusivity of a reservation, the problems posed by non-Indian landowners and residents arose earlier at Port Madison than in Quinault country.

Both the Point Elliott Treaty and the General Allotment Act of 1887 made Indians' individual lots inalienable, but the legislation that ratified the sale of the village site included a special provision permitting Claf-wha George and Qudiskid Big John to sell their personal tracts. Then in 1907, a general act of Congress overrode the treaty and allotment act proscriptions against alienation. The new law allowed US agents, acting as trustees for the Indians, to sell the land of "noncompetent" individuals—people deemed unable to make use of their property or to support themselves otherwise. Agent Pickrell wasted no time before exercising that prerogative. By July 1909, he was entertaining several offers to buy acreage from Port Madison Reservation allottees.[33]

Were Pickrell and his Tulalip Agency colleagues making a sincere effort to fulfill the federal government's self-imposed trust responsibility to needy Indian landowners? Did their decisions reflect a conflicting desire to help fellow whites acquire choice real estate or even to minimize the extent of Indian landholdings? According to Pickrell, infirmities of old age justified the individuals' classification as noncompetent, and their lack of income necessitated the land sales. None of them would be rendered homeless; all would retain small portions of their land for homesites. Yet there are reasons to mistrust officials' justifications for the sales and to doubt that they met their fiduciary obligations. Aged allottees were probably not fluent English speakers or prepared by education or experience to sell real estate on their own. Existing records do not indicate what they thought or whether they even knew about the transactions. The purchasers, in contrast, included some of Seattle's savviest businessmen; Pickrell was a businessman himself and would ultimately acquire some of the alienated land. Not surprisingly, allotments suitable for speculative residential or commercial development—those on the waterfront—were the first to go.

In the early 1980s, the unnamed authors of a manuscript for the Suquamish Cultural Program found Indian agency explanations of the sales unconvincing. In their view, records of "noncompetency rulings" and Indian property transfers to non-Indians showed that "the means by which the Indians were relieved of their land were creative, to say the least." For instance, officials approved the sale of William Rogers's allotment soon after he received it "despite the fact that most family members were capable of managing their affairs." The alleged signs that Rogers and his forty-nine-year-old wife were incompetent included their "advanced age" and their habit of "'expos[ing] themselves to all kinds of weather digging clams.'" Officials dismissed the possibility that a son-in-law could support the elder Rogers. Although the younger man was supporting himself and his own parents, they pronounced him "irresponsible and intemperate."[34]

Government personnel or Indians who wanted to sell allotted reservation land had more legal options than a finding of noncompetency. Another act of Congress in 1906 empowered agents to declare some Indians fully competent, thereby freeing them to dispose of their allotments on their own, without a federal trustee to guard against scammers or the Indians' own imprudence. According to Francis Paul Prucha, a historian of US Indian policy, "On many reservations where land speculators were active, Indian allottees [were] importuned to apply for patents in fee, and in many instances the Indians were defrauded out of a large portion of their lands. . . . For most the patent in fee was soon followed by sale of the land." Since "competency" also made a landowner liable for property taxes, many Indians had to part with their property involuntarily when they did not meet that obligation.[35]

Because non-Indians could bring daunting power to bear on Indians, because allotment sales did not relieve most owners' poverty, and because non-Indian possession of reservation land has subsequently posed a variety of problems for tribes, many federally promoted Indian land sales were arguably betrayals of the US trust responsibility. No doubt some Indians did sell when shrewd buyers took advantage of allottees' limited English skills, poverty, naïveté, or inebriation. But given Suquamish Indians' history of engagement with a market economy and their land's limited uses, it is also likely that some individuals weighed their options sensibly and saw little reason at the time to retain all their acreage. In 1919, for instance, thirty-five of the fifty-one Port Madison Reservation allotments reportedly sat idle.[36]

According to Allen Bartow, "inheritance questions" prevented more than a few Indians from using their allotments. The land of many deceased allottees languished while the Indian Office processed probates at a glacial pace. When an allottee died without a will, as virtually all did, the land usually passed to multiple heirs, who received undivided interests. By federal law, any use of Indian property in such fractionated ownership required the consent of all owners. If unanimous consent was not attainable, responsibility for managing the land fell to the understaffed Indian agency. A statute of 1902 allowed Indians to request the sale of interests they inherited, and many eventually did so for various reasons. Some already had allotments of their own to manage, some inherited land on reservations elsewhere, and some—their numbers increasing rapidly as Indians died intestate—could not foresee any better use for their small shares of undivided property.[37]

The legislation that loosened restrictions on the sale of Indian allotments partially explains how non-Indians acquired 1,262.3 acres of Port Madison Reservation land by 1915 and a total of 2,872.43 acres by 1934.[38] We can infer the motivations of non-Indian buyers with more confidence than the intentions or understanding of Indian sellers. For non-Indian Americans, individual property ownership was a nearly universal aspiration, speculation in land was a strong tradition, and Indian lands were often available at bargain basement prices. Ironically, early purchasers of former Suquamish land proved no more eager than the Indians to farm it or live there full time. Pickrell's report for 1910 stated, "The white settlers in the country adjacent to the reservation have only small clearings, averaging probably less than ten acres and very few of them are able to make a living thereon." Suquamish Cultural Program research revealed that "those most interested in the Indians' land were entrepreneurs attracted to the investment opportunities they saw in the reservation's waterfront location, and lumber companies in search of timber."[39]

Much of the energy and money for such investments emanated from cities across Puget Sound, particularly Seattle, where the Klondike gold rush of 1896–99 triggered dramatic population and economic growth. Seattle-based buyers of Suquamish land included the scion of a prominent "pioneer" family, lawyer Vivian Carkeek, and real estate developer Ole Hanson, a recent immigrant to the region, soon to be Seattle's mayor. Hanson and partner A. H. Reid were among the first to bid on Port Madison

Reservation allotments. They liked their chances of boosting their bank balance by selling vacation homesites to fellow Seattleites. Shortly after acquiring waterfront tracts just north of the military strip in 1909, they incorporated and platted a town there, naming it Silverstrand.[40]

Although their investment did not pay off as handsomely as Hanson and Reid hoped, a summer colony for non-Indians, renamed Suquamish, did take root on the land they platted. After inexpensive daily steamboat service linked the colony to Seattle in 1914, the pool of potential customers for lots grew to include people of modest means seeking year-round residences. Holmes Hyland, a non-Indian born in 1903, spent childhood summers in Suquamish. He recalled later that the Eastman Company acquired a tract there, divided it into small parcels, and sold them to its low-paid Seattle employees at $150 to $200 apiece. The commute between city workplaces and Suquamish cottages cost fifty cents.[41] A newspaper advertisement for lots claimed that the settlement had accumulated five hundred residents as of August 1915. It mentioned the location on former Indian land but implied that all buyers were white.[42]

Some consequences of the influx are apparent from Tulalip Agency correspondence in 1917. William Egbert, one of two agency employees on the Port Madison Reservation, ordered a halt to Sunday baseball games with Indian and non-Indian players because they allegedly attracted crowds of drunken, lawless outsiders. His mandate infuriated Arthur Flynn, a non-Indian with a home in Suquamish town. Flynn sent Egbert's superior two petitions for resumption of the games, one signed by Indians, the other by non-Indians, all found outside the post office on a Sunday. Egbert labeled Flynn "an interloper" with "no rights whatever" on the reservation. "The real question," Egbert insisted, "is whether the white people living off the Reservation, having not the least right or claim, are to be allowed to use the Indian land for Sunday baseball, social gatherings or for whatsoever purpose or time they see fit." Evidently, "people living off the Reservation" referred to residents of the non-Indian-owned Suquamish townsite, reflecting Egbert's dubious assumption that land sales to non-Indians diminished the reservation. Those "Seattle people," Egbert wrote, had already "demanded the use of the school building for their community gatherings, and the school bell to place upon their church." Now they were demanding "the use of a portion of the Reservation for their athletic sports."[43]

By 1920, federal personnel had acceded to the "Seattle people's" demand. The Tulalip Agency annual report explained:

> The little town of Suquamish is built right up against the Agency Reserve. We have permitted the White people to play baseball on our Reserve as the village is built in the timber and they have no available space of that purpose. During the summer Suquamish is quite a resort and on Saturday afternoons and Sundays thousands of visitors invade the town and the Reservation and frequently they have a few drunks in the crowd. This has been an unorganized village until recently they have appointed or elected a constable. If our man there was a special officer he would have authority on and off the reservation to make arrests where he found liquor upon a person and no doubt the moral effect would add greatly to maintaining law and order where there has been some difficulty in the past.[44]

COMMERCE AND COEXISTENCE

While Seattleites came to Port Madison for various purposes, Indians frequently headed the other way. Accustomed to traveling widely in well-engineered canoes, Native people had always seen the deep, cold waters of Puget Sound (*whulge* in their language) as a route rather than a barrier to other shores, and the American settlement in Duwamish territory on the east shore had held attractions for them since its inception in 1851. For Indians with a little money, the Americans' ferries eventually offered a less strenuous alternative to paddling between the reservation and the city.

Many Suquamish earned money in Seattle. To an 1896 report that Port Madison Indians subsisted on fish and shellfish, a Tulalip Agency employee added, "They sell the surplus in Seattle, which is but a short distance away." That commerce was not incidental. "Clam digging for Seattle market is common," subagent Bartow wrote in 1905. "Several men have good fishing outfits which they use to some slight profit. . . . Some women make good baskets [to sell]." For Lawrence Webster and other Indians, Seattle was a source of wages for labor. After his schooling ended in 1916, Webster worked there summers as a longshoreman. In winter, he joined logging crews on the city's outskirts.[45]

By 1911, Indians from the Port Madison Reservation, like these elders photographed at Colman Dock in Seattle, could take the steamer back to the west side of Puget Sound. Identified by early Seattle journalist Thomas Prosch, left to right, as Doctor Peter, Charlie Yukon [Yukted], Mrs. Chief Jacob, Chief Jacob Wahalchu, unknown, Mary Adams. Seattle Museum of History and Industry, Negative 83.10.7723.

By then, loggers were clearing space for non-Indian homes and businesses in many parts of the region. For a national survey of Indian affairs in the 1920s, Tulalip Agency superintendent F. A. Gross wrote, "Western Washington has developed more rapidly in the past seventy five [*sic*] years than probably any other section in the west and possibly in the entire United States." Urban populations had boomed since the 1890s; Seattle's was approaching 500,000. Rural areas within twenty-five miles of the salt water were also "developed to a wonderful degree," and Indian reservations were in the midst of it all. Everett, near the Tulalip Reservation, boasted 40,000 people; Tacoma's 135,000 residents crowded and then crossed into the Puyallup Indian Reservation, buying up Indian allotments. In south-central Kitsap County, adjacent to a site selected for a navy base and shipyard, the town of Bremerton mushroomed, while close to the Port Madison Reservation's northwest boundary, the hamlet of Poulsbo—a once-quiet colony of Norwegian immigrant fishers and loggers—rapidly added commercial establishments and residents. In 1927 Gross observed, "Indians of this jurisdiction mingle a great deal with white people and go to the various towns and cities."[46]

Between 1915 and 1930, non-Indian acquisition and occupation of Port Madison Reservation lands continued apace. In 1920, the United States leased out the tract it had held, unused, for the military since 1905. The non-Indian lessees envisioned farms and resorts there. Over the following six years, a prominent contractor purchased the property for more intensive development, the town of Suquamish installed electric lighting, and Kitsap County Transportation Company built a more substantial dock where a ferry departed daily for Seattle's growing neighborhood of Ballard. According to a non-Indian resident of Suquamish, amenities available to the seven hundred people who summered there in the 1930s included several churches, two stores, two lunchrooms, a barbershop, a garage, a gunsmith, and numerous "beautiful residences."[47]

Meanwhile, ferry owner W. L. Gazzam bought tracts of allotted land in the reservation's eastern portion and began promoting a colony there. His Indianola Company letterhead featured the slogan "Specializing in waterfront property accessible to Seattle." Gazzam told the Tulalip Agency in 1925 that he would lay water mains, put in driveways, golf links, and electricity to "make it very desirable and with its location very valuable as a sort of an exclusive residence property."[48]

In spite of the name Indianola, Gazzam's customers probably thought they were not buying reservation land. Advertisements for Suquamish town lots implied that their history as Indian land was irrelevant. One 1915 ad declared, "This site was chosen by the old Chief Seattle over 50 years ago as the best site for a home on all Puget Sound. The story of great cities is that they are built where the Indians camped."[49] Such references to Indians as if they belonged to the past, not the present, were standard. If buyers asked whether property originally reserved for Indians would come with special conditions, government officials and sellers such as Gazzam likely replied that the land left reservation status when non-Indians acquired it.

By the 1920s, Port Madison Reservation land acquired by non-Indian developers was the site of a nascent waterfront town dubbed Suquamish, which adjoined a tribal tract encompassing a baseball field where Indian and non-Indian teams played. Courtesy of the Suquamish Museum.

Federal laws rarely specified whether sales to non-Indians removed land from a reservation, and judges had answered the question both possible ways.[50] The issue was not firmly settled until 1948, when Congress spelled out that a reservation consists of all land within unaltered reservation boundaries.[51]

Sellers expected names such as Indianola and Suquamish to attract purchasers because Indians had become objects of safe fascination for legions of white Americans, locally and nationally. By the early 1900s, public discourse about Indians characterized them primarily as colorful but vanishing vestiges of the recently tamed Wild West. Since the last armed tribal resistance to US expansion was in the past, some residual aspects of Indian culture could be tolerated, even enjoyed as benignly exotic. Portrayed as pitiable people with such natural virtues as deep attachment to their lands—people who had graciously conceded the superiority of Euro-American civilization and mostly disappeared—Indians warranted whites' nostalgic appreciation.

The Suquamish and Duwamish afforded an example of admirable, vanished Indians in the person of Chief See-athl. His name was commonly associated with stories of his "invaluable services to the white settlers in early days."[52] Businessmen who aimed to populate the Suquamish Reservation area with white people found it useful to promote the image of See-athl as a wise facilitator of interracial peace. Therefore, in 1911, Seattle druggist H. E. Holmes enlisted some of his city's eminent residents, the US Indian agent, military officers, and several tribal elders in staging a day of commemorations and festivities at Suquamish, ostensibly in the great chief's honor. The *Seattle Times* gave prominent coverage to the event, which featured a ceremony at See-athl's grave, speeches by white and Indian dignitaries in three languages—English, Chinook jargon, and "Indian"—navy band music, songs by Indian men, and a baseball game in which a Holmes company team outscored an Indian team seven to five. Citing the "enthusiastic" response of Indians and "the many visitors from Seattle and other points on the Sound," the *Times* accurately predicted many future "Chief Seattle Day" celebrations. Similar ceremonies and dependable *Times* publicity drew substantial white crowds to the reservation every succeeding summer through at least the late 1920s.[53]

Indians on and near the Port Madison Reservation also "mingled" with whites in schools. The first public school at Suquamish opened September 8, 1915, with twenty-six students. By 1920, the year-round non-Indian population within original reservation boundaries was sufficient to support two public schools, both on former Indian allotments. According to a Tulalip Agency report, Indian pupils were received courteously but "not without some opposition in each particular district on the part of White people." The writer shared those opponents' concern about children from "unsanitary homes," but his superiors now wanted Indian families to put their children in public schools. In 1920, the federal government closed the boarding school that most Suquamish children had previously attended.[54]

At Port Madison, Indians and non-Indians also worshipped together in St. Peter's Church. One parishioner recalled summer services during the 1930s for full houses that were "pretty much half and half," Indians and whites. That close association was not entirely comfortable. Most summer residents were "cool" to the Indians and segregated themselves, first in separate pews, then in a new wing of the sanctuary.[55]

Some non-Indians and Indians were not averse to more intimate mingling, as is evident in Indian censuses that recorded individuals' non-Indian ancestry. In 1891, federal supervisors identified eleven "mixed bloods" among 147 Indians on the reservation. Two decades later, the ratio of such persons to so-called full bloods had risen to 83 out of 191; by 1920, it was 101 out of 181.[56] A 1933 Bureau of Indian Affairs survey of Suquamish Indians in Kitsap County listed nine families in which one spouse was white. These figures contrast with comparable statistics for the Quinault Reservation, where just 5 of 801 resident Indians in 1927 were married to whites, with 13 children among them.[57] Although these racial classifications and census numbers were no doubt imprecise, they are reasonably reliable corroborative evidence that Indians of the Port Madison Reservation had grown more accustomed than Quinaults to interactions with non-Indians in matters besides trade or employment.

R. G. Stillman, a Seattle resident who photographed and wrote about local Indians, pronounced the influx of whites to the Suquamish homeland a disaster, but he did not elaborate. In its specifics, his account of cross-cultural relations on the reservation as of 1938 was not notably gloomy. The Indians, he wrote, "are fast becoming a part of the American system, fair farmers, timber workers, fishermen and businessmen. Some of the leaders of the movement to create a great new park in perpetual memory of Chief Seattle and his friendship for the white settlers are Suquamish Natives. Commercial Clubs and Granges of the neighborhood of Port Madison have members whose ancestors of but a few generations past sat at the fires of Old-Man-House and listened to the oratory of Chief Seattle."[58]

EVOLVING TRIBAL RELATIONS

What did a fragmented Indian land base, the breakup of d'suq'wub village, and the influx of non-Indian neighbors mean for Suquamish relations with each other? Did tribal ties and allegiances weaken and rupture, or did they gain importance for disconcerted Indians? Answers are difficult to extract from available records, both because records of tribal relations between 1920 and 1965 are scarce and because information about the nature and strength of earlier Suquamish allegiances is also spotty and ambiguous.

As of 1855, the people known to American treaty makers as Suquamish did not constitute the kind of clearly defined, regulated political entity with which the United States wanted official relations. Rather than a unifying government structure or formally ordained process of governance, intricate kinship networks and shared social practices linked inhabitants of the autonomous house groups in Suquamish territory. Some individuals, such as See-athl, earned wide-ranging prestige and deference, but they held no overarching, institutionalized offices and had no authority to compel obedience from all Suquamish. High-status adults from multiple house groups might meet occasionally to consider issues of common concern, but they could not force anyone to abide by a resulting decision. Most actions that Americans regarded as crimes were problems for affected families to address, usually by exacting restitution but occasionally by retaliating.[59]

American officials, aiming to simplify their oversight of Indians, insisted first that allied bands consolidate into larger "tribes" under "chiefs" who would take responsibility for keeping their people in order. In the longer run, however, the federal government goal was to break down tribal ties and supplant the chiefs as arbiters of individual Indians' relationship to the United States. Across the Puget Sound region, effecting that two-step reorganization and reorientation of Indian societies was more difficult and ultimately less complete than Americans hoped.[60] The fact that many Suquamish and Duwamish did not settle on the reservation hindered efforts to consolidate and control the tribes. Indians who did have homes on the reservation bore the brunt of American interference with tribal life, but they could ease the pressure by leaving. For these reasons, and because the reservation was haphazardly supervised, US agents induced little discernible change in the Indians' conception of Suquamish affiliations, leadership, and allegiances before 1910.

The scanty documentation of Suquamish tribal relations from the 1860s to the 1910s suggests that leadership, while expected from certain men, was limited in purpose and situational. Federal government records are nearly devoid of references to specific leaders. In 1874, when American officials were still trying to conduct relations with "tribes" through cooperative "chiefs," the US agent responsible for Port Madison blamed an unnamed "head man" there for many Indians' reversion to "old Superstitious practices." Better-disposed Indians were allegedly "anxious to have another and better man appointed." Two decades later, the agency's hopes for keeping reservation residents in line rested instead on two Indians in roles the Indian office had instituted nationwide. One was a policeman, the other a judge for the so-called Court of Indian Offenses. Both were agency appointees. Subagent Bartow pronounced the court a "very valuable institution" even though judges had "fallen at times from grace, and had to resign or be discharged." Turn-of-the-century reports mentioned no other Indians who contributed to governance on the reservation or exerted influence in wider Suquamish society.[61]

To legitimize the War Department's acquisition of reservation land in 1905, the US government needed formal approval from the Indians belonging there. Rather than appointing or purporting to recognize a chief who could sign an agreement, officials convened a council of adult male reservation residents—the first tribal decision-making body mentioned in federal records after 1855. Bartow's report on the proceedings said merely, "All the Indians in council thanked Inspector, Col. James Mc'Laughlin [*sic*] for his good advice to put the money coming to them from sale of rights on Govt. strip into improvements upon their claims."[62]

In the 1980s, Lawrence Webster shared recollections that supplement the federal record. He described a reservation community and a leadership culture that US agency personnel either overlooked or did not bother to document. Raised in the home of his grandfather Jacob Wahalchu, a treaty signer who lived until 1911, Webster had a lifelong interest in Suquamish affairs and sharp memories of people he knew as a youth. He recalled that Wahalchu and Big John, another "old timer," served for many years as leaders of the village at d'suq'wub. The two elders opposed the sale for fear that it would "scatter the people" permanently. By then, however, many of the Indians were looking for leadership to some younger men who favored the deal.[63]

The council that debated the 1905 land sale was not an ongoing instrument of tribal governance. Instead, as Webster remembered it, "the agent's word was law" for the following two decades. Then in 1916, the Indians designated new leadership for a new purpose—to represent the Suquamish tribe in the Northwestern Federation of American Indians (NFAI). The impetus for the NFAI's creation in 1913 was a region-wide drive to document US government defaults on treaty promises and get belated satisfaction.

In the 1980s, Lawrence Webster, grandson of the treaty signer Chief Jacob Wahalchu, was chairman of the Suquamish tribal council, an advocate of recovering and preserving stories of Suquamish history, and a respected source of memories about the Suquamish tribal community in the early 1900s. Courtesy of the Suquamish Museum.

Spearheading the campaign was Thomas Bishop, son of a white man and a Snohomish Indian woman living off reservation. Initially focused on federal government failure to provide land for all eligible Indians, Bishop traveled to reservations and Indian homes across western Washington, eliciting memories of government neglect. He published his findings in a pamphlet titled "An Appeal to the Government to Fulfill Sacred Promises Made 61 Years Ago." An appendix supplied the text of the third treaty that Isaac Stevens negotiated and the affidavits of two Duwamish men who said they heard Stevens promise buckets of gold and land for every Indian. Lawrence Webster, recalling Bishop's efforts, remarked, "History could have died if Tommy Bishop did not start asking questions."[64]

Had it not been for the federation Bishop organized, some tribal relations and even identities might also have faced extinction. The NFAI set its sights on suing the United States for treaty violations, and only successors of tribes listed in the treaties would have standing as plaintiffs. Therefore, while membership was open to individuals "of Indian blood," the NFAI functioned through chapters equated with tribes named in the treaties. At the Port Madison Reservation in 1916, forty-two Indians, calling themselves "our Council," endorsed a chapter charter titled "Suquamish Tribal Constitution." A cover sheet bore the words "Central Branch of the Northwestern Federation of American Indians." The constitution's stated purpose was "to assure the tribal rights of all members." The "chief source and motive" of members' "cooperation" was the pending treaty rights and land claim. The sole government structure established was an "executive head" of five elected officers whose only specified power was managing funds, beginning with annual dues of one dollar per general council member.[65] Even so, Webster regarded those officers as his tribe's first "regular tribal council," and he was not the only Indian who dated modern tribal government in western Washington to the creation of the NFAI.[66]

In 1925, the Northwestern Federation secured an act of Congress allowing nineteen tribes to sue the United States. Nine years passed before the Court of Claims rendered a judgment acknowledging some unfulfilled US treaty obligations but denying tribes compensation, largely for technical reasons.[67] The newly constituted Suquamish tribal organization left no record from those years that it functioned for purposes other than NFAI business, but there is other evidence of a Suquamish effort to maintain the leadership structure. A 1934 Indian Office questionnaire about tribal self-governance in western Washington elicited a Tulalip Agency report that Port Madison Reservation Indians had had a five-person business council since about 1925, when the Court of Claims case began.[68]

Lawrence Webster remembered all the first officers—men he thought were "elected for life." (According to the 1934 agency report, the council terms had been "indefinite" since 1928.) They met at the home of Chairman Charles Alexis or in other houses.[69]

Alexis was chairman in 1931 when a Senate investigating committee invited Indians in the Pacific Northwest to make their concerns known. In a letter to committee head Lynn Frazier, Alexis complained of federal law impediments to meaningful tribal self-government and declared, "The ignoring of our tribal councils must be checked. We need some changes in the Indian Office laws governing our affairs, where the Indian may have a voice and be boss of his own business if he is capable. We are all fairly educated and organized so that our tribal and personal property can be lawfully protected in case we were given the right to vote and elect our own men to handle our affairs in the Indian Service locally and at the National Capitol." A second communication from Suquamish Indians—this one signed by Mrs. Gladys Fowler and forty-eight other persons—did not specify the signers' relationship to Alexis and the five-person council, but it also expressed a desire for federally sanctioned tribal self-government: "Most urgently we request that all ancient laws and rigid regulations governing our tribal affairs, and general affairs of the reservation, be revised, and made subject to amendments, and modified to meet present-day conditions. . . . Second. . . . That we have rights to govern our legal and tribal affairs and meet urgent needs of the reservation. Third. That we have proper and adequate protections of all tribal possessions, and private properties within the limits of the reservation."[70]

These pleas for greater freedom to govern tribe members and the reservation came a few years after Tulalip Agency superintendent Gross reported an inquiry from some unnamed Suquamish Indians whose political ambitions were apparently more limited. They asked whether they could organize precincts and elect their own justices of the peace and constables but also be "entirely subject to the state law enforcement bodies." That request suggests that the five-person "business council" did not yet purport to be a general-purpose government of the reservation. If so, Charles Alexis's subsequent letter to senators may indicate a new or growing council desire to take on unprecedented functions, perhaps motivated in part by the fact that the proposal for a precinct under state law went nowhere. According to Gross, local non-Indian authorities declined to consider the idea seriously because their jurisdictions could not tax Indian property.[71]

Three decades later, in 1952, forty-year-old Mary Howard testified before the Indian Claims Commission (ICC) as "chairman" of the Suquamish Tribe. Her people had an unbroken history of tribal relations and leadership, she said, although the form of leadership had recently changed. "Through stories told to every Indian there has always been a Suquamish Indian tribe," Howard declared. "As far back as I can remember we had a Council." She listed a succession of "chiefs," beginning nearly a century before her birth: Kitsap, then See-athl, Jim Seattle, Jacob [Wahalchu], Rogers, her uncle Jack Davis, Sam Wilson, and the current "elected" but "honorary" chief, William Kitsap. She had been at countless tribal dinners, gatherings, and meetings, Howard added, and in her childhood, it seemed that "an awful lot of people" attended.[72]

However, between Howard's childhood and her acceptance of tribal office, many Suquamish appeared to lose interest in tribal affairs, at least those tracked by federal authorities. Outside the Court of Claims, the only recorded collective concern that Suquamish spokespersons brought to officials' attention was fishing rights. In the late 1920s, Superintendent Gross reported that he constantly fielded questions about those rights from Port Madison Indians, probably prompted by non-Indian interference with their fishing.[73] Otherwise, Suquamish political activity was negligible or low-profile, even after federal policy shifted to support for tribal self-government.

In 1935—not long after Charles Alexis and Gladys Fowler entreated US lawmakers to let Indians manage their own affairs—the Bureau of Indian Affairs (BIA) arranged for tribe members to indicate by referendum whether they approved of the new Indian Reorganization Act (IRA). A majority vote in favor would enable them to organize a federally recognized government with powers that Alexis and Fowler said they wanted, such as protecting tribal lands from alienation and advocating for the tribe in the nation's capital. Yet most adults on the Suquamish census did not participate in that milestone event. Of the 110 or 116 individuals who were eligible to vote—BIA records contained both numbers—only 30 cast ballots.[74]

According to the Tulalip Agency superintendent, "It was originally held that the Suquamish had not included themselves under the act because fewer than thirty per cent of the eligible voters participated in the election." However, because more than 30 percent of adult Suquamish reservation residents did vote, because they voted unanimously to accept the IRA, and because BIA personnel deemed it unrealistic to expect the other, "scattered" tribe members to take part in "local suffrage procedures," the bureau ultimately counted Suquamish as a so-called IRA tribe.[75]

Then, three decades passed before the Suquamish established an Indian Reorganization Act government. During that time, any efforts they made as a tribe to address issues of shared concern left few traces for researchers. Participation in tribal affairs dropped between 1935 and 1950. Lawrence Webster mistakenly thought that off-reservation Suquamish stayed away because the Tulalip Agency ruled them ineligible to vote in the IRA referendum. Instead, the agency may have led them to believe they were ineligible to vote on a proposed constitution. In any case, BIA records show that the superintendent in 1940 urged his superiors to authorize a Suquamish vote on a constitution even though off-reservation Suquamish were unlikely to participate. At a recent tribal council meeting, seventeen people had elected new officers and unanimously proposed a constitution that would rest power in a general council of adult tribe members, some of whom would not reside on the reservation. However—apparently expecting that nearly all active council members would be reservation residents—they suggested a quorum of just fourteen people.[76]

Fragmentary records do not reveal why no draft constitution was put to a BIA-sanctioned vote before 1965. Through the late 1930s, 1940s, and early 1950s, people who wished to act collectively as the Suquamish Tribe apparently continued to choose leaders and make decisions much as they had done since joining the Northwestern Federation of American Indians. A 1953 BIA report on tribal organization at Port Madison described it as "semi-active." The council held regular meetings, but interest in tribal affairs was low even though tribe members had long been self-supporting and inclined to assume greater civic responsibilities.[77]

In fact, by the time of Mary Howard's Indian Claims Commission testimony in 1952, she presided over newly heightened tribal activity, spurred mainly by the commission's creation. The ICC offered the Suquamish a second opportunity to seek compensation for wrongs of the US government, and the possibility of sharing in a monetary award evidently made tribal affiliation attractive. By Howard's estimate, fifty to seventy people had applications pending for inclusion on a tribal membership roll that had recently swelled to 270 names. Additionally, pressing a case in the Claims Commission required tribal government decisions about more than membership, starting with the choice of an attorney. Howard described the Suquamish procedure for taking such action in vague terms, albeit emphatically. "We're a purely democratic organization," she said, "in that we vote on any problem that comes up in our reservation. We have a group that decides things."[78]

NEIGHBOR PROBLEMS

Meanwhile, Indians on the reservation faced new problems, some borne in on a shifting nationwide political wind, others on a tide of middle-class prosperity. The wind shifted to the right in the 1940s as Republicans sought to roll back the federal government's recent expansion. Word reached tribes in western Washington that Congress was entertaining proposals to devolve responsibility for Indians to the states, including criminal justice administration. One proposal was a Bill to Authorize and Direct and Conduct an Investigation to Determine Whether the Changed Status of the Indian Requires a Revision of the Laws and Regulations Affecting the American Indian. (The sponsors were apparently less intent on pruning excess verbiage than shrinking federal agencies.) When a House committee held hearings on the bill, the "Suquamish Indian Council" weighed in with a simple written statement: "We are against law enforcement by the State on the reservation."[79]

Grievances against county authorities may account for this opposition to state jurisdiction. In 1948, when the Indian agency deputized Kitsap County sheriff Pete Henderson as a special officer for the reservation, the Suquamish Business Council objected, saying that his practice of entering reservation homes without knocking had caused "considerable resentment." Scorning the sheriff's boast that he had restored law and order on the reservation, the council maintained that he had done nothing to stem a scourge of illegal wood cutting and garbage dumping by whites. The Indians alleged specifically that "during the Christmas Holidays hundreds of trees worth considerable money were removed by people who had no right to do so. . . . [Henderson] saw trees being removed and did nothing about it."[80]

Law officers' interference with Indian use of tidelands particularly angered tribe members. In 1944, when a congressional subcommittee took testimony in western Washington about the circumstances of local Indians, Lawrence Webster appeared for the Suquamish Tribe to complain, "'State officers frequently chase us off the beaches,' although any charges are 'invariably dropped.'"[81]

The lawmen likely acted at the behest of non-Indian owners of waterfront property, whose numbers were rising throughout original Suquamish territory, including the reservation. Middle-class whites' postwar migration to suburbia, abetted by highway and ferry service improvements, had stoked demand for homes in Kitsap County, especially along the salt water. In 1946, a Seattle newspaper announced that developers were breaking ground for a large residential subdivision, dubbed Chief Seattle Park, on the seventy-acre tract that formerly encompassed the

CHIEF SEATTLE PARK
RICH IN HISTORICAL SIGNIFICANCE
. . . AND STEEPED IN INDIAN LORE
With all of the Puget Sound region to choose from, early-day Indians selected the site of Chief Seattle Park as the most desirable location on Puget Sound and established their main village at this location.
It was here that early white settlers found a well-established Indian settlement . . . it was here that friendly Indians led by noble Chief Seattle defended the white men against marauding Chief Kitsap and his bands . . . it was here the Indians carried on trade with the Hudson Bay Company. And it is here one finds today, the shrine to Chief Seattle overlooking the waters once dotted by Indian canoes.
The site of Chief Seattle Park was granted to the Indians through treaties eighty years ago and because of its strategic location in later years, was purchased by the United States and became the Port Madison Military Reservation. Recently this beautifully situated property was made available for private ownership, so now we find this former battle ground of Chief Seattle becoming a peaceful playground for fortunate home owners.
Just as this location was considered the finest on Puget Sound by the Indians, so is it today the finest property available on salt water.
Lots in Chief Seattle Park (both waterfront and "back lots") average 50 ft. x 200 ft. Streets now being cleared, graded and gravelled. Water systems will soon be started. Electricity and phone service will be supplied as construction requires. Beach is sandy and is accessible to all lot owners . . . banks are low and slopes are gradual. There are virgin trees on many of the lots and the soil is good. Ferry from Colman Dock makes 5 trips daily and 7 trips on Sundays to and from Suquamish, a short walk from Chief Seattle Park.
Lots are priced within your ability to pay . . . terms can be arranged. We'd like to show you this property . . . let's make a date!
THE PACIFIC NORTHWEST LAND COMPANY
C. MARC MILLER
ARTHUR D. JOHNSON
FOURTH AND PIKE BUILDING • MAin 1191 • SEATTLE 1, WASHINGTON

In the 1940s, developers selling lots on a large tract of fee land within the Port Madison Reservation thought that romanticized references to the location's Indian history would entice potential buyers, but they ensured that buyers would all be non-Indians. Courtesy of the Suquamish Museum.

Indian village.[82] Some new owners of shoreline land tried to exclude Indians from intertidal terrain where generations of Native families had beached canoes, trapped ducks, and harvested shellfish that were no less important to their well-being than salmon.

In 1950, Washington State offered owners of waterfront lots the opportunity to enhance their value by purchasing adjoining intertidal strips. BIA superintendent Gross responded by asking the state land commissioner to give "full consideration" to the Port Madison Indians' tideland rights. Without specifying the nature of those rights, Gross asserted that the Indians had never relinquished their interest in the tidelands, and many still made a living from resources available there.[83] In 1956, with Indian beach access in continuing jeopardy, Suquamish tribal officers asked the National Congress of American Indians to help. They received in reply only a letter advising them to seek an attorney's advice. A few months later, their exclusion from tidelands was the sole problem that Suquamish representatives brought to the US Indian commissioner's attention when he met separately with a delegation from each western Washington tribe. Councilman Charlie Lawrence, expecting that the state would claim the tidelands because the treaty did not explicitly include them in the reservation, wanted "some provision" ensuring access to clam beds for tribe members who still relied on them for a living.[84]

Suquamish leaders worried that other reservation resources were also at risk for non-Indian takeovers. A rumor circulated in 1956 that whites were challenging the tribe's title to thirty-six waterfront acres adjoining the town of Suquamish. On that tract was the much-used baseball field. Fearing that the site was "on its way to becoming another State Park," the tribal council designated Lawrence Webster and Ed Sigo to seek written BIA confirmation of the tribe's ownership.[85]

If agency officials did provide the desired document or other reassurance, no record of it surfaced in BIA or tribal files. The meagerness of bureau records is not the only indication that the Suquamish received little help in the 1950s from their government guardians. A 1958 Indian Health Service (IHS) publication with data on reservations in the Pacific Northwest, compiled as IHS prepared to transfer its responsibilities to the state, also attests to federal agencies' near neglect of the Suquamish Tribe. The booklet provided informative individual profiles of the larger reservations in Washington State, including Quinault, but relegated the scant data for

Port Madison to a section titled "Other Northwest Washington Reservations" and cautioned that "little factual information" was available for those small tribes. An erroneous identification of the Indians at Port Madison as "Clallam Tribe" and those at the Port Gamble Reservation as "Suquamish Tribe" probably means that the 1956 Indian population figures listed for those reservations—79 and 121 respectively—were also reversed. IHS claimed to know that families at Port Madison were "in particularly poor economic circumstances."[86]

Non-Indians' mounting impacts on the reservation and the potential for Indian residents' thorough marginalization must have been on tribal council members' minds in 1956 when BIA staff presented a sobering proposal: the tribe should request state jurisdiction on the reservation. Three years earlier, bureau personnel had claimed to know that the Suquamish—"competent" and completely accepted into white communities—unanimously favored state jurisdiction over law and order. Indeed, the council ultimately did what the BIA recommended.[87] Unfortunately, the factors that influenced their decision must be inferred from surrounding circumstances, not from their words or the BIA allegation. My search for informative meeting minutes, correspondence, or reports was fruitless.

BIA arguments for state jurisdiction probably emphasized the plan to terminate federal guardianship for tribes and thus end Indians' exemption from state law. As they did at Quinault, agency men would have explained that their funding for law enforcement had already been cut, leaving county sheriffs as the only police available to a growing reservation population. Plainly, the Suquamish tribal council did not have the option of assuming law enforcement responsibility for the reservation. The tribe had no money in the bank, no sources of income, no paid employees. Its only potentially lucrative undertaking was the Indian Claims Commission case in which it alleged that the United States had not paid the full value of aboriginal Suquamish lands and owed the tribe the difference. Those proceedings were moving at a snail's pace. The commission's initial ruling did not come until March 1957, and it merely identified the boundaries of the ceded Suquamish domain. A final cash award, if that were ever to occur, was years away.[88]

Suquamish spokespeople had said on more than one occasion that they wanted their protective relationship with the federal government to continue. Responding to a notice in 1955 that the commissioner of Indian affairs would meet with Indians to explain his agency's new "readjustment program," tribal secretary Patricia Wilcox wrote, "The Port Madison or Suquamish Indian Tribe . . . decided that we do not want a termination for our tribe until our claims are settled. . . . We do for all times and under any circumstances wish to retain our hunting and fishing rights." In a handwritten note, Chairwoman Howard added that her constituents did not want to lose "school aid" or "taxation privileges" and concluded, "We are one of those small reservations that are mentioned who have nothing."[89] However, once it was clear that the tribe would lose even its minimal federal law enforcement services, the Suquamish council approved a formal request for state assumption of criminal and civil jurisdiction on the reservation. As authorized by Public Law 83-280 and recent state legislation, Washington's governor responded in May 1958 with a proclamation of state rule, effective July 14, 1958.[90]

It was not long before a spokesman for the tribe publicly expressed regret about the consent to state jurisdiction. In 1960, the *Kitsap County Herald* quoted Dick DeMain, president of the Suquamish tribal council: "Indians unknowingly may have opened the door to termination when they let the Whiteman's local law and order onto the reservation after a persuasive talk by Indian agency men. Now the sheriff can come on the reservation to enforce local laws. . . . But the Indians feel they have been sold a bill of goods—they let law and order on the reservation to protect members of the tribe, only to find that the whiteman's hunting and fishing laws are enforced too."

The *Herald* detected broader Indian disquiet. "A growing fear of the White-man's congressional scheming" was reportedly "stirring North Kitsap's Indians," who had learned about two bills that would end federal protection for tribes and Indians' right to tax exemption, health care, and trust land management. DeMain and Vice President Chuck Lawrence voiced concern that the legislation "would make older and less well educated members of the tribe prey to the land hungry and glib tongued individuals." The *Herald* added, "The Suquamish are so worried about giving away something unknowingly that they have refused to let the county put a sign on a piece of reservation property."[91]

The story revealed that Suquamish officials were communicating with Indians elsewhere in Washington who feared state jurisdiction in the absence of federal protection for tribal relations and treaty rights. DeMain mentioned a lawsuit "now in the red tape mill" that sought to block the state's expected "back door" nullification of treaty rights. He announced that Port Madison Indians would soon host a clambake where representatives of many tribes could discuss strategies for preventing US renunciation of its obligations to tribes.[92]

Despite their mistrust of state authorities, Indians of the Port Madison Reservation remained under Washington civil and criminal jurisdiction until April 1972, when the secretary of the Interior acknowledged Governor Daniel Evans's order in August 1971 granting the Suquamish Tribe's request for retrocession. Even then, retrocession was incomplete. It applied only to the exercise of powers for which state law required tribal consent. The state could no longer prosecute Indians for criminal offenses on tribal or individual Indian trust land at Port Madison. Still in effect, however, was the complex scheme of state jurisdiction imposed on all reservations in 1963. Washington retained criminal jurisdiction over Indians as well as non-Indians on all other land inside reservation boundaries. In addition, its regulations concerning school attendance, public assistance, mental illness, juvenile delinquency, adoption, dependent children, and motor vehicle operation would apply to Indians anywhere within the reservation, regardless of the land's legal status.[93]

POLITICAL AMBITIONS

By the time that Indians on Port Madison Reservation trust land were relieved of some state criminal law enforcement, the Suquamish tribe had finally adopted a constitution as authorized by the Indian Reorganization Act. Voters approved it on May 23, 1965; one month later the Interior secretary did the same. In Lawrence Webster's memory, that was "when things really got started" for the modern-day tribe. Before then, tribal government was "very lax, really no tribal government."[94]

Webster also said, "The BIA wrote the constitution." The new charter did show the agency's heavy hand in the drafting process. Paternalistic bureau advisers still expected little from the government of such a small tribe. Consequently, the constitution conformed closely to the model that Commissioner Collier's team had recommended to tribes in the 1930s. It conferred only limited powers on the Suquamish governing body, an elected council of seven persons. For example, it authorized the council "to promulgate and enforce ordinances which shall be subject to approval by the Secretary of the Interior governing the conduct of members of the Suquamish Indian Tribe regarding hunting, fishing, and shell fishing." A provision specifying where tribal law might apply was similarly restrictive. It read: "The territory in which the Suquamish Tribe has a beneficial ownership interest includes that portion of the Port Madison Reservation remaining in an unallotted status at the time of the approval of this constitution and bylaws, and any other lands which may be acquired for or by, and held in the name of, the Suquamish Tribe. The jurisdiction of the tribe over such lands, and over the unallotted lands within the original boundaries of the Port Madison Reservation, shall not be inconsistent with applicable Federal and State laws."[95]

According to Martha George, who sat for many midcentury years on the tribal council, the 1965 constitution was the sixth one the Suquamish had proposed since 1922; the previous five did not survive BIA review.[96] The impasse finally broke at a time of motivating national circumstances for tribes, especially the War on Poverty program with its promise of direct federal funding for tribal governments. The number of Suquamish people showing active interest in tribal governance was still small then—the *Seattle Times* reported in 1963 that attendance at membership meetings averaged fifteen people—but those who did participate were alert to the signs of a favorable change in federal policy and in American attitudes about cultural diversity. They publicly proclaimed their determination to maintain tribal relations and preserve Suquamish traditions. They welcomed and possibly promoted a decision of the American Legion post to revive Chief Seattle Days, which in turn energized tribal relations.[97]

The newly installed Suquamish government sought a share of War on Poverty funding, but their ambitions were much more modest than those of the Quinaults. Their lone application to the Office of Economic Opportunity in the 1960s proposed a Head Start program for preschool children.[98] A contemporaneous Suquamish communication to Indian commissioner Robert Bennett also reflected a limited vision of tribal governance. When Bennett met with representatives of Northwest tribes in 1966, no Suquamish were present. Instead, Chairman James Forsman and Secretary Cecilia Hawk sent a short memorandum listing some of their concerns. In contrast to submissions from the Quinaults and several other tribes, which clearly signaled a determination to assume multiple government functions, the Suquamish statement briefly described three specific hardships experienced by tribe members individually: some on the reservation had no electricity, water, or proper sanitation; the state was denying Indians their treaty-guaranteed right to fish and hunt; and county authorities who detained Indian children for alleged violations of law would not release them to parents or honor parents' pleas for information, as they did for white families.

Forsman and Hawk also lamented that the BIA, without explanation, had yet to approve a proposed lease of tribal land that would bring their government much-needed revenue.[99] The land involved was the only reservation tract still in tribal ownership: the water-view acreage that had seemed at risk of becoming a state park in 1956. The apparent holdup at the BIA was not due to doubts there about the wisdom of the lease. On the contrary, the bureau was vigorously advocating that tribes across the West generate revenue with long-term leases of their prime real estate. Thus, national officials did seal a deal for the Suquamish tract by June 1967. The contract gave Philip Malone, a local non-Indian lawyer, a twenty-five-year, renewable hold on the land for a development that would bring many more non-Indian residents to the heart of the reservation. The following spring, Malone made sixty-four house lots available for fifty-year sublets.[100]

That extended assignment of tribal land angered at least one tribe member, who voiced her displeasure to the local press in 1969. The *Kitsap County Herald* identified Vicky Hawk as the leader of an Indian girls' dance group and a "former Suquamish princess" (a teenager who served for a year as a representative of tribal youth at public ceremonies). She had heard that the lease to Malone would preclude Chief Seattle Days activity, and the rumor prompted her to protest "what the white man had taken" from the tribe.[101] Even though Malone's Suquamish Shores development did not ultimately eliminate the space needed for Chief Seattle Days, other tribe members came to share Hawk's objection to the lease. By the 1980s, Suquamish leaders from a new generation, intent on reclaiming the tribe's reserved resources and sovereignty, were seeking ways to challenge the lease or at least to block its renewal.[102]

For Suquamish who envisioned a transition to a take-charge tribal government, circumstances in 1969 might have seemed insurmountably forbidding. The council, which did not maintain an official roll of tribe members, estimated the number of Suquamish Indians at three hundred, fewer than two hundred of them in the Puget Sound region. Indians residing on the reservation were outnumbered approximately five to one by eight hundred non-Indians. The tribal council reportedly convened only "as needed."[103] According to Richard Belmont, who became chairman in 1972, they met at a hall on three acres that the tribe leased to the American Legion for one dollar "so that the community could have a . . . place to meet."[104] Belmont recalled in 2012 that when he took office, his predecessors handed him only a shoebox containing $400 and a few scraps of paper. He and fellow councilors were not trained in running a government, and the tribe had no lawyer on retainer. Following his father's advice, Belmont endeavored to bring issues "that could set a precedent" to meetings of the tribe's membership, but he could get no more than nineteen or twenty people to attend.[105]

Belmont acknowledged these and other challenges early in his second year as chairman, when Suquamish government actions caught the attention of the *Bremerton Sun* newspaper. A resulting article alluded to a Suquamish history of "passivity in the face of encroachment of boundaries" and "gradual relegation to minority status." Having leased out thirty-six of its last forty acres, the tribe was now, "practically speaking . . . , landless." Belmont did not dispute the latter statement; he too suggested that the tribe's very existence was at risk. "The Suquamish have almost completely lost their heritage and their culture," he told the reporter, "because we're in so close to, you might say, civilization. . . . We've got so many white people and non-Indians living on the reservation, and we have no tribal land, no tribal income, so we have to leave the reservation in order to make a living." Belmont himself afforded an example: he was living "away" from the reservation, working as a radiographer at the Puget Sound Naval Shipyard.[106]

But Belmont was bent on "revitalizing" Suquamish government, and he could see a few factors in his favor besides new federal funding for tribal development. One was his acquaintance with Joe DeLaCruz. The two had met at intertribal meetings and become "good buddies." They "had the same views" regarding tribal self-government; they did not want "interference," and they wanted to know what their powers were. In a 2012 interview by telephone, Belmont described DeLaCruz as "kind of an influence" for him.[107]

The youthfulness of Richard Belmont, chairman of the Suquamish tribal council, is evident in this 1975 photograph of him and Willard Bill, chairman of the Duwamish tribal council, flanking Myrtle Loughrey, great-granddaughter of Chief See-athl, whose statue in a Seattle park appears in the background. Courtesy of the Seattle Municipal Archives ID# 30417.

He did not mention other influences, but there is a basis for confident inferences. Thirty-two-year-old Belmont had reached adulthood just as Indians his age—many of them in western Washington—were staging high-profile demonstrations of their desire for US-Indian relations based on the nineteenth-century treaties. Bennie Armstrong, who served on the governing council that Belmont chaired, remembered in 2012 that he was "fresh" in those days from the radicalizing experience of occupying

Alcatraz prison with Indians of All Tribes. The year of that protest occupation, 1969, was also the year that the Quinault and Lummi tribes enforced widely publicized closures of their beaches and reservation waters to nonmembers.[108] Back home, Armstrong was eager to advocate for a radical interpretation of tribal rights.[109]

Belmont and Armstrong decided to seek tribal government office at a time when strong sovereignty rhetoric was increasingly common among Indians, even in historically cautious tribes and intertribal organizations. In 1966, Affiliated Tribes of Northwest Indians approved a cover for their annual meeting program that declared, "The Sovereignty of Indian Rights and Prerogatives shall not be extinguished."[110] Three years later, an Affiliated Tribes resolution recommended that non-Indians on reservations be subject to tribal authority. The next year, the organization pronounced it extremely important that tribes have power over the use of all reservation land. Belmont and Armstrong were exposed to such talk. They surely heard, too, about the Quinault Tribe's zoning of all land within their reservation.[111]

It was in this context, during Belmont's first months in office, that the Suquamish council took several actions reflecting a newly expansive conception of their governing powers. With grant money, the tribe hired its first full-time employee, arranged to purchase land for an office, and launched a search for economic development options. Early in 1972, the council voted to tax on-reservation, Indian-owned cigarette shops, which attracted non-Indian customers with prices that did not include state tax. The tribe's tax enforcement measures embroiled Belmont and BIA police in a federal court lawsuit. Barry Ernstoff, a young lawyer in the Seattle practice established by Alvin Ziontz and Robert Pirtle, took the case on the tribe's behalf and won federal court affirmation of the tribe's power to levy the tax.[112] In July, spurred by a desire to prevent the landfill on county-owned reservation land, the council enacted a zoning ordinance that Pirtle drafted.[113] Six months later the tribe—represented gratis this time by a Seattle Legal Services attorney—sued the US General Services Administration, seeking transfer to the tribe of surplus federal land outside the reservation but within Suquamish ceded territory. The *Seattle Post-Intelligencer* reported that Belmont, "the tribe's quiet young chairman," would "lead a symbolic occupation of the site . . . to dramatize the Indian claim that their need for the excess land should supersede a claim by the

City of Bremerton."[114] Later that year, the tribe announced that it would replace the American Legion as sponsor and host of Chief Seattle Days to ensure that the annual gathering reflected Indian traditions.[115]

About that time, after several years in the air force and Vietnam War, Martha George's grandson Lyle came home to the Suquamish reservation and a surprising encounter. A former teacher, who had always treated him kindly, first tried to avoid him on the street and then said he should not have come back. "He remembered her saying, 'The tribe has brought in radical Indians from the plains. They are trying to take over Suquamish.'" George soon saw the reasons for the non-Indian woman's alarm. He described them in milder terms for a coworker:

> Tribal folks were gaining strength through the movements of the '60s, and there was a feeling of change in the air. The Suquamish people were no longer satisfied with the status quo. Outsiders had been brought in to administer the services that the Federal Government was mandated to provide via the treaties. The tribe was in a growing phase. They were looking to reclaim lost property and to obtain restitution for promises that were made and never honored. Mrs. Donner and the other non-Indian folks, some of whom held leases on premium tribal waterfront property, could sense the change. The Indians were beginning to rock the boat and it threatened their security, so much so that powerful anti-Indian forces were brought to bear on the Suquamish people. And a silent war would be waged that would force our peaceful coexistence to the breaking point.[116]

As Lyle George recognized, national developments had encouraged "tribal folks" to make the changes that were unsettling non-Indians on the Port Madison Reservation, but it was the change makers' sense of Suquamish history that gave their endeavor its purpose and passion. They aimed to reverse historical changes that they regarded as losses for the Suquamish Tribe. Among the lamented losses was thorough, widespread knowledge of the history that tribe members shared as Suquamish Indians, including the full story of their alienated landholdings. Suquamish leaders therefore made it a priority to research and publicize tribal history. In that respect, the resurgent Suquamish and Quinault were alike, but the history of losses was longer, more perplexing, and arguably harder to reverse for the Suquamish than for Quinaults.

7. Encouraging Signs

AT AN INTERTRIBAL MEETING IN 1975, ATTORNEY BARRY ERNSTOFF recounted how he came to be defending the Suquamish Tribe's arrest and prosecution of a non-Indian. Two years earlier, Suquamish officials had told him that they intended to begin policing everyone on their reservation, Indian or not.

> I said, look, I know you guys are anxious to go but it's the wrong tribe and the wrong year and the wrong place to bring that kind of case. They said, thank you very much, they went ahead without asking, and (unintelligible) jurisdiction over all persons. The next thing I knew I got a call and they said, listen, we've had some white guy in jail for five days, and . . . he wants to get out. I said, how did he get there? They said, we arrested him. I said, oh, really. And the case ended up being there. It became a habeas corpus case and a trial which I myself had advised not to get involved in litigation because it was the wrong tribe. . . . I said, let the Camults [Quinaults] handle it. They've got strong tribal government, they have a much larger area of trust land, a lot more Indians than non Indians and the facts were there.[1]

Over time, Ernstoff's view of the Suquamish action changed, as did his memory of learning about Mark Oliphant's arrest. In 2011, replying to an e-mail inquiry, Ernstoff wrote:

> I really do not remember tribes that asserted criminal jurisdiction over non-Indians before Suquamish. . . . While the Suquamish Tribe was not the ideal tribe to do what they did, the facts of the case did work in their favor. The local police almost never responded to calls to the reservation, and without the tribal police, there would have been anarchy. Oliphant himself was an obnoxious drunk kid, who would have caused damage to persons and property had he not been arrested. I don't think that arresting him was a conscious act of assertion of jurisdiction on the part of the tribe. The next morning they called me to tell what they had done and why, but they looked at it as a local police matter and not a cause celebre.[2]

In fact, Ernstoff did know in August 1973 that Quinaults were charging non-Indians who violated tribal law, and he knew they were prepared for challenges to the tribe's authority. Challenges were also possible for tribes elsewhere that claimed jurisdiction over everyone within their boundaries. Thus, the first twentieth-century litigation about Indians' right to prosecute non-Indians might have involved a tribe other than Suquamish. Many people, including Barry Ernstoff, would ultimately wish it had.

Although the Suquamish Tribe's exercise of all-encompassing, on-reservation jurisdiction was not a first for Indians in 1973, it was bold and provocative. For many non-Indians in the area, it was an unwelcome surprise, but when one of them disputed its legality, the tribe argued that inclusive tribal law enforcement was both reasonable in the circumstances and consistent with tenets of American law, particularly the doctrine of tribal sovereignty. After a federal judge accepted that argument in 1974 and sanctioned Suquamish prosecution of a white man, additional tribes asserted comprehensive jurisdiction. Federal government lawyers—reversing a recently announced position—conceded that the power to prosecute non-Indians was a logical corollary of tribal sovereignty, which was an established principle of federal Indian law.

Consequently, efforts to win further acceptance of broad tribal powers took on characteristics of a nationwide political movement even as corresponding fervent opposition developed. Opponents contended that subjection to tribes' jurisdiction deprived non-Indians of liberty and property without due process of law because only tribe members had tribal voting rights. Advocates for tribes countered primarily by reiterating canons of

US law and betting that they could elicit confirming judgments from the federal judiciary.

PRECURSORS

During oral argument in the case of *Mark David Oliphant and Daniel B. Belgarde v. the Suquamish Tribe*, Barry Ernstoff told the US Supreme Court, "Tribes have not done this before." By "this," he meant extending criminal jurisdiction to non-Indians. He did not mean the Suquamish were first or alone in doing that. Indeed, he said earlier that other tribes had already brought "thousands of non-Indians before their courts," and several of those tribes had submitted briefs stating that they began prosecuting non-Indians well before Oliphant's involuntary appearance in the Suquamish court.[3]

Rather than referring vaguely to "thousands" of prosecutions, Ernstoff could have provided examples. For one, he could have related what he knew about Quinault policing of non-Indians. In 1971, the year that Ernstoff finished law school in New York and joined the Ziontz Pirtle firm, Quinaults garnered press coverage in Seattle for interdicting non-Indian activity. Demanding an end to logging practices that choked salmon streams with debris, they blocked timber company access to reservation forests by barricading roads with the tribe's fire truck and other vehicles.[4]

In the *Seattle Times*, Don Hannula attributed Quinaults' audacity and their "on-again-off-again disputes with the white man" to "deep protectionism." They meant to send a "simple" message: "We are going to run our reservation." Characterizing the Indians as "an easy mark" in the past, Hannula announced, "The pint-of-wine-for-a-30-pound-salmon days are long past. Leaders of this 190,000-acre reservation . . . have ruled in recent years with a firm hand and determined management," barring non-Indians from their lake as well as their clam beds and causing "headaches" for real estate developers who hoped to sell reservation fee land.[5]

Quinaults' history of brash actions came to another reporter's mind in early 1973, when armed Indian protesters took over the hamlet of Wounded Knee on the Pine Ridge Sioux reservation. Shortly after that occupation ended, John Bell from the *Seattle Times* solicited Quinault opinions on the protesters' militancy. Tribe leaders told him they had renounced militant confrontation tactics, but their determination to govern their reservation remained firm. Within days, they expected Quinault voters to approve a new law and order code giving the tribal court jurisdiction over non-Indians.

Bell reported these conversations under the headline "Coast Indians Shun 'Warpath' but Assert Tribal Powers." A separate article on Quinaults' "rebirth" featured the photograph of an Indian man seated at a table. The caption read, "There may be a new source of income for the Quinaults after April 1 when Judge Frank Hall begins levying $250 fines—and possible jail terms—against non-Indians caught trespassing on tribal beaches." Hall offered a straightforward explanation of that prospect: "We Quinaults are a law-and-order people." John Bell added that extending tribal jurisdiction was "consistent with the Quinaults' recently developed perception of themselves as a 'nation.'" Tribal president Joe DeLaCruz expressed the idea in one clear sentence: "Self-determination is what the Quinault Nation is all about now, a sovereign nation within Washington state with economic independence and complete control over our lives."[6]

By 1973, Quinaults had been considering full tribal jurisdiction over non-Indians for a few years at least. The tribe's resource development director, Guy McMinds, was well versed on the subject in August 1972 when he complained to a new local attorney about lax federal enforcement of a statute forbidding non-Indians to hunt or fish on Indian lands without permits. Robert Beaty responded by letter that the "conservative course" was to seek help from the US attorney or a federal court. However, he continued, law professor Ralph Johnson "has also called to my attention . . . that at least three Reservations have recently assumed jurisdiction over non-Indians by tribal ordinance." Beaty enclosed one of those ordinances, which specified that entry into the Salt River Reservation in Arizona constituted "implied consent" to tribal law, including penalties for petty criminal offenses and traffic code violations.

Two months later, Beaty sent McMinds the wording for a possible Quinault code section that would likewise authorize tribal jurisdiction over all enumerated offenses "committed by any person within the exterior boundaries" of the reservation. Eleven introductory clauses set out justifications for inclusive jurisdiction, including the US treaty promise of a reservation for "exclusive" Indian use, the numerous "abuses" of tribal lands and resources perpetrated by outsiders, the federal and state statutes that left gaps in law enforcement coverage on reservations, and a lament that the Quinault Tribe was "at the mercy of every non-Indian person who chooses to enter the reservation to do as they want." If Quinaults did adopt the code provision, Beaty advised, they should post signs at reservation entrance points stating clearly that anyone who crossed the boundary would thereby agree to the tribe's jurisdiction.[7]

In December 1972, although the Quinault code did not yet contain language such as Beaty suggested, Joe DeLaCruz told Shelby Scates of the *Seattle Post-Intelligencer*, "We're taking total jurisdiction of the reservation. . . . By treaty we're the sovereign Quinault Nation—and we're prepared to argue the case through the Supreme Court." Scates—alluding to recent activity on non-Indian-owned land within the reservation—elaborated: "Jurisdiction over this strategic corner of the nation has been loose as morals in a massage parlor. . . . From now until a court rules otherwise, says De La Cruz, Quinault Tribal law prevails over the lands of the reservation."[8]

Shortly afterward, Quinaults hired Michael Taylor, handed him drafts of a potential new law and order code, and asked him to produce a version consistent with their desire for self-determination, independence, and control over the reservation. He supplied, and they enacted, a code with three stated purposes: "(1) to protect the lives, property and peace of all persons within the boundaries of the Quinault Reservation . . . , (2) to protect the customs and life-ways of the Indian people living on the Reservation, and (3) to protect the beauty and natural resources of the Reservation." Without purporting to supplant valid federal or state jurisdiction, the new law gave the Quinault court jurisdiction over enumerated crimes on all land or waters within reservation boundaries and over "all persons who enter the exterior boundaries of the Quinault Reservation for whatever purpose, said act of entry being construed as consent to such jurisdiction."[9]

According to Taylor in 2012, the intent of the tribe's move was neither to set an example for other tribes nor to bring on litigation that could confirm the tribe's broad tribal sovereignty. The move was simply a practical response to a local problem of resource protection and control, which Taylor blamed on an inattentive, ineffective federal government that shirked its responsibilities to the tribe. "It seemed that you weren't going to get what the tribes needed by going to the BIA," he recalled. "After dealing with them for a couple years, you realized they were just nowhere. . . . There were two hundred people in that [Western Washington] office . . . , and they didn't do anything except say no."[10]

In a 1973 oral history interview, DeLaCruz spoke with pride of having a tribal code that covered "hunting and fishing trespasses, [cedar] shake theft, sanitation, our building code" and more, even when non-Indians were involved. Then he revealed:

> Our jail right now has two white people in there for two months for shake theft. Their truck is sitting down there full of shakes. If they don't recover it in thirty days, it will forfeit to the tribe. Last weekend the police captain and fish committee members arrested eight people on the lake for fishing without tribal licenses. We'll start arresting people on the beaches too. We had two property owners who were building homes into tribal court for violating the zoning ordinance. Both have come around 100 percent, recognized our court and that they have to comply with our ordinance. One was Quinault. The other one is tearing his house down.[11]

That year, DeLaCruz also expressed satisfaction with Quinault regulation and prosecutions of non-Indians when he testified in *United States v. Washington*, the suit to clarify treaty-guaranteed fishing rights. On his reservation, he said, tribal police and a court with two full-time judges were enforcing fish conservation regulations "whether a violator is Indian or non-Indian." "I think in fact, they had eighteen [non-Indian] violators in there, and our court has tried those cases. . . . I think . . . they have brought non-Indians into court for forestry trespass, for forestry products."[12]

While DeLaCruz all but dared someone to contest Quinault jurisdiction in the courts, Taylor preferred to pursue the tribe's goals without litigation. "I was never one to think about big jurisdictional fights," he said in 2012. "I was always trying to bite off little pieces" of the change needed to secure the control Quinaults wanted in their homeland.[13] Initial reception of the tribe's new law and order code was encouraging in that respect; for a while, it seemed that enforcement of the code might be a relatively uncontroversial or defensible "little piece" of Quinault strategy. Taylor, like DeLaCruz, got word that non-Indians were generally submitting to tribal court jurisdiction. He recalled with a slight smile, "We arrested the owner of the Harvard Exit [a theater in Seattle] for smoking dope on the Quinault Reservation. He pled, paid the fine, and split." Taylor's colleague, Dan Raas, said in 2012, "What I remember is a series of trespass and timber thefts. And one or two DWIs and traffic violations. . . . The timber rats were more than happy to pay a fine to the tribe because that meant they would not get prosecuted in state court, and the state court knew them all very well. And similarly, the traffic violators were generally pleased to do that 'cause nothing ever got reported. Didn't go on their driving record."[14]

Non-Indian drivers responded likewise to citations on the Gila River reservation in Arizona. There, sometime in 1971, Judge William Rhodes instructed the Indian police to summon non-Indian offenders into the tribal court. During Rhodes's preceding years on the bench, the population of nearby Phoenix boomed, traffic on the interstate highway through the reservation multiplied rapidly, non-Indians in growing numbers came to work or live on the reservation, trespasses and vandalism on Indian land became common, and county officers declined to assist with law enforcement. In 1972, Rhodes discussed these problems with legal services attorney Rod Lewis, who approved of the judge's solution. After all, Lewis said in 2012, 98 percent of reservation land was Indian-owned. "We just figured there was no law saying we could not . . . prosecute non-Indians. We would have night court, and the non-Indians cited would all . . . just come in, pay their fines, and go. It seems they never thought that the tribe didn't have jurisdiction; they just saw the tribe as another government or jurisdiction. And the tribe didn't report their fines to the state; it didn't go on their records."[15]

On the other side of Phoenix, where suburbs were expanding rapidly toward the Salt River Reservation, the tribe experienced problems like those at Gila River and responded in 1972 by extending its criminal code to non-Indians. That year, too, the Rosebud Sioux government adopted a code applicable to every "person" on their reservation in South Dakota.[16]

When the Suquamish court jailed Mark Oliphant in August 1973, how many other tribes were policing non-Indians? Apparently, no government or other entity sought that information until the American Indian Lawyer Training Program conducted a survey in 1976. An NCAI amicus curiae brief summarized their data for the Supreme Court. Without providing onset dates, it reported that thirty-three tribes were actively exercising "some measure" of jurisdiction over non-Indians, civil *or* criminal. Twelve more had ordinances authorizing such jurisdiction.[17]

Ultimately, it was not a visitor from Seattle, nabbed by Quinault police for digging clams or smoking pot, who first obtained a US court ruling on a tribe's right to prosecute a non-Indian; nor was it a white Arizonan cited into Gila River tribal court for hurtling through the fragile desert landscape on an ATV. Instead, the precedent-setting contest of tribal jurisdiction arose on the Suquamish reservation, where the protesting non-Indians were not casual visitors or strangers to the community. One was a resident and the son of a reservation business owner, the other a lawyer with a long-term lease on prime tribal land.[18]

In 1975, Barry Ernstoff said he told the Suquamish their reservation was "the wrong place" to provoke a dispute about Indian tribes' power over non-Indian law-breakers; the Quinaults' circumstances were more likely to convince a federal judge that tribal prosecutions were necessary and fair. He did not say whether he restated his qualms when informed of Oliphant's arrest and incarceration. Advice from Ernstoff may have prompted a Suquamish judge to order Oliphant's release and suspend his case five days after the arrest, but the tribe did not drop charges, so Oliphant's lawyer pressed his request for a writ of habeas corpus. Ernstoff therefore plunged into preparations for a hearing on the claim that the arrest and prosecution were illegal.[19]

A habeas corpus petition names the official who has the petitioner in custody—in this case, the Bremerton police chief. Because the Suquamish Tribe was not initially a party to the proceeding, the tribe could offer arguments only as a friend of the court (amicus curiae), and for that it needed the judge's permission. In his successful written request, Ernstoff signaled that the case could require a ruling on a major Indian law issue: "the sovereignty of the Suquamish Indian Tribe and the ability of the tribal government to deal effectively with activities on the Reservation." Ernstoff's subsequent memorandum on the merits of Oliphant's complaint declared, "A prerequisite to a proper determination of this case is a preliminary consideration of the basic nature of the Suquamish Indian Tribe as a political entity," adding that "the original sovereign status of Indian tribes" was "explicated at length" in *Federal Indian Law*, 1958.

The Suquamish memorandum also described "practical matters" that made tribal police and court jurisdiction necessary on the reservation. In the case at hand, the county sheriff and Bureau of Indian Affairs had both declined the tribe's appeal for help with round-the-clock patrols during Chief Seattle Days, when "thousands of people" would "congregate" on tribal land. Consequently, only tribal cops were on duty the night of Oliphant's fistfight.[20] Still, Judge Morell Sharp was on notice that the parties expected a precedent-setting decision on the big question of Indian tribes' power over non-Indians.

With that likelihood in view, the Quinaults also took an active interest in the habeas corpus proceeding. They too requested amicus curiae status, emphasizing what they had at stake in the case. Following a short account of conditions that made "law enforcement on the Quinault Reservation even more difficult than on the Port Madison Reservation," the Quinault motion stated, "Any decision by this Court will affect the legal authority and jurisdiction of the Quinault Tribe to continue to enforce the Tribal Law against non-Indian persons who commit misdemeanor crimes against Indian persons or property or against the Tribal community, lands or property. Because no other law enforcement agency at this time patrols the Quinault Reservation and no other court enforces the Tribal Law, this court's decision will have a major impact."[21]

Judge Sharp received additional briefs bearing similar messages. On behalf of the National Tribal Chairman's Association, the Pima-Maricopa Tribes of the Gila River reservation, and the Nisqually and Squaxin Island tribes in Washington, a Native American Rights Fund attorney contended, "Some measure of responsible police presence is essential to maintain law and order to enhance life in Indian communities," many virtually without state and federal enforcement. Not only could the tribes supply the necessary services, but "their power to do so" was "inherent to their sovereignty." The federal government sided with the Suquamish as well. After certifying that prosecution of non-Indians was within the powers contemplated by the tribe's constitution and code, two US attorneys indicated that the authority of all tribes was at issue. "Notwithstanding a 1970 Solicitor's Opinion to the contrary," they volunteered, "we believe that within their territorial jurisdiction, tribal courts may exercise jurisdiction over the person of non-Indians with respect to their criminal offenses to the extent that such powers of self-government have not been expressly extinguished or limited by federal law."[22]

Affiliated Tribes of Northwest Indians (ATNI) encouraged a corporeal show of support for the Suquamish. Implying that the tribe's adversary represented all opponents of Indian tribal power, an ATNI resolution urged members to have observers at the hearing because the case would have "significant and far reaching effect on the jurisdiction and sovereignty rights of all Indian tribes in the country and on the future of law enforcement and order on all reservations."[23]

For his part, Oliphant's attorney was sure the case mattered to any non-Indian who might be stopped by tribal police. From the outset, Philip Malone intended to challenge his client's arrest and incarceration on more than standard criminal procedure grounds. After replacing the Seattle lawyer who filed the petition for him, Malone named the Suquamish Tribe and its chairman, manager, judges, and arresting officers as additional respondents.[24] His memorandum of authorities disparaged the notion of enduring Indian sovereignty, especially the Suquamish Tribe's sovereignty. Several pages, apparently meant to suggest why non-Indians would reasonably believe themselves exempt from tribal rule, described circumstances that had worried Barry Ernstoff—the large number of non-Indians living on the Port Madison Reservation, the small number of Indian residents, and the Indians' alleged "assimilation . . . sometime long ago" into the world of schools, churches, and "commercial facilities" introduced by non-Indians. The remainder of Malone's fifty-three-page brief was a meandering, often abstruse discourse on the history of federal power and vacillating Indian policy, purporting to show that federal lawmakers had never intended Indian self-government to include jurisdiction over non-Indians.[25]

Judge Sharp gave the parties three months to prepare briefs, but at the hearing on January 25, 1974, Oliphant's lawyer did little to clarify his analysis of the tribal power issue. The transcript shows the judge struggling to understand Malone's statements that the tribe was a "dependent government of the United States" and that "a tribe can have independent self-government but not independent self-sovereignty or power." By the time the last lawyer had spoken, Sharp was persuaded that the tribe and allied amici curiae had a sounder interpretation of existing law than Malone. He denied the writ, saying, "I find that the tribal court is a duly constituted court and has jurisdiction over the subject matter and person of the petitioner, and, in my opinion, accorded him due process."[26]

Almost three years passed before the Ninth Circuit Court of Appeals ruled on Malone's request for reversal of Sharp's decision. In that interval, Suquamish police arrested Daniel Belgarde, another non-Indian. Malone again sought a habeas corpus writ, and the lower court again turned him down, unswayed by his additional argument that the tribe's jurisdiction did not extend to the state highway through the reservation, where Belgarde's arrest occurred.[27] During the same period, two panels of Ninth Circuit judges decided questions of tribal jurisdiction over unlawful non-Indian activity on other reservations. The first panel, referring in strong terms to Indian tribes' "original sovereign powers," upheld Papago police detention and ejection of a non-Indian who had smuggled marijuana contrary to tribal law. The second set of judges concluded that an officer for the Quechan Tribe, exercising inherent tribal power, could rightfully confiscate weapons from non-Indians who hunted on the reservation in violation of tribal law.[28]

Those rulings made sense to two of the three jurists who considered Oliphant's appeal. They took note of recent Supreme Court affirmations that pre-Columbian tribes had full sovereignty and thereafter retained all "powers of autonomous states" not explicitly terminated by US law. The judges found no record of federal action curtailing the Suquamish Tribe's inherent power to punish violators of tribal law. Actions cited by Oliphant's lawyer did not have that effect. On the contrary, prevailing federal policy encouraged tribes to exercise authority over reservation lands. The only "practical consideration" of import, the judges added, was the futility of the Suquamish request for county and BIA police backup, which illustrated the need for tribal jurisdiction. The court therefore sustained Judge Sharp's order denying a habeas corpus writ.[29]

FEDERAL ASSENT

In Indian country, the Ninth Circuit ruling for the Suquamish served less as permission for tribes to expand the jurisdiction they exercised than as confirmation of federal acquiescence to moves that tribes had already made. Since the Suquamish prevailed in the lower court, there had been more signs of federal amenability—reasons to believe that other courts, other branches of the US government, and ultimately most non-Indians would concede the legal validity and wisdom of the arguments for inclusive tribal jurisdiction.

From 1972 to 1976 the Supreme Court seemed favorably disposed to Indian empowerment. Of its fifteen decisions in cases affecting Indians, twelve favored the Indians, including several that affirmed tribes' rights to natural resources and powers to regulate or tax nonmembers. Four of those rulings directly benefited tribes in Washington State.[30] Also in the Pacific Northwest, the outcome of a suit in federal district court fueled optimism about US receptivity to stronger tribal governments. Three weeks after Judge Sharp rejected Oliphant's plea, Judge George H. Boldt rendered an emboldening decision regarding Indian fishing rights.

To the joy of Indians and the consternation of many non-Indians, tribes won a sweeping victory in *United States v. Washington*. The aim of the litigation, as the court stated it, was to settle for good "the divisive problems of treaty right fishing" that had "plagued" the region for decades. After lengthy pretrial preparation and a trial featuring numerous witnesses for tribes and state agencies, Judge Boldt—a Republican appointee newly notorious for harshly penalizing antiwar activists—fully endorsed an interpretation of the treaty language advocated by most plaintiff tribes. He not only affirmed the continuing legal force of the clause that "secured" the Indians' right to fish off reservation "in common with" state citizens; he construed the words "in common" as an Indian agreement to share the fisheries with non-Indians fifty-fifty. Tribes were therefore entitled to half the harvestable fish, and the state had to end management practices that kept most migrating salmon from reaching Indian nets.[31]

A crucial element of Boldt's ruling was his determination that the plaintiff tribes were political successors to self-governing Indian treaty signatories. As such, they could regulate their members' fishing, even outside the reservations, where Indians were usually subject to state law. This conclusion rested on an understanding that Indian tribes' original status as autonomous polities was an enduring principle of US law and policy. As the judge put it, "Ever since the first Indian treaties were confirmed by the Senate, Congress has recognized that those treaties established self-government by treaty tribes, excepting only as limited in the treaties, judicial interpretation thereof or by Congress." A survey of legislative history showed Boldt that "there was a period during which Congress enacted legislation limiting the exercise of tribal autonomy in various particulars," but the tribes' right survived that swing in policy, and federal legislation "in the last decade" had "definitely been in the contrary direction." New laws and measures, Boldt concluded, made it plain that Congress intended "to increase rather than diminish or limit the exercise of tribal self-government."[32]

Mike Taylor credited Quinault testimony for showing Boldt that Indian self-government was more than an abstract principle in 1974; it was a practical reality and a workable basis for sound management of fish resources. Taylor had such testimony in mind when he persuaded the Quinaults to rejoin the lawsuit shortly after taking their private counsel's advice to drop out. "Quinault was going to have something that no other tribe had," Taylor said in 2012—an impressive presentation "to show the court that Indian people themselves could organize a scientific, technical kind of regime . . . that would preserve and enhance the fishery and raise fish and plant fish." Unlike many other tribes, Quinaults also had long had "a kind of . . . Anglicized fisheries regime on the reservation." For decades, they had adopted annual fishing regulations, published them, and enforced them with police and a tribal court. Taylor asked Horton Capoeman, a tribe member who had "lived this," to be a witness. "To talk about *Mason versus Sams* and the history and present some of the regulations and talk about being a fisheries judge. And Horton and Judge Boldt just hit it off right away. . . . They just talked about how this all worked and happened and how the tribe dealt with its responsibilities in fisheries. And when you read the opinion, you can see what Boldt did: he liked us, and he made Quinault a self-regulating tribe. And he said other tribes could get this status if they got what Quinault had."[33]

As Taylor's reminiscence indicates, Judge Boldt's ruling did not by itself free tribes from state regulation of off-reservation fishing. Instead, it made self-regulation contingent on court certification that a tribe could manage fisheries and enforce its own rules. The principal requirements were a "competent" organized government, trained enforcement personnel, access to experts in fisheries science, and maintenance of a complete tribal membership roll. The decision in *U.S. v. Washington* thus gave tribes a new, potent incentive to develop their governmental infrastructure, including law enforcement capability and courts. Consequently, the ink on the court opinion had barely dried before representatives of the tribes arrived in Washington, DC, seeking funding for the tribal government functions that would qualify them to enjoy their triumph in court.[34]

In the nation's capital by then, advocates of greater leeway for tribal governance were increasingly able to find well-disposed listeners in key government positions. Some legislators and administrators were not only familiar with the concept of inherent tribal sovereignty; they were open to relatively generous interpretations. A few proved willing to question a common assumption that the tribes' power to punish criminals could never extend to non-Indians. The district court decision in Oliphant's case partly accounted for that receptiveness, but so did testimony about jurisdictional hodgepodge and law enforcement vacuums on many reservations, especially since that testimony came at a time of political pressure on governments to crack down on crime.

By the 1970s, tribal programs were beneficiaries of new federal aid for local law enforcement. In the Indian Civil Rights Act of 1968 (ICRA), Congress had acknowledged tribal police and courts as ongoing necessities. A provision of the act allowing tribes to opt out of state jurisdiction—a response to enforcement problems under Public Law 280—anticipated more tribal responsibility for policing reservations, as did a requirement that tribal governments honor a bill of rights modeled on the US Constitution. Accordingly, efforts increased to channel federal law enforcement assistance in tribes' direction.[35] In 1968, for instance, the BIA sought legislation making tribes eligible for direct grants proposed in the Crime Control and Safe Streets bill. An assistant commissioner explained to a potential Senate sponsor that tribes were already spending $3.7 million of their own money for law and order services, supplementing the $3 million BIA contribution, but crime rates on reservations were still climbing.[36]

When lawmakers and government planners gave Indians opportunities to describe their law enforcement challenges, the subject of troublesome non-Indians usually came up. That happened in 1971, when planning directors in four southwestern states, expecting to receive federal funds for law enforcement, saw a need to take conditions on reservations into account. They commissioned a study team that included former commissioner of Indian affairs Robert Bennett, two NARF lawyers, a Navajo "police specialist," a law professor, and Quinault "corrections specialist" Wilfred Petit. The resulting report devoted considerable attention to "obvious" jurisdictional problems. It relayed a complaint from tribal police, "especially those near large cities," about "the lack of power over non-Indians who create nuisances on the reservation but who do not commit crimes serious enough to precipitate enforcement by federal or state authorities." The "jurisdictional morass" prompted "frequent informal expression of desires that tribes be given full territorial jurisdiction, at least over minor offenses." Such a measure would improve matters, the consultants agreed, but they doubted that "any such avenue to reduction of the jurisdictional confusion" would open soon. Most tribal police, courts, and correctional systems did not yet have the capacity to assume such responsibility.[37]

Inclusive territorial jurisdiction for tribes seemed unlikely also because key federal personnel thought it was contrary to federal law. In 1970, an Interior Department lawyer issued a formal opinion that "Indian tribes do not possess criminal jurisdiction over non-Indians; such jurisdiction lies in either the state or Federal government."[38] Three years later, the Nixon administration dismissed as unthinkable a demand from Indian rights activists for a congressional mandate "that all persons within the originally established boundaries of an Indian Reservation are subject to the laws of the sovereign Indian Nation." In addition to ruling out tribal criminal jurisdiction over non-Indians, the White House memorandum declared that civil jurisdiction required non-Indians' consent. It maintained that doing what the activists urged would deprive non-Indians of their citizenship rights and prompt them to insist on participating in tribal governments.[39]

And yet, as Thomas Biolsi discovered when researching jurisdiction controversies in South Dakota, by 1975 the Indian commissioner "was comfortable enough with the clarity of the existing case law to advise the . . . solicitor's office that 'Indian tribes are sovereign governments possessed of the same attributes of any government,' including criminal jurisdiction over non-Indians." Sometime before February that year, the Interior Department withdrew the contrary 1970 solicitor's opinion. According to Robert Pirtle, that about-face was the result of Barry Ernstoff's "attacks" on the first opinion's reasoning—his demonstration that no treaty or statute deprived tribes of the jurisdiction they claimed.[40] Whether Ernstoff deserved that credit does not matter here;

reconsideration of the 1970 opinion was ensured in early 1974 when Judge Sharp bought the tribe's arguments in *Oliphant v. Schlie*. The subsequent appellate court approval probably served to ease any lingering doubts in the solicitor's office that tribes could indeed govern non-Indians.

Shortly after that Ninth Circuit decision, Commissioner of Indian Affairs Morris Thompson resolved that his agency would actively support expanded jurisdiction for tribes. He wrote to a deputy solicitor, "The principle of inherent tribal sovereignty appears to give tribes the power to punish offenses committed by non-Indian intruders against their own people." Because no federal laws usurped that authority, "it is our position that the legal principles formulated in the *Oliphant* decision are correct. The right of self-government means more than simple freedom from the laws of others. It means the power to govern over those matters which affect the interests of the tribes regardless of the race or political affiliation of the party involved."[41]

More than court orders spurred and reflected the new federal support for broad tribal jurisdiction. So did the movement of Indians into strategic government positions, largely because of a federal commitment in the 1960s to promote employment and educational opportunities for long-deprived populations. After Robert Bennett's appointment in 1966, every commissioner of Indian affairs was Indian. Upper ranks of the BIA were increasingly filled by Indians as the agency applied the Indian preference provision of the Wheeler-Howard Act to promotions as well as entry-level hires.[42] Granted, Indian identity did not guarantee that an official would advocate expanded tribal power, as Bennett's tenure illustrated.[43] However, by the early 1970s, Indians who subscribed to expansive conceptions of tribal sovereignty were joining agencies and congressional offices with responsibility for Indian affairs.[44]

For instance, the Interior Department solicitor hired Alan Parker in 1972, right out of law school at UCLA, where he studied the history and principles of federal Indian law under instructors who were active advocates for tribes. Parker's principal assignment—research for an updated *Handbook of Federal Indian Law*—would ultimately result in a volume characterizing tribal powers more generously than the 1958 version. Later in the 1970s, Parker served as chief counsel for the Senate Indian Affairs

Committee and helped to secure passage of the Indian Child Welfare Act, which granted tribal governments extraordinary jurisdiction outside the reservations.[45]

Forrest Gerard, although not a lawyer, played a role as a congressional staffer in the shift to a supportive federal policy. Born in 1925 on the Blackfeet Reservation, Gerard began working for agencies and lawmakers concerned with Indian affairs at age thirty-two. In 1972, Senator Henry Jackson, chairing the Interior and Insular Affairs Committee, tapped him to facilitate the transition to a policy of tribal self-determination, which was gradually winning favor as Indian criticism and disastrous consequences discredited termination. In 1977, Gerard accepted appointment as assistant secretary for Indian affairs, a new, higher-status position for the BIA commissioner. When he died, obituaries in Indian publications gave him substantial credit for a string of legislation that enabled tribal governments to flourish, starting with the Indian Self-Determination and Education Act of 1975.[46]

Tribes also had a sympathetic ear in Congress from James Abourezk, a Lebanese-American raised on the Rosebud Sioux Reservation. Abourezk represented South Dakota in the House of Representatives from 1971 to 1973 and then in the Senate until 1979. After leaving Congress, he published a memoir in which he confessed, "Until I left the reservation, I never understood the damage my own racism was doing as I joined the [white] community in its uniformly bad treatment of Indians." Their "principal enemies today," he declared, "are the federal government, which mistreats them and mismanages their resources, and anti-Indian whites who still covet the little land remaining to them."[47]

Early in 1975, as chair of the Senate Subcommittee on Indian Affairs, Abourezk opened a hearing on tribal court reform by assuring "the Indian people" that the proceedings were "not intended as a covert or overt assault on the inherent sovereignty of Indian tribes." After listening without objection as Indian witnesses argued for jurisdiction over non-Indians, Abourezk remarked that "the jurisdiction question" had stirred fear and excitement in South Dakota. His statement implied that federal acceptance of broad tribal jurisdiction was not out of the question but would be contingent on provisions to ensure that Indian courts met non-Indian standards of professionalism and fairness.[48]

PUSHING THE ENVELOPE

Policy makers' willingness to contemplate greater Indian government power evolved in dialectical relationship to the advocacy of tribal leaders and attorneys. Unfavorable legal opinions from federal officials did not silence believers in ample tribal sovereignty. The more those believers stated their case publicly, the more familiar their arguments became to people concerned with Indian affairs, and familiarity lent an aura of authority. In certain political circles by the mid-1970s, the idea that tribal sovereignty was originally unrestricted and never entirely extinguished had attained commonsense status. Affirmative court rulings provided even more reason to press for definitive US acknowledgment of the tribes' right to govern comprehensively on reservations.

Many Indians, their lawyers, and some legal scholars had agreed for years that power to regulate non-Indians was a necessary implication of tribal sovereignty. Resolutions by the Affiliated Tribes of Northwest Indians in 1970 and the National Congress of American Indians in 1973 appealed on that ground for federal legislation prohibiting state control of land use within reservation boundaries.[49] An article in the inaugural issue of the *American Indian Law Review* declared, "A tribe can be sovereign if, and only if, it has the right to establish rules for the conduct of people within its boundaries, and to punish those who violate the rules, regardless of who they are." Many treaties and some US court decisions specified that tribes could exclude non-Indians from reserved territory. Why would they not have a right to govern the non-Indians they admitted?[50]

Word that some tribes had successfully prosecuted non-Indians spread throughout Indian country. During a 1974 NCAI conference workshop on tribal government, Alan Parker cited the Gila River Community experience as a lesson for other tribes. At stake in this "very simple . . . exercise of power" was nothing less than Indian self-government, he said. From the ensuing discussion, workshop participants could have concluded that the odds of success were high. Tribal judge William Rhodes said, "We've had doctors, lawyers, policemen" in court as defendants, and "I can't think of any cases where our authority has been contested." A man from a Northwest reservation, unnamed in the minutes, credited Gila River's example for his tribe's recent assumption of jurisdiction over non-Indians. Mike

Taylor, perhaps fearing that poorly prepared tribes would hop on the bandwagon, said non-Indians were less compliant at Quinault. "Just in the year and a half that I've been there, we've had a total five habeas corpus writs filed against us in the state and federal courts on the issue of jurisdiction over non-Indians and we've had quite a few more threatened." But Taylor added, "None of the writs have been successful."[51]

At a special NCAI conference on jurisdiction the next year, several delegates advertised their tribes' intent to govern non-Indians even before US lawmakers or judges gave their consent. "Mr. Edmo" from the Fort Hall Reservation objected to language in the proposed Indian Justice Improvement Act that seemed to say, "Mr. White Man, we have got to ask you please, won't you let us do this on our reservation?" "*We* have already done it," he snapped. The Nevada Indian Commission director reasoned that making non-Indians submit to tribal law on reservations was no different from his duty to obey the law in Denver. "This is what the tribes back there are saying, that they want complete jurisdiction over everything that goes on except for the major crimes." Quechan delegate Elmer Savilla, cautioning that tribes could be fully sovereign only if economically independent, recommended that they claim as much power as the states but no more. Warier comments from lawyers riled Joe DeLaCruz, who interjected, "I hear attorneys up here saying the tribes can't do things. I think that we have that right, and for going on two years now we did have that right in Quinault or someone would have had us in court by now. We took on some of the biggest real estate companies on the Pacific Coast with our zoning and they didn't take us to court."[52]

Not long afterward, the Quinaults' bet on their right to regulate nonmembers yielded a significant payoff. In September 1975, a US court declined to block the tribe's prosecution of Harry Long, a non-Indian, for trespass on the beach fronting his reservation property. Judge William Goodwin chastised Long for filing suit before answering a Quinault court summons and challenging the tribe's jurisdiction there. He dismissed Long's complaint in words likely to bolster tribal sovereignty advocates' faith in their arguments.

> The long-standing federal policy is to guard and encourage the authority of Indian governments over their reservations. . . . It recognizes the residual sovereignty of the Indian nations and conserves the resources of

> the federal courts. So, when no special circumstances appear, the federal court will require the exhaustion of tribal remedies before itself considering a matter. . . . Despite Mr. Long's pessimism, the Court does not find . . . that he lacks a meaningful remedy in the tribal court. . . . Long's status as a non-Indian is immaterial to this decision. By his voluntary presence on the reservation, and as a landholder there, he subjected himself to the authority of the reservation government to regulate reservation matters.[53]

As news of such encouraging developments circulated, additional tribes moved toward comprehensive regulation of "reservation matters." In mid-1975, Makahs scheduled a vote on a constitutional provision for jurisdiction over everyone in tribal territory, defined as all lands within reservation boundaries.[54] Later that year, the Utes promulgated a code providing for tribal government jurisdiction over non-Indians and towns within the 1.3-million-acre Uintah and Ouray Reservation. Chairman Lester Chapoose declared, "We will no longer stand idly by and watch our resources ruined, our people humiliated and our competency questioned. . . . If state officials can prosecute Indians who violate state laws off the reservation, the Utes can prosecute non-Indians who violate Ute law on or affecting the reservation."[55] Shortly thereafter, an AP correspondent reported "a potentially explosive situation . . . brewing in Montana" over the Blackfeet Tribe's "declared intention to arrest and prosecute non-Indians for violations committed on its reservation."[56] By November, outgoing NCAI president Mel Tonasket was celebrating the tribes' headway toward effective self-government. In his valedictory conference address, he exulted, "Our confidence has grown through the realization of the strength of our sovereign powers, and our growing awareness of the value of our natural resources." Tonasket exhorted his audience to believe "in our status as governments."[57]

In the meantime, armed with reasoning they considered unassailable, tribe leaders who believed that their sovereign powers extended to non-Indians seized opportunities to negotiate the issue with federal lawmakers. They made their case both by invoking legal doctrine and by telling stories about problems stemming from non-Indians' assumed immunity to tribal rule. Representatives of Pacific Northwest tribes took prominent part in this campaign.

As a Colville Confederated Tribes council member elected in 1970, NCAI president from 1973 to 1976, and American Indian Policy Review Commission member in 1977, Mel Tonasket was an ally of leaders in other tribes who aspired to maximize their power on their reservations. Photograph by Theodore Hetzel, courtesy of the Center of Southwest Studies at Fort Lewis College.

Even before Judge Sharp allowed the Suquamish Tribe to prosecute a non-Indian, representatives of several tribes signaled to Congress that they would not be guided by federal lawyers' more restrictive reading of legal history. One vocal challenger was Seattle attorney Robert Pirtle. In June 1973, Pirtle appeared at a Senate hearing on two massive bills to revise the federal criminal code. He was not there on behalf of the Suquamish, who had yet to enact their code and arrest Mark Oliphant. Pirtle had come because three other clients—the Makah, Lummi, and Colville tribes—believed they had a right to govern non-Indians and hoped to correct the senators' apparent ignorance of that right.

In the bills under consideration were references to Indian country where states had "exclusive" jurisdiction. Pirtle complained that the insertion of "exclusive" reflected an erroneous assumption about the Public Law 280 provision for state jurisdiction over Indians. In written testimony, he urged lawmakers to affirm that PL 280's authorization of state jurisdiction on reservations did not oust tribal jurisdiction. Instead, he contended, "the jurisdiction which the tribes have always retained as a matter of internal sovereignty and which is now concurrent with either federal or state jurisdiction, must be recognized." Committee members heard the same arguments from a lawyer speaking for eight other tribes and the NCAI.[58]

More provocatively, Pirtle warned senators not to codify "another major erroneous assumption that Indian tribes have no jurisdiction over non-Indians as to either felonies or misdemeanors." The prospect of full tribal jurisdiction on reservations might strike some people as a "novelty" and stir fears of unjust treatment by tribes, he conceded. But surely the United States would fulfill its duty under the Major Crimes Act, thus relieving tribes of the need to prosecute felons. For their part, tribal judges—thoroughly trained and aware of the Indian Civil Rights Act requirement to ensure due process of law—could handle misdemeanor cases. "Our tribal judges," Pirtle insisted, "are entitled to as much confidence as is accorded to local magistrates in any town or village through which one happens to be passing in these United States."

A senator proposed that tribes, by "non-exercise" of jurisdiction, might have lost the power Pirtle claimed for them. Pirtle demurred, implying that years of oppression had not dulled his clients' sense of their original sovereignty. "Their rights they speak about very clearly," he said, "and they sometimes draw me up short . . . if I suddenly begin thinking like a white man." For them, having jurisdiction to protect their lands, lakes, natural resources, and property was "extremely important." Therefore, Pirtle announced, "the tribes that we represent are each enacting new criminal law codes which specifically provide for jurisdiction over non-Indians on the reservation" and "that entry on the reservation constitutes a consent to the jurisdiction of the Indian tribes, just as the States have similar provisions in their statutes." Pirtle concluded, perhaps with more hope than confidence that he was stating a fact, "We believe we have the full support of the United States government in our efforts toward achieving a real self-determination including revitalization of our Law and Order Codes and our court systems." It would be "tragic if this Congress in a worthy effort to revise the criminal code inadvertently destroyed an inherent tribal right which has fallen into disuse and is now being exercised by tribes in their effort to govern their reservations properly."[59]

Makah chairman Joseph Lawrence contributed a written statement of his tribe's motivation for taking the steps Pirtle described: state law enforcement was virtually nonexistent on the isolated reservation, and non-Indians consequently wreaked havoc on natural resources there. Colville chairman Mel Tonasket declared forcefully that his people would not wait for congressional permission to govern non-Indians. They had sent him specifically "to impress upon this committee the importance of Indian sovereignty, sovereignty of our tribe to have jurisdiction within the boundaries of our reservation. That means jurisdiction over non-Indians." Sensing some fear that "non-Indians would not get . . . fair treatment" from tribes, Tonasket said, "I think that they are afraid that maybe we will act the way they act. . . . But our new law and order codes guarantee them a fair trial and also give them the right to appeal to Federal Court."[60]

Tonasket urged the senators to hear from other tribes. A month later, they did. Rod Lewis and Judge Rhodes came from Gila River to support the Makah, Lummi, and Colville position and to describe their own reasons for asserting jurisdiction over non-Indians. Their written statement described problems they "confronted on a daily basis." "One of the most significant problem areas concerns the destruction and theft of our natural resources. Mesquite wood, cactus, and other native plants are often carelessly and thoughtlessly destroyed by non-Indian visitors. . . . There seems to be the feeling among our non-Indian neighbors that the Reservation is an ideal place to race motorcycles, recklessly drive their dune buggies, or test out any type of vehicle which happens to be new and exciting. The result is frequent trespass on land allotted to tribal members or upon land belonging to the tribe." Another menace was non-Indians who "specialized in preying on tribe members," particularly the elderly and recent recipients of "welfare checks."

"Efforts to work with the surrounding communities were futile," Rhodes elaborated. Counties lacked personnel enough to patrol the 1,300-square-mile reservation. In contrast, an Interior Department solicitor and a US attorney did provide useful assistance. "With their help," tribe members in 1971 adopted "an implied consent ordinance," which the secretary "allowed . . . to become policy." Since then, the tribal court had

had "full cooperation" from non-Indians who appeared there. "To date," Rhodes testified, "we have tried 635 traffic cases, more or less; approximately 75 criminal cases, an average per year; and approximately 75 civil cases involving mostly restitution cases, bad debt cases." Gila River Community therefore urged senators "to recognize the tribes' sovereign authority. Otherwise, it's inefficient and uneconomical law enforcement, with the possibility that Indians would be punished but non-Indians not."[61]

No recognition of tribes' authority over non-Indians came from that Congress or the next few, and neither did a comprehensive revision of the federal criminal code. Tribe leaders, national Indian organizations, Senator Abourezk, and Senate Indian committee staff meanwhile set their sights on an intermediate goal: bringing the existing US code into compliance with Congress's new commitment to tribal self-determination. The specific objective was legislation allowing tribes individually to rid themselves of state jurisdiction.

By December 1975, the desired bill—the Indian Law Enforcement Improvement Act (S. 2010)—was the subject of Senate hearings. With the stated aim of reducing "jurisdictional uncertainties" in Indian country, it would authorize any tribe to reclaim some or all jurisdiction "lost" due to Public Law 280. The tribe could decide whether its laws would apply concurrently with state or federal law. In opening remarks, committee chair Abourezk said the bill was a response to Indian organizations' persistent campaign for repeal of PL 280, which was a legacy of "discredited 'termination'" policies. "If one believes in the concept of tribal government," Abourezk added, "it seems to me the tribes must have jurisdiction over their own people within the boundaries of the reservation." Did the senator use that wording to discourage tribes from construing the legislation as permission to govern people besides tribe members? If so, the next few speakers either missed his meaning or chose to ignore it.[62]

The first witnesses—all from reservations in Washington State—interpreted the bill as an opening for significantly stronger tribal governments. Some explicitly construed it as enabling tribal control of non-Indian activity within reservation boundaries. Mel Tonasket, speaking as president of NCAI, expressed delight that the legislation would effectively rescind PL 280, "a noose which has been gradually choking Indian tribes and the Indian way of life out of existence." He emphasized that S. 2010 reflected not "an Indian position" but "*the* Indian position"—"a consensus of all the Indian tribes of America" achieved with "great effort and expense" on NCAI's part. Tribe leaders with experience under state jurisdiction had crafted the bill, incorporating advice from "knowledgeable lawyers" and discussions at a conference attended by people from every tribe, Congress, the BIA, universities, and national organizations.

Tonasket's closing admonition makes one wish for a transcript describing committee members' expressions. He said, "The American Indian people will never rest secure until the doctrine of self-determination is again embodied in the area of civil and criminal jurisdiction on Indian reservations. . . . The Senate, and the House must not be deterred by the non-Indian vote, by frightened people afraid of the resumption of Federal jurisdiction and strengthened tribal law and order systems. You know your duty."[63]

Of the other speakers that day—Quinault chairman DeLaCruz, Yakima councilman Roger Jim, Colville council member Lucy Covington, and lawyers Robert Pirtle and James Hovis—it was DeLaCruz who most clearly indicated that he would take S. 2010 as an acknowledgment of tribes' right to impose their laws on non-Indians. "This legislation," he said, "will for the first time in over 100 years, provide a firm foundation for the exercise of tribal self-government in a meaningful way." It is meant "to place the Indian people back in a position where they can exercise their rightful authority to control the land and people of their reservation as strong governments based upon clear legal jurisdiction over their territory and peoples." Defining that "rightful authority" was a matter of simple logic:

> The Quinault Reservation is our country, set apart in a unique way from your country by promise, by agreement, by negotiated treaty, when we accepted the sovereignty and protection of the United States over us. The population of the United States as a whole received all the rest of our country and they own and control it. The laws of the non-Indian citizens of the United States govern all the land except for the reservation. When my people go outside the reservation we expect to obey the laws of the non-Indian government, except where our treaty rights protect us from those laws. . . . When any person comes to the reservation we expect him to obey our laws.

DeLaCruz assured senators that Quinaults would not "injure" non-Indians who came on the reservation to live, sightsee, or work. The tribal government would not treat them differently from Indians or take their property, as so many feared. But Quinaults would not tolerate state or county interference with efforts to build "a tribal way of life" on the reservation, whether interference consisted of removing Quinault children, attempting to tax tribal enterprises, or adopting land use regulations favoring speculators.[64]

Yakima and Colville witnesses, who also stressed the crippling effect of state jurisdiction on Indian self-government, did not echo DeLaCruz's position on tribal power over non-Indians, but Abourezk returned to that issue. Noting that "a lot of non-Indians live on Indian land within the boundaries," he asked Pirtle whether the bill would give tribes jurisdiction over them. Pirtle's answer was ambiguous. Hovis interjected that his clients in the Yakima Tribe had assumed responsibility for regulating all land use but thought it "better" not to assume jurisdiction over non-Indian crimes. Then DeLaCruz stepped in with an example of the need for a simpler allocation of jurisdiction. "Right now in the Quinault Tribal jail we have an alien, a man from Colombia, South America. . . . He happened to burglarize four non-Indian summer homes on the Quinault Reservation. Our officers investigated him. . . . The county prosecuting attorney chose to leave the matter of justice to the tribal court. The FBI and U.S. attorney chose to leave two of the counts within the jurisdiction of the tribal court. The man right now is serving time on one of the counts in the Quinault jail."[65]

Abourezk asked various speakers how non-Indians would likely react to tribal jurisdiction "over their persons." Tonasket remarked that non-Indians of his region were "starting to have a little more confidence" in tribal law enforcement. DeLaCruz was even more sanguine. Quinault courts, he revealed, had tried about seventy non-Indians "with legal counsel." "I think there have only been one or two cases that were appealed to the Federal Court," he said. "The Federal court in Tacoma sent those cases back to the tribal court to go through the due process of appeals to the tribal courts." The main opponents of tribal jurisdiction were land speculators and developers who resented the tribe's zoning restrictions.[66]

Senate Bill 2010 was destined to remain just a proposal while a newly created commission considered the issues it raised. One strong impetus for the commission's creation was legislators' desire for clarification and perhaps simplification of existing jurisdiction law. Critics of the status quo had exposed contradictions between the recent federal government commitment to Indian self-determination and the complex jurisdictional arrangements that were discouraging tribal governance.

Among those troubled by the discrepancy was Sherwin Broadhead, who wrapped up a stint as Abourezk's legislative assistant for Indian affairs in 1974. In a parting memorandum for his boss, Broadhead expressed gratification that the Senate was taking "a more positive direction . . . than there has been for the past 40 years, if not in history." But the gains for Indians were overshadowed by their unmet needs, including those arising from states' assumption of jurisdiction on reservations. Hearings in the summer of 1973, Broadhead observed, "brought forcefully to our attention" the fact that Public Law 280 "caused severe problems in family relationships, cultural ties, and traditional ceremonies, as well as problems in protecting fishing and hunting and other resource rights." It was apparent that "states lack the understanding, the willingness, and the financial capability to adequately fill the needs of the Indian communities." Indeed, state enforcement efforts were "far more oppressive than even the inadequate system that the Indians had previously."[67]

Broadhead was moving on to an assignment in which his top priority would be devising solutions to unworkable and harmful allocations of jurisdiction. The new job was part of a congressional initiative to replace the messy palimpsest of Indian policy and law with an updated, coherent framework for US-tribe relations. In January 1975, Congress had approved Abourezk's proposal to establish an American Indian Policy Review Commission (AIPRC), a body of six lawmakers and five Indians selected by the lawmakers. The authorizing legislation also provided for eleven task forces, each assigned a specific "study area," and each consisting of three persons from relevant professions, two of them Indians.[68]

In Abourezk's conception—at least as described in his memoir—the AIPRC's work was necessarily and appropriately a project for and by Indians. "There had never been a study done by the Indians themselves, which was one of my principal objectives," he wrote. Another of his objectives "was to build cadres of Indian leadership." Abourezk implied that he felt no obligation as commission chairman to set aside his pro-Indian bias or to mediate differences between Indians and non-Indians. He recalled that early Indian complaints "about an Indian study commission controlled by whites [in Congress] ended when it was discovered that I voted with the Indians 100 percent of the time."[69]

One of the eleven task forces was to investigate and make recommendations concerning federal, state, and tribal jurisdiction. Broadhead, a non-Indian lawyer, agreed to chair it. Members and staff of the task force provided a sympathetic audience for people who wanted greater Indian control of resources and activities on reservations. Task force legal adviser Paul Alexander had directed the production of a report for the US Commission on Civil Rights titled "The Navajo Nation: American Colony." "Specialist" Don Wharton was formerly counsel for the Klamath Indian Tribe. Chairman Broadhead was the BIA superintendent on the Colville Reservation when the tribe approved a code asserting criminal jurisdiction over everyone there.[70] At task force hearings, witnesses who advocated full territorial tribal government jurisdiction were preaching to at least two members of their own choir: sitting at the head table with Broadhead and Matthew Calac, a California Indian, was Judge Rhodes of the Gila River Community. When the task force took testimony in Yakima, Washington, speakers found themselves also addressing Mel Tonasket, a member of the AIPRC task force on federal administration.[71]

Following that session in Yakima, Mrs. H. A. Dewar of the Suquamish Community Club complained by letter to Washington State congressman Lloyd Meeds, a member of the policy review commission, that her testimony had fallen on closed ears. A non-Indian, she faced people who were "almost entirely Indian" and, in her view, out to put non-Indians on the defensive. She thought they "seemed most interested in that information which strengthens their own point of view: to perpetuate the Indian sovereign nation concept and govern everyone living within the original exterior boundaries of their reservations."[72]

Task force members were overtly and understandably keen to hear from tribes already exercising jurisdiction over non-Indians. But if the proceedings in Yakima cowed speakers who opposed such jurisdiction, their intimidation is not evident from hearing transcripts. Besides

Mrs. Dewar, several local government representatives and other non-Indians took the witness chair, each of them protesting that subjection to tribal law would deprive non-Indians of their rights as Americans. The chairman of the Yakima County Commission, claiming to speak for "all people" of the county, said they were "very concerned about returning jurisdiction of activities within the Reservation boundaries to the Tribal Council" because the council "would have no responsibility to protect the rights" of the reservation's 18,000 non-Indian residents. The Suquamish Community Club submitted a memorandum recommending that treaties with Indians be disregarded because they were a US government "mistake" when signed and now gave Indians "more rights than other citizens." Elizabeth Morris, representing an organization of Quinault Reservation fee landowners, relayed their complaint that "their taxes go to pay salaries for three tribal lawyers who work full time for the tribe to deprive them of the use of their land and freedoms guaranteed under the Constitution."[73]

Morris's written statement declared, "This is not a race problem." "I have done everything all my life to help Indians," she testified. She claimed "very good success" as a local schoolteacher with the parents of her "many Indian children." But Morris denounced the tribal government's assertion of jurisdiction over privately held land in heated terms. Their regulation of land use was a "nightmare," rendering affected property "useless" and breaking the hearts of people like her who had bought reservation lots with dreams of retiring to live quietly on "untamed" land of unique beauty.

> We find ourselves the innocent victims in the no-man's-land between government politicians and Indian militancy. Current jurisdictional abuses are breeding a hatred unrecognized by the young militant leaders, heady with their new power. Apparently they will employ any means to run us off the reservation. We understand their strategy: create a hysterical feeling of guilt throughout the land; assume jurisdiction by claiming jurisdiction; threaten county officials with another Wounded Knee if you don't get what you want; hassle fee patent owners physically and emotionally; zone them off their lands; arrest them; make them subject to tribal court; threaten to tax them off their land; shoot at them, bomb them; order them off their own land, or ban them from the reservation.

In response to this broadside, task force chairman Broadhead requested documentation of alleged shootings and suggested that some of the private owners' woes were the federal government's fault. When Morris said that fear of violent tribal action caused her to limit her use of her land, Mel Tonasket replied, "I understand. I used to be afraid to go across certain parts of Omak because the little white kids would bust my head with rocks so I learned to swim up the river."[74] What direct criticism Morris and other non-Indian witnesses endured came from spokesmen for the Suquamish and Quinault tribes, but they devoted most of their testimony to explaining the circumstances and motivations of their efforts to govern non-Indians. Mike Taylor was there to speak for Quinaults; the Suquamish delegation consisted of chairman Richard Belmont, attorney Barry Ernstoff, and the tribe's manager, Don Bread.

Taylor faulted the fee landowners' group for snubbing an invitation to talk with tribal representatives, but he did not answer Morris's extreme rhetoric in kind. Instead, recalling her statement that she did not realize her land was "still reservation" when she bought it in 1966, Taylor conceded that people in her situation had reason to feel wronged by developers who led them to believe they could avoid tribal regulation. Regulation was nonetheless necessary, he said, to prevent problems such as raw sewage that pooled on the ground where soils could not accommodate septic tanks. Taylor assured the task force that the tribe, as a government, was "very concerned with according people their rights, according them the possibility and the probability of putting the developments that they want on the reservation." The tribe had even included a non-Indian on its zoning commission and non-Indians on tribal court juries. Still, Quinaults remained firm in their conviction, grounded in settled federal law, that non-Indians who entered the reservation thereby put themselves under Quinault jurisdiction. Quinaults were also "in the forefront of two or three or four other tribes who have decided that it is not possible to operate a government where you don't have jurisdiction over the person and property of all the individuals who come within the boundaries of the reservation." Taylor added,

> When I first began to study Indian law I read all of the textbooks which seem to say that they have this jurisdiction. . . . The Quinaults . . . have been asserting their authority right along. But a lot of other tribes are not

> well versed in the authority that they do have to exercise. I think this is the direct responsibility of the [federal government] trustee. The trustee has been hiding the ball for a long time because he essentially has been in league with the people who want to exploit the resources of the reservation.[75]

The three Suquamish spokesmen emphasized in turn that the tribe's assumption of jurisdiction was necessary because neither the BIA nor Kitsap County would provide adequate law enforcement on the reservation. Richard Belmont had a seemingly unsympathetic rejoinder to the objections of non-Indian landowners: "There's an old cliché 'Buyer Beware.' I just figure that the people there aren't satisfied with the government, then they can leave." A little later, Belmont softened his stance, saying, "We try to serve the whole population of the reservation. . . . We hope to furnish law enforcement for not only Indian but non-Indian people. But, as you can see in the testimony, I guess they don't want us around and it really saddens my heart that I have to listen to something like this."[76]

To Mrs. Dewar and others who registered opinions like hers, the ultimate AIPRC position on tribal jurisdiction seemed predetermined, but it likely shocked most other Americans who learned of it. As summarized in the *New York Times*, the commission's final, eight-hundred-page report, sent to Congress in March 1977, proposed "that tribes be recognized as sovereign entities with the right to tax, maintain their own courts and control all resources on their own lands." The *Times* mentioned three specific recommendations, two of which spelled out what recognition of tribal sovereignty would mean for non-Indians: "Indians should be guaranteed the right to try offenders against tribal law, whether the offenders be Indians or non-Indians, in tribal courts," and "tribes should be allowed to tax citizens, Indians or not, who live on Indian land."[77]

Those AIPRC proposals reflected testimony and data collected by the jurisdiction task force and by other task forces as well. The Reservation Resource Development and Protection panel, for example, lamented the effects of "checkerboard landownership" on law enforcement and natural environments. It concluded, "Clear jurisdiction over reservation lands is necessary for a tribe to plan and control development."[78] The Tribal

Government task force reported that "time and again in task force meetings and hearings," tribal leaders stressed the need to develop governments capable of regulating all facets of reservation society, land use, and commerce. Appended to that report was a NARF study of land management on the Quinault Reservation, which arrived at the following bottom line: "In order to implement a rational planning program, it is essential that all jurisdictional doubts concerning reservation fee patent lands be resolved in favor of the tribe." A second attached study found non-Indian support for the Gila River Community Court's jurisdiction over non-Indians.[79]

Even with plentiful task force data and analysis favoring tribal government primacy on reservations, a final AIPRC recommendation of congressional support for tribal jurisdiction over non-Indians was not a foregone conclusion. When commissioners met to mark up their report, staff director Ernie Stevens—noting the trend on reservations and in courts toward greater tribal power—asked whether the wise course for lawmakers was to leave well enough alone. "The Indian people are now in a position where we are assuming jurisdiction," he said. Addressing the subject in the AIPRC report could harm Indians by misleadingly seeming to suggest that Congress needed to make new law. In fact, Stevens emphasized, "We feel secure in the law as it exists."[80] Ultimately, the commissioners did include an explicit call for recognition of tribal court jurisdiction over non-Indian offenders. Meeting transcripts do not show why. Perhaps they felt less "secure in the law" than Stevens did.

AIPRC members approved the full report by an eight-to-one vote. The lone dissenter was six-term congressman Lloyd Meeds, a Democrat from a district north of Seattle. It was Meeds to whom Mrs. Dewar complained about the jurisdiction task force, and it was his fellow commissioners' endorsement of broad jurisdiction that particularly offended Meeds. He maintained in comments to the press that the Supreme Court had repeatedly rejected the doctrine of inherent tribal sovereignty. He predicted that commission proposals for increased tribal power had "absolutely no chance of being enacted into law" because they were "oblivious to political reality." Nevertheless, Meeds promised to seek legislation expressly prohibiting Indian courts from exercising criminal jurisdiction over anyone but tribe members because, he said, "doing justice by Indians does not require doing injustices to non-Indians."[81]

On the policy review commission, Meeds was the odd man out, but he accurately foresaw that he would have abundant company in Congress when the issue was tribal power. His disdain for Indian claims of sovereignty both expressed and encouraged a position taken by thousands of his constituents and voters in other states. Several years of well-publicized, successful Indian claims to valuable resources and powers had stirred resentment among people who felt their interests threatened. In Washington State, the principal flashpoint was Judge Boldt's ruling, which required big cuts in non-Indian commercial and recreational fishing. Consequently, even as the AIPRC did its work, opponents of distinctive legal rights for Indians mobilized in the Pacific Northwest and across the country.[82] That development alarmed Indians and their allies, but rather than judging it prudent to slow the drive for expanded tribal government power, staunch advocates argued for an unrestrictive interpretation of tribal sovereignty with redoubled determination, in court and out.

Washington Post coverage of Meeds's stance on the AIPRC report emphasized rising resistance to Indian "demands." Three years earlier, Meeds said, he was happy to be "something of a champion" for Indians. "No one was paying much attention" to them, and "there was this feeling around the House that these were pretty good civil rights votes." Since then, the tribes' claim on Northwest salmon had ignited something "close to open warfare." Voters in the usually liberal district that included Seattle elected a Republican who promptly fulfilled a promise to sponsor legislation "terminating" all treaties with Indians. Meeds nearly lost his own reelection bid, apparently for saying he would accept Boldt's interpretation of Indian fishing rights. Now his mailbox was inundated with letters praising his dissent from the AIPRC majority report. Meanwhile, Indians in eastern states had sued for land long held by non-Indians, and western tribes had asserted priority rights to scarce water, causing some "former Indian supporters in Congress . . . to shy away from Indian issues." Meeds detected "an increasing feeling that most people have the right to claim title to the continent after living here 400 years."[83]

In an op-ed follow-up to the *Post* article, Meeds cautioned against oversimplifying the controversy about Indian rights as "a confrontation between Indian-Demands-Gone-Wild and The-Racist-Backlash." While other legislators and western state officials cheered the bill to nullify Indian treaties, Meeds pronounced the measure "too severe"—"a kind of cultural genocide," although probably "proposed more out of ignorance than meanness." But he complained, "Most Indians see no difference between this total-abrogation approach and my concern about some of their more extreme demands for expansion of their sovereign rights."[84]

To the Indians Meeds had in mind, it was probably the congressman's "compromise" proposal that seemed extreme—a bill that would extend state civil jurisdiction to Indian country in all fifty states, waive tribes' sovereign immunity to suit, deny them jurisdiction outside Indian country, even over their own members' fishing, and limit their on-reservation jurisdiction to their members. Prefacing the bill's substance was a "finding" that "subjection of nonmembers to the powers of Indian tribes is not . . . consistent with basic American principles of democratic control of governmental power."[85] What Meeds portrayed as a defense of democratic principles some people called a racist backlash. In fact, "backlash" quickly became a common term for arguments that "granting" Indians "special rights" deprived non-Indians of *their* unquestionable rights.

Like the *Washington Post*, observers commonly cited non-Indian fishers' defiance of Judge Boldt's ruling in *U.S. v. Washington* as an early expression and important catalyst of the widening opposition to Indians' unique rights. At the same time, but less visibly, reservation property owners were organizing to oppose tribal regulation, particularly in western Washington. Seattle resident Howard Gray told a local reporter about their efforts in September 1976. Gray identified himself as a founding member of the Interstate Congress for Equal Rights and Responsibilities, which had recently lobbied federal lawmakers for language in the proposed Indian Jurisdiction Act that would limit the powers of tribal governments. Claiming to speak also for landowner associations on the Lummi and Quinault Reservations, Gray complained that a "real problem" there stemmed "from the fact that although the Indians have sold huge quantities of the reservation to non-Indians, nevertheless they still insist on exclusive jurisdiction over everything and everyone on the reservation." Non-Indian property holders were consequently enduring "harassment," impediments to building on their land, and the pain of having to sell "at a sacrifice."[86]

Such organized opposition to tribal regulation was familiar to Quinault officials in 1976. For several years, Quinault Property Owners Association (QPOA) leaders had exhorted members to unite and fight for their "rights as citizens" against a "movement" of Indian tribes "trying to develop a power of independence that will give them jurisdiction over all the offenses by non-Indians, taxes, zoning, environmental control, etc." At a public meeting to discuss zoning on the reservation, the arguments of a QPOA speaker struck one county commissioner as unacceptably threatening, and Joe DeLaCruz labeled the association newsletter "racist."[87]

To many Indians and allies in their quest for empowerment, criticism of the tribes' recent successes did look like bigotry or knee-jerk defense of privileges that non-Indians enjoyed because of injustices inflicted on Indians. As evidence of racial and cultural intolerance, they could cite comments such as one from a non-Indian resident of the Port Madison Reservation: "I damn well think . . . they (Indians) ought to be forced to be assimilated like all other immigrants to this country. They are immigrants, too. They came over on the land bridge from Russia."[88]

In the National Congress of American Indians, the specter of disgruntled citizens and legislators collaborating to limit tribes' powers was a concern well before 1977. Someone brought to a 1974 NCAI conference a petition drafted by a Washington State senator calling on Congress to "renegotiate existing [Indian] treaties in order to achieve the goal of equal rights for all" and reaffirm states' right to regulate their natural resources.[89] In September 1975, a letter from Richard Belmont reached an unrecorded number of people in the NCAI, informing them that a new "non-Indian organization" had vowed to fight the Suquamish and "all Indian Tribes." Attached was a "solicitation" from the United American Rights Association urging "all persons on all property residing or traveling on the Port Madison Indian Reservation" to help finance appeals from the lower court rulings against Oliphant and Belgarde and, if needed, a subsequent campaign for legislation prohibiting tribal jurisdiction over nonmembers. Why wait, the flyer asked, for individuals to lose their rights "one by one" as the tribe's "federally supported power" grew?[90]

By early 1976, the Interstate Congress for Equal Rights and Responsibilities (ICERR) had announced its intent to coordinate the scattered opposition to special Indian rights. Assembled under the ICERR umbrella were groups with names such as Montanans Opposed to Discrimination and South Dakotans for Civil Liberties. A Washington State chapter claimed thirteen constituent groups: Associated Property Owners and Residents of Port Madison Area, Civil and Equal Rights for All, Concerned Citizens for the Constitution and Conservation, Glenwood Water Users Association, Lummi Property Owners Association, Quinault Property Owners Association, five recreational fishing clubs, and two associations of commercial fishers.[91]

In publications and public statements, these organizations denied any anti-Indian animus. At the Quinault Reservation, with its history of tensions between Quinaults and nonresident allottees from other tribes, the property owners association maintained that their quarrel was with a new generation of political radicals whose plans would rob landowners of their constitutional rights. To their Indian critics, a QPOA newsletter addressed this boast:

> It may come as a surprise to you that we have Indian land owners who have asked to become, and are, members, too. We understand that there are many Indian land owners without representation in their tribal affairs. Hopefully, our fight for our rights may help some of them. Rather an interesting thought, isn't it? Other Indians have wanted to know the purpose of our organization. To them we shall address this note. We hope to live in harmony with you and among you. We treasure the land just as you do.

Other QPOA contentions were implausibly extreme. An association officer, fresh from a meeting called by Montanans Opposed to Discrimination, relayed rumors that "a thread running through the whole thing" was manipulation by American Indian Movement militants who had "encouragement and help from members of the Communist party in this country." He added, "There are strong indications that Indians are being used in a scheme to destroy America."[92] By contrast, the more common charge that tribal jurisdiction would deprive non-Indians of their political rights seemed reasonable to many people, including members of Congress. Washington's Senator Slade Gorton endorsed the ICERR goal of denying tribes jurisdiction over non-Indians and declared in a letter to a Suquamish reservation resident, "I do not believe that any group, including Indians, should, by reason of race, have special legal rights which differ from those of their neighbors." A Kitsap County commissioner successfully appealed to Congressman Norm Dicks for a similar statement on behalf of his white constituents with homes or business on the Suquamish reservation.[93]

TO THE SUPREME COURT

Announcements by the ICERR that it aimed to "terminate" tribal self-government drew prompt NCAI responses, including an executive committee resolution:

> WHEREAS, the inherent governmental powers of Indian tribes derived from their sovereign status, and further defined by federal treaties and statutes, explicitly authorize Indian tribes to exercise jurisdiction over all persons and property on Indian reservations; and WHEREAS, courts, without exception, have held that the exercise of governmental powers by Indian tribes is in no way incompatible with rights guaranteed to non-Indians by the United States Constitution; . . . RESOLVED . . . the NCAI will not be deterred in its efforts to defend and promote tribal sovereignty.[94]

Nor would the Suquamish Tribe be deterred from claiming the power to punish non-Indians for some criminal acts. The ultimate adjudicator of that claim was therefore likely to be the US Supreme Court, and turning to the court for a definitive ruling would be consistent with something Joe DeLaCruz said in 1976. Disparaging "the propaganda and political route" favored by people who opposed tribal jurisdiction, DeLaCruz declared, "There's a bigger hope than 'Congress' to resolve the white man's disputes with Indians. . . . An excellent judicial system."[95] And so in late 1977, as a chorus of opposition to tribal rights swelled outside the halls of justice, Barry Ernstoff knew that he could soon be arguing in the Supreme Court for a contentious, far-reaching implication of Indians' historic sovereignty.

Despite DeLaCruz's declaration of faith in the US judiciary, Ernstoff could not take for granted that the high court would do what he, his clients, and many other Indians considered the right thing. He would be asking the justices to set aside a long-accepted assumption about the effect of US supremacy on Indian tribal power. Although DeLaCruz said the tribes were exercising jurisdiction that had always been within their power, Ernstoff's colleague Al Ziontz, who agreed in principle, described the lower court rulings in Oliphant's case as "a drastic change in what has been understood to be the law the last 100 years." That understanding would surely be on justices' minds as they entertained the tribe's argument for jurisdiction over non-Indians. If it were to influence their interpretation of pertinent treaties, laws, and court opinions, they could well render a decision that limited the powers of all tribes. Ernstoff also had reason to fear the effect on the justices of the ongoing agitation against special Indian rights. He himself had said publicly that non-Indians who fell under tribal law were in "an unfortunate situation because they have no voice in tribal governments."[96] The nine men on the Supreme Court were not Indians.

The ever-present risk of adverse, precedent-setting Supreme Court decisions had already spurred an NCAI effort to promote collaborative strategizing by tribes engaged in litigation. Robert Pirtle traced that initiative to a conversation with Mel Tonasket.

> I complained that young lawyers, fresh out of law school . . . , were appearing with many tribal delegations, all bright-eyed and bushy-tailed idealists hoping to make a huge impact for their tribal clients but still green behind the ears with no concept of Indian law. And since any single sovereign tribal governmental power damaged in a lawsuit for one tribe has effect on every other tribe, I worried about the future of tribal sovereignty. Mel's response was to lead NCAI to establish a Litigation Committee and to urge every tribe about to undertake a major case to present it to the Committee for national approval before proceeding.[97]

After the committee's creation in 1976, a tribal newspaper announced, "For the first time, the Indian community will attempt to coordinate its strategy in the courtroom." Tonasket characterized the plan as a response to anti-Indian backlash led by "red-neck" organizations that were "by their own admission against tribal governments expanding their jurisdiction." "'We're being surrounded,' Tonasket warned, 'Not by bullets or cannons, but by the law.'"[98]

The first special NCAI conference on litigation revealed that uncomfortable dilemmas were inherent in the role envisioned for the new committee. One sticky question concerned the makeup of the committee:

should tribal officials or lawyers dominate? Comments from some tribal delegates betrayed discomfort with the need to trust attorneys' motivations and expertise. Lawyers were indispensable to any decision about litigation, and some of them were Indians, but tribal officials wanted to call the shots. Not surprisingly, lawyers were the butt of a few sarcastic remarks. Tonasket, revealing that his tribe had spent over $100,000 on attorney fees in one year, quipped that a coordinated attempt to litigate selectively might encounter "subtle opposition" from attorneys who feared an adverse effect on their pocketbooks. Tonasket hastened to add that he meant no criticism of lawyers—they were a "costly necessity." He just wanted tribes to control their counsel, lest they get the tribes "in trouble."

There were proposals to limit the number of lawyers on the litigation committee, to include them only as unpaid "volunteers," to relegate them to an "advisory council," and to ensure that "tribal people" outnumbered lawyers. Elmer Savilla declared, "I hate to see any committee of tribal people overpowered by talkative attorneys." Tonasket, explaining his aims as conference chairman, said, "I don't want to even take the chance that this conference is going to be dominated from the floor by attorneys." Unless tribal delegates wanted their lawyers to speak, he would "make the Indians be the boss." Ultimately, the committee members with law degrees were all Indians and not in private practice. They worked in organizations such as the Native American Rights Fund, the American Indian Law Center, the American Indian Lawyers Training Program, and California Indian Legal Services.[99]

Rod Lewis from Gila River was on the committee. NCAI records confirm his memory that jurisdiction over non-Indians was always at the top of committee and conference agendas during that period. Invariably, some participants wanted to avoid litigation unless all conceivable factors favoring success were in place. At the 1976 litigation conference, attorney Steven Boyden reported that Utah's governor had told non-Indians to ignore citations from the Ute tribal court. Although Boyden thought the factual "backdrop" for the Utes' claim of jurisdiction was strong—they had an "excellent" courtroom, new jail, good judges, and well-trained police—he was reluctant to litigate because judges on that region's federal appeals court had not been friendly to Indians. At the 1977 NCAI convention, Albert Trimble kicked off a panel discussion on sovereignty with an account of the defiance that his Oglala Sioux Tribe encountered as they tried to control "lawless behavior of non-Indians." Instead of litigating the matter, Trimble proposed that the NCAI lobby for legislation "to sustain sovereignty where local tribal government cannot do so unassisted."[100]

On the question whether tribes should take action that might provoke lawsuits, Justice Department attorney Peter Taft observed, "If the first test case is in a reservation 80 percent Indian and 20 percent non-Indian, your chances of success are greater." Noting that some tribes were already exercising what they believed to be their rights, he conceded, "You are going to be in court whether you like it or not."[101] At every meeting, there were people who did seem to like that prospect. Arguably the most enthusiastic was Al Ziontz. "Many of us believe that these are questions that are going to have to be tested," Ziontz said in 1976, "but we think ultimately in this area, that is, tribal jurisdiction over fee land on the reservation, the Indians can win."[102] At the following year's meeting, John Echohawk also sounded optimistic about the tribes' chances in court. "Maybe the problem anymore is not that we are not doing litigation the right way," he said. "I think we are doing it pretty well, and a testimony to that is the fact that now we are getting organized opposition."[103]

The NCAI litigation committee was created with the hope of ensuring that tribes did litigation "the right way," but its effectiveness was limited by a reality Echohawk identified in 1975: the organization could not stop a member tribe from proceeding with an inadvisable case; trying to do so would constitute interference with the attorney-client relationship. Still, Echohawk proposed, "We could sure go in and maybe make them see the light of day" so that their lawyer would advise them to hold off. Barry Ernstoff—apparently thinking that Echohawk had Ernstoff's defense of Suquamish actions in mind—did not let the implicit criticism go unanswered. After claiming that the Suquamish Tribe's extension of jurisdiction was contrary to his advice, he said, "I'm sure all of you involved in law know that ego is about two thirds of the makeup of a good lawyer, a good tribal councilman. And I've never seen a tribal councilman say . . . , You're right, it makes much more sense to let the tribe and the reservation two miles down the road from us bring the case. Because they have better facts of the situation. Tribal councils just don't do that."[104]

Decision-making for tribal councils and their lawyers was more fluid and less dualistic than Ernstoff's comment implied. Until litigation was under way and lawyers' recommendations necessarily carried great weight, councilors and their counsel influenced and responded to each other. As legal scholars Austin Sarat and Stuart Scheingold have observed, lawyers ideally help their clients "define the realm of the possible" so that the clients can make informed decisions about what to do.[105] Indian officials thus heard from their lawyers about pertinent law and the odds of prevailing in court, but what they understood and how those understandings influenced their decisions were not under the lawyers' control. Councils could indeed insist that attorneys advocate for them in long-shot cases. Tribe leaders' fierce determination might even affect the lawyers' calculations of the odds. Lawyers' confidence in their own skill at crafting persuasive arguments or their relish for the adversary process (not to mention their incentive to earn fees in some cases) also factored into decisions.

A question at the forefront of many minds in 1976 and 1977 was whether Ernstoff and his partners had calculated the odds correctly in the Suquamish jurisdiction case. If urged by other lawyers to recalculate, would he or the tribe do so? At the meeting to establish the NCAI litigation committee, Ziontz did not wait for someone else to raise the question; he mentioned Mark Oliphant's suit and tried to allay the concerns of delegates from other tribes.

> Possibly if that case could come before a committee, the committee might have said, "This is a lousy case, don't bring that case. Let the white man go. If he sues you, settle with him, don't challenge him." But the tribe insisted on going forward with that case. The tribe had an excellent fact situation. We had a well-equipped police force, they were trained, we had a contract with the county for the use of the county jail, they read him his rights . . . , and everything was lined up. . . . We are very optimistic.

In any event, Ziontz stressed, a basic fact and principle of law portended success: Congress had never terminated tribes' inherent authority to punish people for crimes on reservations.[106]

Ziontz's assurance did not squelch fears of a ruling that would adversely affect all tribes. To Rod Lewis, for instance, it seemed that the Suquamish case was "not the best fact situation." In 2012, he remembered being "pretty sure" the tribe's argument for jurisdiction "would fail." Pessimists argued that the prudent Suquamish course was to end the case by dropping the charges against Oliphant and Belgarde. NCAI records suggest that their arguments were persuasive. At the conference on litigation in 1977, Ziontz announced a new consensus: "the tribes" and their lawyers had decided as a policy matter "that it would not be in our interest to have this case go to the Supreme Court at this time, because we feel that the tribes in Washington and around the nation should have an opportunity to show what they can do, given the authority to handle law enforcement over white people."[107]

That may have been the occasion Justine James, Sr., described during a 2012 interview. The Quinault councilman remembered that the Suquamish Tribe's lawyers told tribal delegates at an NCAI meeting, "It looks like we're losing the case . . . so we'll pull out of it if that's the consensus of this body." But then Joe DeLaCruz "got up to the microphone and told 'em, 'The courts are with us. Go for it!'" James took issue with DeLaCruz's advice, he said, and he could sense that many tribal leaders in the crowd disapproved of his pessimism about the case.[108]

Five months later, the court of appeals decision in the Suquamish Tribe's favor must have eased some pessimists' fears. However, no one doubted that Oliphant's attorney would seek Supreme Court review, and no matter how sanguine Ernstoff was about the tribe's chances in the high court, he preferred not to take the risk. The Suquamish had the ruling they wanted from the next highest court. If the justices did not review that ruling, it would stand, leaving Oliphant to his fate in the Suquamish court. Ernstoff therefore answered Philip Malone's petition for a writ of certiorari, which would signal the court's decision to review the case, with a brief opposing review. He pointed out that a common reason for Supreme Court review—the existence of conflicting circuit court decisions on the key issue—was not present. "In fact, Petitioner's allegation that this case is of such great moment and public import so as to require review by this Court is impeached by the notable absence of litigation in other courts concerning this subject matter, despite the exercise of jurisdiction by Indian tribes over non-Indians throughout the nation over the past several years."[109]

In June 1977, the Supreme Court nevertheless agreed to consider Oliphant's appeal, perhaps swayed more by a recommendation from the Interior and Justice Departments than by Malone's plea.[110] The news triggered a round of phone calls among tribal lawyers, many no doubt reminding Ernstoff that his clients might yet avoid the risky Supreme Court review if the tribal court dropped the disputed charges.[111] But a consensus of tribes and their lawyers was not an enforceable mandate. In a memorandum addressed to unidentified recipients, Ernstoff announced a different course of action. A number of lawyers, uneasy about the facts of the case and "the current views of the Supreme Court," had raised the question of "mooting" the issue, he noted. His response: "I have had extensive discussions with many of you as well as other lawyers in the Indian field and after much deliberation have come to the conclusion that we should proceed with the case. Members of the Suquamish Tribal Council discussed the matter in great detail with other Indian Tribal leaders at N.C.A.I. and have advised me that they also, despite some misgivings, would prefer to go on with the case."[112]

Thus, at a time described by the *Washington Post* as "an era of unprecedented controversy over Indian claims to land and its resources," a tiny Washington tribe and two young white men would take their dispute about tribal jurisdiction to the Supreme Court, where a ruling for the tribe could effectively hand Indians "the real reins of power on any reservation."[113]

8. Telling Stories in Court

In *Telling Stories*, a special issue of *Michigan Law Review*, sociologist Kim Lane Scheppele observed that "the resolution of any individual case in the law relies heavily on a court's adoption of a particular story." Thus, "there are few things more disempowering than having one's own self-believed story rejected, when rules of law (however fair in the abstract) are applied to facts that are not one's own, when legal judgments proceed from a description of one's own world that one does not recognize."[1] Milner Ball's contribution to the volume identified several such instances of American Indian disempowerment—cases in which the US Supreme Court espoused a prevalent "American origin story to the detriment of tribes." Among the cases on Ball's list was *Oliphant v. Suquamish Indian Tribe*.[2]

To resolve the dispute that began with the Suquamish Tribe's arrest of Mark Oliphant, the Supreme Court did adopt a particular story—one consisting largely of facts that Suquamish and other Indians would not have considered their own. In an opinion approved by five of his colleagues, Justice William Rehnquist related a variant of a common American history narrative in which a principled republic fulfills its destiny by bringing a vast territory and all inhabitants under the rule of law. Rehnquist described a world where no one doubted US supremacy or the Euro-American state's right to define indigenous peoples' possibilities. Not included as essential facts were Indian beliefs about the original and contemporary nature of their societies, Indian conceptions of their evolving relationship to the United States, or Indian stories about their struggles to keep and control their territories and resources.

Rehnquist's account of history explained the ruling for the Suquamish Tribe's opponents but did not entirely adopt their version of the facts. It disregarded their "self-believed" story that a handful of people claiming dubious Indian tribal identity were bent on subjecting disfranchised non-Indians to unconstitutional Indian government rule. In Rehnquist's narrative, the key characters were neither Indians nor their non-Indian neighbors; the protagonists who mattered were agents of the US government.

After its publication in March 1978, the majority opinion in *Oliphant v. Suquamish Tribe* drew intense criticism from a variety of perspectives: predictable protests from Indians aligned with the Suquamish but also condemnation from presumably disinterested scholars of law and history. The scholars accused Rehnquist of drawing on the historical record selectively, even disingenuously, to describe a US government that had always denied tribes' right to sanction non-Indians for criminal acts. They stopped short of censuring Rehnquist for a blinkered focus on non-Indian intentions, probably because they knew that a corresponding record of Indian history was not available to the court.

ADVERSARIES' STORIES

The adversaries in *Oliphant et al. v. Suquamish Indian Tribe* first had an opportunity to tell the Supreme Court their stories when they submitted written arguments on the central issue in the case: whether the tribe had jurisdiction to prosecute Mark Oliphant and Daniel Belgarde for criminal violations of Suquamish law. Lawyers wrote those briefs—Philip Malone for petitioners Oliphant and Belgarde and Barry Ernstoff for the tribe. Malone filed the first one, with copies to his opponents; Ernstoff submitted a response, and Malone had the last word in a reply brief. At lengths that belied the name "briefs," those documents on both sides chiefly recounted how federal lawmakers, judges, and executive officials, over the course of US history, had conceived of Indian tribes' powers and relations with non-Indians. How the Suquamish thought about such matters garnered scarcely a mention.

Malone began with a chronology of governmental actions affecting the Suquamish Tribe. Most were federal actions—the "establishment" of the Port Madison Reservation "with the signing" of the Point Elliott Treaty, the General Allotment Act of 1887, Washington's admission to statehood in 1889, US acquisition of the Suquamish village site in 1905, federal allotment of reservation lands in 1910, the Indian Reorganization Act of 1934, Public Law 83-280's authorization of state jurisdiction on reservations, federal approval of a Suquamish constitution in 1965, the Indian Civil Rights Act of 1968, a 1968 BIA-approved lease of "all remaining tribal lands except for 5 acres," and federal regulations for tribal law and order codes, promulgated in 1973.[3] Three state actions made the list: the legislation in 1957 and 1963 by which Washington assumed jurisdiction on the reservation and the partial retrocession of that jurisdiction in 1971. Only two items were Suquamish actions: "passage" in 1916 of "the first Suquamish constitution"[4] and the 1973 enactment of a law and order code.

Malone offered no explanation of the chronology's significance for the Suquamish claim of jurisdiction over non-Indians. If he intended to provide that analysis in the body of the brief, he did not follow through. In one hundred pages of argument, he said far less about events on the list than about other acts of Congress, none of them specific to the Suquamish Tribe. He also discussed numerous federal court rulings, contending that they implicitly precluded tribal prosecutions of non-Indians, even rulings that affirmed a US policy of supporting tribal self-government. He surveyed general legislation concerning federal jurisdiction over Indian affairs, particularly statutes from 1790 through 1854 that regulated non-Indian relations with autonomous Indian nations. Opinions by federal lawyers in 1834, 1934, and 1970 also figured in Malone's narrative of a United States government that consistently denied tribes jurisdiction over non-Indians.

The consistency Malone claimed to see was a conception of US supremacy that left no room for independent tribal sovereigns. By declaring its own sovereignty, Malone contended, the United States gained the right to determine the limit of Indians' powers. Starting with the Constitution, American law assumed and ensured the tribes' subordination simply by declining to affirm their sovereignty. For evidence that Congress took that stance from the beginning of the republic, Malone cited early legislation authorizing federal trials of non-Indians who committed crimes in tribal territory. He also mentioned treaties allowing tribes to punish their own wayward people but stipulating that non-Indians would be tried in US courts. Such records were Malone's basis for arguing that "tribes were never given or considered to have jurisdiction over non-Indians."[5]

Malone disputed a key premise of the 1976 appellate court ruling for the Suquamish—that Indian tribes were originally sovereign and retained all essential attributes of sovereignty except those they surrendered. He denied that any statutes or Supreme Court opinions acknowledged inherent sovereignty as the basis for tribes' self-governance. In his view, the court merely blocked state interference with federal management of Indian affairs while upholding federal actions that progressively curtailed Indian self-governance until it could be phased out entirely. In 1953, declaring that time at hand, Congress permitted states to take jurisdiction in Indian country. Not until 1959, according to Malone (ignoring *Worcester v. Georgia* in 1832), did the Supreme Court recognize "an independent Indian interest in self-government which stood as a barrier to state powers," and it qualified that conclusion in 1972 when it observed, "'The trend has been away from the idea of inherent Indian sovereignty as a barrier to state jurisdiction and toward federal preemption.'"[6]

Malone then hedged his bet with an alternative argument: even if the Suquamish Tribe had once been a sovereign polity with jurisdiction over non-Indian offenders, Congress had exerted its "plenary power" to prohibit such tribal action. Malone again cited the early legislation that gave federal courts jurisdiction to try non-Indians for offenses in tribes' territory. He quoted a provision directing trial judges to apply "the general US laws as to the punishment of offenses committed in any place within the sole and exclusive jurisdiction of the United States." Mistaking that language as an extension of all federal law to Indian country, Malone called it evidence of "Congress's steadfast refusal to grant tribal governments criminal jurisdiction over non-Indians."[7] The Indian Civil Rights Act of 1968 did not mark a change in policy, he added, even though it appeared to accept tribal governments and courts as permanent institutions. Instead, because the ICRA required tribes to provide accused persons with most of the protections guaranteed by the Bill of Rights, it was yet another US-imposed limitation on tribes' autonomy and range of authority.

Although the Brief for Petitioners gave pride of place and space to non-Indian constitution drafters, treaty negotiators, lawmakers, and jurists, it also tried to influence how the justices thought about the Suquamish and their history. To make the point that non-Indians far outnumbered Indians on the Port Madison Reservation, Malone inserted current population and landownership figures, broken down by "race." He conceded that lower courts had not made "thorough findings" on the subject, and he admitted to casting available information "in the light most favorable to Petitioners" but claimed that his version of the facts had "gone uncontested." He also ventured an assertion not conceded by the tribe: "The Suquamish Indians have not had a tribal community at Port Madison for quite some time."[8]

Elsewhere in the memorandum, Malone suggested that the Suquamish had never constituted an organized, autonomous polity. "The degree and nature of powers originally possessed by Indian tribes is quite unclear," he began. "There is no evidence that the Suquamish Tribe was a sovereign entity exercising powers over non-members either before or after the relevant treaty."[9] A sentence referring to all Point Elliott Treaty tribes as a group cited only an unpublished law student essay and a general text on American Indians to support the contention that there was "no identification of any particular area of land individual tribes and bands occupied to the exclusion of others in the Washington Territory."[10]

Unfortunately for the jurists and lawyers who had to read Malone's analysis of law and legal history, he did not make cogent points in logical order. The brief's organization, long declarative headings, and prose were as convoluted as the history of Indian policy they attempted to explain. Justice Blackmun's law clerk, charged with preparing a synopsis of the parties' written arguments, lamented, "I am afraid that petitioners' brief is of the Faulkner genre, and it is difficult to summarize faithfully." In the margin of that memo, Blackmun jotted, "Oh, yes!"

"For more coherent statements of essentially the same arguments," the clerk recommended that Blackmun turn to briefs filed by South Dakota and Kitsap County as friends of the court. Both of those governments, viewing tribal regulation of non-Indians as encroachment on state sovereignty, argued that tribes could exercise jurisdiction over non-Indian offenders only if the federal government had used its power to preempt state jurisdiction and sanction Indian jurisdiction, and it had not. The county and South Dakota parsed the same statutes Malone cited, acknowledging that they were ambiguous but promoting an inference of intent on legislators' part to restrict tribal jurisdiction to Indians. In addition, South Dakota alluded to a history in the Bureau of Indian Affairs of advising tribes that they had no criminal law jurisdiction over non-Indians.[11]

The Suquamish Tribe's response to Malone's brief was an opportunity to dispute his broad account of history, but at the outset, Ernstoff seemed disinclined to do that. The case before the court, he wrote, was a narrow one involving a single tribe and its specific history.[12] Nevertheless, as most counsel would have done in the circumstances, Ernstoff let few of Malone's assertions go unanswered. He devoted most of his fifty-two-page memorandum to a similarly extensive analysis of past US Indian policies, treaties, and judicial pronouncements.

As evidence that history was on his clients' side, Ernstoff could and did cite the lower court rulings against Oliphant and Belgarde. To refute his opponents' depiction of legal history, he offered alternative interpretations of the treaties, statutes, court opinions, and government actions that Malone mentioned, and he analyzed additional events, from a treaty with Delaware Indians in 1778 to several Supreme Court decisions in the 1970s. Overall, the Suquamish Tribe's argument mirrored the petitioners' focus on non-Indian views of Indian tribes' status and powers. The adversaries' stories differed primarily in the lessons they drew from the words in written artifacts of United States governance.

Like Malone, Ernstoff urged the justices to see crucial continuity in the twists and turns of legal history. The continuity he described was repeated recognition in all branches of US government that tribes were sovereign before European colonization and had not ceded all the prerogatives of their sovereignty. Following an introductory summary of that reasoning, Ernstoff's brief promised to demonstrate five things: "Through early Statutes and treaties, the United States recognized tribal authority over non-Indians; that authority has not been subsequently extinguished by statute; the Treaty of Point Elliott did not extinguish the Suquamish Tribe's authority over non-Indians; [Supreme Court decisions] affirm tribal authority over non-Indians on all lands within the reservation as to matters in which there is a sufficient tribal interest; [and] Congress has confirmed by statute the continuing existence of tribal authority over non-Indians."

The basis for this take on history was a passage in the 1958 *Handbook of Federal Indian Law* that stated "a cardinal principle of federal Indian law."

> The whole course of judicial decision on the nature of tribal powers is marked by adherence to three fundamental principles: (1) An Indian tribe possessed, in the first instance, all the powers of any sovereign State. (2) Conquest rendered the tribe subject to the legislative power of the United States and, in substance, terminated the external powers of sovereignty of the Tribe, e.g., its power to enter into treaties with foreign nations, but did not by itself terminate the internal sovereignty of the tribe, i.e., its powers of local self-government. (3) These internal powers were, of course, subject to qualification by treaties and by express legislation of Congress, but, save as thus expressly qualified, many powers of internal sovereignty have remained in the Indian tribes and in their duly constituted organs of government.

By incorporating this concise legal history in his brief, Ernstoff made a long exposition on the "course of judicial decision" unnecessary. He cited and quoted just six Supreme Court opinions, the first in 1832 and the latest in 1975, pointing out that they characterized Indian tribes variously as distinct political communities, separate peoples, and unique aggregations with sovereign or quasi-sovereign attributes. Rather than specifying that territorial jurisdiction to punish all offenders was an attribute of sovereignty, Ernstoff simply reiterated that the tribes originally "possessed the usual accoutrements of a sovereign government."[13]

One by one, Ernstoff considered numerous treaties and laws for what they might reveal about relevant federal intentions. None of them contained explicit language curtailing tribes' preexisting sovereign right to govern non-Indians in tribal territory. He also reviewed more than half a dozen cases in which a federal court or the Supreme Court affirmed Indian jurisdiction over non-Indians for purposes other than punishing crimes. Finally, he argued that two acts of Congress in the twentieth century—the Indian Reorganization Act of 1934 and Indian Civil Rights Act of 1968—promoted the "revitalization" of tribes' inherent sovereignty and the development of tribal courts.

Before 1934, Ernstoff conceded, there were "several decades" when tribes exercised very little of their sovereignty. The reasons were "not legal but historical and socio-political." "Overly paternalistic" federal policy discouraged tribal governance. By exerting US "plenary control" in ways that hamstrung and exploited Indians, the Office of Indian Affairs "created a sense of despair and impotence among the tribes. People so indoctrinated do not aggressively assert the full measure of their rights. In the area of criminal jurisdiction, this sense of powerlessness was aggravated by a federal policy discouraging tribal assertion of jurisdiction over non-Indians."[14] Ernstoff neither made this observation specific to the Suquamish nor distinguished Suquamish experience from this generality.

Ernstoff's brief did not directly refute Malone's contention that the pretreaty Suquamish were not a sovereign polity with a distinct geographical domain. In fact, it said little more than the petitioners' brief about pertinent Suquamish history. Rather than addressing that subject in full, Ernstoff adopted the statement of facts in the amicus brief of the United States, which in turn referred the justices to "facts set forth in the district court opinion," adding only that the reservation provided for the Suquamish was a "remnant" of their "aboriginal territory" and still "their home."[15] Otherwise, the Suquamish history that Ernstoff mentioned was recent. Regarding the Suquamish ordinance asserting jurisdiction over non-Indians as well as Indians, he averred merely that the tribe deemed it a necessary response to "many years of ineffective federal and state law enforcement on the isolated Port Madison Indian Reservation."[16]

For his reply brief, Malone had a cosigner—Jesse Trentadue, a recent law school graduate whose contribution may explain why the brief was noticeably more cogent than Malone's first effort.[17] It maintained a focus on acts of Congress, court opinions, and administrative records, describing them again as evidence that the US government had never considered Indian tribes fully sovereign or consented to tribal jurisdiction over non-Indians. The brief also tendered a new argument. Under the General Allotment Act, it noted, allottees were to have "the benefit of and be subject to the laws, both civil and criminal, of the state or territory in which they may reside." By leaping from there over considerable unmentioned factual ground, Malone and Trentadue reached a conclusion of marginal relevance to the dispute about jurisdiction on the Suquamish reservation: "A non-Indian settling on the Port Madison Reservation . . . was thus told by the federal government that his Indian neighbor would become subject to state law, and not that he would become subject to the law of his Indian neighbor."[18]

The reply brief returned to the issue of aboriginal Suquamish sovereignty with more forcefulness than Malone had previously mustered. To view tribes of the Puget Sound area as sovereign nations in 1855, it declared, was "to ignore historical reality." In *U.S. v. Washington*, Judge Boldt acknowledged the reality in a finding that "no formal political structure had been created by the Indians living in the Puget Sound area at the time of initial contact with the United States Government. Governor Stevens, acting upon instructions from his superiors and recommendations of his subordinates, *deliberately created political entities* for purposes of delegating responsibilities and negotiating treaties." Not mentioned in the reply brief were Boldt's additional findings that each tribe in the fishing rights case had "established its status as an Indian tribe recognized as such by the federal government," each was "a political successor in interest to some of the Indian tribes or bands which were parties" to a treaty, and "those treaties established self-government by treaty tribes."[19]

In the petitioners' narrative, Suquamish motivations for governing everyone on the reservation were significant only in that they were allegedly racist. Non-Indian residents of the reservation could not participate as voters in the Suquamish government; the tribe reserved that privilege for its members. Therefore, Malone contended, subjecting non-Indians to tribal jurisdiction deprived them of their right as Americans to have a voice in their own governance. The tribe's intended prosecution of people they had "completely disenfranchised" was also a violation of the US Constitution's Fifth and Fifteenth Amendments and the Indian Civil Rights Act (ICRA) because the reason for the disenfranchisement was "race."[20]

The petitioners likewise labeled Suquamish jury service qualifications a racially motivated denial of non-Indians' rights rather than equating the requirement of tribal membership with state laws that limited jury duty to US citizens. "Defendants are entitled to a jury trial," Malone noted, referencing the ICRA, "but the Suquamish, by vote of *thirty-two members*, passed [a resolution] to exclude non-Indian [*sic*] from the jury panel." Furthermore, because jurors could reside off the reservation, juries could potentially consist entirely of Indians who were not residents of the petitioners' home community.[21] The intensity of Malone's belief in the righteousness of this argument was apparent, as was his mangled syntax, in a passage of the opening brief.

> What is the difference between the *Suquamish Indian Tribe* as a quasi-governmental organization based upon racial ancestry of their members exercising for the benefit and protection of their members only powers of government over non-members and their property when chartered by the United States, receiving funds from the United States Government for Law and Order, being dependent upon and subject to the laws of Congress of the United States in its relationship with the United States and that of a *State* of the Union, using its powers of government to support a racial organization to which other citizens of the state and the United States cannot belong because of their race that exercises general powers of government over them in violation of the privileges and immunities clause of the United States Constitution.[22]

The Supreme Court received nine amicus briefs favoring Suquamish jurisdiction, most of which addressed the issue much as Ernstoff did. Aside from a few stipulated facts about the Suquamish Tribe and the reservation, the history they recited was a succession of federal statutes, court decisions, and government pronouncements or practices. However, four of the briefs did urge the court to consider tribal community histories and Indian perspectives on US policy.

A brief from the National Congress of American Indians and three tribes emphasized the practical consequences of shifting federal policies for historically self-governing tribes. Allotting tribal lands to individuals, it argued, did not achieve the stated goal of converting Indians to "the white man's competitive, acquisitive ways." Instead, "by distributing tribal property and bringing whites onto reservations," allotment laws and their implementation "worked to impair the ability of tribes to govern themselves." To correct the consequent "appalling social conditions" and "crippling loss of tribal lands," Congress approved the 1934 Indian Reorganization Act, under which "tribes slowly began to reacquire the strength and land base necessary for effective self-government." After the postwar period, when the federal aim "was to terminate federal protection of tribes and let their future development be a part of state structures and government," the United States returned by the 1970s to a policy of encouraging tribal development, thus enabling many Indian reservations to become "effective, modern, self-governing communities."[23]

The National American Indian Court Judges Association (NAICJA) offered a history of tribal judicial systems, beginning with Courts of Indian Offenses created by the Interior Department in the 1880s. While conceding that many reservation courts remained arms of the Indian bureau until federal policy "shifted . . . to a greater recognition of the powers of self-government," NAICJA asserted that "tribes themselves retained the inherent power to administer justice," and many acted "to establish their own legal systems and . . . courts." In the 1960s and 1970s, a "major resurgence in the Indian court system . . . occurred simultaneously with the federal policy of Indian self-determination."[24]

A memorandum from three Southwest tribes explained their stake in the Suquamish case by recounting law enforcement challenges stemming from "exponential" population growth in their region. As Phoenix and two other Arizona cities expanded, thousands of outsiders regularly traversed the Salt River Pima-Maricopa reservation. Many viewed the Indian lands "as a place to dump refuse, speed from one city to another, and in recent years, use marijuana and narcotics beyond the control of City or County police." "To control all criminality within their borders," the Salt River Community enacted an ordinance giving their police and court jurisdiction over all persons regardless of race. Gila River Tribal Community officials took the same step in response to similar problems plaguing their reservation. At the Colorado River Reservation on the Arizona-California border, non-Indian farms and recreational opportunities attracted seasonal influxes of workers and tourists, giving rise by 1974 to a need for comprehensive policing. The Indian government decided to meet it in the same fashion as those at Salt River and Gila River.[25]

A slim brief on behalf of the Quinault Indian Nation and the Lummi Tribe reported that the Quinault government had been prosecuting non-Indians even longer than the three Southwest tribes. The tribe's judicial branch traced its roots to a fisheries court established in 1917. As of the 1960s, on a 200,000-acre reservation with 2,500 Indian residents, approximately 600 non-Indian residents, and a timber industry that brought non-Indian workers to the reservation every day, law enforcement was provided almost exclusively by tribal and BIA police. "The Quinault Nation began taking jurisdiction over non-Indians in some land-use matters in 1967," the brief related, and two years later "took jurisdiction over non-Indians involved in various criminal trespass offenses." A revised law and order code, in effect since March 21, 1973, gave the tribal court "civil and criminal jurisdiction over all persons acting within the boundaries of the reservation."[26]

After all briefs were in, the adversaries in *Oliphant v. Suquamish Tribe* had one more opportunity to tell stories that might inspire the rulings they wanted. The justices heard oral arguments on January 9, 1975. On that occasion, however, no one could present a complete narrative. The attorneys faced numerous interruptions from the bench, often with

At oral argument in *Oliphant v. Suquamish Indian Tribe*, lawyers faced eight of the Supreme Court justices who sat for this 1976 portrait. Left to right in front they are Byron White, William Brennan (absent that day), Warren Burger, Potter Stewart, Thurgood Marshall, and in back William Rehnquist, Harry Blackmun, Lewis Powell, and John Paul Stevens. Courtesy of the Library of Congress, LC-USZ-62-60135.

comments and questions suggesting that the justices expected to adopt a story substantially different than the speaker proposed.

Court members asked a few preliminary questions about the present-day Suquamish Tribe, the reservation, and the law enforcement situation there. Overall, however, they did not show interest in contemporary facts of life for people on the Port Madison Reservation, let alone the deeper history of the tribe. One justice even suggested—whether sarcastically or sincerely is not apparent in the transcript—that the court need not trouble itself with such specifics.[27] The comment came after Phil Malone said his arguments would be no different if circumstances at Port Madison were like those on the vast Navajo Reservation with its overwhelmingly Indian population and landownership. A justice replied, "Well, then, some of the facts are not particularly important," and Malone responded, "That is true"—one of the few coherent sentences he managed when addressing a justice's question.

If Barry Ernstoff had a different opinion about the importance of population and landownership statistics, he did not say so. Nor did he devote much of his allotted time to explaining the jurisdiction dispute from a Suquamish perspective. Rather than describing the history and local conditions that presented the Suquamish and other tribes with jurisdictional dilemmas or recounting developments that prompted them to assert inclusive territorial sovereignty, Ernstoff adhered to the strategy of emphasizing federal law and policy. Congress had created the troublesome "anomaly" of non-Indian residents and landowners in areas reserved for exclusive Indian homelands, Ernstoff argued. Congress should therefore solve the problem with legislation, especially since it had reversed its longtime policy of disabling tribal self-government. But even without explicit congressional approval, Ernstoff insisted, tribes had sufficient basis for the jurisdiction they were asserting. They could cite supportive "case law" and the Constitution's delegation of power over Indian affairs solely to the federal government. This argument brought a surprising statement from one member of the court, not named in the transcript. Because Ernstoff could cite no authority for the desired tribal jurisdiction *except* principles set out in Supreme Court opinions, he had nothing, the justice said.

Malone ceded some of his time on the hot seat to Washington attorney general Slade Gorton, who spoke before Ernstoff did. Although Washington's governor had asked the court not to review the lower court rulings,

Gorton submitted a separate brief advocating review and reversal. At oral argument, he downplayed the relevance of "case law," urging the court to rely instead on statutory law, but a barrage of questions and comments from justices forced him to talk first about court rulings. He eventually managed to say that the words of the Point Elliott Treaty and congressional legislation were decisive, and they did not explicitly acknowledge or authorize tribal jurisdiction. In the closing minutes of his allotted time, Gorton invoked post-treaty history as another reason to deny the tribe jurisdiction. "Literally tens of thousands of United States citizens," he said, "in reliance on" lawmakers' and officials' "consistent, longstanding" views that tribes could not govern non-Indians, "purchased land and settled on Indian Reservations in full confidence that they have not waived their rights to self-government and to participation in the administration of their criminal justice system." It was now too late to tell them they were effectively in a foreign country, one where they could never become "naturalized citizens."[28]

The court heard last from S. Barton Farr III, representing the United States government. Of the four lawyers who spoke that morning, Farr was presumably best suited to discuss federal policy history, but justices grilled him instead about Indians' thinking. Under questioning by Justice Potter Stewart, Farr found himself speculating about Indians' original conception of their tribal dominions. When Stewart posited that tribes' sovereignty did not begin as full sovereignty, Farr said, "We think it did," but Stewart countered, "Not a territorial sovereignty" and asked, "Was that not a concept wholly alien to Indian Tribes?" Unaccountably, giving no indication that he had more than supposedly common knowledge to go on, Farr responded, "That is correct . . . , they did not have a sophisticated concept of land ownership and there was not anybody else to govern. It was just them. . . . But that is because they did not view territories belonging to particular individual tribes . . . ; that is a concept in which the European settlers quickly educated them." To a justice who subsequently faulted Farr for failing to show that tribes originally had criminal jurisdiction at all, Farr answered, "I have given it my shot."[29]

Two days later, during oral argument in a case from the Navajo Reservation, court members initiated more discussion about Indian tribes' imputed sovereignty. The man accused of a crime in that case was Indian but not Navajo, and the tribe was not a party. Once again, some justices expected an attorney for the United States to know the history of tribal governance, and the attorney—tapping into common stereotypes—simply guessed at how the Indians historically punished wrongdoers. "I understand that there is [*sic*] rudimentary institutions of justice," he said. 'I think they were called family courts. I think crimes of violence were not too well known to the Navajos until the introduction of alcohol by non-Indians, and I don't think that was much of a problem. So they had informal institutions of justice."[30]

The parties and justices agreed that resolution of the Navajo case—*United States v. Wheeler*—would turn on whether Indians' right of self-government was inherent in their history as a "tribe" that predated the United States. The court expected to answer the same question in *Oliphant v. Suquamish Tribe*, and during oral arguments in both cases, questioning from justices suggested an interest in comparing Suquamish and Navajo political history and contemporary circumstances. In neither case, however, did the court hear about those histories and circumstances from the Indians who experienced them.

THE COURT'S STORY

On March 6, 1978, the Supreme Court reversed the two lower court judgments in *Oliphant v. Suquamish Tribe*. Mark Oliphant and Daniel Belgarde would not face a Suquamish judge or jury after all. Eight justices had considered "whether Indian tribal courts have criminal jurisdiction over non-Indians," and six agreed on an answer, announced early in the Opinion of the Court: "We decide that they do not."[31]

In seventeen following pages, Justice Rehnquist gave two principal reasons for that decision. First, federal records supported an inference that the United States Congress and executive, for two centuries, had consistently viewed tribes as having no right to penalize non-Indians for crimes. Second, and crucially, the power to prosecute non-Indians was "inconsistent with [tribes'] status" as "dependents" of the United States, which controls the territory Indians occupy and has steadfastly aimed to protect US citizens from "unwarranted intrusions on their personal liberty." (The latter phrase was as close as the court came to a stand on petitioners' argument that tribal jurisdiction over "disenfranchised" people of another race would violate their rights under the US Constitution.)[32]

Most of the court opinion was a narrative about the intentions of non-Indian legislators, administrators, legal advisers, and jurists—people who had roles in governing the United States and creating the records from which Rehnquist crafted his story. Following a standard introduction identifying the adversaries and describing their dispute, the opinion said almost nothing about Suquamish or other Indian experiences, actions, or aims, let alone Indian conceptions of their tribal powers and territorial rights. In other words, the court narrative's focus corresponded to the focus of litigants' stories.

A footnote acknowledged that courts should interpret ambiguous wording of relevant US treaties or statutes "in favor of the weak and defenseless" Indians, taking into account their circumstances at the time of the agreements or legislation. Yet Rehnquist, considering no circumstances except the American-authored language of the Point Elliott Treaty, inferred that the Suquamish "in all probability" understood "the United States would arrest and try non-Indian intruders."[33]

The history of Indian self-governance garnered just one brief mention from Rehnquist, in a passage concerned solely with courts. Citing no sources, he wrote that the Indian effort to exercise criminal jurisdiction over non-Indians was "a relatively new phenomenon, and where the effort has been made in the past, it has been held that the jurisdiction did not exist." "Until the middle of this century," he continued, "few Indian tribes maintained any semblance of a formal court system. Offenses by one Indian against another were usually handled by social and religious pressure and not by formal judicial processes; emphasis was on restitution rather than on punishment." The sole identified basis for this generalization was a report to Congress in 1834 from an Indian affairs commissioner who purported to know that "with the exception of two or three tribes . . . , the Indian tribes are without laws, and the chiefs without much authority to exercise any restraint."[34]

From that point in Rehnquist's account, the significant actors were all in the federal government's employ. Among them were treaty negotiators in 1830 who supposedly spurned a Choctaw Nation request for a provision acknowledging its right to punish white violators of Choctaw law. Also featured were early Congresses that authorized federal trials of non-Indians for alleged crimes in Indian territory, bill drafters who were "careful" in 1834 "not to give the tribes of the [proposed Western] territory criminal jurisdiction over United States officials and citizens traveling through the area," and authors of a 1960 Senate report who assumed that "Indian tribal law is enforcible [*sic*] against Indians only."

Judges at all levels of the federal court system were essential to Rehnquist's story as well. Most went unnamed, their roles indicated only by the mention of cases they decided. Of the three jurists Rehnquist did name, two served on the Supreme Court during its earliest decades, when it first saw a need to define Indians' relationship to the United States in American legal terms. One was Chief Justice John Marshall, whose conception of history was the basis for rulings on cases in 1824, 1831, and 1832. From Marshall's two opinions that firmly acknowledged Cherokees' status as an inherently self-governing nation, Rehnquist chose to quote only an assertion of Indians' need for "protection from lawless and injurious intrusions into their country," a reference to Cherokees as "quasi-sovereign," and a statement that they were "completely under the sovereignty and dominion of the United States."

A contemporary of Marshall, Justice William Johnson, made a cameo appearance in Rehnquist's account because—in an 1810 contest between two non-Indians—he wrote an individual opinion on the limits of Indian tribes' sovereignty. That was not the central issue in the case, but Rehnquist highlighted Johnson's gratuitous statement that US sovereignty prohibited tribes from governing "every person within their limits except themselves."[35]

The third jurist with a featured role in Rehnquist's story was Isaac Parker, a district judge in Arkansas Territory. Parker ruled in 1878 that a Cherokee Nation court did not have jurisdiction over a white man accused of theft. The fact that the theft occurred outside Cherokee Nation boundaries was sufficient basis for that ruling, as Parker conceded, but Rehnquist chose to quote another, unnecessary assertion. For the tribe's court to have jurisdiction over an offender, Parker wrote, "such offender must be an Indian." The accused man, the widower of a Cherokee woman, was a Cherokee citizen admittedly subject to Cherokee jurisdiction in Cherokee country, but neither Parker nor Rehnquist said so. Rehnquist took unusual pains to justify the attention he devoted to the uncalled-for opinion of a single lower court judge. In a long footnote, he claimed that Indian tribes in Parker's district held him in high esteem. No supporting evidence followed that claim.[36]

DISSENTERS AND DOUBTERS

Two members of the Supreme Court dissented from the majority opinion in *Oliphant v. Suquamish Tribe*. Thurgood Marshall explained why in one terse paragraph: he and Chief Justice Warren Burger agreed with Ninth Circuit judges that the tribe could try any tribal law violator in its territory because the "power to preserve order on the reservation . . . is a sine qua non of the sovereignty that the Suquamish originally possessed," and no treaty or federal statute had expressly annulled that power. Marshall and Burger thus firmly endorsed the principle of law and the reasoning on which the Suquamish had based their bid for inclusive territorial authority.

Dissenters, both on the court and outside it, attracted little attention from mainstream news media. The *Washington Post*, *Wall Street Journal*, and *New York Times* reported the outcome of the case without commentary. The *Seattle Times* solicited reactions from people with personal stakes in the litigation and gave top billing to Frank Ruano, president of the Association of Property Owners of Port Madison. Ruano had formerly "accused the Suquamish of repeatedly attempting to claim sovereignty . . . , avoid compliance with state and federal laws," and "force its will on non-Indian residents regarding land use, utilities, roads, and other matters." The Supreme Court decision, he exulted, would "establish that Indians are not a sovereign nation within this country, any more than is the People's Republic of China." Triumphant state attorney general Gorton pronounced the ruling "very, very profound."

The *Seattle Times* also relayed comments from two disappointed men. Barry Ernstoff, rather than decrying the court's decision, downplayed its importance. Oliphant's case involved only criminal law enforcement, he said. The ruling would not affect "other issues of sovereignty, such as those mentioned by Ruano," which were civil law matters. The non-Indian editor of the *Indian Voice*, a locally produced monthly with modest national circulation, was less accepting. "It's patently obvious," Bob Johnson rumbled, "if they'll allow rednecks to go driving drunk tearing up property through a reservation, the Supreme Court . . . is countenancing a situation that breeds lawlessness."[37]

Meanwhile, experts on federal Indian law scrutinized the ruling for Oliphant and Belgarde and found much to disparage. Among the first to publish a thorough analysis were Russel Barsh and James Youngblood Henderson, who began their highly critical *Minnesota Law Review* article with studied restraint: "A close examination of the Court's opinion reveals a carelessness with history, logic, precedent, and statutory construction that is not ordinarily acceptable from so august a body." Alex Skibine did not bother with measured language. In the journal of the Institute for the Development of Indian Law, he slammed the *Oliphant* holding as "perhaps the most political, racist and detrimental Supreme Court opinion in a long time," a signal that "the so-called trust relationship . . . can be used against the Indians and make a mockery out of Indian sovereignty."[38]

The legal analysts generally reproached the court for disregarding established doctrine. Most deplorably, in their view, the justices ignored the tenet that tribes retain all their original sovereign powers except those that they explicitly relinquished or Congress explicitly nullified.[39] Rehnquist conceded that neither exception applied in the Suquamish case; no treaty clause or act of Congress stated that the tribe could not punish non-Indians. Rehnquist simply fashioned a third exception to the rule of retained tribal power when he declared that Indians' "dependent status" could nullify an inherent power. Historian Bethany Berger stressed that the court thus "created something wholly new in Indian law, the principle that simply by incorporation within the United States tribes had been divested of criminal jurisdiction over non-Indians." The innovation dismayed law professor Sarah Krakoff because it disregarded another foundation of Indian law: congressional supremacy. The justices, bypassing Congress, claimed the right to determine whether a specific power is inconsistent with tribes' status. To Krakoff, this usurpation of legislators' prerogative was "the most important aspect" of the court's regrettable decision.[40]

Scholars also aimed scathing criticism at Rehnquist's assertions about history. Some found his choices and use of historical evidence so inapt, misleading, and illogical as to suggest deliberate deception, disingenuousness, or cynicism. The critics saw Rehnquist engaging in roughly five kinds of flawed argument: disregarding indisputably relevant evidence, denying the relevance of recent circumstances, generalizing from isolated examples, interpreting the "silence" of historical actors as consistent with his hypothesis, and failing to recognize and compensate for his own bias.

Several analysts found Rehnquist's evidence of single-minded US opposition to tribal jurisdiction unfairly selective. To show a constant assumption that Indians could not prosecute non-Indians, the justice ignored significant contrary evidence in federal records. Barsh and Henderson offered a lengthy list of disregarded items. Berger saw deceitful selectivity throughout the entire "two thirds of the opinion in which the Court discussed historic non-judicial assumptions about tribal jurisdiction over non-Indians." For example, Rehnquist pulled from Cohen's *Handbook of Federal Indian Law* a statement that US courts, since 1871, had generally condemned tribes' attempt to exercise jurisdiction over non-Indians. He omitted "what Cohen actually wrote . . . , that originally a tribe 'might punish aliens within its jurisdiction according to its own laws and customs,' and '[s]uch jurisdiction continues to this day, save as it has been expressly limited by the acts of a superior government.'" This omission was not inadvertent, Berger emphasized; the court had received two briefs quoting the very language he ignored. A more glaring instance of biased evidence selection, in Berger's view, was Rehnquist's use of an 1834 congressional report on a bill that never became law. He chose a sentence suggesting that legislators intended to make federal court the only place to try non-Indians for crimes in a proposed Western Indian Territory. He did not mention statements on the same page of the report that "clearly showed the opposite" intent.[41]

Political scientist David Wilkins pointed out other disregarded evidence that ran contrary to the court's characterization of federal policy. For instance, Rehnquist cited two obscure opinions by government lawyers who denied tribal jurisdiction but did not mention Nathan Margold's influential contrasting opinion endorsed by Commissioner John Collier. The court's statement that tribal efforts to police non-Indians were "a relatively new phenomenon" also elided inconvenient evidence, including facts recited in an 1824 Supreme Court opinion.[42]

To Wilkins's consternation, more recent history carried no weight with the court majority. In depicting a federal government that had always rejected tribal jurisdiction over non-Indian offenders, Rehnquist wrote off a decade or more of late twentieth-century developments. Although he acknowledged that US policy and legislation since the 1960s had enabled some tribes to provide "sophisticated" law enforcement and justice services, that was a throwaway concession. In Rehnquist's analysis, the contemporary policy era, like the New Deal period of fostering tribal government, was an immaterial exception to the United States' persistent denial of tribes' right to punish non-Indians. This indifference to changed circumstances would be "especially troublesome to larger tribes," Wilkins warned; they had acted on the belief that recent cases affirming tribal sovereignty and ongoing federal support for tribal court development, together with the predominance of Indians on their reservations, would weigh in favor of their "strong right to prosecute non-Indian criminals."[43]

Krakoff and Berger, among others, emphasized that the justices' opinion disregarded and misconstrued pertinent decisions of the Supreme Court itself. Rehnquist did not even cite the 1959 ruling in *Williams v. Lee*, identified by Krakoff as the leading case on "the proper analytical approach to determining the existence of inherent tribal powers." Instead, Rehnquist cited and quoted older cases that stressed the forced dependency and political weakness of tribes in the late 1800s. He relied on early nineteenth-century rulings for the notion that the court could determine whether a tribe's asserted power was consistent with its "status," but in all those cases, Krakoff observed, the issue was only the tribes' power over external affairs, which had been explicitly limited in nation-to-nation agreements with the United States. Rehnquist ignored the fact that the court at that time did not claim authority to "ferret out" implicit limitations on Indians' power over "purely domestic" matters.[44] Berger took issue with Rehnquist's citation of Justice Johnson's unnecessary concurring opinion in 1810. Why rescue from obscurity the only denial of tribal jurisdiction over non-Indians to be found in early court opinions? It was "a slender reed" on which to rest the claim that the court could suddenly redefine the powers of Indian nations, especially since Johnson's concurrences "always expressed radically different views on Indian law than the opinions of the Court."[45]

To Barsh and Henderson, the scandal of Rehnquist's skewed historical evidence was compounded by false claims for the representative nature of items he cited. He ignored records that did not fit his narrative and alleged that some unusual ones exemplified an entire pattern of federal understanding and intent. For instance, to show constant US opposition to tribal prosecution of non-Indians, Rehnquist wrote that the "'earliest treaties *typically* expressly provided' for punishment of non-Indian offenses in Indian country 'according to the laws of the United States.'"

That language, Barsh and Henderson found, "appears in only one treaty."[46] Law professor Robert Clinton observed that Rehnquist paired this pattern of privileging isolated documents with the misrepresentation of records that could undercut his thesis. He "brushed aside a number of early Indian treaties" containing declarations "that non-Indian United States citizens who illegally entered and settled in Indian country were subject to tribal punishment. Since these treaties were seemingly inconsistent with the remainder of Justice Rehnquist's theory, he simply misinterpreted them by suggesting that they did not really provide what they seemed to say."[47]

To show what Rehnquist overlooked, Barsh and Henderson compiled a table of the numerous and varied Indian treaty clauses that expressly addressed jurisdiction over non-Indian criminal conduct. "In the final analysis," they summarized, "Justice Rehnquist cited only six treaties out of 366. None of the articles he quoted appear . . . to have been representative; one treaty he relied on is unique, and another has been materially misquoted. From this insubstantial foundation, Justice Rehnquist concluded that tribal treaties acquiesced in a historical federal policy against tribal criminal jurisdiction over non-Indians."[48]

The Suquamish treaty was one of many without an explicit provision concerning tribal punishment of non-Indians. It included only the Indians' promise "not to shelter or conceal offenders against the laws of the United States, but to deliver them up to the authorities for trial." Several scholars identified that as a simple agreement to extradite people accused of breaking US laws, not tribal law. Rehnquist himself noted the treaty's silence on the subject at issue in the Suquamish case, but in a footnote he mentioned that an early draft of the treaty did contain a clause providing for federal prosecution of non-Indians charged with on-reservation crimes. Dismissing the possibility that its omission from the final agreement was due to Indian objections, Rehnquist simply deemed it "probable" that the Indians understood the treaty "as acknowledging exclusive federal criminal jurisdiction over non-Indians."

This reasoning struck Barsh and Henderson as "the ultimate absurdity of historical inference: resolving silence in favor of the hypothesis" when there was "no evidence to support either view of the matter." It was the kind of reasoning Rehnquist used more than once to infer US officials' thinking. He purported to intuit the unspoken assumptions of people who wrote documents that said nothing at all about the issue at hand. Barsh and Henderson called that "*Gestalt* jurisprudence."[49]

Critics directed some of their sharpest barbs at the surprisingly ahistorical analysis in the following passage of the court opinion.

> From the formation of the Union and the adoption of the Bill of Rights, the United States has manifested . . . [a] great solicitude that its citizens be protected from unwarranted intrusions on their personal liberty. The power of the United States to try and criminally punish is an important manifestation of the power to restrict personal liberty. By submitting to the overriding sovereignty of the United States, Indian tribes therefore necessarily give up their power to try non-Indian citizens of the United States except in a manner acceptable to Congress. This principle would have been obvious a century ago when most Indian tribes were characterized by a "want of fixed laws [and] of competent tribunals of justice . . . ." H.R. Rep. No. 474, 23d Cong., 1st Sess., 18 (1834). It should be no less obvious today, even though present-day Indian tribal courts embody dramatic advances over their historical antecedents.

David Wilkins, his tongue perhaps in his cheek, responded to this passage with questions the court did not address. If the federal government wanted to protect its citizens' rights, and if tribal courts would presumably impose "unwarranted intrusions" on citizens' liberty, why had Congress or the justices not protected Indians from the jurisdiction of tribal courts? Indians—citizens at least since 1924—were still tried in tribal courts. The Indian Civil Rights Act of 1968 guaranteed essential protections for defendants in tribal courts. Why was that not an assurance for non-Indians too? As Rehnquist himself noted, lawmakers amended a draft of the ICRA so that its guarantees would apply to "any person" who came under tribal jurisdiction.

One passage in the opinion hinted at how the justices might have answered Wilkins's questions. Rehnquist quoted a Supreme Court ruling from 1883 that explained why a federal statute left the punishment of Indian-on-Indian crimes to the tribes: Indians were "aliens and strangers . . . , separated by race and tradition" from non-Indians; it would be wrong to judge Indians in US courts "by a standard made by others and not for them." The converse of that idea, Rehnquist reasoned (as if a nineteenth-century characterization of Indians needed no reevaluation), was that trying non-Indians by the standards of Indian-made laws would also be unfair. If so, Wilkins remarked, then Indians are aliens to the state courts where they are often tried.[50]

More directly than Wilkins, law professor Robert A. Williams, Jr., denounced the court opinion in *Oliphant* for its "rigid adherence" to old doctrine rooted in European colonizers' assumption that indigenous American societies were deficient, particularly in matters of law and governance. Because of that assumption, Williams observed, Indians had endured decades of US disrespect for their "self-defining vision." Over the decade preceding 1978, however, the "tradition" of disrespect "had begun to dissolve with the dramatic shift of federal policy." Now the court had suddenly "revived the [objectionable] tradition." In ruling against the Suquamish, a few white men had reflexively rendered a decision reflecting discredited premises of Indian inferiority and lawlessness rather than a conception of Indian-US relations as a process of give-and-take between nations whose legal traditions deserved equal respect.[51]

Ultimately—in the eyes of Wilkins, Barsh, Henderson, Williams, and others—the most shameful thing about the decision in *Oliphant v. Suquamish Tribe* was not the justices' detection of a long-standing US government desire to protect non-Indians from punishment by Indian tribes; it was the justices' endorsement of that desire in 1978, apparently because they expected tribal courts to treat non-Indian defendants unfairly. As Barsh and Henderson wrote, "Justice Rehnquist seemed to assume that the protection of citizens' liberty only required that whites be immunized from the risk of tribal prosecution." Did he assume that tribal courts would improperly interfere solely with non-Indians' liberty? "Or has Justice Rehnquist told us that Congress only cares what happens to white people? . . . In effect, Justice Rehnquist's policy argument . . . discriminates against Indians because of their ethnicity and customs."[52]

Barsh and Henderson labeled the court's decision a "betrayal" for revoking a recent US bargain with Indian tribes. Policy changes since the 1950s, new federal laws, and corresponding administrative actions had signaled to Indians that the reward for "modernizing" their legal systems would be United States recognition of tribal governments as the appropriate managers of reservations. Tribal courts had consequently been evolving, with federal help, toward an Anglo-American legal model, and tribes had reasonably come to expect respect for those courts. Now six high court jurists had intervened to prohibit the fulfillment of that expectation.

This argument implied that the tribes' expectations were more consistent with historical facts than the court's story of unchanging federal assumptions and policy. Throughout the history of US-Indian relations, from the 1770s to the 1970s, the power balance and the degree of Indian autonomy had been in continual negotiation, changing over time to reflect fluctuating Indian circumstances as well as new US government considerations. In 1978, when the court stepped in to foreclose one area of tribal governance, it preempted that political process, preventing Indians and the United States from continuing to adjust an important term of their historic nation-to-nation relations.

MISSING STORIES

While the justices' desire to protect non-Indians from tribal prosecutions drew charges of racial bias from members of the legal profession, their one-sided view of history did not incur equivalent censure. That tacit acceptance of the court's near-exclusive concentration on US government beliefs and intentions is notable because a rule of federal law requires that Indian treaties be interpreted according to the Indian parties' reasonable understandings.

Even critics evidently expected the court to focus on the thinking of federal officials and lawmakers. After all, the Supreme Court is an organ of the US government charged with upholding US laws. More to the point, appellate courts in the United States rely on case records to provide nearly all the facts the judges should consider, and in *Oliphant v. Suquamish Tribe*, the record contained almost no evidence of pre-1970s Indian expectations or practices related to crime and punishment, tribal powers, tribal territory, and tribes' relationship to the United States.[53]

The nature of the litigation partly accounts for the case record's dearth of Indian history. There is seldom much testimony in habeas corpus proceedings because essential facts are not numerous or disputed. Documents confirm a petitioner's detention and circumstances affecting its legality; the judge determines as a matter of law whether that detention is proper. The initial court review of Oliphant's detention fit this pattern. The parties agreed on the facts that presented the question of law: an Indian tribe had arrested and charged a non-Indian for actions he did not deny. The lean record therefore consisted of a petition and written reply, a few affidavits, and briefs arguing legal points. The tribe did not offer live testimony or documentation of past Suquamish beliefs about tribal power and jurisdiction, let alone evidence regarding other Indians over a century or more. Barry Ernstoff counted on an argument grounded in law—a treaty, federal statutes, rulings by other courts, and established legal principles—to carry the day.

Consequently, the files that reached the Supreme Court revealed nothing about the deep history of Indian self-governance, methods of social control, or expectations of autonomy and territorial control after their treaties with the United States. No one had testified to nineteenth-century Suquamish concepts of crime or practices that corresponded to American law enforcement. No one had submitted evidence of Suquamish reactions to criminal acts by early American settlers. The habeas corpus pleadings and affidavits scarcely mentioned Suquamish relations with non-Indian neighbors or other governments, historical or contemporary.

What little information the justices did have about the Suquamish was surely on their minds as they pondered the tribe's assertion of sovereignty. The briefs told them—without further explanation—that non-Indians in 1973 vastly outnumbered the few Indians on the Port Madison Reservation and owned most of the land there, that the tribe's current formal government was barely a decade old, that its criminal law code and court were new when a Suquamish judge arraigned Mark Oliphant. Kitsap County urged the court to consider facts of another sort: the array of services the county ostensibly provided on the reservation, including law enforcement.

Common sense suggests that such information could inhibit the justices' receptivity to arguments for tribal jurisdiction. Indeed, three years later a political scientist compiled data suggesting just such an effect. Philip Lee Fetzer examined Supreme Court decisions in eleven recent jurisdictional disputes between tribes and state governments. He found, with one exception, that the ruling favored the state every time the non-Indian population of the reservation exceeded the Indian population.[54]

In the words of legal scholar Stephen Winston, "The issues before a court, no matter how broad their potential impact, are framed in a microcosm. . . . It is only in concrete, specific factual situations that a court issues its rulings on the law."[55] Mindful of this reality, some tribe leaders and attorneys feared the effect that the unique Suquamish facts might have on justices' feelings about tribal trials of non-Indians. Several amicus briefs therefore aimed to expand the court's view of relevant facts. The NCAI brief characterized Port Madison Reservation demographics as atypical and urged the court not to let non-Indians' predominance "cloud the issue"; there were more representative situations to consider. "The issue . . . might have arisen on, say, the Quinault Reservation in Washington State, which has an area of 190,000 acres (entirely rural), a population of about 1,100 Indians and 200 non-Indians, and a comparatively well-equipped law and order system." Even on some reservations with larger minority non-Indian populations, inclusive tribal law enforcement was already standard and not controversial. Around the country, the Bureau of Indian Affairs counted three hundred tribal arrests of non-Indians for nontraffic offenses in the first half of 1977, and traffic citations were surely more numerous.[56]

Yet amicus briefs could not make up for a case record lacking evidence of pertinent Indian expectations. Indian experiences described in the briefs were either recent or general consequences of repressive US policies. Moreover, justices likely gave little weight to unsworn factual assertions in amicus briefs. Mike Taylor thought they simply ignored his. Asked in 2012 whether he had had qualms about the Supreme Court's decision to review the Suquamish case, Taylor said, "No. . . . We used to think the Supreme Court read amicus briefs though."[57]

It is reasonable to imagine that the justices' vote on the tribal jurisdiction issue might have been closer or their ruling less sweeping if a tribe such as Quinaults had made the disputed arrest, then documented their decades of formal self-governance, their long-running determination to control affairs on their reservation, and their persistent expectation of US respect for their political autonomy. As it was, even if the justices read and believed briefs from the Quinaults and other amici, Suquamish reservation demographics probably did cloud their analysis. Still, that shadow may not have darkened their view of tribal jurisdiction significantly more than if the case had originated elsewhere. After all, the court ruled out tribal prosecution of non-Indians everywhere, including reservations with large majority Indian populations, and Rehnquist expressed concern for the rights of non-Indians in all tribal courts, even the well-established, "sophisticated" ones.

In the end, because the Supreme Court—with the parties' consent—chose to answer the jurisdiction question for every tribe in the United States, it ruled as if the specific experiences of the Suquamish or other Indians did not matter much. A single local dispute had become the occasion to announce a new rule of law that would apply nationwide to hundreds of diverse tribes. In that situation, the Suquamish understandably opted to emphasize general legal principles rather than their unusual local history and circumstances. They hoped to win judicial approval of their recent political resurgence by claiming a part in the larger story of US-Indian relations and federal Indian law.

A bare-bones case record is not the only reason for the court's concentration on non-Indian characters in the story; another, more potent factor was at work. The intentions of federal government personnel were the focus of the litigation from the beginning because no interested party made an issue of US hegemony. No lawyer directly questioned the right of the United States to make and enforce law that limited or denied tribes' sovereignty. No one contested the court's role as enforcer of tribes' subordination to the colonial power of the United States. In effect, even the Indians tacitly acknowledged that US government intentions were what ultimately mattered in *Oliphant v. Suquamish Tribe.*

Weighty factors either deterred a challenge to US hegemony or kept attorneys for tribes from imagining such a stratagem. For one, the Supreme Court had long since approved the United States' claim of nearly unlimited power to govern Indian tribes and their members. Indian law experts have found that approval in two opinions—*United States v. Kagama* (1886) and *Lone Wolf v. Hitchcock* (1903). Both rulings upheld acts of Congress inconsistent with prior US acknowledgment of the tribes' sovereignty. In Kagama's case, the court converted an early metaphorical characterization of the United States' relationship with the Cherokee Nation to a federal legal status for all Indians. Justice Marshall had suggested in 1831 that the relationship *resembled* a guardian's protection of a ward. The *Kagama* opinion declared that Indians in 1886 *were* dependent wards of the federal government, and Congress could therefore "protect" them by authorizing federal prosecutions of tribe members for Indian-on-Indian crimes, which had previously been the tribes' exclusive concern. In Lone Wolf's case,

Kiowas could not prevent US abrogation of a treaty. With reasoning that allowed Congress to make virtually any law affecting its putative wards, the court held that lawmakers could disregard treaty-secured Kiowa property rights to achieve well-intentioned US objectives.[58] The court described the government's "plenary authority" over Indian affairs as "a political one, not subject to be controlled by the judicial department." In other words, courts had no business second-guessing legislators' Indian policy decisions.[59]

After the 1970s, some scholars of Indian law disputed the court's premise that the United States can unilaterally nullify tribes' sovereign rights. Their argument—an attack on the conception of federal plenary power announced in *Kagama* and *Lone Wolf*—was one that the Suquamish might have made if they had chosen to contest the supremacy of US law. The critics deplored the opinions in those cases as creative rationalizations of colonial control, lacking a legal foundation. The court in *Kagama* cited no judicial precedent for unlimited US power, nor could it have found that power spelled out in the Constitution. Under the Constitution, which clearly identified Indian tribes as politically separate peoples, Congress's power in Indian affairs was supreme or "plenary" only vis-à-vis state governments. Robert Clinton suggested that even Congress's 1871 ban on future Indian treaties was unconstitutional, and nowhere did the Constitution authorize direct congressional rule of Indian nations' internal affairs. In the critics' view, the *Kagama* and *Lone Wolf* rulings were so flawed that the Supreme Court should and could now reverse them.[60]

Petra Shattuck and Jill Norgren attributed those flaws to historical circumstances. By the late 1800s, tribes were weak, and pressures on the federal government to serve non-Indian interests were strong. The court, like Congress, felt free then to disregard their own precedents that had "defined the limits of federal power" over Indians "by reference to" Indian nations' rights under international law. Ignoring tribes' inherent rights as well, the justices went along with lawmakers' renunciation of relations with tribes as nations. To meet contemporary "political demands for the dispossession of the Indian," they assigned new meaning to Congress's "plenary" power so that "questions of Indian rights" could "be decided according to the preponderance of white power without giving the appearance of lawlessness." Thenceforth, the court would recognize "no limits to the federal power over Indians other than those the United States government had chosen to impose on itself."[61]

Shattuck and Norgren argued that the present-day court could reverse the insupportable *Kagama* and *Lone Wolf* holdings. By doing so, it would reaffirm the original Indian law principles derived from international law, especially the principle of inherent tribal sovereignty. It would acknowledge that the US refusal to make more treaties with tribes did not invalidate the tribes' claim of nationhood. Unilateral federal government decisions were just that; they did not extinguish tribes' inherent sovereignty. Because the United States had undeniably superior power, it might in practice limit the powers that tribes exercised, but it could not dictate how Indians conceived of their tribes, law, or justice. Furthermore, tribes would still have grounds in American legal doctrine as well as international law to maintain their sovereignty and contest the US claim of unlimited power.[62]

That the Suquamish Tribe in 1977 did not mount this challenge to the doctrine of federal plenary power is hardly surprising. Pragmatic considerations and the culture of the legal profession effectively precluded such a radical tack. On the practical front, the research and analysis needed to discredit *U.S. v. Kagama* and *Lone Wolf v. Hitchcock* would have been a tall order for a small-firm lawyer with limited time and resources. Critiques of those cases were not yet available in publications an advocate could conveniently cite. At best, tribal attorneys would have to draw on basic reasoning in a few law review articles and Felix Cohen's work from decades earlier, but they would not find a robust refutation of *Kagama* and *Hitchcock* spelled out there.[63]

Professional commitments and culture would also have deterred lawyers such as Ernstoff from contesting the unilateral imposition of US law on tribes. By joining the legal profession, attorneys accepted the authority of their country's courts on a wide range of subjects, including Indian affairs. They presumably shared with judges a basic respect for American legal culture, its tenets, its methods of reasoning, and its procedures for resolving disputes. They were trained to help clients achieve goals in a system where the usual objective was to persuade judges that those goals were consistent with previous judicial decisions, statutes, and other legal authorities. Arguing that relevant precedents favored a judgment for their clients was certainly preferable to seeking a reversal of long-standing precedent, and Ernstoff could invoke recent as well as old Supreme Court opinions that did affirm tribes' inherent sovereignty. In those circumstances, questioning the very foundation of federal government power to determine the limits of tribal sovereignty—had that occurred to him or his colleagues—would have seemed unnecessary as well as unwise.

There was another possible way to discredit the case law that allowed unilateral US denial of tribal sovereignty. Ernstoff alluded to it without developing an argument. He quoted the Supreme Court's admission in *Morton v. Mancari* (1974) that "overly paternalistic" US exercise of its plenary power had been "both exploitative and destructive to Indian interests." That paternalism was contrary to the more enlightened federal policy in effect since the mid-1960s.[64] If Ernstoff or Justice Department attorneys had taken this thought farther, their reasoning could have gone as follows. The court's formulation of the unlimited power doctrine in 1886 and 1903 was the product of a time in history when judges and government officials harbored a since-discredited belief in Indians' inferiority and whites' moral superiority. The tribes' defeat and dependency had enabled the federal government to impose severe practical limits on their autonomy without fear of effective retaliation. The court simply recognized the imbalance of power and called it "law." By the 1970s, however, circumstances had changed again as long-disadvantaged US populations mobilized to demand fairness and empowerment. Federal policy makers, recognizing Indians' enduring expectations of tribal self-government and their capacity for managing their own affairs in the contemporary American context, had agreed to a redistribution of power in Indian country. Such change required reconsideration of the assumptions about Indians that underlay the *Kagama* and *Lone Wolf* holdings.

To this argument, the Suquamish Tribe's opponents would likely have replied that Indians had long since acquiesced to ultimate United States control. When the court decided *United States v. Kagama*, most Indians had effectively conceded the US government's authority or would soon do so. Over the next half century or more, in practice if not in their hearts, they had acknowledged their subjection to American law in many aspects of life. They had asked US courts to ensure fulfillment of federal Indian law principles, including the rule that the government's self-assigned guardianship role came with solemn obligations to tribes. As Shattuck and Norgren observed in 1991, Indians had tried to hold "the law to its own promises and pretensions of justice" and at times had succeeded.[65] Thus, tribes and their lawyers had come to think of federal Indian law as a body of doctrine they could invoke for Indians' protection so long as court procedures were fair and judges followed accepted methods of achieving doctrinal coherence. Some Indian leaders in the 1970s sounded happy with the results. Joe DeLaCruz, for instance, said in 1976, "Today we have 250 lawyers fighting for our rights. We learned the laws of this great land. We like them." Ernie Stevens told members of the American Indian Policy Review Commission in 1977, "We feel secure in the law as it exists."[66]

To refute the implication that Indians' acknowledgment of US hegemony was an intentional, permanent renunciation of their sovereign powers over outsiders in tribal territory, tribes would have needed historical evidence that they did not provide in Oliphant's case. Ideally, that evidence would have included accounts from at least the 1850s to the 1970s of Indians policing non-Indians, imposing consequences for their crimes, or resisting US opposition to such tribal actions. Indian responses to criminal non-Indian conduct before the American conquest could also have been instructive.

Such evidence would not have been easy to muster, if indeed it had ever existed, particularly for the Suquamish and neighboring tribes. As of the 1970s, historical research about the Suquamish was all but nonexistent, and published histories of other tribes in western Washington were nearly as scarce. Nationwide as well, few historians had documented Indians' experiences for their own sake. Over the following four decades, scholars did begin to uncover and tell more history of indigenous peoples, some of which detailed Indian tribes' efforts to retain or regain as much self-governing power as possible under colonial domination. Ethnohistorians and authors of "new Indian history" employed innovative methods that could have enabled the Suquamish and their supporters to offer a fuller story of relevant Indian history. But in 1973, that surge of Indian-centered research was yet to come.[67]

Furthermore, even if the Suquamish could have commissioned such research for the habeas corpus hearing, a rich yield of material suitable for trial testimony and exhibits was hardly guaranteed. For several reasons, evidence of Indian beliefs and intentions would likely have been sparse, spotty, and ambiguous. Much of it would have taken forms such as orally transmitted memories, which a judge was apt to find unconvincing or inadmissible as evidence.[68]

The Suquamish had one close-to-home example of litigation that did produce a rich trial record of historical Indian expectations and understandings, but the persuasiveness of that record became apparent only after Judge Sharp denied Oliphant's petition. In *U.S. v. Washington*, a key witness for the United States and tribes was an anthropologist who had thoroughly researched how Indians understood the treaty clause securing their right to fish, both in 1855 and over ensuing decades. In ruling for the tribes, Judge Boldt described that witness's conclusions, based on fieldwork interviews with Indians and historical documents, as "well taken, sound, and reasonable" and found her "summaries of relevant aspects of Indian life" "authoritative."[69]

Even if the tribes could have generated a comparable record in *Oliphant v. Suquamish Tribe*, such as evidence of reasonable past Indian expectations that the reservations would be Indian-regulated enclaves, would that have overcome the Supreme Court's unease about tribal prosecutions of non-Indians? It seems unlikely. Still, such evidence might at least have bolstered an argument that the court should respect the recently renewed US government support for expanded tribal government powers and tribal courts. The Suquamish could have argued that tribes, as they gathered new strength over the twentieth century, had essentially engaged federal lawmakers and administrators in negotiations for more power, and they had won concessions that the court should not gainsay, including federal approval of codes that extended tribal governments' reach to non-Indians. The court could then have done what it purportedly did in *Lone Wolf v. Hitchcock*: it could have declined to decide whether tribal jurisdiction over non-Indians was proper and left the issue to be settled in the ongoing political process.

A record richer in testimony about Indian community history might have had another salutary effect for tribes. Telling Indian stories about the past in American courts has long been part of tribes' efforts to negotiate better terms of relations with non-Indians. The more such stories become public records and gain credibility in institutions that non-Indians respect, the more power those stories are likely to carry for tribal negotiators in other situations. That was an apparent consequence of the effort to educate the trial judge in *U.S. v. Washington*. Indians gained a hearing and ultimately a public outlet for history they could subsequently invoke for new purposes in their relations with non-Indians. If Indians in the Suquamish jurisdiction case had told more stories about matters related to the non-Indian problem on reservations—for example, stories about the circumstances of reservation land sales to non-Indians, county officials' disdain for tribal government, tribe members' eviction from reservation beaches, tribes' efforts to work with non-Indian authorities, and Indians' demonstrated respect for American legal culture and institutions—the Supreme Court might still have ruled as it did, but the tribes would have created a record and memories of potential use to them in future negotiations for control of their homelands.

In sum, when Mark Oliphant and his lawyer chose to resist Suquamish tribal prosecution on federal Indian law grounds, tribe leaders—despite a history of US policies that saddled them with a reservation populated largely by non-Indians—put their fate and perhaps their faith in the hands of non-Indian judges and lawyers. That strategy recommended itself in large part because of past Indian victories in federal courts, some in the early years of the American republic, some very recent, and some close to home. But the Supreme Court betrayed the Indians' faith (if faith it was). Rather than affirming the tribes' power based on foundational principles of Indian law that neither Congress nor the court had renounced—inherent tribal sovereignty and the enduring legal force of unabrogated Indian treaties—the court invoked judicial pronouncements that reflected a late-nineteenth-century conception of tribes whose sovereignty existed only at the pleasure of the federal government and its top jurists. Ignoring a trend in the US government of respecting tribes' aspirations for meaningful power, six justices decided that Indian tribes could not be allowed to judge non-Indians' guilt. To them, it seems, Indian societies were still too alien to ensure fairness for non-Indian defendants but no longer independent enough to define their own powers.

9. Obstacles, Options, and Opportunities

On many Indian reservations, the first and most critical consequence of Mark Oliphant's litigation victory was a law enforcement quandary. The weekly *Seattle Sun* announced the problem under an eye-catching headline: "Suquamish: Who's in Charge Here?" "The small town of Suquamish on the Kitsap peninsula spent last week virtually without police protection. In the wake of last Monday's United States Supreme Court decision denying the tribe's right to prosecute non-Indians for violations of the law while on reservation land, tribal police, under direction of the tribal council, refused to arrest non-Indians until the ramifications of the decision were clarified."[1]

Clarification would not come easily or soon. Indeed, clarity would be an elusive goal for decades to come. As Assistant Interior Secretary Forrest Gerard observed, "The Oliphant decision probably raised as many questions as it had resolved." Government officials, lawyers, and judges offered differing, contested responses to the new questions. Even Gerard's most urgent query for the Justice Department—"whether there is a law enforcement void on reservations now, and if there is, who is going to fill it"—did not have a ready, simple answer.[2]

The *Seattle Sun* reporter found various people pondering implications of the *Oliphant* decision for Indian tribes' legal status and place in the

American political system. It had "sparked a far-ranging debate among the tribal authorities, Kitsap County, and the attorney general of the state of Washington over the questions of Indian sovereignty and jurisdiction for criminal activity on the Port Madison Indian Reservation." Similar debates were under way in other tribes, counties, and states, wherever Indians maintained governments in federally recognized Indian country. Issues ranged from the competence of tribal police and courts to the concept of inherent tribal sovereignty and the desirability of expanding tribes' jurisdiction by federal legislation. Just the effort to answer Gerard's question about an enforcement void would be an open-ended, multifaceted process of tribal government experimentation, intergovernmental negotiations, congressional investigations, federal court litigation, and changes to the US code.

Advocates for Indian governments participated in that process with continuing determination to maximize their jurisdiction over reservation affairs. They did not concede Washington attorney general Slade Gorton's claim that the concept of tribal sovereignty—"a phony issue from the start"—had been put to rest for good.[3] Without disputing that the Supreme Court had foreclosed tribal prosecutions of non-Indians, they neither abandoned nor suspended the drive for tribal government authority over everyone within reservation boundaries. They did not even write off the possibility of penalizing non-Indians for violating tribal law. They did, however, try to achieve their goals by means other than litigation, especially as the Supreme Court rejected more tribal claims of jurisdiction. Thus, Joe DeLaCruz advised the Quinault general council in 1980, "To be successful in this fight we will have to increase our commitment to self regulation and discipline while we move from the court room to the US Congress and even to international commissions and organizations."[4] In some cases, Indian tribes' growing political sophistication and economic clout made power-sharing arrangements with other governmental entities a better option than the risks of winner-take-all litigation.

TESTING *OLIPHANT*'S LIMITS

Many people expected the outcome of *Oliphant v. Suquamish Tribe* to have the effect suggested by the *Seattle Sun* article: no government would take responsibility for policing non-Indians on reservations. Some tribal officials explained again that they had taken that responsibility earlier precisely because of enforcement gaps. State and federal police, spread thin in rural areas, could not or would not provide adequate patrols or respond reliably to criminal activity on reservations. Overburdened federal prosecutors pursued very few of the Indian country cases that fell within the jurisdiction of congested federal courts. Non-Indian troublemakers knew they could defy the law with impunity. Congressman Don Bonker, whose district included the Quinault Reservation, agreeing with these claims, told a reporter, "The availability of law and order to the million Indian and non-Indian citizens who live on reservations is in jeopardy."[5]

Indian leaders warned that the effectiveness and morale of tribal police would suffer. Where reservation land was a crazy quilt of Indian and non-Indian ownership, it was often hard to determine quickly which government had jurisdiction at the site of a crime in progress. Police could not tell on sight whether a suspect was Indian. Encounters with non-Indian lawbreakers could put tribal officers in a bind that DeLaCruz described for senators in 1980. Forbidden to process a non-Indian found engaged in crime, Quinault police had to call for state assistance, and when they got no response, as was common, they had to let the person go. "In one case," DeLaCruz said, "the non-Indian was driving while drunk. Upon his release he drove a mile down the road and ran into a guardrail. The officers involved may be liable for false arrest if they detain such a man and may be liable for the damage he causes if they release him. You can see what an impossible situation has grown up."[6] The situation exasperated Al Aubertin, vice chairman of the Colville Tribes. "How can tribal police work under the present set-up?" he asked. "I wish the Supreme Court had to live on the reservation."[7]

The Argus, a Seattle newspaper, offered evidence that the feared law enforcement voids were "not hypothetical." After Stan Robinson caught a thief inside his business on the Puyallup Reservation, he spent more than three hours "trying to persuade law enforcement officers to come and get his prisoner."

> Fife police, whose headquarters are 600 yards from the Teepee Shop, said they couldn't help because the smokeshop was on Indian land. Pierce County police told Robinson to call King County police, because that's where the crime was committed. King County police referred him back

> to Fife police. Fife police referred him back to King County police. Meanwhile, the prisoner locked himself in a restroom and flushed evidence down the toilet. . . . After that, Puyallup tribal police put the man in custody until the FBI finally agreed to intervene.[8]

At the Suquamish reservation, residents said the county sheriff could not be trusted to fill the vacuum left by the tribal officers' withdrawal. Some non-Indian residents lamented the loss of Suquamish enforcement services. One called the tribal cops "a good police force" and added, "It's a shame not to use them." Another described them as "small town cops in the best sense of the word. They'll take you home before they'll take you downtown."[9]

While complying with a strict interpretation of the Supreme Court opinion, Suquamish officials investigated potential work-arounds, alternative ways to stop or deter harmful non-Indian activity. One possible option—expelling or excluding offenders from the reservation—had limited appeal. Joe DeLaCruz, predicting a rise in "forestry thefts," announced that beleaguered tribes might "close borders." On his reservation, he warned, that would "create tremendous hardships" for the 1,700 non-Indians who worked there and the 500 who lived there. A state attorney, noting non-Indians' predominance on the Port Madison Reservation, foresaw that "the practical problems of . . . excluding a non-Indian resident" would be "considerable."[10] Additionally, a non-Indian landowner was certain to challenge an exclusion order, and few tribal officials or lawyers were eager for that legal battle or optimistic about winning it.

Because the Supreme Court explicitly prohibited only tribal prosecution and incarceration of non-Indians, some people asked whether tribal police could at least stop crimes by arresting non-Indians and delivering them to state or federal custody. Law professor Ralph Johnson thought they could. Shortly after the *Oliphant* opinion came down, he advised Northwest tribal judges that the court did not forbid tribes to apprehend non-Indian violators of state or federal law. He later told a reporter that the Assimilative Crimes Act enjoined tribes "not to shelter or conceal offenders against the law of the United States," but to hand them over for trial instead.[11]

The *Seattle Sun* story was thus outdated before the paper reached newsstands. Suquamish chairman Richard Belmont had decided by then to let

CAUTION

- Board contains magnetic shavings which can settle and cause discolouration if left in one position for extended time.
- Some pixels may be discoloured-this is an affect of the magnetic shavings and can sometimes be helped by passing a strong magnet over the entire board to lift shavings.
- Small black marks may appear on board-this is caused by air bubbles and cannot be helped. Please disregard such marks as part of the manufacturing process.
- Please keep board in cotton bag provided to protect from harmful sun/flourescent rays which can damage board and cause yellowing.
- Only a thin layer of paint is used to show the natural grain of the wood.
- Slide bar might be stiff at first but after regular use, should become easier to move.
- Edge of the board may show signs of discolouration. This is a side effect of the manufacturing process.
- If the board is stepped on or cracked, you may see liquid inside- this is non-toxic and not dangerous.

本製品に関しての使用および保管上の注意

- 本体を長期間、横に倒している状態もしくは使用されない場合、ボード内のパウダー成分が沈下する為、ボードの発色が不鮮明になる場合がございます。付属のペン・スタンプで発色が不鮮明な場合は、磁力の強い磁石（ご家庭のメモクリップやホワイトボード等で使用されている強めの磁石）を使いボード全面を発色させてお使い頂きますようお願い致します。
- 直射日光や室内灯等の外光下にて、長期間使用された場合、ボード部全体に黄ばみが生じることがございます。使用後も出来るだけ外光は避け付属のバッグ等に入れ保管して下さい。
- ボード表面は樹脂製の為、付属のペンで強く押さえたり、たたきつけた場合、傷や発色不良の原因となりますのでお気を付け下さい。
- ボード表面や際に見受けられる黒い小さな点は気泡によるものですのでご了承ください。
- 木目がうっすら見える塗装に仕上げております。そのため、濃い木目などは目立ちやすくなっております。
- 天然木を使用しているため商品には個体差があり、中には犬のスライド部がひっかかる物もございます。
- ボードと木製フレームとの境目部分に黒い気泡が出ている場合がございますが、これはボードの特性上ボード際までは色がつかない仕様となっております。ご了承下さい。
- ボードを足で踏みつけたり、落としたりした場合破損の原因となりますのでご注意下さい。その際、中の液体が流出することがございますが、有毒物質ではございませんのでご安心下さい。

CAUTION

- Board contains magnetic shavings which can settle and cause discolouration if left in one position for extended time.
- Some pixels may be discoloured-this is an affect of the magnetic shavings and can sometimes be helped by passing a strong magnet over the entire board to lift shavings.
- Small black marks may appear on board-this is caused by air bubbles and cannot be helped. Please disregard such marks as part of the manufacturing process.
- Please keep board in cotton bag provided to protect from harmful sun/flourescent rays which can damage board and cause yellowing.
- Only a thin layer of paint is used to show the natural grain of the wood.
- Slide bar might be stiff at first but after regular use, should become easier to move.
- Edge of the board may show signs of discolouration. This is a side effect of the manufacturing process.
- If the board is stepped on or cracked, you may see liquid inside- this is non-toxic and not dangerous.

本製品に関しての使用および保管上の注意

- 本体を長期間、横に倒していた状態もしくは使用されない場合、ボード内のパウダー成分が沈下する為、ボードの発色が不鮮明になる場合がございます。付属のペン・スタンプで発色が不鮮明な場合は、磁力の強い磁石（ご家庭のメモクリップやホワイトボード等で使用されている強めの磁石）を使いボード全面を発色させてお使い頂きますようお願い致します。
- 直射日光や室内灯等の外光下にて、長期間使用された場合、ボード部全体に黄ばみが生じることがございます。使用後も出来るだけ外光は避け付属のバッグ等に入れ保管して下さい。
- ボード表面は樹脂製の為、付属のペンで強く押さえたり、たたきつけた場合、傷や発色不良の原因となりますのでお気を付け下さい。
- ボード表面や際に見受けられる黒い小さな点は気泡によるものですのでご了承ください。
- 木目がうっすら見える塗装に仕上げております。そのため、濃い木目などは目立ちやすくなっております。
- 天然木を使用しているため商品には個体差があり、中には穴のスライド部がひっかかる物もございます。
- ボードと木製フレームとの境目部分に黒い気泡が出ている場合がございますが、これはボードの特性上ボード際まで色がつかない仕様となっております。ご了承下さい。
- ボードを足で踏みつけたり、落としたりした場合破損の原因となりますのでご注意下さい。その際、中の液体が流出することがございますが、有害物質ではございませんのでご安心下さい。

his officers arrest non-Indians when they could arrange transfers to non-tribal authorities. Other tribes in the region did the same, but without much reason to expect improved law enforcement. After all, tribes had asserted jurisdiction because they could not count on state or federal police to come. Now, some sheriffs and state police were questioning tribal cops' competency and legitimacy while emboldened non-Indians threatened to defy tribal officers, contending that even short detentions contravened the *Oliphant* ruling. Frank Ruano, spokesman for some non-Indian reservation property owners, growled, "If they (tribal police) take me in, they will be sued for every penny they have. It is false arrest."[12]

A third possible way to control non-Indian troublemakers—civil regulation—was under discussion moments after the Supreme Court ruled. Recall Ernstoff's statement to the *Seattle Times* that the ruling did not limit the reach of tribal civil law.[13] Ralph Johnson agreed and advised tribal judges accordingly: the decision pertained only to enforcement of laws that defined violations as crimes; it had no bearing on tribal government power to require compliance with the regulation of matters such as land use, commerce, and public health hazards.[14] NCAI member tribes eventually received the same assurance from the organization's legal advisers.[15]

Suquamish leaders no doubt welcomed that assurance. Like several other tribes in Washington State, they had asserted a right to regulate reservation land use and environmental conditions well before they sought to bring pugnacious non-Indian drunks or reckless drivers to trial in tribal court. They had been contesting county zoning power for at least six years.[16] Most recently, the *Seattle Sun* reported, the tribe had asserted a right to block a proposed commercial landfill inside the reservation. A county commissioner, claiming the Indians would make the reservation "a legal no-man's land . . . not subject to environmental and solid waste regulations," expected the landfill to comply with county regulations. "I have no quarrel dealing with the tribe if they conceive of themselves as a municipal entity," he said, "but I do have problems if they see themselves as a third sovereign, not subject to federal or state law." Dick Belmont retorted that the tribe was indeed a separate sovereign and—by the way—would probably use its sovereign power to veto the garbage dump for fear of adverse environmental impacts.[17]

One federal judge in western Washington thought the *Oliphant* opinion did preclude tribal regulation of non-Indian commercial activity.

A Canadian company planning a trailer court and shopping center on the Muckleshoot Reservation had sued to bar enforcement of the tribe's business licensing ordinance. Judge Walter McGovern denied the company a preliminary injunction in January 1978, but after the decision in *Oliphant* he ruled that the tribe—lacking "an outright grant of power from Congress"—had no civil jurisdiction over non-Indians "because that's inconsistent with the status of Indian tribes." (The court of appeals subsequently ordered McGovern to dismiss the case for lack of federal court jurisdiction, and the tribe blocked the development by proving its title to a dry riverbed running through the project site.)[18]

Belmont told the *Argus* reporter that a pending lawsuit by the Yakima Nation "could resolve the civil jurisdiction question for all tribes." The case he had in mind, not named in the article, was likely a challenge to the 1963 Washington legislation that imposed state jurisdiction on eight kinds of Indian reservation activity, most of them civil law matters.[19] If so, the Supreme Court dashed Belmont's and Yakima hopes. In *Washington v. Confederated Bands and Tribes of the Yakima Indian Nation*, the justices declined to find the state's complex jurisdiction scheme inconsistent with Public Law 280, and their reason was unrelated to questions about tribal government jurisdiction.[20]

Meanwhile, tribes hoping to subject non-Indians to civil regulation took heart from other high court rulings. *United States v. Wheeler*, a unanimous decision two weeks after the *Oliphant* setback, characterized tribes as "independent sovereigns" rather than creations of the federal government. Two months later, in *Santa Clara Pueblo v. Martinez*, the Supreme Court again confirmed tribes' sovereignty when it declared them immune from suit without their consent, adding that tribal courts had "repeatedly been recognized as appropriate forums for adjudicating disputes involving important interests of both Indians and non-Indians" and were therefore "available to vindicate rights created" by the Indian Civil Rights Act.[21]

Tribal governments saw another opening in a Supreme Court decision sharply limiting the civil jurisdiction that Public Law 280 conferred on states. The Chippewa plaintiff in *Bryan v. Itasca County* contested Minnesota's right to tax his on-reservation personal property. To the surprise of many Indian law experts, the justices agreed with him and held that PL 280 allowed only state court adjudication of private disputes arising on reservations; it did not permit across-the-board state regulation or taxation of Indians. The ruling also dispelled a common notion that state jurisdiction precluded concurrent tribal regulation or taxation.[22]

After that, tribes' right to police non-Indians seemed to hinge on doing it with regulations that treated unacceptable conduct as something other than crime.[23] Washington State set an example in 1980, when it converted most traffic rule violations from crimes to civil infractions with only monetary penalties. A number of tribes followed suit, motivated by practical enforcement considerations as well as a desire for regulatory power. After all, the Minnesota tax case decision meant that switching to civil citations had divested the state of jurisdiction to ticket Indian drivers on reservations. Tribal officers would have to do it, and how would they know whether a speeding driver was Indian or non-Indian? The tribes therefore decriminalized most driving offenses in ordinances that applied to any motorist within reservation boundaries.[24]

The Suquamish tribal council adopted such an ordinance in 1982. Ensuing events, recounted by their attorney a decade later, were sobering if not surprising. No sooner did Suquamish police begin enforcing the civil code than "certain non-Indians" raised "a stink." They caught the attention of the county prosecutor, who pronounced the tribe's new ordinance an unsuccessful "lawyer-like attempt to take the matter out of the realm of *Oliphant*." On behalf of non-Indian drivers who complained about their tribal citations, he wrote to Suquamish officers, "You have no authority whatsoever over traffic offenders . . . who are not Indians." A like-minded state attorney instructed the Washington licensing department not to enter tribal citations on non-Indians' driving records. The Suquamish council, foreseeing another round of resource-draining litigation and hoping another tribe would shoulder that burden this time, suspended their ordinance's application to non-Indians.[25]

Meanwhile, a case concerning the Crow Tribe's civil regulation of hunting and fishing had worked its way up to the Supreme Court. In *Montana v. United States*, six justices—citing *Oliphant*—held that the tribe could not regulate non-Indian hunters or fishers on non-Indian reservation land because tribes, "through their original incorporation into the United States, as well as through specific treaties and statutes . . . , lost many of the attributes of sovereignty, particularly as to the relations between a tribe and nonmembers of the tribe." Then Justice Stewart threw tribes a consolation bone. "To be sure," he wrote, "Indian tribes retain inherent sovereign power to exercise some forms of civil jurisdiction over non-Indians on their reservations, even on non-Indian fee lands." The next two sentences were ostensibly a guideline to help Indian officials and non-Indians determine whether a particular tribal regulation was one such "form of jurisdiction." "A tribe may regulate, through taxation, licensing, or other means, the activities of nonmembers who enter consensual relationships with the tribe or its members, through commercial dealing, contracts, leases, or other arrangements. . . . A tribe may also retain inherent power to exercise civil authority over the conduct of non-Indians on fee lands within its reservation when that conduct threatens or has some direct effect on the political integrity, the economic security, or the health or welfare of the tribe."[26]

Rather than clarifying the scope of tribes' civil jurisdiction, this passage ensured that their attempts to regulate or tax non-Indians would provoke more lawsuits. For years to come, many a federal judge would preside over litigation to determine whether a tribe's action fell within one of the permissible categories mentioned in *Montana v. United States.*

The earliest of those suits to reach the Supreme Court made one thing clear: there was a bias in that tribunal against tribal jurisdiction. Most justices seemed inclined to veto any tribal regulation of non-Indians, at least on non-Indian property. They not only required the tribe to prove that its assertion of power fit an exception specified in the Crow case; they construed those exceptions narrowly.[27] For example, in 1989, the Yakima Nation was unable to persuade a majority of justices that its political integrity or its members' health and welfare necessitated tribal jurisdiction to zone non-Indian land in a part of the reservation "open to the public." Four years later, in a case from South Dakota, the court ruled unambiguously that the sale of tribal land to a non-Indian by itself deprived the tribe of jurisdiction to regulate non-Indian hunting or fishing there.[28]

When the issue was taxation, the high court initially appeared more receptive to tribal jurisdiction over non-Indians. In 1982, six justices affirmed the Jicarilla Apache Tribe's right to impose a severance tax on oil and gas that non-Indians extracted from tribal land. Their rationale seemed to sanction even broader tribal tax power. "The power to tax is an essential attribute of Indian sovereignty because it is a necessary instrument of self-government and territorial management. This power enables a tribal government to receive revenues for its essential services. The power does not derive solely from the Tribe's power to exclude non-Indians from tribal lands, but from the Tribe's general authority, as sovereign, to control economic activities within its jurisdiction, and to defray the cost of providing governmental services by requiring contributions from persons or enterprises engaged in such activities." Three years later, all participating justices agreed that the Navajo government could tax companies doing business on tribal land.[29]

In 2001, however, the justices unanimously blocked Navajo taxation of a hotel operating on a small parcel of non-Indian property surrounded by tribal lands. Their opinion stated bluntly, "A tribe's sovereign power to tax reaches no further than tribal land." Paradoxically, the justices then considered whether the tribe had met the tests for jurisdiction set out in *Montana v. U.S.* Because the tribe had no contracts with the company or its guests, they found no consensual relationship. The virtual certainty that the company or its guests would call on the tribe for police, fire, or medical services did not create such a relationship, they decided; nor was the tribe's economic and political security at risk even though the tribe would bear nearly all costs of servicing such isolated, hemmed in non-Indian properties. "Whatever effect" the company's operation "might have upon surrounding Navajo land," the court concluded, "it does not endanger the Navajo Nation's political integrity."[30]

Federal courts also entertained a line of cases in which the issue was not tribal regulation or taxation but tribal court jurisdiction of civil disputes. Advocates for tribes thought they had convincing arguments that tribes' adjudicatory power was broader than their regulatory power.[31] Supreme Court rulings in 1985 and 1987 were encouraging; the justices allowed personal injury suits to proceed in tribal courts despite objections from non-Indian parties.[32] Then came two contrary decisions. In 1997, when ruling that the Fort Berthold Reservation court could not handle a suit between non-Indians who collided on a state highway through the reservation, its rationale included a statement that the tribe could not govern activity on that highway. Four years later, the justices ruled out tribal court jurisdiction even when non-Indians' injurious actions occurred on Indian land. In *Nevada v. Hicks*, it prohibited a civil rights suit in tribal court against a state law officer who had entered the reservation to investigate an off-reservation crime.[33]

In 2014, law professor Matthew L. M. Fletcher surveyed the previous three decades of federal litigation about tribal jurisdiction and sympathized with judges as well as Indians who wanted a clearer delineation of tribes' civil authority. "Indian tribes," he wrote, "struggle with governing nonmembers that pollute tribal lands and waters, allegedly cause deadly automobile and railroad accidents, accidentally cause far-ranging forest fires, discriminate against Indian people in business financing, and commit numerous criminal infractions over which tribes have no jurisdiction except through the issuance of civil citations." Because "the Supreme Court had not squarely addressed [even] simple cases arising on tribal lands," lower federal courts were also "struggling" with many lawsuits triggered by tribes' regulatory measures.[34]

The stream of litigation about tribes' jurisdiction would have dried up if the outcomes of *Oliphant v. Suquamish Tribe*, *Montana v. United States*, and subsequent cases had discouraged Indians from strengthening their governments and seeking more control over conditions on reservations. Instead, many tribes continued apace to develop their codes, courts, and other government infrastructure while watching for opportunities to demonstrate the necessity, practicality, and fairness of some tribal jurisdiction over non-Indians. Their drive for tribal power suited to contemporary circumstances had momentum that a few disappointing Supreme Court decisions did not immediately kill.

The drive continued in part because it was yielding occasional rewards at local and regional levels, where astute tribal governance and litigation could work together at times to boost tribes' leverage. Joe DeLaCruz drew this lesson from Quinault experiences. In his 1980 address to the Union of British Columbia Indian Chiefs and National Indian Brotherhood, he advocated the development of governments able to engage and negotiate effectively with non-Indian counterparts. "If our people are to survive the long term," he said, "alternative means must be found for resolving conflict besides seeking relief through prolonged and heated litigation that enriches attorneys while polarizing the public. The most promising way we now have to protect our interests is to strengthen our governments. We must encourage our governments to actively assert our rights in the non-Indian world."[35]

The Quinault government had recently experienced a cycle of developing its functions, asserting its right to regulate non-Indians, persuading federal judges not to intervene, winning compliance from more non-Indians, and gaining the confidence to call more shots on the reservation. In 1977 the tribe—unable to generate sufficient revenue solely from tribe-owned resources—had instituted a license fee and tax on all reservation businesses. Eight non-Indian business owners refused to pay and sued even though they did business with the tribe and benefited from its services. On appeal from a federal district court decision in the businesses' favor, Ninth Circuit judges pronounced the tribal tax a "valid exercise of inherent sovereignty." The Supreme Court declined to review that decision.[36] In the meantime a large timber company, ITT-Rayonier, dropped its court challenge to the tax, and the tribe began collecting new annual revenue that would fund reservation-wide services as well legal expenses.[37]

In two other cases, a federal district judge allowed the Quinault Nation to block a non-Indian's development on private land zoned by tribal law for forestry, and the court of appeals permitted Quinaults to enforce health and safety regulations against the non-Indian operator of a store on private land. In the latter instance, the judges disagreed with the lower court's conclusion that *Oliphant v. Suquamish Tribe* precluded Quinault civil jurisdiction. They held that the tribe could shut the store until the owner complied with the regulations because the circumstances met the test set out in *Montana v. United States*. The store owner had commercial dealings with the tribe and conducted a business likely to affect tribe members' health and safety. Once again, the Supreme Court chose not to second-guess the circuit court's decision.[38]

PLUGGING A GAP

When tribe leaders warned that *Oliphant v. Suquamish Tribe* created law enforcement voids, the voids they saw were primarily in practice, not in law. Taken together, federal and state codes did authorize punishment of non-Indians for most crimes they committed on reservations. Not long after the Supreme Court's decision, Justice Department analysts therefore concluded that few reservation communities needed to worry about untouchable non-Indian lawbreakers. At a conference convened by the American Indian Lawyer Training Program, Roger Adams from the department's criminal division said their investigators had identified possible "gaps" only in Washington and South Dakota—states that had taken jurisdiction on reservations selectively.[39]

Five other panelists—a tribal judge, Secretary Forrest Gerard, and three attorneys with Indian law expertise—questioned the accuracy of Adams's survey. But apparently, no one on the panel anticipated the gap in government authority that the Supreme Court would identify a decade later. The unforeseen loophole would affect Indian country everywhere, and the untouchables would not be white, black, or Asian Americans; they would be Indians.

The man who asked a federal court to acknowledge that loophole, Albert Duro, was enrolled in a California Indian band but resided on the Salt River Reservation in Arizona, where tribal prosecutors charged him with unlawful firearm use. The judge in a federal habeas corpus proceeding ordered Duro's release. Since tribes could not prosecute non-Indian outsiders, he reasoned, allowing them to prosecute Indian outsiders would constitute impermissible discrimination based on race. Eighth Circuit judges disagreed, but in 1990 the Supreme Court reversed that reversal. The decisive ruling in *Duro v. Reina* exempted all Indians from prosecution by tribes other than their own.[40]

The justices did not endorse the district judge's finding of discrimination based on race. Doing so would have contradicted a Supreme Court ruling in 1974 that "Indian" is a political status in federal law, not a racial category.[41] Instead, the justices elaborated on that ruling by distinguishing tribe members from nonmember Indians for jurisdiction purposes. They noted that *Oliphant v. Suquamish Tribe* and *Montana v. U.S.* used the term "nonmembers" instead of "non-Indians" when discussing limits on tribal sovereignty and stated clearly that tribes' dependency on the United States restricted their criminal law powers to "internal relations." "Internal," the justices elaborated, should be construed to exclude nonmembers, even Indians of other tribes. In sum, Indian tribes' "retained authority" was nothing more than "authority the tribes maintain over Indians who consent to be tribal members."[42] Implicitly, the court in *Duro v. Reina* signaled that no one should take the term "American citizens" in the *Oliphant* opinion as code for "whites." Indians, too, should enjoy protection from prosecution in the courts of "alien" tribes.

By thus invoking one set of precedents, the court defied others that legitimized tribes' jurisdiction over all Indians within their borders. The ruling for Duro was contrary to statutes on the books since 1817, when Congress first extended limited federal jurisdiction to Indian country. Those statutes exempted all Indian-on-Indian crimes from federal prosecution without a qualification that they be intratribal crimes. When lawmakers later authorized US prosecution of Indians for specified major crimes against Indians, they renewed the original exception for other Indian-on-Indian crimes and for "any Indian" who had been "punished by the local law of the tribe." They reaffirmed that exception in 1988.[43] Congressional records indicated that lawmakers consciously used the phrase "any Indian" to designate Indians in general; they did not intend to limit tribes' jurisdiction to members. Both the Supreme Court and the executive branch had consistently interpreted "any Indian" accordingly. Consequently, as of 1988 there were still Indians who could not be tried in federal court for crimes on other Indians' reservations.[44] Where states had not assumed jurisdiction under Public Law 280, those Indians could not be tried in state courts either; only tribal courts could try them—until *Duro v. Reina*.

Because nonmember Indians were ubiquitous on reservations, the decision landed like a live, unexploded grenade in federal and tribal government offices. Alarmed tribe leaders headed for Congress, seeking emergency action. The National Congress of American Indians and Native American Rights Fund, working with key committees and agencies, secured short-term legislative consent to tribal prosecutions of nonmember Indians. The measure not only limited *Duro*'s adverse consequences for tribal communities but also attested to the indispensability of tribal justice systems.[45] Lawmakers then fashioned an amendment to the Indian Civil Rights Act that acknowledged the "inherent power of Indian tribes . . . to exercise criminal jurisdiction over all Indians." A companion amendment reaffirmed that the term "Indian" in the federal criminal code meant a person belonging to any recognized tribe.[46]

As lawmakers considered whether to "fix" the *Duro v. Reina* decision permanently, representatives from Pacific Northwest tribes described the urgent need in their region. They explained that a reservation community typically encompassed Indians of many tribes—spouses, children, and other relatives of tribe members, employees of the tribe, even tribal police officers. Two witnesses said thousands of nonmember Indians visited the Yakima and Warm Springs Reservations every year for social and cultural purposes. Joe DeLaCruz emphasized that the allotment of Quinault Reservation land to Indians of several other tribes had guaranteed a multitribal resident population. Nonmember Indians had been respecting Quinault laws for decades and participating in all aspects of Quinault civic life except voting. Yakima councilman Harry Smiskin estimated that one-third to half of Indians on his large reservation were enrolled in other tribes, and the same proportion of tribal court criminal cases in 1989 involved nonmember Indians. "During the few months that the *Duro* ruling was in effect last year," he said, "we had to dismiss pending charges against 43 Indians because they were not enrolled."[47]

The speakers explained why they could not depend on state or federal authorities to police nonmember Indians. Two hundred fifty such persons lived on the Makah Reservation, which was 175 miles from federal law enforcement officials in Seattle and seventy-five miles from county and state patrol stations. Makah chairman Donald Johnson recalled a negligent homicide on the reservation that state authorities declined even to investigate. Harry Smiskin lamented an "extremely high" rate of state and federal police failure to act when victims were Indian. He offered the sobering example of two men—one Yakima, one from another tribe—who raped a Yakima woman. Although the Major Crimes Act gave the federal government jurisdiction, the US attorney declined to prosecute, leaving the tribe to charge the tribe member with a lesser crime and watch the other man go free.

Smiskin, DeLaCruz, and Johnson insisted that the public could have confidence in Indian police and judges, whose thorough training stressed the importance of adhering to strictures of the Indian Civil Rights Act. The Makah, Quinault, and Yakima governments provided public defenders for the accused. Makahs and Quinaults allowed nonmember Indians to sit on tribal court juries. DeLaCruz, who had served on two commissions that evaluated tribal justice programs, praised tribes for committing substantial monetary and human resources to the development of courts that other Americans would regard as fair. "I would say," he ventured, "that our systems have advanced and become superior to some of the systems that you have in 4,400 counties in the United States."[48]

After Congress overrode the *Duro* ruling, some nonmember Indian facing charges in a tribal court was bound to challenge that act. Less predictable, perhaps, was that the legislation survived Supreme Court scrutiny. In 2004, by a vote of seven to two, the court allowed both the federal government and a tribe in North Dakota to prosecute a nonmember Chippewa man. Billy Jo Lara's claim of double jeopardy failed because the justices did not regard the legislative "fix" for *Duro* as a delegation of federal power to the tribe. Instead the tribe was exercising its inherent sovereign power with Congress's blessing. The court opinion in *United States v. Lara* did not say that *Duro v. Reina* was wrongly decided; it just validated the superceding legislation. Justice Stephen Breyer wrote that Congress had relaxed "restrictions on the bounds of inherent tribal authority."[49]

Missing from Breyer's analysis was an observation that the restrictions in question were first identified and arguably imposed by the court itself in the *Duro* decision. Still, Breyer used language that champions of strong tribal government could appreciate. His opinion not only confirmed federal lawmakers' power to ease supposed limits on tribal governance; it also declared such action consistent with United States recognition of tribes' inherent authority to control events on their own lands.

RESETTING TERMS

If Congress could countermand a Supreme Court decision regarding tribal jurisdiction over nonmember Indians, could it not do the same for the case about non-Indians? Justice Rehnquist suggested as much in the *Oliphant* opinion. In view of tribal courts' increasing sophistication, Indian Civil Rights Act protections for defendants, and high reservation crime rates, Congress might conclude that "Indian tribes should finally be authorized to try non-Indians," Rehnquist wrote.[50] Not long before, Joe DeLaCruz had spoken optimistically about the same possibility. Probably encouraged by recommendations of the American Indian Policy Review Commission, he told the *Seattle Times* that Indians were looking to legislation rather than courts for a solution to the unworkable jumble of jurisdiction on reservations.[51]

Suquamish chairman Dick Belmont was not enthusiastic about Rehnquist's suggestion. When reminded of it, he recalled that Lloyd Meeds had recently introduced a bill to forbid tribal jurisdiction over non-Indians, and past congressional action had often restricted Indians. "Especially with the Washington delegation," Belmont said, "we don't think we are in the best position to get good legislation." Representative Bonker shared that assessment. "I can't imagine anyone in the Washington delegation giving tribes jurisdiction over non-Indians," he declared. "It's such a volatile situation, it's all we can do to prevent a backlash."[52]

Even so, because law enforcement gaps troubled state and federal agencies as well as tribes, some members of Congress and Indian leaders did consider legislative corrections to the outcome of *Oliphant v. Suquamish Tribe*. One option would have authorized state-tribal agreements to share responsibility for policing reservations. Another proposal would have commissioned special federal magistrates with jurisdiction over Indian country offenses. DeLaCruz, warning that such a move "would only complicate things more," told senators, "A better approach would be to return to tribal courts jurisdiction over all reservation activity, including crimes by non-Indians." But his prediction that "some" Washington State officials would object was more realistic than expecting lawmakers in 1980 to take the "better approach."[53]

The odds of congressional support for expanded tribal law enforcement improved gradually over the next two decades. Three interrelated factors promoted more acceptance of Indian governments' permanent role in a tripartite American allocation of police power. Congress and the executive branch held to the policy of government-to-government relations with tribes and tribal self-determination that it had proclaimed in 1975. The Supreme Court concurrently and repeatedly affirmed that inherent tribal sovereignty and enduring treaty rights remained tenets of American law, however attenuated their implementation might be. And the tribes—viewing this legal context as an opening for greater control over their futures—continued to develop political structures, practices, and expertise that earned respect from some federal and state counterparts. As their capacity for governance increased and many tribes made headway against community problems such as high rates of unemployment and ill health, reversion to the federal detribalization policy of the 1950s became more unlikely.[54]

Quinaults' story illustrates the interplay of these three factors: Indians' desire for meaningful power on their reservations, circumstances encouraging that desire, and tribes' development of their government functions.

In 1988, approving a proposal advanced by DeLaCruz and other members of a ten-tribe Alliance of American Indian Leaders, Congress amended the 1975 Indian Self-Determination and Education Assistance Act to create the Tribal Self-Governance Demonstration Project. The proponents resented paternalistic BIA regulations and red tape that were thwarting the aims of the Self-Determination Act. Under the new legislation, a select few tribal governments could negotiate to assume full responsibility for services that the BIA and other federal agencies administered. Participating tribes could even ask to manage resources held in trust for them, such as timber. Of the seven tribes in the demonstration project, three were in western Washington, including the Quinaults. DeLaCruz called it "a historic opportunity to get rid of the people who thrive off the miseries of Indians." Other proponents described it as an opening for "the strongest assertion of Indian sovereignty in years."[55]

The pilot project, authorized for five years, was so successful that Congress extended it after just three years, adding thirty more tribes. In 1994, the permanent Tribal Self-Governance Act opened the program to all tribes. Within two decades, 50 percent of tribes were setting policies and administering programs in numerous areas formerly under federal control.[56] Mel Tonasket, comparing Indians' prospects in 2005 to circumstances when he became a Colville Confederation councilman three decades earlier, saw potential for tribes finally to "take over their own futures, run their own reservations."[57]

By the 1990s, many Indians brought more than political savvy to the business of influencing federal legislation; they came to the Capitol from tribes with growing economic clout. New tribal enterprises fueled much of that prosperity, including recreational gaming establishments. Feasible initially because of tribes' immunity from state regulation, tribe-owned casinos gained congressional approval in 1988, partly because Indian governments had few other revenue sources at a time of big federal funding cuts. The most lucrative casinos not only generated money for tribal government services but also provided employment for hundreds of Indians and non-Indians, funded charities that served non-Indians as well as Indians, and yielded large sums that tribes donated to political campaigns. A *Fortune* magazine headline in 1993 declared, "American Indians Discover Money Is Power." A more appropriate title might have been "Americans Discover That Indians Know Money Is Power."[58]

Increasingly confident of their governments' credibility in the American political arena but alarmed by high reservation crime rates, some tribe leaders in the early 2000s thought the time was right to press harder for congressional endorsement of tribal jurisdiction over non-Indians, if only for limited purposes.[59] The purpose that ultimately proved acceptable to key legislators was stemming domestic violence on reservations and securing justice for its many Indian victims.

In 2003, tribes prevailed on the NCAI to create a task force that would educate lawmakers about the stunning prevalence of rape and domestic abuse in Indian country. A 1996 Senate Judiciary Committee study had shown that one-third of Native American women were or would likely be rape victims, and two out of five could expect to suffer domestic violence. Congress responded in 2005, when renewing the 1994 Violence Against Women Act (VAWA), by funding tribal programs to address the problem. It did nothing, though, to change the jurisdictional patchwork that enabled many of Indians' abusers to avoid punishment. With VAWA set to expire again in 2011, two Senate proponents of renewal decided to sponsor an added provision sanctioning tribal jurisdiction over non-Indian batterers.[60]

Victims of abuse joined tribal governments, intertribal organizations, and international human rights groups in documenting and publicizing how often Indian women on reservations endured assaults by husbands or boyfriends, many of them non-Indians never charged with the crimes.[61] At a press conference called by Washington senator Patty Murray, the newly elected vice chair of the Tulalip Tribes' Board of Directors, Deborah Parker, broke a lifelong silence about her own victimization in childhood and pleaded for the bill's passage.[62] At a Senate hearing, Carmen O'Leary spoke for a coalition of Great Plains tribes about the need for Indian nation jurisdiction "over crimes of domestic violence, stalking, dating violence and sexual assault by non-Indians." "Many episodes of violence against Native women," she said, "include perpetrators of another race who know that they can continue to offend without any consequences due to the unique and confusing jurisdictional rules present in Indian country." Muscogee Creek law professor Sarah Deer testified for Amnesty International, which released a report in 2007 criticizing the jurisdictional maze that so often frustrated abused Native women's search for justice. She said, "True tribal empowerment and sovereignty will not be possible without addressing the Supreme Court's 1978 ruling on Oliphant vs. Suquamish, which . . . denies due process and equal protection of the law to survivors of sexual violence. We therefore urge Congress to re-recognize the concurrent jurisdiction of tribal authorities over all crimes committed on tribal lands, regardless of the Native identity of the accused, legislatively overriding the U.S. Supreme Court's decision."[63]

Opponents of new tribal jurisdiction and other changes to VAWA delayed its renewal for two years, but the act that cleared Congress in February 2013 did recognize tribes' "inherent power" to exercise "special domestic violence criminal jurisdiction" over certain non-Indian defendants. Most tribes had to wait until 2015 to prosecute non-Indian abusers, but five named tribes, including the Tulalips in Washington, received permission for a head start.[64] While victims' advocates celebrated, tribal officials took quieter satisfaction at getting a toe in a door that might someday open farther to tribal court jurisdiction over non-Indians. Suquamish chairman Leonard Forsman said, "It's a small but measurable step toward restoring our sovereignty in our tribal courts, and I am happy about that."[65]

As Indian governments gained experience, visibility, and standing in Washington, DC, some also gained credibility with officials in jurisdictions close to home. Their enhanced leverage opened opportunities to negotiate new terms of relations at a variety of political levels for diverse purposes, from natural resource management and the protection of children to law enforcement. Harry Smiskin described one cooperative local relationship. "Interestingly enough," he told senators in 1991, "50 percent of calls for assistance coming into the tribal police department . . . come from non-Indians, including some who have been referred through the Yakima County Sheriff's Office." In many cases, the tribe's officers responded and did the necessary investigations for county or federal prosecutors whose police admittedly would not or could not provide those services.[66]

While Yakima Nation and county personnel cooperated ad hoc, other tribes sought or considered formal jurisdiction-sharing agreements. In Washington attorney general Gorton's opinion, that was the reasonable approach to law enforcement issues on reservations—the only way to address each reservation's distinctive "people problems." At the Symposium on Tribal Sovereignty and Jurisdiction in 1979, Gorton had opined that a federal statute giving tribes jurisdiction over non-Indians would be "blatantly unconstitutional." Tribes and their antagonists should "stop battling over fascinating theoretical problems, such as notions of sovereignty," he said. They should negotiate instead and, specifically, "should promote cross-deputization."[67]

Cross-deputization of law enforcement officers, also known as cross-commissioning, was not a new idea for tribes in 1979. Some had already made or proposed such arrangements with counties and other nontribal governments. Usually the aim was a contract authorizing police from either jurisdiction to answer calls about on-reservation crimes, then cite offenders into the appropriate courts. Despite some initial state and county assumptions that the *Oliphant* decision precluded tribal arrests of non-Indians, many tribal governments hoped more than ever to secure county and federal commissions for their officers.[68]

Where state, county, or federal officers had corresponding needs for help from Indian police, tribal governments had good shots at getting cross-deputization agreements. For instance, as illegal drug traffickers increasingly exploited the spotty law enforcement on reservations, federal and state authorities recognized their interest in enabling tribal police to arrest non-Indian culprits. Representative John McCoy, a Tulalip Tribes member, made that argument for a bill he sponsored during the Washington legislature's 2008 session. He had once caught a non-Indian burglar in his reservation office and waited almost two hours for a sheriff. Tribal cops were available; why not let them make the arrest and conduct the investigation? Tribal police on the Colville Reservation had had such county commissions for years by then. State legislators bought McCoy's argument. Undeterred by opposition from most county sheriffs, they approved his bill, and the governor signed it. Thenceforth, officers employed by "sovereign" Indian nations could act as general authority peace officers under Washington law so long as they had specified training and liability insurance.[69]

In at least one instance, litigation motivated a tribal government and state opponents to consider a settlement that included cross-deputization of fish and game officers. A year after the Supreme Court blocked tribal regulation of non-Indian fishers on the Crow Reservation, Colville Confederated Tribes agreed to shelve their suit challenging state jurisdiction over non-Indians who fished or hunted on their reservation, but they elicited a pledge that the Washington Department of Game would work with them to formulate joint regulations and would commission tribal officers as state wildlife agents.[70]

Conversely, a Suquamish Tribe lawsuit intensified county resistance to cross-commissioning. In 1986, the tribe's police chief thought he had a good argument for authorizing his officers to arrest non-Indians. On a reservation with a liquor store, two taverns, four other businesses selling alcohol, and eighty-seven miles of roads, drunk drivers were common. Only two sheriff's deputies patrolled that half of Kitsap County, while four tribal cops were always on duty within the reservation. Yet when Suquamish officers stopped intoxicated non-Indian drivers and transferred them to the state patrol, the county court—doubting tribal police authority—dismissed the charges. The prosecutor and sheriff flatly refused to consider cross-commissions as a solution. Although Suquamish officers and sheriffs graduated from the same police academy and took the same psychological tests, Undersheriff Chuck Wheeler told the *Seattle Post-Intelligencer*, "The state and Kitsap County do not recognize tribal officers as commissioned peace officers." Prosecutor C. Danny Clem, citing the *Oliphant* holding, said, "There is no way you can compromise. They (the tribal police) either have jurisdiction, or they don't have jurisdiction." Clem also attributed the county's position to the tribe's "attitude," exemplified by its pending lawsuit seeking a federal court declaration that tidelands adjacent to non-Indian-owned reservation lands were tribal property. "The tribe 'can't sue the citizens of Kitsap county' and then ask the county government to help them," Clem grumbled.[71]

Mistrust between Suquamish and county officials persisted for years, but by the 1990s their police forces had an understanding that tribal officers could apprehend a non-Indian lawbreaker and call the sheriff to take the case from there. In 1993, the state supreme court approved that practice in an opinion acknowledging "inherent" Suquamish police authority "to stop and detain a non-Indian who has allegedly violated state and tribal law while on the reservation until he or she can be turned over to state authorities."[72] That ruling, the tribe's subsequent launch of a casino that drew throngs of non-Indian customers, and key personnel changes—the departures of Clem and longtime sheriff Pat Jones—created conditions more favorable to cross-deputization. Even so, it was not until 2015—seven years after the state recognized tribal police as general authority officers—that Suquamish and county representatives finally reached a formal agreement. Under their memorandum of understanding, tribal police would detain non-Indian suspects and notify the sheriff, but if sheriffs declined to come, Suquamish officers could also make formal arrests, conduct investigations, and transfer the suspects to county custody.[73]

The Suquamish Tribe's resurgence—exemplified and facilitated by remarkable economic advances—earned its government and leaders respect from some other governments as well. As of 2015, the tribe's development agency, Port Madison Enterprises, encompassed more than a successful casino and resort. Its payroll of 752 people made it the second-largest private-sector employer in the county. With revenue generated from several businesses, the tribe funded vital on-reservation services, bought back privatized reservation land, and contributed millions of dollars to charities and public services in surrounding communities.[74] In the nearby city of Poulsbo, a councilman who also chaired a regional economic development board described the Suquamish Tribe's accomplishments as "breathtaking." "It's exciting for Poulsbo," Ed Stern said, "because we're within the radius for spinoff business." Stern expressed special pride in his city's government-to-government relationship with the tribe, formalized in a 2001 memorandum of understanding.[75]

The Quinaults, too, could boast of government infrastructure and economic power that had the attention of neighboring jurisdictions as well as state and federal civic and political leaders. In 2016 the Quinault Indian Nation, as a government and as owner of six enterprises, was the source of 1,200 jobs, making it the largest employer in Grays Harbor County. President Fawn Sharp, a licensed attorney, promoted Quinault interests and cultivated intergovernmental relations by assuming such roles as president of Affiliated Tribes of Northwest Indians, governor of the Washington State Bar Association, and trustee of Grays Harbor Community College.[76]

The growing acceptance of tribes as essential participants in intergovernmental affairs did not immunize them against resentment or resistance from non-Indians in their midst. Some non-Indians who lived or owned property on reservations viewed the tribes' increasing self-confidence as a threat to their interests. For instance, when the Suquamish planned housing for low-income members on tribe-owned reservation land, non-Indians in an adjacent neighborhood expressed animosity that apparently had simmered for years. Although the housing project would not entail tribal regulation of the non-Indians, some claimed that the tribe saw its alleged sovereignty as a license to push non-Indians around.[77]

In 2001, Associated Property Owners/Residents of the Port Madison Reservation and twelve individuals tried to block the tribal housing with litigation. The plaintiffs, adopting a conception of Indian reservations long since corrected by Congress and the Supreme Court, requested an injunction against Suquamish and US authority over nontribal members on "lands no longer part of the Port Madison Reservation." They contended that sales of Indian allotments and the old village site had removed those lands from the reservation. The suit also recycled an old claim that the Suquamish Tribe organized under federal law in 1965 was not the aboriginal tribe that signed the Point Elliott Treaty.[78] The district judge held that the plaintiffs lacked standing to sue, and appellate judges sustained his dismissal of the lawsuit.[79]

At the Quinault Reservation, too, nonmembers who contested tribal authority periodically gave tribal staff attorneys extra litigation experience. In 2007, the tribe sued a developer who defied Quinault land use regulations and a Quinault court order, but it dropped the case after a state judge declared that the tribe's claim of jurisdiction failed the test established in *Montana v. United States*. In 2015, a property management company and two individual landowners were in court disputing the Quinaults' long-acknowledged right to control activity on Lake Quinault and its shoreline.[80]

CLOSING THOUGHTS

Indian reservations have never been impenetrable havens, even when their creators specified that they were for Indians' exclusive use. From the start, non-Indians could enter as visitors or as trespassers, and some lived there as US agents, missionaries, storekeepers, or Indians' kin. But when the federal government allotted the reserved tribal lands and then promoted the sale of many lots, non-Indians moved onto reservations in much greater numbers and in new capacities, as property owners and resource users. Nevertheless, the government neither abolished reservations and dispersed the tribes nor, in most cases, redrew reservation boundaries to omit land acquired by non-Indians. Furthermore, although the United

States eventually claimed nearly unlimited power over Indians, it failed to realize its stated goal of governing them entirely by the same laws as non-Indians. Indians on reservations thus remained in a distinctive status under US law, one rooted in indigenous nations' historical, intrinsic sovereignty.

On allotted reservations, Indian reactions to the presence of non-Indian neighbors have run the gamut of possibilities, from fearful or resentful avoidance to friendly fraternization. But some long-term repercussions of opening the reservations to non-Indians have stirred resentment among Indian residents by severely limiting their influence over conditions in their homelands.

Allotment contributed to a crazy-quilt allocation of government powers and responsibilities on reservations. Federal, state, and tribal governments all made claims to some authority there. Under federal law, for example, jurisdiction to punish criminal conduct depended not only on the authority of the punishing government but also on the "race" or citizenship of offenders and victims. Jurisdiction could hinge, too, on who owned the land where an offense took place. Divided and often-uncertain authority left gaps in law enforcement, thus fostering crimes of opportunity, litigated disputes about jurisdiction, and intergovernmental tensions.

For much of the twentieth century, circumstances ranging from federal paternalism and Indian impoverishment to highway construction and encroaching suburbia limited tribes' ability to prevent unwanted activity on their reservations. By the 1960s, however, many Indians saw reason to hope and work for a power balance shift in their direction. Converging factors encouraged them to seek clarification or reconsideration of key assumptions about tribal governments' status vis-à-vis the United States and other polities. They wanted acknowledgment that tribes had a legal basis for regulating activity affecting their people and their reserved resources. A crucial impetus for this Indian initiative was federal and state agencies' preemption of control over activity, property, and conditions that Indians expected to manage. The preemption was not exclusively a reservation problem; tribe members also endured restrictions on treaty-guaranteed off-reservation access to fish, game, and vegetation. But in most cases, the issue of jurisdiction over land and resources was framed by reservation boundaries. And in many parts of Indian country, tribal governments envisioned regulations that would apply to non-Indians as well as Indians.

Local histories were fundamental stimuli for Indians' efforts to expand tribal government jurisdiction. On many reservations, a history of tribal decision-making and Indian leadership created motivating memories and expectations. So did remembered grievances, be they US mismanagement of forests, non-Indian poaching of fish and game, state and federal neglect of law enforcement responsibilities, land use and business activity inconsistent with tribal community standards, or state and federal government practices reflecting disdain for tribal culture and autonomy. Histories of resistance to such affronts, including legal action in US courts, also inspired some tribes' ambitions.

Indians with such ambitions knew very well that tribal communities depended for their continuing existence on a specialized body of US law. The first of their forebears to encounter Euro-American colonizers had recognized the centrality of law to the newcomers' conduct of intercommunity relations. Elders who experienced Americans' coercive power and will to dominate during the nineteenth century impressed on their offspring the need to learn the colonizers' legal culture and invoke their rules strategically.[81] Thus, tribe leaders of the 1960s and 1970s expected to make their arguments for control of reservation conditions in the language and institutions of American law. Chief among the laws to invoke were treaties, because they represented United States affirmation of the tribes' nationhood and rights to resources. Modern tribal governments accepted US law's application to them with the understanding that it embraced and guaranteed multiple sovereignties, including the tribes' original, precolonial sovereignty.

As Sally Engle Merry observed when analyzing Native Hawaiians' adaptation to colonial rule, "Those who import [or accept] new systems of law often seek a new place in the global order even though this may require dramatic and even traumatic changes in the social life of the nation."[82] American Indian tribes' engagement with colonial legal culture did require changes to internal as well as external relations. By the late twentieth century, when tribal governments extended jurisdiction to non-Indians in their midst, they had laws, courts, and police procedures modeled in many respects on American counterparts. They had even acceded to federal lawmakers' requirement that tribes observe nearly the same constraints on their use of government power as the US Constitution imposed on state and federal governments.

To promote their interests and defend their communities in US legal forums, tribes needed the services of licensed attorneys. Whether they initiated contacts with attorneys or attorneys approached them to offer support, most tribal governments by the 1960s had employed such advocates, at least for limited purposes. In those relationships, Indians told lawyers what they needed or wanted to accomplish, and lawyers explained the constraints as well as the possibilities that rules of American law and legal procedures presented, but that process of reciprocal education necessarily induced more Indian adjustments to American legal culture than adjustments by attorneys to Indian practices.

By employing attorneys and appealing to American judges, tribes put the fate of their quests for justice in the hands of people with professional investments in the colonial legal system. Attorneys for tribes might share their clients' goal of shifting power relations in Indians' favor; they might hope to curtail US authority in certain respects; but few were inclined to challenge the ultimate sources or foundational principles of the legal system in which they worked. Their usual aim was to hold adversaries to established rules of American law that served their clients' interests. Existing law determined how lawyers framed arguments and told stories in court. In practice, attorneys for tribes acted as intermediaries between the tribes and the US legal establishment. To elicit the desired judicial decisions, they would not necessarily tell their clients' stories as the Indians told them outside of court. Indians would sometimes find that tribal stories did not translate well into the intermediaries' language of law.

A legal concept of European origin that inspired tribal attorneys and their clients was Indian sovereignty. The use of that term by courts and by Indians' legal advisers to denote indigenous peoples' political autonomy predated the United States' creation. American judges and officials periodically affirmed that the United States initially recognized Native peoples as nations, inherently self-governing and therefore sovereign. Through decades of repressive federal policy and apparent Indian submission, when US relations with tribes hardly seemed like those with independent nations, there were always Indians and allies of Indians with knowledge of tribal sovereignty doctrine. When new opportunities for self-government energized reservation communities in the 1960s, talk of sovereignty seemed increasingly appropriate to tribe leaders—sovereignty not only as a status their ancestors had enjoyed but also as an attribute that tribes could claim at present. Legal precedents offered a framework for viewing history and recounting it in a way that could justify bold claims about the significance of tribal sovereignty in modern times.

Opponents of tribal sovereignty commonly characterized it as unacceptable legal plurality. They argued that the US Constitution and Indians' US citizenship guaranteed and required legal equality or uniformity for Indians and non-Indians, thus precluding rights for Indians that non-Indians did not enjoy. In their view, non-Indians on reservations needed protection from the jurisdiction of Indian political bodies that denied them a right they would have outside Indian country: the right to vote. This argument disregarded the fact that legal plurality had always been a feature of American government as well as US-Indian relations. The United States is a federation of sovereign states. Americans have accepted and generally cherished the states' power to make and enforce laws separate laws, applicable within their boundaries, and apply them to people who cannot vote there. However, from the inception of the Union, Indian tribes' claim of comparable sovereign power was an impediment to the settler colonial project. Construed as the power to deny non-Indians control of coveted land and resources, the principle of tribal sovereignty thus repeatedly drew cries of unfairness.[83]

Some people also scoffed at ascribing sovereignty—often defined as supreme power or authority—to peoples who had little actual power vis-à-vis the United States. International law principles acknowledged by the Supreme Court furnished a response. National sovereignty in practice is relative rather than an absolute or predefined degree of authority. It is an attribute whose reality and operative extent are affirmed or challenged in relations with other self-governing peoples. Hence, the United States and the tribes could and did agree that Indian nations had accepted some limitations on their original sovereignty without surrendering all of it.[84]

Indians who favored "sovereign" as a term for their communities' political status in the 1960s knew that the scope and elements of their governments' power in practice were contingent on a conception of tribal sovereignty acceptable to the more powerful United States. Any extension of the government functions they exercised, or any resumption of precolonial governing practices, could be stymied unless the US government acquiesced. Congress seemed unlikely then to approve expanded jurisdiction, but lawyers for tribes thought it reasonable to expect acquiescence from the judicial branch because the nation's highest court had affirmed that tribes' sovereignty was inherent and never yet wholly relinquished.

Even so, in staking their bid for broader jurisdiction on judges' interpretation of the sovereignty doctrine, tribes ran the risk that history would be used against them. The danger arose from contradictory implications of the doctrine's historical basis. US recognition of Indian sovereignty was originally premised on the tribes' perceived foreignness. The Constitution and early federal laws concerned themselves with Indians only as alien polities with which the nation might trade, make war, or make peace. Affairs in Indian territory were the Indians' to manage, including relations with non-Indians there, although US officials could seek agreements to extradite American troublemakers. As the United States attained dominant power, however, Indians' foreignness and their societies' alleged deficiencies became grounds for US legal measures intended to eradicate the differences and bridge the jurisdictional boundaries—measures such as the assertion of plenary power and unilateral extension of citizenship to all US-born Indians. Implicit in those measures was the possibility that Indian acculturation and assimilation might someday call the tribes' very sovereignty into question. For the most part, though, federal policies perpetuated Indians' exceptional legal status, and continuing differences of other kinds sustained non-Indian aversion to tribal jurisdiction.

By proclaiming jurisdiction over non-Indians in the 1970s, tribal governments effectively asked non-Indians to recognize both the tribes' persistence as distinctive sovereign polities and the changes they had made to their governing practices that reduced their foreignness, particularly the "modernization" of their laws, law enforcement, and court systems. When non-Indians responded by seeking a federal court declaration that tribal sovereignty did not extend to non-Indian lawbreakers, the outcome was bound to reflect judges' views of persistence and change in Indians' history. The tribes needed an argument or story that denied the mutual exclusivity of those two historical forces. On one hand, they needed to win jurists' acceptance of the idea that some differences in culture and ideals still justified separate, Indian-governed enclaves, and case law did seem to indicate that judges expected a significant degree of immutability and insularity in the Indian communities that claimed sovereignty. On the other hand, emphasizing Indian traditionalism and otherness could make judges as concerned with protecting non-Indians from tribal justice as nineteenth-century officials were. Thus, whether Indians did or did not emphasize their communities' enduring distinctive Indian character, the United States, including its judiciary, might balk at drawing the desired conclusion about the scope of the tribes' sovereignty.

In *Oliphant v. Suquamish Tribe*, rather than focusing on the question of continuity or change in reservation communities, lawyers on both sides chose to direct the jurists' attention almost entirely to the history of the tribal sovereignty doctrine in the US government and courts. Advocates for the tribes' position argued that the important continuities were federal law's acknowledgment of Indian nations' inherent sovereignty and the absence of explicit exceptions for jurisdiction over non-Indians. To the non-Indian petitioners and ultimately the Supreme Court, the important continuity was a supposedly consistent intention on the part of US officials, lawmakers, and judges to prevent Indians from punishing non-Indian criminals. No one addressed head-on the question whether Indians' conception and experience of their sovereignty had changed over time and whether any changes or continuities helped or hurt their argument for jurisdiction.

Six Supreme Court justices thought they saw evidence of persistent US government determination to deny Indians jurisdiction over non-Indian offenders. Even if they were correct, that determination continued through decades during which the American government's willingness to accommodate Indian tribal enclaves and Indian self-government waned, waxed, waned, and waxed again in the face of changing circumstances. The court did not consider the likelihood that relevant Indian history was a comparable chronicle of persistence paired with change: persistent Indian determination to maintain their autonomous tribes' existence in protected homelands even as the tribes' strength waned, waxed, waned, and waxed again over the decades.

If Indians had made substantial changes, it was with the hope of preserving the essential thread of their existence as distinct indigenous peoples. However, legal doctrine, trial procedure, and the difficulty of telling complex stories about history discouraged them from highlighting the changes they had made for the sake of essential continuity—legal continuity. Doctrine also discouraged them from casting their new assertions of jurisdiction as proposals for reconsideration and substantial adjustment of the terms of nation-to-nation relations with the United States.

In fact, the terms of tribes' relations with the United States were already changing in practice, but to the court, those changes were largely immaterial. Aside from a brief mention that Congress could "grant" the tribes the jurisdiction they claimed, the court did not depict or seriously consider tribal sovereignty as an ongoing, bilateral political process that had resulted in changes the court could recognize. Rather than acknowledging and deferring to tribes' ongoing negotiations with other branches of the US government, the court authored a history in which tribes had no meaningful agency.

For the tribes, that was a problem, but it was not the end of the story. Neither *Oliphant v. Suquamish Tribe* nor subsequent litigation provided conclusive answers to the questions at the heart of the tribes' quest for broad jurisdiction: What does it mean for a tribe to have a reservation if non-Indians live and own property there too? If those non-Indians do not have to live by the tribe's laws, what does the tribe's ascribed sovereignty mean? What is or will be the meaning of the reservation and its boundaries?

Legal processes will certainly continue to inform efforts to answer these questions. As political scientist Jeffrey Dudas put it, in the courts of their colonizers, Indians have challenged the colonizers' hegemony "on the terms of hegemony itself," and they will do so again. Such familiarity with legal culture shapes "collective memory" and "channels" imaginations. However, Dudas adds, it is unlikely that "legal logics and conventions" have colonized Indians' minds entirely.[85] More than law has influenced Indians' evolving conceptions of reservations and tribal sovereignty. The same is surely true of non-Indians.

The story of Indian tribes' responses to the presence of non-Indians on reservations is bigger and more open-ended than their futile bid for blanket Supreme Court approval of tribal jurisdiction to prosecute non-Indians. The jurisdiction story is embedded in the epic, still-unfolding story of Indians' efforts to arrange satisfactory relations with non-Indians, to gain respect from other American governments for their inherent nationhood and right of self-governance. There have been and will be subsequent chapters of that saga as Indians employ a variety of strategies aimed at securing and ensuring the conditions for self-determination essential to their communities' survival.

NOTES

Full information for shortened archival sources can be found in Selected Archival Collections, following notes.

ABBREVIATIONS

AAIA	Association on American Indian Affairs
AIPRC	American Indian Policy Review Commission
ARCIA	Annual Report of the Commissioner of Indian Affairs
ATNI	Affiliated Tribes of Northwest Indians
BIA	Bureau of Indian Affairs
CCF	Central Classified Files
LAT	*Los Angeles Times*
NA	National Archives
NA PAR	National Archives, Pacific Alaska Region
NCAI	National Congress of American Indians
NYT	*New York Times*
RG	Record Group
ST	*Seattle [Daily] Times*
TNT	*Tacoma News Tribune*
UW	University of Washington
UWL	University of Washington Libraries
WDF	Washington Department of Fisheries
WP	*Washington Post*
WSJ	*Wall Street Journal*
WWA	Western Washington Agency

INTRODUCTION

1 "Indians Close Littered Beach," *NYT*, Aug. 26, 1969, 43; "Indians Close Beach Littered by Tourists," *WP*, Aug. 26, 1969, A8; "Quinault Beach," Vanderbilt Television News Archives, Record No. 20521.

2 Don Hannula, "Quinaults Get 1,000 Letters Applauding Beach Closure," *ST*, Sept. 4, 1969, 11; "Tribal Council Receives Award," *ST*, Nov. 19, 1969, 14.

3 Don Hannula, "Quinault Indians Now Run Reservation with a Firm Hand," *ST*, Sept. 26, 1971, 72.

4 Iron Crow v. Oglala Sioux Tribe of the Pine Ridge Indian Reservation, 231 F. 2d 89 (8th Cir. 1956), 91, 98–99.

5 "Summary of Some of the Major Points Mentioned in the Small Group Reports," Dec. 19, 1969, 13, NCAI Records, Series 4, Intertribal Organizations, Box 139, N–P, Folder: "Affiliated Tribes of Northwest Indians [1959–1975]."

6 Oliphant v. Suquamish Indian Tribe, 431 U.S. 191 (1978).

7 Paul C. Rosier, "'They Are Ancestral Homelands': Race, Place, and Politics in Cold War Native America, 1945–1961," *Journal of American History* 91:4 (2006): 1302, 1324.

8 Edward M. Kennedy, American Indian Lawyer Training Program (AILTP), *Indian Self-Determination and the Role of Tribal Courts* (Oakland, CA, 1982), i.

9 The broad scope and political emphasis of this book's story does not allow me to include a deep, comprehensive study of Suquamish and Quinault culture and history—something scholars have yet to produce.

10 Thomas King, *The Back of the Turtle* (Toronto: Harper Collins, 2014).

11 Steven Hahn, *A Nation without Borders: The United States and Its World in an Age of Civil Wars, 1830–1910* (New York: Penguin Random House, 2016), 281; Karen Ordahl Kupperman, *Indians and English: Facing Off in Early America* (Ithaca, NY: Cornell University Press, 2000), 92; Cynthia Cumfer, "Local Origins of National Indian Policy: Cherokee and Tennessean Ideas about Sovereignty and Nationhood, 1790–1811," *Journal of the Early Republic* 23 (Spring 2003): 21–46; Frederick E. Hoxie, "Why Treaties?," in *Buried Roots and Indestructible Seeds: The Survival of American Indian Life in Story, History, and Spirit*, ed. Mark A. Lindquist and Martha Zanger (Madison: University of Wisconsin Press, 1994), 88; Lisa Ford, *Settler Sovereignty: Jurisdiction and Indigenous People in America and Australia, 1788–1836* (Cambridge, MA: Harvard University Press, 2010), 3.

12 Cherokee Nation v. Georgia, 30 U.S. (5 Pet.) 1 (1831); Worcester v. Georgia, 31 U.S. (6 Pet.) 515 (1832).

13 United States v. Kagama, 119 U.S. 375 (1886).

14 Johnson v. M'Intosh, 21 U.S. (8 Wheat.) 543, 573–74 (1823); United States v. Rogers, 45 U.S. (4 How.) 567, 572 (1846).

15 United States v. McBratney, 104 U.S. 621 (1881).

16 Alexandra Harmon, *Indians in the Making: Ethnic Relations and Indian Identities around Puget Sound* (Berkeley: University of California Press, 1998), chapter 3.

17 Opening Native property to white farmers and businesses was a "colonial land policy" intended "to integrate native resources into the American economy." Frederick E. Hoxie, *A Final Promise: The Campaign to Assimilate the Indians, 1880–1920* (Lincoln: University of Nebraska Press, 1984), 187.

18 Major Crimes Act, 23 U.S. Stat. 385, 18 U.S.C. Sec. 1153; U.S. v. Kagama.

19 *Felix S. Cohen's Handbook of Federal Indian Law* (1942; repr. Albuquerque: University of New Mexico Press, 1971), 8; 18 U.S. Code Sec. 1151 (1948).

20 AILTP, *Indian Self-Determination and the Role of Tribal Courts*, 17.

21 David Rich Lewis, "Reservation Leadership and the Progressive-Traditional Dichotomy," *Ethnohistory* 28 (Spring 1991): 124–48; David LaVere, "Minding Their Own Business: The Kiowa-Comanche-Apache Business Committee of the Early 1900s," in *Native Pathways: American Indian Culture and Economic Development in the Twentieth Century*, ed. Brian C. Hosmer and Colleen M. O'Neill (Boulder: University Press of Colorado, 2004), 52–65.

22 Choctaw children were sent to Choctaw Academy to learn to conduct business with non-Indians. Christina Snyder, "The Rise and Fall and Rise of Civilizations: Indian Intellectual Culture during the Removal Era," *Journal of American History* 104:2 (2017): 390–91.

23 Frederick E. Hoxie, *This Indian Country: American Indian Activists and the Places They Made* (New York: Penguin Press, 2012); Katrina Jagodinsky, *Legal Codes and Talking Trees: Indigenous Women's Sovereignty in the Sonoran and Puget Sound Borderlands, 1854–1946* (New Haven, CT: Yale University Press, 2016); Jeffrey R. Dudas, "Law at the American Frontier," 29 *Law and Social Inquiry* 859 (2004): 862.

24 Brad Asher, *Beyond the Reservation: Indians, Settlers, and the Law in Washington Territory, 1852–1889* (Norman: University of Oklahoma Press, 1999), 196; Michael C. Blumm and James Brumberg, "'Not Much Less Necessary . . . Than the Atmosphere They Breathed': Salmon, Indian Treaties, and the Supreme Court—a Centennial Remembrance of *United States v. Winans* and Its Enduring Significance," *Natural Resources Journal* 46 (2006): 489, 506, 510 et seq.; Harmon, *Indians in the Making*, chapters 5 and 6.

25 American Indian Citizenship Act, 8 U.S. Code 1401 (b); United States v. Nice, 241 U.S. 591 (1916).

26 Philip J. Deloria, "American Master Narratives and the Problem of Indian Citizenship in the Gilded Age and Progressive Era," *Journal of the Gilded Age and Progressive Era* 14 (2015): 3–12.

27 Nelson A. Miles, "The Indian Problem," *North American Review* 128 (Mar. 1879): 304–14, published online by University of Northern Iowa, accessed courtesy of JSTOR.

CHAPTER 1: FACTS ARE TOUGH

1 Blackmun Papers.

2 Stephen L. Wasby, "Justice Harry A. Blackmun: Transformation from 'Minnesota Twin' to Independent Voice," in *The Burger Court: Political and Judicial Profiles*, ed. Charles M. Lamb and Stephen C. Halpern, 63–99 (Urbana: University of Illinois Press, 1991), 70–71; Bob Woodward and Scott Armstrong, *The Brethren: Inside the Supreme Court* (New York: Simon and Schuster, 1979), 412, 359.

3 As of 1978, the Indian Civil Rights Act, 25 U.S.C. 1301–3, limited tribal court penalties to jail terms of six months and/or fines of $500.

4 Cynthia Gorney, "Tribal Powers Challenged," *WP*, Feb. 20, 1978, A1.

5 Justice William Brennan did not take part in consideration of the case.

6 Justice Powell's papers, provided in electronic form by Washington and Lee Law School, shed little light on his thoughts except in a memorandum stating that policy considerations weighed in the state's favor because of the high ratio of non-Indians to Indians on the reservation.

7 A Suquamish memorandum filed in district court made a claim the tribe apparently did not pursue: the tribe had "reason to believe" Belgarde was Indian but not Suquamish. Appendix: On Writ of Certiorari to the United States Court of Appeals for the Ninth Circuit, 35, Oliphant v. Suquamish Tribe (Petition filed Nov. 22, 1976; cert granted June 13, 1977).

8 Oliphant v. Schlie.

9 Gorney, "Tribal Powers Challenged."

10 Petition for Writ of Habeas Corpus, Oliphant v. Schlie.

11 Appendix, Oliphant v. Suquamish Tribe, 31.

12 Appendix, Oliphant v. Suquamish Tribe, 75, 94.

13 Appendix, Oliphant v. Suquamish Tribe, 78.

14 Appendix, Oliphant v. Suquamish Tribe, 75. Malone's figures differed from brief to brief. Brief for Petitioners, 8, and Appendix: Supplement to Petition for Writ of Habeas Corpus, Oliphant v. Suquamish Tribe.

15 Brief for Petitioners, Oliphant v. Suquamish Tribe, 8, 29; Appendix: Supplement to Petition, Oliphant v. Suquamish Tribe, 28–29.

16 Appendix: Supplement to Petition, Oliphant v. Suquamish Tribe, 30; Brief for Respondents, Oliphant v. Suquamish Tribe, 4–5.

17 Memorandum of Authorities of Amicus Curiae Suquamish Indian Tribe, Oliphant v. Schlie.

18 Brief for Petitioners, Oliphant v. Suquamish Tribe, 9; Appendix: Supplement to Petition, Oliphant v. Suquamish Tribe, 28–29.

19 Memorandum of Authorities of Amicus Curiae United States and Additional Memorandum of Authorities of Amicus Curiae Suquamish Indian Tribe, Oliphant v. Suquamish Tribe.

20 Records re Oliphant v. Schlie, Records Regarding Litigation, RG 48, Secretary of the Interior, Regional Solicitor's Office, Pacific NW Region, Portland, Indian Land Administration, 1957–1981, Box 2.

21 Oliphant v. Schlie, 544 F. 2d 1007 (9th Cir. 1976), 1013.

22 Eric Hobsbawm, *On History* (New York: New Press, 1997), 24.

23 Hobsbawm, *On History*, 26; Charles A. Miller, *The Supreme Court and the Uses of History* (Cambridge, MA: Harvard University Press, 1969), 6.

24 D. G. Bell, "Historians and the Culture of the Courts," *Acadiensis* 28:1 (Autumn 1998): 23–26, part 3 of "History, Native Issues and the Courts: A Forum," 3–26; Miller, *The Supreme Court and the Uses of History*, 122.

25 Hein Online US Supreme Court Library, keyword search for "Blackmun and Indian."

26 Morton v. Mancari, 417 U.S. 535 (1974), 554.

27 Frederick E. Hoxie, "War of the Worlds: History versus the Law in Charles Wilkinson's *American Indians, Time and the Law*," *Law and Social Inquiry* (1988): 791–99, 798.

CHAPTER 2: PROMISES OF POWER

1 Statement of James Jackson, *Constitutional Rights of the American Indian*, US Senate Subcommittee on Constitutional Rights, Committee on the Judiciary, 89th Cong., 3d sess. (June 22–24, 1965), CIS-NO 89, S1693-3, SUDOC: Y4.J89/2:In2/6/965, 100–103.

2 *Constitutional Rights of the American Indian*, 89th Cong., 133; Summary Report of Hearings and Investigations, US Senate, *Constitutional Rights of the American Indian*, 88th Cong., 2d sess. (1964), 10.

3 *Constitutional Rights of the American Indian*, 89th Cong., 103, 148, 207, 338, 347, 352, 354, 347.

4 *Constitutional Rights of the American Indian*, 89th Cong., 99.

5 *Constitutional Rights of the American Indian*, 89th Cong., 235, 240, 352. Since the mid-1990s, the Yakima Tribe, using the term "Nation," has spelled its name Yakama, as in its treaty with the United States. See www.yakamanation-nsn .gov/history3.php.

6 For a partial explanation, see Erich Steinman, "The Contemporary Revival and Diffusion of Indigenous Sovereignty Discourse," *American Studies* 46:3/4 (Fall 2005/Spring 2006): 89–113. Historian Daniel M. Cobb traced the ideas among

militant "activists at the national level." *Native Activism in Cold War America: The Struggle for Sovereignty* (Lawrence: University Press of Kansas, 2008), 3.

7 Harold E. Fey, *Indian Rights and American Justice* (Chicago: Christian Century Foundation, 1955), 3, 5.

8 Worcester v. Georgia, 31 U.S. 515, 561 (1832).

9 Lone Wolf v. Hitchcock, 187 U.S. 553 (1903).

10 Paul Rosier linked termination policy to the "Cold War imperative of 'ethnic integration.'" "'They Are Ancestral Homelands': Race, Place, and Politics in Cold War Native America, 1945–1961," *Journal of American History* 92:4 (2006): 1301.

11 Kenneth R. Philp, *Termination Revisited: American Indians on the Trail to Self-Determination, 1933–1953* (Lincoln: University of Nebraska Press, 1999), xiii, 12, 94–95; Thomas W. Cowger, "'The Crossroads of Destiny': The NCAI's Landmark Struggle to Thwart Coercive Termination," *American Indian Culture and Research Journal* 20:4 (1996): 123–24.

12 US House of Representatives, Committee on Indian Affairs, *Investigate Indian Affairs*, 78th Cong., 1st sess., Hearings on H. Res. 166 (June 1944); File: ["H.R. 4725—Confer State Jurisdiction over Indian Reservations, 1948"], NCAI Records, pre-1994, Series 6, Box 258.

13 US Senate, Subcommittee of the Committee on Interior and Insular Affairs, *New York Indians*, Hearings on S. 1683, S. 1686, S. 1687, 80th Cong., 2d session (March 9–11, 1948) (Washington, DC: USGPO), 24, 30, 109–10.

14 David E. Wilkins, "Native Peoples and American Indian Affairs during the Truman Presidency," in *Native Americans and the Legacy of Harry S. Truman*, ed. Brian Hosmer, 69–75 (Kirksville, MO: Truman State University Press, 2010), 69–70; Paul C. Rosier, *Serving Their Country: American Indian Politics and Patriotism in the Twentieth Century* (Cambridge, MA: Harvard University Press, 2009), 135–36.

15 Larry W. Burt, *Tribalism in Crisis: Federal Indian Policy, 1953-1961* (Albuquerque: University of New Mexico Press, 1982), 25.

16 House Concurrent Resolution 108, 67 US Statutes at Large B132 (Aug. 1, 1953).

17 Cowger, "'Crossroads of Destiny,'" 131; File: "Public Law 280 (84th–85th Cong.) 1955–1957," NCAI Records, Pre-1994. Series 6, Box 258; Folder: "Affiliated Tribes of Northwest Indians [1959–1975]," NCAI Records, Series 4, Intertribal Organizations, Box 139, N–P.

18 Rosier, "'They Are Ancestral Homelands,'" 1302, 1304, 1315, 1324.

19 Fey, *Indian Rights and American Justice*, 3.

20 Rosier, *Serving Their Country*, 158–59.

21 File: "[H.R. 4725—Confer State Jurisdiction over Indian Reservations, 1948]."

22 John Collier to Superintendents, Tribal Councils, and Individual Indians, 11, Jan. 20, 1934, NA RG 75, CCF, Records Concerning the Wheeler-Howard Act,

1933–37, Box 1, pt. 1-A, File 4894-34-066; Henry F. Dobyns, "Therapeutic Experience of Responsible Democracy," in *The American Indian Today*, ed. Stuart Levine and Nancy O. Lurie, 268–91 (Baltimore: Penguin Books, 1970), 271.

23 Russel Lawrence Barsh and James Youngblood Henderson, *The Road: Indian Tribes and Political Liberty* (Berkeley: University of California Press, 1980), 104, 99. Also, John Collier, "The Purpose and Operation of the Wheeler-Howard Indian Rights Bill," Feb. 19, 1934, Collier Papers, UWL Microfilm A-6833, Reel 30, Part II, 505.

24 25 U.S.C. 476.

25 [John Collier], Editorial, *Indians at Work* (Office of Indian Affairs, Washington, DC), July 1, 1934.

26 ARCIA (1934), in *Documents of United States Indian Policy*, ed. Francis Paul Prucha (Lincoln: University of Nebraska Press, 1975), 227–28.

27 For example, Felix S. Cohen, "The Spanish Origin of Indian Rights in the Law of the United States" (1942), in *The Legal Conscience: Selected Papers of Felix S. Cohen*, ed. Lucy Kramer Cohen, 230–52 (New Haven, CT: Yale University Press, 1960), 234.

28 Philp, *Termination Revisited*, 3–7; Felix S. Cohen, "Indian Self-Government" (1949), in *The Legal Conscience*, 305–14.

29 25 U.S.C. 478.

30 "Facts about the Indian Reorganization Act" [n.d.], Collier Papers, Reel 30, Part II, 505, Item 90027. Emphasis added.

31 Felix S. Cohen, *On the Drafting of Tribal Constitutions*, ed. David E. Wilkins (Norman: University of Oklahoma Press, 2006), 55, 35. On Indian Office suppression of the opinion, Cohen, "Indian Self-Government," 307.

32 *Felix S. Cohen's Handbook of Federal Indian Law* (1942; repr. Albuquerque: University of New Mexico Press, 1971), v–vi, xvii, 122, 33. Cohen's work was meant for Interior Department employees, "not for tribes." Barsh and Henderson, *The Road*, 113.

33 Felix S. Cohen, "How Long Will Indian Constitutions Last?" (1939), in *The Legal Conscience*, 222–29, 222; Cohen, "Indian Claims" (1943), in *The Legal Conscience*, 264–72, 269.

34 Barsh and Henderson, *The Road*, 103; Laurence M. Hauptman, *The Iroquois Struggle for Survival: World War II to Red Power* (Syracuse, NY: Syracuse University Press, 1986), 207; Hauptman, *Seven Generations of Iroquois Leadership: The Six Nations since 1800* (Syracuse, NY: Syracuse University Press, 2008), 70; Kenneth William Townsend, *World War II and the American Indian* (Albuquerque: University of New Mexico Press, 2000), 103–6, on Hickiwan Papagos in Arizona.

35 John Collier, "The Purpose and Operation of the Wheeler-Howard Indian Rights Bill," Collier Papers, Reel 30, Part II, 505.

36 John Collier, "The Indian in a Wartime Nation," *Annals of the American Academy of Political and Social Sciences* 223 (Sept. 1942): 26.

37 For example, Raymond D. Austin, *Navajo Courts and Navajo Common Law: A Tradition of Tribal Self-Governance* (Minneapolis: University of Minnesota Press, 2009), 13.

38 Theodore H. Haas, *Ten Years of Tribal Government under the Indian Reorganization Act* ([Washington, DC]: United States Indian Service, 1947), 1.

39 Richmond L. Clow, "The Indian Reorganization Act and the Loss of Tribal Sovereignty: Constitutions on the Rosebud and Pine Ridge Reservations," *Great Plains Quarterly* 7 (Spring 1987): 125–34.

40 Cohen, *On the Drafting of Tribal Constitutions*, xxi. Also, Editorial, *Indians at Work*, May 1, 1934; Paul C. Rosier, *Rebirth of the Blackfeet Nation, 1912–1954* (Lincoln: University of Nebraska Press, 2001), 21.

41 Minutes, Northwest Indian Congress, March 8, 1934, NA PAR RG 75 WWA, Tribal Operations Branch General Correspondence, 1914–1951, Box 257; *Indians at Work*, April 15, 1934, 24–25.

42 US House of Representatives, *Investigate Indian Affairs*, 78th Cong., 1st sess., Hearings on H. Res. 166, Part I, 106; Thomas Biolsi, *Organizing the Lakota: The Political Economy of the New Deal on the Pine Ridge and Rosebud Reservations* (Tucson: University of Arizona Press, 1992), 68.

43 Cohen, *On the Drafting of Tribal Constitutions*, 19, 55; Biolsi, *Organizing the Lakota*, 70.

44 Biolsi, *Organizing the Lakota*, 85–87, 98; Constitution and Bylaws of the Puyallup Tribe, http://thorpe.ou.edu/IRA.puycons.html; Nisqually Indian Tribe Constitution and By-Laws, www.nisqually-nsn.gov/index.php/council/constitution.

45 Clow, "Indian Reorganization Act and the Loss of Tribal Sovereignty," 131–32.

46 Biolsi, *Organizing the Lakota*, 126; Donald L. Parman, *Indians and the American West in the Twentieth Century* (Bloomington: Indiana University Press, 1994), 100.

47 Haas, *Ten Years of Tribal Government*, 5; Parman, *Indians and the American West*, 93, 100; Biolsi, *Organizing the Lakota*, 140.

48 Graham D. Taylor, *The New Deal and American Indian Tribalism: The Administration of the Indian Reorganization Act, 1934–45* (Lincoln: University of Nebraska Press, 1980), 21; Barsh and Henderson, *The Road*, 116.

49 Alexandra Harmon, *Indians in the Making: Ethnic Relations and Indian Identities around Puget Sound* (Berkeley: University of California Press, 1998), 204; US House of Representatives, *Investigate Indian Affairs*, Part I, 111. Also, Rosier, *Rebirth of the Blackfeet Nation*, 143.

50 Dobyns, "Therapeutic Experience of Responsible Democracy," 272; 48 U.S. Statutes 596.

51 Taylor, *The New Deal and American Indian Tribalism*, 94.

52 Shirley Hill Witt, "Nationalistic Trends among American Indians," *Midcontinent American Studies Journal* 6:2 (Fall 1965): 58.

53 Alison R. Bernstein, *American Indians and World War II: Toward a New Era in Indian Affairs* (Norman: University of Oklahoma Press, 1991); Suquamish Museum, *The Eyes of Chief Seattle* (Suquamish: Suquamish Museum, 1985), 46.

54 John Fahey, *Saving the Reservation: Joe Garry and the Battle to Be Indian* (Seattle: University of Washington Press, 2001), 10.

55 Bernstein, *American Indians and World War II*, 133, 134–35; Townsend, *World War II and the American Indian*, 215–16, 221; Parman, *Indians and the American West*, 115; Peter Iverson, "Building toward Self-Determination: Plains and Southwestern Indians in the 1940s and 1950s," *Western Historical Quarterly* 16:2 (April 1985): 165; Peter Iverson, "Legal Counsel and the Navajo Nation since 1945," *American Indian Quarterly* 3:1 (1977–78): 2–3; Witt, "Nationalistic Trends among Indians," 59.

56 Bernstein, *American Indians and World War II*, 171, 117; Parman, *Indians and the American West*, 121.

57 Cowger, "'Crossroads of Destiny,'" 121–25. Also, Affiliated Tribes of Northwest Indians Bulletin, April 1955, 5–6, AAIA Papers, Series 2, Subject Files, 1851–1995, Subseries 1, General Correspondence, Miscellaneous, Box 57, Folder 13.

58 Parman, *Indians and the American West*, 122.

59 H. D. Rosenthal, *Their Day in Court: A History of the Indian Claims Commission* (New York: Garland Publishing, 1990), 19, 57, 251; Indian Claims Commission Act, 60 Stat. 1049–58.

60 "Tribe to Get 'Fair Value' of Downtown Seattle—1859," *ST*, Mar. 29, 1957, 1; "Suquamish Tribe Still Awaits Claim Decision," *Bremerton Sun*, Feb. 26, 1969, 17; Rosenthal, *Their Day in Court*, 246, 248, 250.

61 Rosenthal, *Their Day in Court*, 48–49, 246; Witt, "Nationalist Trends among American Indians," 60–61.

62 Rosenthal, *Their Day in Court*, 247.

63 Rosenthal, *Their Day in Court*, 26.

64 The ICC opened 617 "dockets" in total. Indian Claims Commission Final Report, September 1978, courtesy of National Indian Law Library, https://www.narf.org/nill/documents/icc_final_report.pdf.

65 Billy Frank, "Florence James Kinley, Lummi, 1916–2003—a Life's Unwritten Chapter" [Text Reflection on Oral Eulogies by Billy Frank], www.scribd.com/doc/55141925/Florence-Dutch-FINAL.

66 Dobyns, "Therapeutic Experience of Responsible Democracy," 275, 276; Rosenthal, *Their Day in Court*, 23, 255; Iverson, "Legal Counsel and the Navajo Nation," 2; Robert McLaughlin. "Training Ground for the New Warriors," inset in "Who Owns the Land? A Native American Challenge," *Juris Doctor* 6 (Sept. 1986): 20.

67 Norman M. Littell, *Reflections of a Tribal Attorney* (booklet in the Library of Congress, n.p., n.d.), 1–3, 5; Iverson, "Legal Counsel and the Navajo Nation," 2–4; Daniel M. Burnham, "Indians Press Attack on Uncle Sam, Score Victories in Court," *WSJ*, Jan. 6, 1961, 1.

68 "Lawyer Just Couldn't Pass Up a Fight," *Arizona Republic*, Jan. 2, 1977, A-1, and Earl Zarbin, "Gila Indians Win Claim against U.S. for $1.5 million," *Arizona Republic*, Oct. 1, 1976, B-1, clippings in Lyman Papers, Box 26, News Clippings, Folders 33 and 14, respectively.

69 "Indian Affairs: Circular to Indian Agents Relating to Persons Acting as Attorneys for Indians," *NYT*, July 12, 1875, 5; Rosenthal, *Their Day in Court*, 21, 23; 48 Stat. 984, 987, 25 U.S.C. 476; Public Law 726, 60 Stat. 1049, sec. 15.

70 US Senate, Committee on Interior and Insular Affairs, *Attorney Contracts with Indian Tribes*, Senate Report 8, 83rd Congress, 1st sess. (1953), Serial Set Vol. No. 11659, Session Vol. No. 1, 4, 5–17.

71 Anthony Leviero, "Two Capital Hearings Set to Air Rules for U.S. Indians' Lawyers," *NYT*, Nov. 9, 1951, 1, 14; "Bureau's New Rules for Indians Stir Row," *NYT*, Nov. 18, 1950, 7; Leviero, "Curb on Lawyers of Indians Lifted," *NYT*, Jan. 25, 1952, 11. Also, Felix S. Cohen, "The Erosion of Indian Rights, 1950–1953: A Case Study in Bureaucracy," 62 *Yale Law Journal* 355 (1952–53).

72 US Senate, *Constitutional Rights of the American Indian* (1965 hearings), 4, 376; US Senate Committee on the Judiciary, Subcommittee on Constitutional Rights, *Constitutional Rights of the American Indian*: Summary Report of Hearings and Investigations, 88th Cong., 2d sess. (1964), 18; Helen Schierbeck, comments, transcript, Institute of the American West, Indian Self-Rule Conference, Aug. 19, 1983, "Toward Self-Determination, 1960–1976," 30–33, O'Neil Papers, Box 43, Folder 6.

73 O [La Farge] to Al [Ziontz], Feb. 22, 1952, AAIA Papers, Miscellaneous, Series 2, Subject Files, Subseries 3, Legislation, Box 312, Folder 4, Law Enforcement.

74 Worcester v. Georgia, 31 U.S. 414 (1832).

75 Williams v. Lee, 358 U.S. 217 (1959), 221–23 (notes omitted).

76 Begay v. Miller, 70 Arizona 380 (1950), 385, 222 P. 2d 624; Iron Crow v. Oglala Sioux Tribe of the Pine Ridge Indian Reservation, 231 F. 2d 89 (8th Cir., 1956), 91, 98–99.

77 Bethany R. Berger, "Williams v. Lee and the Debate over Indian Equality," 109 *Michigan Law Review* 1463 (June 2011): 1467, 1503.

78 Dewi Ioan Ball, "*Williams v. Lee* (1959)—50 Years Later: A Re-assessment of One of the Most Important Cases in the Modern-era of Federal Indian Law," *Michigan State Law Review* 391 (Summer 2010): 394.

79 "Arthur Lazarus Jr.," Wikipedia, https://en.wikipedia.org/wiki/Arthur_Lazarus_Jr.

80 La Verne Madigan to Jeffrey Fuller, Feb. 9, 1959, AAIA Papers, Miscellaneous, Series 2, Subject Files 1851–1995, Subseries 1, General Correspondence; Minutes of May 25, 1959, meeting of Committee on Indian Law of FBA, Folder: "Federal Bar Association, 1959–1960," NCAI Records, Series 8, Attorneys and Legal Interest Groups, Box 11.

81 NCAI Records, Series 8, Attorneys and Legal Interest Groups, Box 11; Wolfgang Saxon, "Marvin J. Sonosky, 88, Lawyer Who Championed Indian Cause," *NYT*, July 21, 1997, B9. For example, John W. Cragun memo to tribes "for whom we are general counsel," Jan. 13, 1956, re: pending bills on tribal consent to P.L. 280 jurisdiction, File: "Public Law 280 (84th–85th Cong.) 1955–1957," and Wilkinson, Cragun & Barker memo to "Tribal Clients," Dec. 3, 1959, re: South Dakota State Court ruling that state has no jurisdiction over Indian crimes on reservations, File: "Jurisdiction [1954–1961]," both in NCAI Records, Pre-1994. Series 6, Box 258.

82 Fahey, *Saving the Reservation*, 6.

83 Cragun memo to tribes "for whom we are general counsel"; File: "Jurisdiction Matters: Proposed Amendments to Public Law 280, 1955–1961"; Fahey, *Saving the Reservation*, 5.

84 Assistant Secretary of the Interior to Senator Murray, Aug. 1957, File: "Public Law 280 ('Law and Order Act'), 1957–1959," NCAI Records, Pre-1994, Series 6, Box 258.

85 US Senate, *Constitutional Rights of the American Indian*, Part 2 (Nov. 29, 1961, Phoenix), 87th Cong., 1st sess., 406–7.

86 Terry Brady, "Law, Order Struggle Splits Lummi Tribe," *Bellingham Herald*, Feb. 10, 1961, 1, 2, clipping, AAIA Papers, Series 2, Subject Files, 1851–1995, Subseries 2, Tribal, Box 285, Folder 7, Lummi.

87 Petition, "Law and Order," Dec. 1959, AAIA Papers, Series 2, Subject Files, 1851–1995, Subseries 2, Tribal, Box 285, Folder 12, Nisqually.

88 Sebastian Williams to Helen L. Peterson, April 24, 1959, AAIA Papers, Series 2, Subject Files, 1851–1995, Subseries 2, Tribal, Box 286, Folder 13, Tulalip, 1959–1962; Controversy over State Assumption of Law & Order on Indian Reservations (Case in point: Tulalip), NA PAR RG 75 WWA, Box 315, Law and Order Correspondence & Reports, 1952–68, File 170.1.

89 Alice Myers Winther, "Indian Parley Sifts Jurisdiction Issues," *Christian Science Monitor*, Feb. 20, 1960, copy in NCAI Records, Pre-1994, Series 6, Box 258, File: "Jurisdiction [1954–1961]."

90 Donald Janson, "Anti-Indian Bias Is Laid to States," *NYT*, Sept. 8, 1962, 17.

91 Stephen Conn, "Mid-Passage—the Navajo Tribe and Its First Legal Revolution," 6 *American Indian Law Review* 329 (1978): 332; Austin, *Navajo Courts and Navajo Common Law*, 27–28.

92 Edward Charles Valandra, *Not without Our Consent: Lakota Resistance to Termination, 1950–59* (Urbana: University of Illinois Press, 2006), 120, 9, 221.

93 Donald Janson, "South Dakota Indians Complain Their Highways Are Unpoliced: Officials Cite Confusion of Jurisdiction," *NYT*, June 14, 1962, 36; "South Dakota Vote Is Forced by Tribes, *NYT*, June 2, 1963, 8; Donald Janson, "Sioux Fight South Dakota Law for Authority on Reservations," *NYT*, June 3, 1963, 55; "Sioux Fight Curb on Independence: Indian Nation Is Sponsoring South Dakota Referendum," *NYT*, Aug. 30, 1964, 72; "Indians in Dakota Oppose Law Shift," *NYT*, Oct. 25, 1964, 62; "Sioux Indians Fight to Keep Tribal Rights," *LAT*, Jan. 7, 1965, OC14; La Verne Madigan to Betsy Ann Trick, Aug. 5, 1959, AAIA Papers, Series 2, Subject Files, 1851–1995, Subseries 2, Tribal, Box 285, Folder 6, Washington, Law & Order, 1959–1963; Wilkinson, Cragun & Barker to "Tribal Clients," Dec. 3, 1959, NCAI Records, Pre-1994, Series 6, Box 258, File "Jurisdiction [1954–1961].

94 Bill Becker, "Squatters Bring New Indian War," *NYT*, May 1, 1960, 62; "10-Indian Police Force Patrols Tribal Lands," *LAT*, May 24, 1961, A12. Also, Daniel M. Burnham, "Indians Press Attack on Uncle Sam, Score Victories in Court," *WSJ*, Jan. 6, 1961, 1; Carole Goldberg-Ambrose, "Public Law 280 and the Problem of Lawlessness in California Indian Country," 44 *UCLA Law Review* 1418 (1997).

95 Burt, *Tribalism in Crisis*, 74, 84, 114.

96 "Tribe on Wrong Trail: Appeals in Vain for 3 Foreign Envoys' Aid on Land Claims," *NYT*, Nov. 19, 1958, 39; "Chiefs Back Plan to Unite Indians," *NYT*, Apr. 2, 1959, 25.

97 Harry A. Kersey, Jr., "The Havana Connection: Buffalo Tiger, Fidel Castro, and the Origin of Miccosukee Tribal Sovereignty, 1959–1962," *American Indian Quarterly* 25 (Fall 2001): 496–97; Burt, *Tribalism in Crisis*, 120 (Ute secession declaration).

98 Burt, *Tribalism in Crisis*, 117, 118, 120, 122.

99 "Iroquois at U.N. 'House of Peace,'" *NYT*, Jan. 31, 1957, 10; "Disgruntled Chippewas Ask U.N. Membership," *NYT*, July 9, 1960, 2.

100 Kersey, "The Havana Connection," 496–97.

101 Report and recommendations on NCAI letterhead, Dec. 1, 1960, Tom Greenwood Papers, Ayer Modern MS Greenwood, Newberry Library, Box 1, Folder 1 [Chicago American Indian Conference, 1961].

102 Nancy Oestreich Lurie, "Commentary: Sol Tax and Tribal Sovereignty," *Human Organization* 58 (Spring 1999): 108, 114, 115; "Declaration of Indian

Purpose," in *Documents of United States Indian Policy*, ed. Francis Paul Prucha (Lincoln: University of Nebraska Press, 1975), 244–46; George Pierre Castile, *To Show Heart: Native American Self-Determination and Federal Indian Policy, 1960–1975* (Tucson: University of Arizona Press, 1998), 18.

103 Cobb, *Native Activism in Cold War America*, 33, 41.

104 Greenwood Papers, Newberry Library, Box 1, Folder 12, Report # 4, April 26, 1961. Indians in Washington State "called for a return to their 'original status of tribal self-government in the absence of dominance from another.'" Cobb, *Native Activism in Cold War America*, 47.

105 Witt, "Nationalistic Trends among American Indians," 64; NIYC Constitution and Statement of Purpose at http://en.wikipedia.org/wiki/National_Indian_Youth_Council; Cobb, *Native Activism in Cold War America*, 79, 52, 54.

106 Lurie, "Commentary," 110–11.

107 D'Arcy McNickle, Proposal for a Training Program for Indian Leaders, [1960], Ayer MS Modern McNickle Papers, Newberry Library, Box 23, Folder 196.

108 D'Arcy McNickle testimony, June 1, 1962, *Constitutional Rights of American Indians* hearings, Part 3, CCIS-NO: 87 S1570-3 (87th Cong., 1st sess.)

109 Cobb, *Native Activism in Cold War America*, 64, 27.

110 1964 Workshop Papers, Ayer MS Modern McNickle Papers, Newberry Library, Box 23, Folder 205; 1962 Workshop Papers, Newberry Library, Box 24, Folder 212; Cobb, *Native Activism in Cold War America*, 66.

111 Burt, *Tribalism in Crisis*, 127–28; Stephen Cornell, "Crisis and Response in Indian-White Relations: 1960–1984," *Social Problems* 32 (October 1984): 46; Witt, "Nationalistic Trends among American Indians," 63; Donald Janson, "U.S. Moves to Spur Tribal Economies: Change in Policy is Outlined at Indian Convention," *NYT*, Sept. 5, 1962, 61.

CHAPTER 3: COLONIAL CONTROLS IN QUINAULT TERRITORY

1 Author's telephone conversation with Richard Belmont, Jr., Feb. 1, 2012.

2 US Senate Select Committee on Indian Affairs, *Jurisdiction on Indian Reservations*, Hearings on S. 1181, S. 1722, S. 2832, 96th Cong., 2d sess., May 17, 18, 19, 1980 (Washington, DC: US Government Publishing Office, 1980), 80.

3 Joe DeLaCruz, keynote address, National Fisheries Conference, Union of British Columbia Indian Chiefs National Indian Brotherhood 5/20/80, Fourth World Documentation Project Archives, Center for World Indigenous Studies, www.cwis.org.

4 Quinault population was larger before the introduction of new lethal pathogens in the 1780s. Taholah village, reportedly named for "Chief" Taxo'la, was at the site of the aboriginal village kwi'nail, source for the name Quinault. Ronald L.

Olson, *The Quinault Indians*, University of Washington Publications in Anthropology 6 (November 1936), 3.

5 Olson, *Quinault Indians*, 11.

6 Oregon Donation Land Claim Act (1850), 9 U.S. Stat. 496.

7 12 U.S. Stat. 971.

8 Charles J. Kappler, *Indian Affairs: Laws and Treaties* (Washington, DC: Government Printing Office, 1904), 923; Gary Seiji Morishima, "A Systems Study of Natural Resource Development on the Quinault Indian Reservation," PhD diss., University of Washington, 1979, 29–30.

9 Office of Indian Affairs, ARCIA (1878), 137; Olson, *Quinault Indians*, 12–13; Pauline K. Capoeman, ed., *Land of the Quinault* (Taholah: Quinault Indian Nation, 1990), 123, quoting Ferrand's *Traditions of the Quinault Indians* (New York: American Museum of Natural History, 1902).

10 ARCIA (1878), 135; ARCIA (1874), 335; ARCIA (1877), 196; ARCIA (1886), 240. Also, Capoeman, *Land of the Quinault*, 12.

11 ARCIA (1869), 148; ARCIA (1878), 137; ARCIA (1875), 365; ARCIA (1882), 161; Morishima, "Systems Study," 3.

12 ARCIA (1873), 312; ARCIA (1877), 195; ARCIA (1880), 162; ARCIA (1884), 164.

13 Capoeman, *Land of the Quinault*, 122; ARCIA (1869), 148; ARCIA (1874), 334; ARCIA (1877), 195; ARCIA (1880), 162; ARCIA (1887), 212.

14 "State News," *Seattle Republican*, May 10, 1902, 7; "Indians Make Protest," *San Francisco Call*, April 14, 1907, 33.

15 Capoeman, *Land of the Quinault*, 111, 136; Aaron Goings, "Hoquiam—Thumbnail History," History Link, www.historylink.org/index.cfm?DisplayPage=output.cfm&file_id=8652.

16 Olson, *Quinault Indians*, 13, 95, 114. "Property . . . was not desired for its own sake, but rather for the social and material benefits" that accrued to the person who had it. "To possess was not to hoard, but to give and spend." Ram Raj Prasad Singh, "Aboriginal Economic System of the Olympic Peninsula Indians, Western Washington," PhD diss., University of Washington, 1956, 204, 206.

17 ARCIA (1869), 148; ARCIA (1875), 365; ARCIA (1880), 162; Capoeman, *Land of the Quinault*, 104–5.

18 Capoeman, *Land of the Quinault*, 104, 116–17.

19 ARCIA (1880), 162; ARCIA (1887), 212; ARCIA (1889), 228; ARCIA (1890), 227; ARCIA (1891), 452.

20 ARCIA (1904), 354; Goings, "Hoquiam."

21 Capoeman, *Land of the Quinault*, 138.

22 Capoeman, *Land of the Quinault*, 177; Morishima, "Systems Study," 36; "Plans Miscarry: A Shrewd Move to Control Quinault Lands," *Aberdeen Herald*, Jan. 28, 1904, 1.

23 "Lobby Talk" column: "Quinault Indians Richest Tribe," *San Francisco Call*, July 26, 1913, 1.

24 Tribe member Francis Rosander recalled that some Quinaults in the 1960s expressed resentment at having to share reservation resources with Quileutes. Author's interview with Rosander, Taholah, July 16, 2012.

25 ARCIA (1904), 354.

26 Morishima, "Systems Study," 38–44; Capoeman, *Land of the Quinault*, 178; Robert E. Beaty, "A Study of B.I.A. Timber Management on the Quinault Indian Reservation, 1950–1970," in *Studies in American Indian Law*, vol. 2, ed. Ralph W. Johnson (unpublished student papers, University of Washington Law School, June 1970), 403–51, 410.

27 Act of March 4, 1911 (Public Law 486); Second Assistant Commissioner to H. H. Johnson, May 20, 1911, NA PAR RG 75, WWA, Box 282, 064, Tribal Operations Branch "Tribal" Files, ca. 1919–68, Quinault, file: "Acts of Tribal Council, 1907–13."

28 Capoeman, *Land of the Quinault*, 177; Morishima, "Systems Study," 41.

29 Capoeman, *Land of the Quinault*, 177.

30 Morishima, "Systems Study," 38, 55; 36 U.S. Stat. 1345.

31 E. B. Meritt to Secretary of the Interior, Oct. 28, 1919, NA PAR RG 75 WWA, Box 281, Tribal Operations Branch "Tribal" Files, ca. 1919–68, Quinault.

32 "Quinaut's [*sic*] Adopt Different Indians into Their Tribe," *Real American* (Hoquiam, WA), July 3, 1925, 1.

33 Hilary Halbert v. United States, 283 U.S. 753 (1931).

34 For instance, Eugene Hill to CIA, June 22, 1920, NA PAR RG 75 WWA, Box 282, 064.

35 Morishima, "Systems Study," 41, 52, 55–56, 40, citing Taholah Agency records, NA PAR RG 75, Box 1, File VIII, 54, 51–52, 55–59, and Kinney, "The Administration of Indian Forests," *Journal of Forestry* 28:8 (1930): 1046; Capoeman, *Land of the Quinault*, 117. Also, [Quinault Indian Tribe, Forestry Division], *Portrait of Our Land: A Quinault Tribal Forestry Perspective* (Taholah, 1978), 10.

36 Morishima, "Systems Study," 39, 52–54.

37 Capoeman, *Land of the Quinault*, 183.

38 Morishima, "Systems Study,"101–2, 88–89; Capoeman, *Land of the Quinault*, 183, 190.

39 Capoeman, *Land of the Quinault*, 141; Morishima, "Systems Study," 84.

40 US Department of Agriculture Soil Conservation Service, "Reconnaissance Survey of the Quinaielt Indian Reservation," April 1939, NA PAR RG 75, Portland Area Office, Tribal Operations Branch, General Subject Files, ca. 1934 (George P. LaVatta), Surveys and Reports, 1936–41, Box 1499; Squire v. Capoeman, 351 U.S. 1, 10 (1956).

41 Quinault-BIA Relations, 1920s–1950s, Taholah Indian Agency Decimal Files, 1925–1950, NA PAR RG 75, 064.0 Tribal Meetings, Councils, Constitutions, TAH 07, Box 66, Quinault Folder 2; Morishima, "Systems Study," 87; Beaty, "Study of B.I.A. Timber Management," 442.

42 DeLaCruz interview.

43 Beaty, "Study of B.I.A. Timber Management," 410, 418–19.

44 United States v. Mitchell, 463 U.S. 206 (1983). The Supreme Court case consolidated four Court of Claims actions on behalf of 1,465 individuals with interests in reservation allotments, an association of Quinault Reservation allottees, and the Quinault tribe.

45 [Quinault Indian Tribe], *Portrait of Our Land*, 11, 27. Also, Charles Wilkinson, *Blood Struggle: The Rise of Modern Indian Nations* (New York: W. W. Norton, 2005), 18.

46 William Garfield et al. to F. H. Abbott, Feb. 7, 1913, NA PAR RG 75 WWA, Law and Order Correspondence, 1908–1922, Box 1, TAH-33; "Sea Only Left, Say Indians; Already Driven to the Brink, They Tell Congressman," *San Juan Islander*, Oct. 17, 1913.

47 Quinault Department of Natural Resources and Economic Development, *QDNR&ED Newsletter* (Taholah, WA), May 1979, 4; undated memorandum, "Origin of Quinault Fishing Regulations," NA PAR RG 48, Secretary of Interior, Regional Solicitor's Office, Pacific Northwest Region, Indian Land Administration, Fishing and Hunting Rights, U.S. v. Washington Historical Background Documents, 1960–1975, Box 27; Morishima, "Systems Study," 100; Capoeman, *Land of the Quinault*, 211.

48 Rules, Taholah Sub Agency, May 22, 1909, Fishing Industry Correspondence, 1908–1921, TAH-74, NA PAR RG 75, Taholah Agency, Box 1, Folder: "ED Industries Fishing 1908 to 1914."

49 Petition of 42 Indians, May 4, 1914, Rules, Taholah Sub Agency, May 22, 1909; Frank W. Law to Commissioner of Indian Affairs, Dec. 4, 1918, and J. M. Phillips to Miles Pointdexter [*sic*], Jan. 10, 1919, Fishing Industry Correspondence, 1908–1921, TAH-74, NA PAR RG 75, Taholah Agency, Box 1, Folder: "Fishing/Education Law & Order 1919–21."

50 Sources for the preceding two paragraphs are letters in Folders "Ed. Fishing Industry 1915–1918"and "Fishing/Education Law & Order 1919–21," Fishing Industry Correspondence, 1908–1921, TAH-74, NA PAR RG 75, Taholah Agency, Box 1. Indians expected a say in selecting officers to enforce regulations. Johnson Waukenas to E. B. Meritt, Jan. 2, 1914, Law and Order Correspondence, 1908–1922, Quinault Taholah Agency Correspondence, NA PAR RG 75, Taholah Indian Agency, TAH-33, Box 1, Folder: "Education, Law & Order [1914]."

51 Superintendent to Commissioner of Indian Affairs, Oct. 30, 1919, Fishing Industry Correspondence, 1908–1921, NA PAR RG 75, Taholah Agency Box 1, TAH-74.

52 Capoeman, *Land of the Quinault*, 77.

53 Mason et al. v. Sams, 5 F. 2d 255 (1925). Word of this ruling reached Indians and non-Indians throughout Washington via newspapers such as the *Seattle Times* and the *Real American, A National Indian Weekly Newspaper*, published by a Quileute Indian ("Indians Regain Fish Rights at Quinault," Apr. 24, 1925, 1). How the Indians found or paid lawyers Stuart A. Elliott, H. G. Rowland, and Dix H. Rowland I could not determine. NA PAR RG 75, Taholah Indian Agency Decimal Files, 1925–1950, Quinault Folder 171, Quinault-BIA Relations, 1920s–1950s.

54 E. B. Meritt, to Wm. B. Sams, Oct. 9, 1928, and W. B. Sams to Commissioner of Indian Affairs, Aug. 29, 1928, folder: "Petitions, Tribal, William Mason et al. v. W. B. Sams, Superintendent," NA PAR RG 75, Quinault-BIA Relations, 1920s–1950s, Taholah Indian Agency Decimal Files, 1925–1950, No. 069, Box 112.

55 Undated memorandum, "Origin of Quinault Fishing Regulations."

56 "Quinault Fishing Ban Reviewed at Capitol," *ST*, Feb. 13, 1927, 14; Supt. to Hoquiam Chamber of Commerce, Dec. 2, 1926, NA PAR RG 75 WWA, Tribal Operations Branch "Tribal" Files, ca. 1919–68, Box 282, Quinault, 064.

57 Pioneer Packing Company v. Winslow, 159 Wash. 655 (1930); *QDNR&ED Newsletter*, Feb. 1980, 2; WDF Files, Indian Affairs, Box 32, Quinault Files, Folder: "Quinault, 1925–52."

58 Blanche McQ. Nicholson to W. B. Sams, March 16, 1927, Quinault-BIA Relations, 1920s–1950s, NA PAR RG 75, Taholah Indian Agency Decimal Files, 1925–1950, 07 Decimal File Correspondence, 1926–1950, Box 50, Folder 050 Statistics [1926–1941].

59 DeLaCruz interview; Capoeman, *Land of the Quinault*, 210. A 1934 amendment to the bylaws provided for a Business Committee of four officers and five additional persons. John Collier to N. O. Nicholson, Sep. 24, 1934, NA PAR RG 75 WWA Tribal Operations Branch "Tribal" Files, ca. 1919–68, Quinault.

60 Capoeman, *Land of the Quinault*, 126.

61 "Summer Home Sites to Be Sold by Indians," *ST*, Nov. 14, 1927, 5; US Department of Agriculture, "Reconnaissance Survey." Reports in 1930, 1935, and 1946 of logging harm to fisheries are in *QDNR&ED Newsletter*, May 1979–February 1982, 4.

62 Extract, ARCIA (1933), in *Documents of United States Indian Policy*, 3rd ed., ed. Francis Paul Prucha (Lincoln: University of Nebraska Press, 2000), 225.

63 48 U.S. Stat. 984, secs. 16 and 18.

64 General Correspondence (Old Taholah/Tulalip), ca. 1914–51, NA PAR RG 75 WWA, Box 258.

65 William Zimmerman, Jr., to George P. LaVatta, July 14, 1936, NA RG 75, Records of the BIA Indian Organization Division, General Records Concerning Indian Organization, 1934–56, Box 32; Charles A. Hobbs to James E. Officer, May 4, 1965, Officer Files, Box 37, Folder 2 of 6 labeled "Quinault." According to Morishima, reservation residents voted 107 to 36 against accepting the IRA; off-reservation Indians voted 148 to 69 in favor. Morishima, "Systems Analysis," 156–57. Also, Justine E. James, Jr., with Leilani A. Chubby, "Quinault," in *Native Peoples of the Olympic Peninsula: Who We Are*, ed. Jacilee Wray, 99–117 (Norman: University of Oklahoma Press, 2002), 110.

66 William Zimmerman, Jr., to N. O. Nicholson, Aug. 12, 1938, Quinault-BIA Relations, 1920s–1950s, NA PAR RG 75, Taholah Indian Agency Decimal Files, 1925–1950, 064.0, Tribal Meetings, Councils, Constitutions, TAH 07, Box 66. Folder 4.

67 James and Chubby, "Quinault," 110; Morishima, "Systems Analysis," 56–57.

68 Minutes, council meetings June 24, 1939, and June 23, 1942, Quinault-BIA Relations, 1920s–1950s, NA PAR RG 75, Taholah Indian Agency Decimal Files, 1925–1950, 064.0 Tribal Meetings, Councils, Constitutions, TAH 07, Box 66 Quinault, Folder 2, Councils, Acts of Tribal (Minutes of Meetings, Quinaielt).

69 AAIA Papers, Series 2, Subject Files, 1851–1995, Subseries 2, Tribal, Box 287, Folder 6: "Washington General, 1951–1960," and Box 286, Quinault, 1952–1962.

70 Singh, "Aboriginal Economic System of the Olympic Peninsula Indians," 96, 103; author's interview with Francis Rosander.

71 Quinault-BIA Relations, 1920s–1950s, NA PAR RG 75, Taholah Agency Decimal Files, 1925–1950, 064.0 Tribal Meetings, Councils, Constitutions, TAH 07, Box 66, Quinault Folder 1.

72 Frank Hyasman, resignation as judge, Jan. 12, 1925, Quinault-BIA Relations, 1920s–1950s, NA PAR RG 75, Taholah Indian Agency Decimal Files, 1925–1950, 076, Folder: "Judges, Indian—Taholah, Washington," 1 of 2. Also, Resolution of Business Committee approving appointment of Oscar McLeod, Nov. 28, 1942, Quinault-BIA Relations, 1920s–1950s, NA PAR RG 75, Taholah Indian Agency Decimal Files, 1925–1950, 064.0—Tribal Meetings, Councils, Constitutions, TAH 07, Box 66, Quinault Folder; correspondence, Tribal Operations Branch "Tribal" Files, ca. 1919–68, Quinault, NA PAR RG 75 WWA, Box 282, 067 Business Committee Tribal Council 1930–39. On Courts of Indian Offenses, Laurence F. Schmeckebier, *The Office of Indian Affairs: Its History, Activities, and Organization* (Baltimore: Johns Hopkins University Press, 1927), 259–60.

73 Quinault-BIA Relations, 1920s–1950s. BIA regulations issued in 1935 allowed tribes organized under the IRA to establish their own courts, appoint and

remove judges, and employ police forces. Quinaults did that in the 1970s. Kenneth R. Philp, *Termination Revisited: American Indians on the Trail to Self-Determination, 1933–1953* (Lincoln: University of Nebraska Press, 1999), 8.

74 Cleveland Jackson to Floyd H. Phillips, April 26, 1940, and Melvin Helander to Jackson, Aug. 3, 1948, Quinault-BIA Relations, 1920s–1950s, NA PAR RG 75, Taholah Indian Agency Decimal Files, 1925–1950, 064.0, Tribal Meetings, Councils, Constitutions, TAH 07, Box 66, Quinault Folder 1.

75 Anna A. Jackson to Vincent Keeler, Mar. 15, 1948, Quinault-BIA Relations, 1920s–1950s, NA PAR RG 75, Taholah Indian Agency Decimal Files, 1925–1950, 064.0, Tribal Meetings, Councils, Constitutions, TAH 07, Box 66, Quinault Folder 1. Also, Queets residents petition, July 25, 1938, Quinault-BIA Relations, 1920s–1950s, NA PAR RG 75, Taholah Indian Agency Decimal Files, 1925–1950, 064.0, Tribal Meetings, Councils, Constitutions, TAH 07, Box 66, Folder 4.

76 Tribal council minutes, June 23, 1943, and minutes of the "tribal committee," Mar. 2, 1946, Quinault-BIA Relations, 1920s–1950s, NA PAR RG 75, Taholah Indian Agency Decimal Files, 1925–1950, 064.0, Tribal Meetings, Councils, Constitutions, TAH 07, Box 66, Quinault Folder 2, Councils, Acts of Tribal (Minutes of Meetings, Quinaielt).

77 Quinault-BIA Relations, 1920s–1950s, NA PAR RG 75, Taholah Indian Agency Decimal Files, 1925–1950, 064.0 Tribal Meetings, Councils, Constitutions, TAH 07, Box 66, Quinault, Folder 2; N. O. Nicholson to Mr. Frank Law, Taholah, May 11, 1938, and N. O. Nicholson to Simon Charley, Dec. 3, 1937, Quinault-BIA Relations, 1920s–1950s, NA PAR RG 75, Taholah Indian Agency Decimal Files, 1925–1950, 076—Folder: "Judges, Indian—Taholah, Washington," 1 of 2.

78 Quinaielt Tribal Business Committee to Melvin Robertson, July 29, 1954, NA PAR RG 75 WWA, General Correspondence, 1952–68, Box 10.

79 P.L. 83–280, Aug. 15, 1953, codified as 18 U.S.C. § 1162, 28 U.S.C. § 1360, and 25 U.S.C. §§ 1321–1326.

80 Author's interview with Justine James, Sr., Taholah, Washington, July 16, 2012; author's interview with Harold L. Patterson, Taholah, Washington, July 17, 2012.

81 Capoeman, *Land of the Quinault*, 198; Philp, *Termination Revisited*, 96; Larry W. Burt, *Tribalism in Crisis: Federal Indian Policy, 1953–1961* (Albuquerque: University of New Mexico Press, 1982), 60.

82 Real Property Reports, 1950–1969, NA PAR RG 75 WWA, Box 29, Folder: "Report of Land Transactions 1956–58."

83 Beaty, "Study of B.I.A. Timber Management," 410; C. W. Ringey to John W. Libby, Oct. 4, 1960, General Correspondence, NA PAR RG 75 WWA, 1952–1960, Box 10. Joe DeLaCruz said in 1983 that Quinaults "lost" more than 35,000 acres of timberland during this period. Kenneth R. Philp, ed., *Indian Self-Rule:*

First-Hand Accounts of Indian-White Relations from Roosevelt to Reagan (Logan: Utah State University Press, 1995), 182; Quinault Business Committee and Planning and Review Committee, *Quinault Comprehensive Plan: Existing Conditions* (Taholah, Aug. 1974), 20.

84 Horton Capoeman to Robert Schoettler, May 26, 1955, and Capoeman to Aloha Lumber Company, April 26, 1956, WDF Files, Indian Affairs, Box 32, Quinault Files, Folder "Quinault 1953–62."

85 Minutes of meeting, April 3, 1956, NA PAR RG 75, Portland Area Office, Tribal Operations Branch, General Subject Files, 1953–67, Tribal Council Minutes, ca. 1950–1965, Box 1575. Capoeman and Cleve Jackson challenged the BIA from their first years in Quinault government. They were on the Business Committee that complained to Superintendent Nicholson, "Your office is always very insistant [*sic*] on having the Tribal council approve of things that do not amount to anything but when we put in a complaint about something that we could get some benefit from, it is always ignored. If this protest is shelved the same as our last one, we shall hound the Washington Office with letters and telegrams until we get some action." Business Committee to N. O. Nicholson, Nov. 2, 1938, Quinault-BIA Relations, 1920s–1950s, NA PAR RG 75, Taholah Indian Agency Decimal Files, 1925–1950, 064.0, Tribal Meetings, Councils, Constitutions, TAH 07, Box 66, Quinault Folder 1.

86 Horton Capoeman to C. W. Ringey, Aug. 31, 1960, NA PAR RG 75 WWA, General Correspondence, 1952–68, Box 10.

87 Claude H. Heyer to La Verne Madigan, AAIA Papers, Series 2, Subject Files, 1851–1995, Subseries 2, Tribal, Box 287, Folder 6, Washington General, 1951–1960; "Lake Quinault to Be Closed to White Fishers, Boaters," *ST*, Mar. 25, 1961.

88 Cleve Jackson to NCAI, April 25, 1956, NCAI Records, pre-1994 accessions, Series 4, Box 122, Tribal Files, Qu–Se, Folder: "Quinault Tribe (Washington) 1956–1961"; John Fahey, *Saving the Reservation: Joe Garry and the Battle to Be Indian* (Seattle: University of Washington Press, 2001), 154–56; *Squire v. Capoeman*, 351 U.S. 1 (1956).

89 Capoeman, *Land of the Quinault*, 122.

90 The Quinault Tribe of Indians v. The United States, 102 Ct. Cl. 822 (1945).

91 General council minutes, June 23, 1943, and minutes of other 1940s meetings in Quinault-BIA Relations, 1920s–1950s, NA PAR RG 75, Taholah Indian Agency Decimal Files, 1925–1950, 064.0, Tribal Meetings, Councils, Constitutions, TAH 07, Box 66, Quinault Folder 2. Also, March 31, 1956, meeting, NA PAR RG 75, Portland Area Office, Tribal Operations Branch, General Subject Files, 1953–67, Tribal Council Minutes, ca. 1950–1965, Box 1575. I found no records of the car tax case.

92 Fred Saux to Oliver La Farge, April 27, 1956, AAIA Papers, Series 2, Subject Files, 1851–1995, Subseries 2, Tribal, Box 286, Quinault, 1952–1962.

93 Supt. to CIA, Nov. 27, 1923, enclosing minutes of meeting Nov. 1923 to consider adoptions. NA PAR RG 75 WWA, Tribal Operations Branch "Tribal" Files, ca. 1919–68, Box 282, Quinault. In 2012, Francis Rosander said he knew Gladys Phillips well. Asked how the tribe happened to consult her, he said, "Oh, she was an Indian." Author's interview with Rosander.

94 Heyer to Madigan, Nov. 6, 1960, AAIA Papers, Box 287, Folder 6, Washington General, 1951–1960; minutes, special council meeting April 10, 1936, Quinault-BIA Relations, 1920s–1950s, NA PAR RG 75, Taholah Indian Agency Decimal Files, 1925–1950, 064.0, Tribal Meetings, Councils, Constitutions, TAH 07, Box 66, Quinault Folder 2; Ralph H. Case, University of South Dakota Libraries, http://libguides.usd.edu/case.

95 General council minutes, June 23, 1943; clipping "Attorney Hired by Quinault Indians," *Daily World*, May 3, 1951, in WDF Files, Indian Affairs, Box 32, Quinault Files, Folder "Quinault, 1925–52."

96 General council minutes, Quinault-BIA Relations, 1920s–1950s, NA PAR RG 75, Taholah Indian Agency Decimal Files, 1925–1950, 064.0, Tribal Meetings, Councils, Constitutions, TAH 07, Box 66, Quinault Folder 2. Until 1964, Gladys Phillips reportedly provided services to the tribe without charge. C. J. Higman to Tribal Operations File, Feb. 26, 1964, Quinault BIA Correspondence, NA PAR RG 75 WWA, Tribal Operations Branch Tribal Files, ca. 1919–1968, Box 282, Folder 060.

97 Minutes of meeting, Mar. 31, 1956, NA PAR RG 75, Portland Area Office, Tribal Operations Branch, General Subject Files, 1953–67, Tribal Council Minutes, ca. 1950–1965, Box 1575; Wilkinson, Cragun & Barker to "Tribal Clients," Dec. 3, 1959, NCAI Records, pre-1994, Series 6, Box 258, file "Jurisdiction [1954–1961]."

98 ATNI Bulletin, April 1955, 1 and 3, AAIA Papers, Miscellaneous, Series 2, Subject Files, 1851–1995, Subseries 1, General Correspondence, Box 57.

99 Fahey, *Saving the Reservation*, 53.

100 Executive Director Madigan described the AAIA in 1957 as a "national organization of mixed Indian and non-Indian membership with about 15,000 members and many more supporters" focused on national problems "which can be solved in Washington, just as the Indian focus has also been." The AAIA litigated to protect Indians' civil rights. When US policy shifted to termination, the AAIA "united forces to combat or slow those trends." "Program and Proceedings—Third Annual Conference on Indian Affairs: Indian Problems of Law and Order," at State University of South Dakota, June 16 and 17, 1957, O'Neil Papers, Box 46, Folder 1, p. 57. According to historian Daniel M. Cobb, the AAIA "carried considerable influence in national Indian politics." *Native*

Activism in Cold War America: The Struggle for Sovereignty (Lawrence: University Press of Kansas, 2008), 14.

101 Joseph R. Hillaire to AAIA, Oct. 13, 1951, and May 31, 1953. AAIA Papers, Series 2, Subject Files, 1851–1995, Subseries 2, Tribal, Box 285, Folder 7: Lummi.

102 "Destruction of Trusteeship Status Still before Indians," AAIA Bulletin, April 1955, 3, AAIA Papers, Miscellaneous, Series 2, Subject Files, 1851–1995, Subseries 1, General Correspondence, Box 57, Folder 13: "Affiliated Tribes of Northwest Indians, 1955–1989"; LaVerne Madigan to Betsy Ann Trick, Aug. 5, 1959, AAIA Papers, Series 2, Subject Files, 1851–1995, Subseries 2, Tribal, Box 285, Folder 6, Washington, Law & Order, 1959–1963.

103 On relations among indigenous peoples of the region, Alexandra Harmon, *Indians in the Making: Ethnic Relations and Indian Identities around Puget Sound* (Berkeley: University of California Press, 1998).

104 Fred Saux to Oliver La Farge, April 27, 1956, and La Verne Madigan to Fred Saux, May 17, 1956, AAIA Papers, Series 2, Subject Files, 1851–1995, Subseries 2, Tribal, Box 286, Quinault, 1952–1962.

105 Papers of Erna Gunther, UWL Special Collections, Accession 614-001, Box 1, Folder 1.

106 Quinault Fact-Finding Committee to Oliver La Farge, June 21, 1960, AAIA Papers, Series 2, Subject Files, 1851–1995, Subseries 2, Tribal, Box 286, Quinault, 1952–1962.

107 Minutes, ATNI Executive Council Meeting, Neah Bay, Nov. 14–15, 1958, AAIA Papers, Box 287, Folder 6, Washington General; H. Con. Res. 108, 67 Stat. B122, Aug. 1, 1953; R.C.W. 37.12.021.

108 Minutes of meeting, April 3, 1956. NA PAR RG 75, Portland Area Office, Tribal Operations Branch, General Subject Files, 1953–67, Tribal Council Minutes, ca. 1950–1965, Box 1575.

109 "Tribal Units Jurisdiction Transfer Hit," *ST*, July 22, 1958, 4.

110 Madigan to Betsy Ann Trick, Aug. 5, 1959.

111 Quinault Fact-Finding Committee to La Farge, June 21, 1960.

112 Quinault Fact-Finding Committee to La Farge; Transcript, Institute of the American West, Indian Self-Rule Conference panel, "Tribal Sovereignty," Aug. 20, 1983, O'Neil Papers, Box 44, Folder 3, Session 403.

113 Robert E. Ratcliffe to Leon Jourolmon, Mar. 13, 1961, *State of Washington v. Bertrand* related correspondence and record, NA RG 48, Secretary of Interior, Regional Solicitor's Office Records, Pacific NW Region, Indian Land Administration, 1957–1981, Box 1, Folder 602.500. Frank Pickernell likewise testified that he signed the original request for state jurisdiction and subsequently a resolution declaring the first action "null and void." Some records of this case

are missing. Wilkinson, *Blood Struggle*, 19, 20; author's interview with Francis Rosander.

114 Mrs. Cleve Jackson (Anna A.) to C. W. Ringey, April 12, 1958, NA PAR RG 75 WWA, General Correspondence 1952–68, Box 10; author's interview with Harold L. Patterson.

115 Transcript of meeting—C. W. Ringey, Cleveland Jackson with William G. Wilson and Leon Jourolmon, Regional Solicitor's Office, May 12, 1960, *State v. Bertrand* file, 20.

116 Frederick W. Saux, to Oliver La Farge, July 20, 1960, AAIA Papers, Series 2, Subject Files, 1851–1995, Subseries 2, Tribal Box 286, Quinault, 1952–1962.

117 List of Quinault allotments and owners, Feb. 20, 1930, Timber Allotments and Contracts, Quinault Indian Reservation, 1927–1930, NA PAR RG 75, Taholah Indian Agency, TAH-60 Box 1; Hannah Bowechop to Robert L. Bennett, Aug. 22, 1966, Quinault General Correspondence, July 1964 thru FY 1968, NA PAR RG 75 WWA, Box 282, 060.

118 Proposed statement of facts for rehearing on appeal, *State of Washington v. Bertrand*; Complaint, Hannah Mason Bowechop and Hazel Strom Smith for themselves and a class of members of the Quinault Tribal Council v. Cleveland Jackson, Horton Capoeman, Francis McCrory, David Purdy, Frank Pickernell, and the Tribal Business Committee of the Quinault Tribe of Indians, filed in US District Court, W. Wash., Southern Division, by Brockman Adams, Mar. 28, 1960; also US District Court docket register, W. Wash., Southern Division, entry for *Bowechop et al. v. Jackson et al.*, Docket # 2525, NA PAR RG 21; correspondence and records concerning *State of Washington v. Bertrand*, NA, RG 48, Secretary of Interior, Regional Solicitor's Office Records, Pacific NW Region, Indian Land Administration, 1957–1981, Box 1, Folder 602.500; clipping, "Indian Case to Be Argued," *TNT*, Mar. 15, 1960, in NCAI Records, pre-1994, Series 6, Box 258, file: "Jurisdiction [1954–1961]." Bowechop was the daughter of traditional chief William, or Billy Mason, who had been lead plaintiff in *Mason v. Sams*.

119 Quinault Fact-Finding Committee to La Farge, June 21, 1960; *State of Washington v. Bertrand* correspondence and record, NA RG 48, Secretary of Interior, Regional Solicitor's Office Records, Pacific NW Region, Indian Land Administration, 1957–1981, Box 1, Folder 602.500. The rehearing testimony also included a disputed claim that Saux's minutes of the March meeting did not record the final vote empowering the Business Committee to take action on law and order matters.

120 State v. Bertrand, 61 Wash. 2d 333, 378 (1963); Glenn L. Emmons to Don C. Foster, Dec. 24, 1959, *State of Washington v. Bertrand* related correspondence and record, NA RG 48, Secretary of Interior, Regional Solicitor's Office

Records, Pacific Northwest Region, Indian Land Administration, 1957–1981, Box 1, Folder 602.500.

121 Comments of Wilford Pettit, minutes of meeting, Taholah, Oct. 20, 1962, NA PAR RG 75, Portland Area Office, Tribal Operations Branch, General Subject Files, 1953–67, Box 1520, File: "Minutes Taken Verbatim from Misc. Tribal Meetings [1962, 1965]"; John W. Cragun, Statement in Explanation of a Bill to Extend State Jurisdiction over the Quinault Indian Reservation Only with Tribal Consent, May 2, 1963, Quinault BIA Correspondence, NA PAR RG 75 WWA, Tribal Operations Branch Tribal Files, ca. 1919–1968, Box 282, Folder 060; "Indian Chief Kills Himself," *ST*, Nov. 8, 1960, 17.

CHAPTER 4: "ARISING" IN THE SIXTIES

1 Quinault Acculturation Report, April 9, 1963, NA PAR RG 75 WWA, General Correspondence, 1952–68, Box No. 0006, Folder 024.1.

2 Marshall Wilson, "Quinaults Accused of Blocking Off Peninsula," *ST*, Apr. 17, 1961, 16; Marshall Wilson, "Quinaults Open Battle for Survival," *ST*, Apr. 16, 1961, 18; Marshall Wilson, "Quinault Plans Working Out," *ST*, Nov. 25, 1963, 49; Quinault Tribal Council to BIA Portland Area Office, Nov. 25, 1961, NA RG 75, Officer Files, Box 37, Folder 5 of 6.

3 Ron Fowler, "Quinault Indian Tribe Looks to the Future," *Seattle Post-Intelligencer*, June 14, 1964, Pict. 10–11.

4 James Jackson to George M. Felshaw, Feb. 27, 1964, Quinault BIA Correspondence, NA PAR RG 75 WWA, Tribal Operations Branch Tribal Files, ca. 1919–1968, Box 282, Folder 060.

5 NCAI Records, pre-1994 accessions, Series 6, Committees and Special Issues, Box 122, Tribal Files (Series 4) Qu–Se, Folder "Quinault (Washington) 1961–1970."

6 Transcript, Oral Decision of Court, State of Washington, ex rel. v. Honorable Warner Poyhonen, Washington State Supreme Court, NA RG 75, Officer Files, Box 37, Folder 4 of 6.

7 Report, Jan. 1963, NA PAR RG 75 WWA, Law and Order Correspondence & Reports, 1952–68, File 170.1—Law and Order—L&O Reports (monthly), Box 315.

8 James Officer to regional solicitor, Nov. 8, 1961, NA RG 75, Officer Files, Box 37, Folder 3 of 6; Quinault BIA Correspondence, NA PAR RG 75 WWA, Tribal Operations Branch Tribal Files, ca. 1919–1968, Box 282, Folder 060.

9 "Quinaults Told They Are under State Law," *Bellingham Herald*, Jan. 31, 1963, 1; Resolution of April 8, 1963, NA PAR RG 75, Portland Area Office, Tribal Operations Branch, General Subject Files, 1953–67, Tribal Council Minutes, ca. 1950–65, Box 1575.

10 R.C.W. 37.12.010; John W. Cragun, Statement in Explanation of a Bill to Extend State Jurisdiction over the Quinault Indian Reservation Only with Tribal Consent, May 2, 1963, Quinault BIA Correspondence, NA PAR RG 75 WWA, Tribal Operations Branch Tribal Files, ca. 1919–1968, Box 282, Folder 060.

11 Marshall Wilson, "Indian Brochure Doesn't Tell All, Say Quinaults," *ST*, Apr. 20, 1961, 2; "3 Indian Treaties Meaningless, State Argues in Fishing-Rights Case," *ST*, May 31, 1966, 5.

12 Charles Wilkinson, *Blood Struggle: The Rise of Modern Indian Nations* (New York: W. W. Norton, 2005), 20; American Friends Service Committee, *Uncommon Controversy: Fishing Rights of the Muckleshoot Puyallup, and Nisqually Indians* (Seattle: University of Washington Press, 1970).

13 Acting regional solicitor to [?] Adams, Oct. 17, 1961, NA PAR RG 48, Secretary of the Interior, Regional Solicitor's Office, Pacific Northwest Region, Indian Land Administration, Fishing and Hunting Rights, U.S. v. Washington Historical Background Docs, 1960–1975, Quinault fishing and hunting history, Box 27.

14 Lucile McDonald, "Proposed Coast Highway Cuts No Indian Paradise," *ST*, Oct. 29, 1961, Mag. 4.

15 Elling Simonsen, "Indians, Legislators Puff Peace Pipe Over Steelhead," *Bremerton Sun*, Apr. 30, 1962, 1; Wilson, "Quinaults Open Battle for Survival"; "Quinaults Oppose Change in Treaties," *ST*, Mar. 5, 1962, 14.

16 "Indians Refuse Span OK; Quinaults Vote Down Request," *Seattle Post-Intelligencer*, May 13, 1961, 1, 4. To prevent poaching of fish and game, the tribe conditioned approval of the highway on tribal control of access. Author's interview with Harold Patterson, Taholah, July 17, 2012.

17 George Felshaw to Northwest Realty and Appraisal Company, July 22, 1965, NA RG 75, Officer Files, Box 36, "Puyallup to Quinault," Folder 1 of 6.

18 Claude H. Heyer to LaVerne Madigan, April 26, 1961, AAIA Papers, Series 2, Subject Files, 1851–1995, Subseries 2, Tribal, Box 286, Quinault, 1952–1962.

19 Leslie Gay to James Officer, June 19, 1963, NA RG 75, Officer Files, Box 37, Folder 4 of 6.

20 Assistant Area Director to George Felshaw, Oct. 1, 1963, NA PAR RG 75 WWA, Quinault BIA Correspondence, Tribal Operations Branch Tribal Files, ca. 1919–68, Box 282, Folder 060.

21 Quinault Business Committee Resolution No. 2, AAIA Papers, Series 2, Subject Files, 1851–1995, Subseries 2, Tribal, Box 286, Quinault, 1952–1962; Frederick Saux to Julia Butler Hansen, July 25, 1962, Hansen Papers, Box 8, Folder "Dept. of Interior: Indian Affairs, Quinault."

22 Wilson, "Indian Brochure Doesn't Tell All."

23 Wilson, "Quinaults Open Battle for Survival."

24 In some records, Petit's first name appears as Wilford.

25 Few Indian parents considered formal education necessary until the mid-1940s, "when Quinault ex-service men [*sic*], who had taken advantage of the G. I. Bill, began returning to the Reservation," "strengthened the school curriculum," and "a new attitude toward education . . . evolved among many of the Tribe." Pauline K. Capoeman, ed., *Land of the Quinault* (Taholah: Quinault Indian Nation, 1990), 130–31. Petit had been an army colonel; Capoeman served in the air force during World War II. Squire v. Capoeman, 351 U.S. 1, 3 (1956).

26 "Jim 'Jug' Jackson: Former Quinault Tribal Leader Found Dead; Suicide Suspected," *Kitsap Sun* (Bremerton, WA), Apr. 4, 1999; author's interview with Michael Taylor, Stanwood, WA, Jan. 30, 2012.

27 Author's interview with Pearl Capoeman-Baller, Kamilche, WA, July 18, 2012; author's interview with Justine James, Sr., Taholah, WA, July 16, 2012; author's interview with Harold L. Patterson.

28 Author's interviews with Justine James and Harold Patterson.

29 Julia Butler Hansen to Alex Saluskin, Mar. 13, 1962, and Hansen telegram to Wilfred Petit, Feb. 28, 1962, Hansen Papers, Box 43, Folder "Quinault Indians, Indian Affairs," and Box 8, Folder "Indian Affairs, Quinaults—Lake Quinault."

30 Fowler, "Quinault Indian Tribe Looks to the Future."

31 Larry Burt, "Western Tribes and Balance Sheets: Business Development Programs in the 1960s and 1970s," *Western Historical Quarterly* 23 (Nov. 1992): 465–95, 479.

32 Transcript, Stewart L. Udall Oral History Interview III, 1 (4/18/69) by Joe B. Frantz, LBJ Library, www.lbjlibrary.net/assets/documents/archives/oral_histories/udall/UDALL03.PDF; "Government Task Force Urges More Fiscal Aid to Indians," *WP*, Mar. 16, 1961, A7; Julius Duscha, "Udall Maps 'New Trail' for U.S. Indians: More Federal Funds, Economic Growth," *WP*, July 13, 1961, A7; Donald Janson, "U.S. Moves to Spur Tribal Economies: Change in Policy Is Outlined at Indian Convention," *NYT*, Sept. 5, 1962, 61; Burt, "Western Tribes and Balance Sheets," 480; George Pierre Castile, *To Show Heart: Native American Self-Determination and Federal Indian Policy, 1960–1975* (Tucson: University of Arizona Press, 1998), 20–21; Pub. L. 87-27, 75 Stat. 47.

33 Wilson, "Quinault Plans 'Working Out.'"

34 Lyndon Baines Johnson, address, Jan. 8, 1964, http://www2.hn.psu.edu/faculty/jmanis/poldocs/uspressu/suaddresslbjohnson.pdf.

35 Pub. L. No. 88-452, 78 Stat. 508.

36 Robert Burnette, *The Tortured Americans* (Englewood Cliffs, NJ: Prentice-Hall, 1971), 88; Burt, "Western Tribes and Balance Sheets," 481–82; Robert Bennett, Statement, Institute of the American West, Indian Self-Rule Conference panel, Aug. 19, 1983, "Toward Self-Determination, 1960–1976," O'Neil Papers, Box 43,

Folder 6. The OEO insisted on tribes' control over their budgets. Daniel M. Cobb, *Native Activism in Cold War America: The Struggle for Sovereignty* (Lawrence: University Press of Kansas, 2008), 122. Also, Castile, *To Show Heart*, 30; Alyosha Goldstein, *Poverty in Common: The Politics of Community Action during the American Century* (Durham: Duke University Press, 2012), 185.

37 Harriet Rennie to Chief Tribal Operations Office, Jan. 22, 1964, Quinault BIA Correspondence, NA PAR RG 75 WWA, Tribal Operations Branch Tribal Files, ca. 1919–68, Box 282, Folder 060; Hilda Bryant, "Quinaults Start New Housing Project," *Seattle Post-Intelligencer*, Sept. 28, 1969, 43; DeLaCruz interview.

38 Author's interview with Harold Patterson. Home construction in the 1960s almost doubled Taholah's population to 750. Marilyn Bentz, "The World View of Young Quinault Indians," PhD diss., University of Washington, 1984, 39.

39 James E. Officer to J. B. Hansen, Jan. 11, 1965, NA RG 75, Officer Files, Box 37, Folder 3 of 6; Quinault Business Committee Resolution, Oct. 26, 1964, ICAP Files Box 53, Reservation Files: Washington IX, Quinault, Folder 1.

40 Author's interview with Harold Patterson.

41 Quinault Business Committee Resolution, Oct. 26, 1964.

42 Quinault Tribal Council Application, Dec. 8, 1965, Community Services Administration, Office of Economic Opportunity, Office of Operations, Indian Division, Grant Correspondence and Evaluations, 1965–71, NA RG 381, Box 14, Folder—"Quinault Tribal Council."

43 Chuck McEvers to Kay Haws, Mar. 26, 1966, and William George Harris, undated memorandum, ICAP Files, Box 45, Reservation Files: Washington—I, Folder 5. Emphasis in the original.

44 James J. Lopach, Margery H. Brown, and Kathleen Jackson, eds., *Tribal Constitutions: Their Past—Their Future*, proceedings of conference at Billings, Aug. 12–13, 1977 (Bureau of Government Research, University of Montana, Missoula, Aug. 1978), 23.

45 Sherwin Broadhead, memorandum, Sept. 12, 1966, Broadhead Papers.

46 Castile, *To Show Heart*, 33, 81.

47 Cobb, *Native Activism in Cold War America*, 200–202.

48 Henry W. Hough, *Development of Indian Resources* ([Washington, DC]: ICAP, 1967), 241–42; Cobb, *Native Activism in Cold War America*, 107, 126.

49 Alexandra Harmon, *Indians in the Making: Ethnic Relations and Indian Identities around Puget Sound* (Berkeley: University of California Press, 1998), 178–85, 213–15, 234–35; Billy Frank, "Florence James Kinley, Lummi, 1916–2003—a Life's Unwritten Chapter" [Text Reflection on Oral Eulogies by Billy Frank], www.scribd.com/doc/55141925/Florence-Dutch-FINAL.

50 Harmon, *Indians in the Making*, 207–9; ICAP Files, Box 45, Reservation Files: Washington—I.

51 Robert Heilman, "Destination Olympia: Indians Meet to Plan Protest," *ST*, Feb. 2, 1964, 16; Cobb, *Native Activism in Cold War America*, 95; Bradley G. Shreve, "'From Time Immemorial': The Fish-In Movement and the Rise of Intertribal Activism," *Pacific Historical Review* 78 (Aug. 2009): 403–34. Shreve credits NIYC alone with conceiving and organizing the protest.

52 WDF Files, Indian Affairs, Quinault Files, Box 32, Folder "Quinault 1953–62"; Department of the Interior Bureau of Sport Fisheries and Wildlife Management, undated statement with cover letter and Fish and Wildlife Service commissioner to Julia Butler Hansen, Feb. 9, 1968, Hansen Papers, Box 43, Folder "Quinault Indians, Indian Affairs."

53 Frank, "Florence James Kinley."

54 US Senate Committee on the Judiciary, Subcommittee on Constitutional Rights, *Constitutional Rights of the American Indian*, Summary Report of Hearings and Investigations, 88th Cong., 2d sess. (1964).

55 Robert D. Dellwo to Portland Area Office, attention Paul Weston, April 22, 1963, and Weston to Leland C. Strait, July 1, 1964, NA PAR RG 75, Portland Area Office, Tribal Operations Branch, General Subject Files, 1953–67, Box 1521, File: "Indian Leaders Workshop, Olympic College, Bremerton, Wash."

56 File: "Tribal Leadership Seminar, Olympic Comm. College, 4/30–5/1-65," NA PAR RG 75, Portland Area Office, Tribal Operations Branch, General Subject Files, 1953–67, Box 1521.

57 Program, Tribal Leaders Conference, 1967, NA PAR RG 75, Portland Area Office, Tribal Operations Branch, General Subject Files, 1953–67, Box 1522.

58 File: "Olympic College Workshop, April 29–30, 1966," NA PAR RG 75, Portland Area Office, Tribal Operations Branch, General Subject Files, 1953–67, Box 1521; author's interview with Justine James. Some sources identify Helen Mitchell as Quinault, others as Chehalis. US BIA, "New Horizons": Indian Leaders Conference with Robert L. Bennett, Spokane, Oct. 17–19, 1966, UW Libraries Special Collections.

59 Anna Jackson served at times as tribal secretary. Report of council elections June 25, 1938, NA PAR RG 75, Taholah Indian Agency Decimal Files, 1925–1950, Quinault-BIA Relations, 1920s–1950s, Quinault Folder 3; Anna A. Jackson to Vincent Keeler, Mar. 15, 1948, Quinault-BIA Relations, 1920s–1950s, NA PAR RG 75, Taholah Indian Agency Decimal Files, 1925–1950, 064.0, Tribal Meetings, Councils, Constitutions, TAH 07, Box 66, Quinault Folder 1; Mrs. Cleve Jackson to C. W. Ringey, Apr. 12, 1958, NA PAR RG 75 WWA, General Correspondence, 1952–68, Box 10.

60 Author's interview with Daniel Raas, Bellingham, Washington, April 4, 2012.

61 "Quinaults Get Historic Call to Inauguration," *ST*, Jan. 13, 1965, 29.

62 Cobb, *Native Activism in Cold War America*, 119.

63 Vine Deloria Jr., to James Jackson, Feb. 17, 1965, NCAI Records, Pre-1994 accessions, Series 6, Committees and Special Issues, Box 122, Tribal Files (Series 4) Qu–Se, Folder: "Quinault (Washington) 1961–1970."

64 Cobb, *Native Activism in Cold War America*, 128.

65 NA PAR RG 75, Portland Area Office, Tribal Operations Branch, General Subject Files, 1953–67, Box 1520, File: "Conferences."

66 Agenda, Western Inter-Tribal Coordinating Council Convention, Oct. 5, 1966, Portland, Oregon, ICAP Files, Box 53, Folder 4, Quinault; Program, NA PAR RG 75, Portland Area Office, Tribal Operations Branch, General Subject Files, 1953–67, Box 1522, File: "NCAI Convention, Portland, OR, 10/2–6, 1967."

67 File: "Affiliated Tribes of the N.W. Indians, 8/30–9/1, 1966," NA PAR RG 75, Portland Area Office, Tribal Operations Branch, General Subject Files, 1953–67, Box 1521; Cobb, *Native Activism in Cold War America*, 141; "Comments on the Federal-Indian Relationship," *NCAI Sentinel* 13 (Fall 1968).

68 Lyndon B. Johnson, "Remarks at the Swearing In of Robert L. Bennett, Commissioner of Indian Affairs," April 27, 1966, American Presidency Project, www.presidency.ucsb.edu/ws/?pid=27563.

69 Folder 10: "Bennett, Robert L," AAIA Papers, Miscellaneous, Series 2, Subject Files, 1851–1995, Subseries 1, General Correspondence, Box 69.

70 US Bureau of Indian Affairs, "New Horizons: Indian Leaders Conference with Robert L. Bennett," Spokane, October 17–19, 1966, 222, copy in UW Libraries Special Collections.

71 US BIA, "New Horizons," 229–33.

72 US BIA, "New Horizons," 80–81, 96–98.

73 Stan Steiner, *The New Indians* (New York: Harper & Row, 1968), 270; transcript, Robert Bennett Oral History Interview I (11/13/68) by Joe B. Frantz, LBJ Library PDF.

74 Conference in LaConner, July 27–29, 1967, ICAP Files, Bureau of Indian Services Training Programs, Workshops, and Conferences, Acc. 026, Box 1, Folder 15.

75 Quinault Tribal Council minutes, Feb. 22, 1964, NA PAR RG 75, Portland Area Office, Tribal Operations Branch, General Subject Files, 1953–67, Box 1575; "Quinaults Challenge State Jurisdiction," *ST*, June 17, 1964, 5.

76 Quinault Tribal Council minutes, Mar. 27, 1965, NA PAR RG 75, Portland Area Office, Tribal Operations Branch, General Subject Files, 1953–67, Box 1575; Quinault Tribe of Indians v. Gallagher, 368 F. 2d 648 (9th Cir. 1966).

77 Report, July 1963, NA PAR RG 75 WWA, Box 315, Law and Order Correspondence & Reports, 1952–68, File 170.1—Law and Order—L&O Reports (monthly). .

78 Charles J. Kappler, *Indian Affairs: Laws and Treaties*, vol. 1 (Washington, DC: Government Printing Office, 1904), 923–24.

79 Report, June 1, 1964, NA PAR RG 75 WWA, Box 315, Law and Order Correspondence & Reports, 1952–68, File 170.1—Law and Order—L&O Reports.

80 Minutes, Aug. 30, 1965, NA PAR RG 75, Portland Area Office, Tribal Operations Branch, General Subject Files, 1953–67, Box 1575.

81 George M. Felshaw to Northwest Realty and Appraisal Company, July 22, 1965, NA RG 75, Officer Files, Box 36, "Puyallup to Quinault," Folder 1 of 6.

82 Clippings, unidentified Grays Harbor County newspaper(s), Aug. 3 and July 31, 1965, NA RG 75, Officer Files, Box 37, Folder 3 of 6: "Quinault."

83 "Indian Jurisdiction," *ST*, Aug. 13, 1965, 2.

84 Clippings, Grays Harbor County newspaper(s), Aug. 3 and July 31, 1965; Charles A. Hobbs to James E. Officer, Aug. 16, 1966, NA RG 75, Officer Files, Box 37, Folder 2 of 6, "Quinault."

85 Chief, Tribal Government Section to Chief Tribal Operations Officer, July 13, 1966, James Officer to James Jackson, Dec. 3, 1966, and James Jackson to J. B. Hansen, July 29, 1966, Officer Files, Box 36, "Puyallup to Quinault," Folder 1 of 6.

86 "Moclips Clams for Tribe, Says Leader," *ST*, Aug. 14, 1966, 27.

87 Minutes, July 18 and Aug. 18, 1966, NA PAR RG 75, Portland Area Office, Tribal Operations Branch, General Subject Files, 1953–67, Box 1575; "Tribe Asks for Use Survey," *Nugguam* [Taholah] 1 (Sept. 23, 1966): 1.

88 Joe DeLaCruz, testimony, US Senate, Subcommittee on Indian Affairs of the Committee on Interior and Insular Affairs, Hearing on S. 2010, Indian Law Enforcement Improvement Act of 1975, 94th Cong., 1st sess., Dec. 3 and 4, 1975, Part 1, CIS-NO: 76-S441-28, 15.

89 Alice Chenois, "Information Needed!," *Nugguam* 1 (Sept. 23, 1966): 2.

90 In July 1968, twenty-five individuals were on the planning commission and two other CAP committees. Alice Chenois to Mr. Old Elk, Bureau of Indian Services, July 11, 1968, ICAP Files, Box 53, Folder 4, Quinault.

91 Tribal Operations Office report, Oct. 28, 1965, Quinault BIA Correspondence, NA PAR RG 75 WWA, Tribal Operations Branch Tribal Files, ca. 1919–68, Box 282, Folder 060.

92 Author's interview with Justine James; "Moclips Clams for Tribe, Says Leader," *ST*, Aug. 14, 1966; Quinault Business Committee application, ICAP Files, Box 53, Reservation Files: Washington IX, Quinault, Folder 1.

93 Author's interview with Francis Rosander, Taholah, WA, July 16, 2012.

94 Author's interview with Harold Patterson.

95 Minutes, Quinault General Council Annual Meeting, Mar. 25, 1967, Records Relating to the Office of Economic Opportunity Programs, 1964–68, NA RG 75, Records of the BIA, Division of Community Services, Box 21, Portland Area, Folder: "Quinault."

96 Minutes, Quinault General Council, Mar. 25, 1967; author's interview with Harold Patterson.

97 "Timber Production on Quinault Reaches All-Time High," BIA Western Washington "Quinault Newsletter," no. 31, Aug. 3, 1965, NA RG 75, Officer Files, Box 37, Folder 3 of 6, "Quinault."

98 Capoeman, *Land of the Quinault*, 201; Ron Fowler, "The Quinault Indians Launch 'Operation Bootstrap,'" *Seattle Post-Intelligencer*, Jan. 16, 1966, Mag. 3.

99 James Jackson to Julia Butler Hansen, May 20, 1968, Hansen Papers, Box 43, Folder "Quinault Indians, Indian Affairs."

100 Harold Patterson to Julia Butler Hansen, May 1, 1967, Hansen Papers, Box 43, Folder "Quinault Indians, Indian Affairs"; author's interview with Harold Patterson; *Nugguam* 1 (Mar. 3, 1967): 4.

101 Minutes, meeting at Taholah, Oct. 21, 1966, NA PAR RG 75 WWA, Box 282, 060 Quinault General July 1964 thru FY 1968.

102 Quinault Tribal Council application, Dec. 8, 1965. The tribe subsequently withdrew this request; OEO records do not indicate why.

103 Harold L. Patterson to Mike McCormack, Washington State Senate, Feb. 5, 1965, ICAP Files, Box 53, Folder 3, Quinault Correspondence.

104 In 1968, B. F. Whittaker of Santiago Realty reportedly told a BIA investigator he would not stop development without a court order. Meanwhile, the BIA expedited sales of reservation land. Jackson to Hansen, May 20, 1968, Hansen Papers, Box 43, Folder "Quinault Indians, Indian Affairs."

105 Law and Order Report, Jan. 27, 1967, NA PAR RG 75, Portland Area Office, Tribal Operations Branch, General Subject Files, 1953–67, Tribal Council Minutes, ca. 1950–65, Law and Order Reports, 1967–70, Box 1801; Harold Patterson to Julia Butler Hansen, May 1, 1967.

106 James Jackson to John Belindo, Nov. 8, 1967, US House of Representatives, *Rights of Members of Indian Tribes*, Hearing before Subcommittee on Indian Affairs of the Committee on Interior and Insular Affairs, 90th Cong., 2d sess., Mar. 29, 1968, Serial 90-23, 126–27.

107 *Nugguam* 1 (Jan. 20, 1967): 4; Harold Patterson to Julia Butler Hansen, May 1, 1967, and Robert Bennett to Hansen, July 6, 1967, Hansen Papers, Box 43, Folder "Quinault Indians, Indian Affairs." The Interior Department approved the tribe's zoning ordinance May 2, 1968, with the proviso that the county "'enact the same ordinances to cover lands and persons within the Quinault Indian Reservation which may be subject to its jurisdiction.'" The county produced an ordinance Aug. 4, 1969, but did not provide zoning for reservation lands. Timothy A. LaFrance, "A Case Study of Land Management and Land Use Planning on the Quinault Indian Reservation," Appendix III, AIPRC Task

Force Two: Tribal Government, *Report on Tribal Government* (Washington, DC: US Government Printing Office, 1976), 145–59, 153.

108 James Jackson to Wilkinson, Cragun, et al., May 2, 1967, NA PAR RG 75 WWA, 060 Quinault General July 1964 thru FY 1968, Box 282.

109 Desmond Wilcox, "The Indian Chief: Joe DeLaCruz," *Americans* (New York: Delacorte Press, 1978), 148; author's interview with Harold Patterson.

110 Harold Patterson to Julia Butler Hansen, May 1, 1967.

111 Robert Bennett to Julia Butler Hansen, July 6, 1967, Hansen Papers, Box 43, Folder "Quinault Indians, Indian Affairs"; Memo, Tribal Operations Assistant to Chief, Branch of Tribal Operations, July 18, 1967, NA PAR RG 75 WWA, Box 282, 060 Quinault General July 1964 thru FY 1968.

112 Harold L. Patterson to Mike McCormack, Feb. 5, 1965, ICAP Files, Box 53, Folder 3, Quinault Correspondence.

113 *Nugguam* 1 (Mar. 3, 1967): 4.

114 James Jackson to Julia Butler Hansen, May 20, 1968, Hansen Papers, Box 43, Folder "Quinault Indians, Indian Affairs."

115 Western Washington Agency Law and Order Reports, Oct. 6 and Oct. 31, 1966, and May 1967, NA PAR RG 75, Portland Area Office, Tribal Operations Branch, General Subject Files, 1953–67, Law and Order Reports, 1967–70, Box 1801.

116 Indian Civil Rights Act, P.L. 90-284, 82 Stat. 77, 25 U.S.C. §§ 1301–1304; Proclamation by Gov. Daniel J. Evans, Aug. 15, 1968, Ray Records, Folder "Indians—Quinault tribe"; Monthly Narrative & Statistics, West. Wash. & Warm Springs, FY 69 and part of 1970, NA PAR RG 75, Portland Area Office, Tribal Operations Branch, General Subject Files, 1953–67, Law and Order Reports, 1967–70, Box 1801.

117 Author's interview with Harold Patterson. DeLaCruz was appointed tribal business manager in 1967. Ross Anderson, "Quinault Indian Leader Joe DeLaCruz Dies," *ST*, April 18, 2000.

118 Jim "Jug" Jackson obituary, *Kitsap Sun;* Joe DeLaCruz, testimony, US House of Representatives, Subcommittee on Department of Interior and Related Agencies Appropriations, Committee on Appropriations, Hearing HRG-1073-0041, May 7, 9, 10, 1973, 93rd Cong., 1st sess., CIS-No. 73-H181-37, 241. DeLaCruz also said, "I was business manager for six years . . . , and the previous chairman I more or less worked for, he trained me, he had warned me every time the tribe turned around, that the state was trying to infringe on the tribal rights." Joe DeLaCruz, testimony, United States of America, Plaintiff; Quinault Tribe of Indians, et al. Intervenor-plaintiffs v. State of Washington, Defendant; Thor C. Tollefson, et al. Intervenor-Defendants, Civil No. 9213, United States District Court, Western District of Washington at Tacoma, Sept. 13, 1973, 3478.

CHAPTER 5: LAWYERS ON THE SCENE

1 "1969: An Eventful Summer," CNN, Aug. 9, 2009, www.cnn.com/2009/US/08/09/summer.1969.timeline/index.html?iref=24hours; Earl Caldwell, "Indians Discuss a 'Turning Point': A Swing to Harsh Militancy Is Evident at Parley," *NYT*, Oct. 12, 1969, 41.

2 "Best Sellers in Seattle," *ST*, Oct. 19, 1969, 175.

3 Author's interview with Michael Taylor, Camano Island, Washington, Jan. 30, 2012; Columbia Legal Services, http://columbialegal.org/about/history. About VISTA, see Ryan Wells, "Volunteers in Service to America," https://www.britannica.com/topic/Volunteers-in-Service-to-America.

4 Author's interview with Michael Taylor.

5 Author's interview with Michael Taylor.

6 Author's interview with Michael Taylor; Mike Taylor, "Remembering Guy McMinds," *Nugguam* (Oct. 2012): 4; Barry Siegel, "Tribes Seek to Govern Non-Members: Indians' New Powers Bring Gains, Conflicts," *LAT*, May 27, 1986, 4.

7 Author's interview with Michael Taylor.

8 Robert McLaughlin. "Training Ground for the New Warriors," inset in "Who Owns the Land? A Native American Challenge," *Juris Doctor* 6 (Sept. 1986): 17–25, 20, S. Tyler Papers, Box 119, Folder 5.

9 Helen L. Peterson to Eagle Selatsee, May 18, 1954, NCAI Records, Pre-1994 accessions, Series 4, Tribal Files, Box 135, Wa–Ya, Folder: "Yakima (Washington) 1949–1955."

10 Bulletin, April 1955, AAIA Papers, Miscellaneous, Series 2, Subject Files, 1851–1995, Subseries 1, General Correspondence, Box 57, Folder 13: "Affiliated Tribes of Northwest Indians, 1955–1989."

11 Henry W. Hough, *Development of Indian Resources* ([Washington, DC]: National Congress of American Indians, 1967), 178.

12 Claude H. Heyer to LaVerne Madigan, April 26, 1961, AAIA Papers, Series 2, Subject Files, 1851–1995, Subseries 2, Tribal, Box 286, Quinault, 1952–1962.

13 Helen L. Peterson to Edward L. Bernays, May 25, 1961, NCAI Records, Series 8, Attorneys and Legal Interest Groups, Box 11, Folder: "[Correspondence—1956–1964]." Emphasis in the original.

14 Peterson to Bernays.

15 Daniel M. Cobb, *Native Activism in Cold War America: The Struggle for Sovereignty* (Lawrence: University Press of Kansas, 2008), 118.

16 Alvin J. Ziontz, *A Lawyer in Indian Country: A Memoir* (Seattle: University of Washington Press, 2009), 4–7.

17 Robert L. Pirtle, *To Right the Unrightable Wrong: An Autobiography of Robert L. Pirtle, Tribal Lawyer* (Bloomington, IN: Xlibris, 2007), 269.

18 Pirtle, *To Right the Unrightable Wrong*, 274.

19 Ziontz, *A Lawyer in Indian Country*, 192, xi; interview with Charles F. Wilkinson, Aug. 19, 1983, University of Utah Marriott Library Manuscripts Division, Accession 2186, Indian Self-Rule Oral Histories.

20 Ziontz, *A Lawyer in Indian Country*, 267, 192; Pirtle, *To Right the Unrightable Wrong*, 270.

21 For example, Lewis A. Bell, Tulalip Tribes' general counsel for many years, or Malcolm McLeod, a sole practitioner. Constantine Angelos, "Quinault Indian Closes Road, Blocks Logging Operations," *ST*, June 13, 1961, 1.

22 Transcript, NCAI conference on jurisdiction and PL 280, Feb. 24–25, 1975, 23, NCAI Records, Pre-1994, Series 6, Box 259 (Committees and Special Issues—Jurisdiction), File: "PL 280 Videotape"; James B. Hovis to NCAI, Feb. 24, 1958, NCAI Records, Pre-1994 accessions, Series 4, Tribal Files, Box 135, Wa–Ya, Folder: "Yakima [Washington] 1957–1961"; James Hovis obituary, https://www.dignitymemorial.com/obituaries/yakima-wa/james-hovis-4513555.

23 Pirtle, *To Right the Unrightable Wrong*, 346.

24 Pirtle, *To Right the Unrightable Wrong*, 272, 290, 493; Ziontz, *A Lawyer in Indian Country*, 193.

25 Ziontz, *A Lawyer in Indian Country*, 193–94.

26 Alan W. Houseman and Linda E. Perle, "Securing Equal Justice for All: A Brief History of Civil Legal Assistance in the United States," Center for Law and Social Policy (2007), 7, www.clasp.org/docs/0158.pdf; Robert C. Swan, "Indian Legal Services Programs: The Key to Red Power," 12 *Arizona Law Review* 594 (1970).

27 Monroe E. Price, "Lawyers on the Reservation: Some Implications for the Legal Profession," 1969 *Law and Social Order* [12 *Arizona State Law Journal*] 161 (1970); McLaughlin, "Training Ground for the New Warriors."

28 Application, ICAP Files, Box 29, Indian Legal Services Files, Folder 1.

29 Application, Letter of James Jackson, Mar. 14, 1967, Charles L. McEvers to Lyman Tyler, July 13, 1966, and Leo J. LaClair to James B. Coleman, Jan. 10, 1968, ICAP Files, Box 53, Reservation Files: Washington IX, Quinault, Box 29, Folder 2.

30 Houseman and Perle, "Securing Justice for All," 9, 11–12.

31 Pub. L. 89-635, §1, Oct. 10, 1966, 80 Stat. 880, 28 U.S. Code § 1362.

32 Confederated Salish and Kootenai Tribes of the Flathead Reservation v. Moe, 425 U.S. 463 (1976); Daniel H. Israel, "The Reemergence of Tribal Nationalism and Its Impact on Reservation Resource Development," 47 *University of Colorado Law Review* 617 (1975–76): 624–25; Rennard Strickland, "Take Us by

the Hand: Challenges of Becoming an Indian Lawyer," *American Indian Law Review* 2 (Summer 1974): 47–59, 49.

33 Pub. L. 90-284, 82 Stat. 77, 25 U.S.C. § 1301–1304; Israel, "Reemergence of Tribal Nationalism"; meeting record, May 11, 1973, American Indian Lawyers Association, *The Indian Civil Rights Act, Five Years Later* [Denver, 1973], 52, 54.

34 Native American Rights Fund, www.narf.org.

35 Interview of Monroe Price, UCLA, Jan. 28, 1971, University of Utah, J. Willard Marriott Library Special Collections, Doris Duke Indian Oral History Transcripts, MS 0417, Item 1006, 1–2.

36 Interview of David Getches, Oct. 11, 2006, Boulder, Colorado, www.crwua.org/documents/about-us/oral-histories/David-Getches.pdf.

37 David Getches, "Difficult Beginnings for Indian Legal Services," *NLADA Briefcase* 30 (May 1972): 181–85, 181; Native American Rights Fund, www.narf.org/about/history; interview with Charles F. Wilkinson, 4–5.

38 Interview with Charles Wilkinson, 1, 3, 4, 7.

39 Getches, "Difficult Beginnings for Indian Legal Services, 181–85.

40 Getches, "Difficult Beginnings for Indian Legal Services," 185; data from résumés of early CILS and NARF attorneys, AAIA Papers, Series 2, Subject Files, 1851–1995, Subseries 1, General Correspondence, Box 146, Folder 13, "Native American Rights Fund."

41 Interview with Charles Wilkinson, 11.

42 John Echohawk, "Termination, Indian Lawyers, and the Evolution of the Native American Rights Fund," in *Native Americans and the Legacy of Harry S. Truman*, ed. Brian Hosmer, 82–86 (Kirksville, MO: Truman State University Press, 2010), 83.

43 Getches, "Difficult Beginnings for Indian Legal Services," 185; interview with Charles Wilkinson, 11.

44 Echohawk, "Termination, Indian Lawyers," 82–83; William E. Schmidt, "An Indian Lawyer Leads in Fight for Tribal Rights," *NYT*, June 24, 1988, B5.

45 Interview of Monroe Price, 10–11; Philip S. Deloria, "The American Indian Law Center: An Informal History," 24 *New Mexico Law Review* 285 (1994): 285–86.

46 Echohawk, "Termination, Indian Lawyers," 82.

47 Interview of Monroe Price, 10; Ralph W. Johnson, "Indian Tribes and the Legal System," 72 *Washington Law Review* 1021 (1997): 1029; interview with Charles Wilkinson, 21; Thomas Fredericks, "A Visionary in Indian Affairs," http://alumni.colorado.edu/2013/11/13/visionary-indian-affairs; McLaughlin, "Training Ground for the New Warriors," 20, 24.

48 Mario Gonzalez and Elizabeth Cook-Lynn, *The Politics of Hallowed Ground: Wounded Knee and the Struggle for Indian Sovereignty* (Urbana-Champaign: University of Illinois Press, 1999), 383.

49 Author's interview with Alan Parker, Evergreen State College, Olympia, WA, Nov. 30, 2011.

50 Earl Johnson, Jr., *Justice and Reform: The Formative Years of the American Legal Services Program* (New York: Russell Sage Foundation, 1974), 178–80; author's telephone interview with Rodney Lewis, May 1, 2012.

51 Author's interview with Michael Taylor.

52 Linda Medcalf, *Law and Identity: Lawyers, Native Americans, and Legal Practice* (London: Sage Publications, 1978), 33; American Indian Law Students' Association session transcript, Denver, Colorado, March 26, 1971, American Indian History Project, Doris Duke #1039, Western History Center, University of Utah; Native American Law Students Association, http://nationalnalsa.org/about-us; Richard Trudell to William Byler, Sept. 25, 1972, and memorandum of William Byler, Nov. 6, 1972, AAIA Papers, Series 2, Subject Files, 1851–1995, Subseries 1, General Correspondence, Box 60, Folder 13, American Indian Lawyers Association; "The Mission of NNABA," National Native American Bar Association, www.nativeamericanbar.org/the-mission-of-nnaba; Minutes of Puget Sound Indian Law Society, Oct. 26, 1972, Johnson Papers, General Correspondence folder, Nov. 1972.

53 Pirtle, *To Right the Unrightable Wrong*, 345.

54 Medcalf, *Law and Identity*, 22; Deloria, "The American Indian Law Center," 293–94; Native American Rights Fund, www.narf.org/nill; "American Indian Law Review: Purposes and Goals," *American Indian Law Review* 1 (1973): 3; *Indian Law Reporter*, www.indianlawreporter.org.

55 Vine Deloria, Jr., to Sherwin Broadhead, May 24, 1971, Broadhead Papers.

56 Echohawk, "Termination, Indian Lawyers," 82.

57 Daniel M. Cobb, "Talking the Language of the Larger World: Politics in Cold War (Native) America," in *Beyond Red Power: American Indian Politics and Activism since 1900*, ed. Daniel M. Cobb and Loretta Fowler (Santa Fe, NM: School for Advanced Research, 2007), 162.

58 Stephen Cornell, "Crisis and Response in Indian-White Relations, 1960–1984," *Social Problems* 32 (Oct. 1984): 44–59, 46.

59 Cobb, "Talking the Language of the Larger World," 162; Stan Steiner, *The New Indians* (New York: Harper & Row, 1968), 279.

60 Sherry L. Smith, "Indians, the Counterculture, and the New Left," in Cobb and Fowler, *Beyond Red Power*, 148.

61 Trova Heffernan, *Where the Salmon Run: The Life and Legacy of Billy Frank, Jr.* (Seattle: University of Washington Press, 2012), 73–79.

62 Stephen E. Cornell cites earlier demonstrations of defiance by Mohawks and Lumbee Indians in *Return of the Native: American Indian Political Resurgence* (New York: Oxford University Press, 1988), 189.

63 Remarks of George E. Brown, Jr., *Congressional Record*, Mar. 5, 1970, E169, NCAI Records, Series 5, Indian Interest Organizations, Box 144, A—Folder: "Alcatraz—Indians of All Tribes."

64 Judith Randal, "Alcatraz Indians Hire Lawyer," *Evening Star* (Washington, DC), Dec. 5, 1969, A-9, NCAI Records, Series 5, Indian Interest Organizations, Box 144-A, Folder: "Alcatraz—Indians of All Tribes."

65 John Bell, "Coast Indians Shun 'Warpath' but Assert Tribal Powers," *ST*, Mar. 18, 1973, 1; Ada Deer, keynote address, "Why Does the American Indian Movement Attack and Threaten Tribal Sovereignty?," NCAI Records, pre-1994 accessions, Series 1, Conventions, Box 22, 1973–1974, Folder: "1973 Speeches."

66 Author's conversation with Bennie Armstrong, Jr., Suquamish Tribal Center, Mar. 26, 2012; Earl Caldwell, "Indians Discern a 'Turning Point': A Swing to Harsh Militancy Is Evident at Parley," *NYT*, Oct. 12, 1969, 41; Vine Deloria, Jr., "The War between the Redskins and the Feds," *NYT*, Dec. 7, 1969, SM 47.

67 Vine Deloria, Jr., "This Country Was a Lot Better Off When the Indians Were Running It," *NYT*, Mar. 8, 1970, SM 17.

68 Hank Adams résumé, Adams Papers, Box 80, Folder 10 of General Correspondence; Hank Adams biography [n.p., n.d.], https://www.sos.wa.gov/_assets/legacy/biographies/pages/Hank-Adams-bio.pdf.

69 Hank Adams to Gov. Albert D. Rosellini, July 26, 1963, and Adams to Rosellini, Aug. 21, 1963, Ray Records, Box 2T-6-003.

70 Cobb, *Native Activism in Cold War America*, 155.

71 Cobb, *Native Activism in Cold War America*, 157, 162, 178, 182; Joe DeLaCruz to George Harris, April 29, 1968, enclosing articles from the Port Angeles *Evening News*, Quinault, ICAP Files, Box 53, Folder 4; Sherry L. Smith, *Hippies, Indians, and the Fight for Red Power* (New York: Oxford University Press, 2012), 40.

72 Transcript and Commentary re: Position Statement of Attorneys Hired to Represent American Indians in the Forthcoming United States v. State of Washington Case, Adams Papers, Box 82, Folder 4.

73 Medcalf, *Law and Identity*, 50. Medcalf referred to interviewing thirteen "anonymous" attorneys, but her appendix indicates that she talked with sixteen. Ibid., 33, 137.

74 Interview with Charles Wilkinson, 14.

75 Interview with Charles Wilkinson, 35.

76 Medcalf, *Law and Identity*, 33–35.

77 Medcalf, *Law and Identity*, 49, 50, 76.

78 Author's interview with Michael Taylor.

79 Author's interview with Daniel Raas, Bellingham, Washington, April 4, 2012.

80 *NCAI Sentinel* 13 (Fall 1968).

81 AIPRC Records, NA RG 220.17.8 (A1 Entry 38060), Box 60, Transcripts of Task Force Hearings, State of Washington, Vol. 2, Feb. 3, 1976, 413.

82 Barry Siegel, "Tribes Seek to Govern Non-Members," *LAT*, May 27, 1986, 4.

83 "Indians Close Beach Littered by Tourists," *WP*, Aug. 26, 1969, A8; "Indians Close Littered Beach," *NYT*, Aug. 26, 1969, 43; "Quinault Beach," CBS Evening News, Vanderbilt Television News Archives Record No. 20521, Aug. 27, 1969.

84 "Closure of the Beaches," *Nugguam* 5 (Sept. 5, 1969), Hansen Papers, Box 100, Folder "Quinault Indians 1969 (BIA)."

85 DeLaCruz interview; "Indians Arrest Four Men for Illegal Fishing," *ST*, Jan. 11, 1970, 40; Bill Mertena, "Protests by Quinaults Kill Coast Highway," *ST*, Dec. 22, 1970, 11; "Tribe Disputes State on Dropping Highway," *ST*, Dec. 23, 1970, 6; "Indians Bar Loggers at Barricade," *ST*, Sept. 16, 1971, 6; Dick Young, "Quinault Timberland Tragedy," *Seattle Post-Intelligencer*, Sept. 26, 1971, A3; Pauline K. Capoeman, ed., *Land of the Quinault* (Taholah: Quinault Indian Nation, 1990), 205–6; Charles Wilkinson, *Blood Struggle: The Rise of Modern Indian Nations* (New York: W. W. Norton, 2005), 319–21.

86 Highlight Report of ICAP staff visit Nov. 17–18, 1969, ICAP Files, Box 54, Folder 1.

87 Don Hannula, "Land Is Life: Quinault Indians Now Run Reservation with Firm Hand," *ST*, Sept. 26, 1971, 72.

88 Ross Anderson, "Quinault Indian Leader Joe DeLaCruz dies," *ST*, April 18, 2000.

89 Reservation Development Program, May 10, 1971, Reservation Planning Reports, 1968–71, NA RG 75, Records of the BIA, Division of Tribal Resources Development, Box 2.

90 Reservation Development Program; DeLaCruz interview.

91 Anna Micklethwait to "People working for, or interested in, the development of Quinault Natural Resources," Nov. 8, 1971, Johnson Papers, Box 2, Folder: "Quinault Project."

92 Charles A. Hobbs to Julia Butler Hansen, Oct. 21, 1971, Hansen Papers, Box 100, Folder: "Indian Affairs—Tribes—Quinault, 1971"; United States v. Mitchell, 463 U.S. 206 (1983).

93 "Jim 'Jug' Jackson: Former Quinault Tribal Leader Found Dead," *Kitsap Sun*, Apr. 4, 1999.

94 "Quinault Indians Win Round in Dispute with Logging Firms," *ST*, Sept. 23, 1971, 32; "Quinault Indians Ordered to End Logger Blockade," *ST*, Sept. 30, 1971, 6; "Indians Restrained from Blocking Loggers," *ST*, Oct. 1, 1971, 8; "Quinaults to Seek Order Halting Logging," *ST*, Oct. 5, 1971, 56.

95 Author's interview with Dan Raas.

96 Author's interview with Michael Taylor.

97 Author's interview with Dan Raas.

CHAPTER 6: COLONIAL CONTROLS IN SUQUAMISH TERRITORY

1 Bruce Johansen, "They Greeted Whites: And Lost Their Way of Life," *ST*, May 12, 1976, 55.

2 Marjorie Jones, "Suquamish Zoning Bans Garbage Dump," *ST*, July 9, 1972, 31; Warren King, "Lines Drawn in Suquamish Squabble," *ST*, Aug. 10, 1977, 15; documents in folder "Sovereignty," Bradley H. Patterson Files, Gerald R. Ford Presidential Library, Box 5, https://www.fordlibrarymuseum.gov/library/document/0142/1103434.pdf.

3 Bainbridge Island History, www.ci.bainbridge-isl.wa.us/195/Island-History; "Kitsap County," Legacy Washington, http://www.sos.wa.gov/legacy/cities_detail.aspx?i=35; "Port Madison: First Area Settled on Bainbridge Island by Non-Natives," www.bainbridgehistory.org/virtual_exhibit/vex5/76E8452C-7089-4DB4-ADE7-360672104922.htm.

4 Deposition of Sam Wilson, Duwamish et al. v. United States of America, US Court of Claims, No. F-275, UWL Microfilm A-7348, Testimony, 416, 418, 420.

5 Leonard Andrew Forsman, "The Dyes Inlet Indian Communities: An Analysis of the Historic Significance of an Off-Reservation Settlement," MA thesis, Goucher College, 2004, 11, 14–15.

6 Treaty with Dwamish, Suquamish, and Other Allied and Subordinate Tribes of Indians in the Territory of Washington, http://digitalcollections.lib.washington.edu/cdm/ref/collection/lctext/id/1592.

7 D'suq'wub was also called ita kbw (lots of people). T. T. Waterman, "Puget Sound Geography," [192?] excerpt, Suquamish Tribal Archives. Also, Coll Thrush, *Native Seattle: Histories from the Crossing-Over Place* (Seattle: University of Washington Press, 2007), 23; Ernest B. Bertelson, "Historic Indian Spot Wiped Out by Progress," *ST*, April 28, 1946, 51.

8 Records of the Washington Territory Superintendency of Indian Affairs (1854–55), 452–53, UWL Microfilm A-171; Suquamish and Klallam Tribes Title IV Committee and North Kitsap School District, "The Suquamish Tribe: A History from Manuscripts and Memories" (mimeograph, 1975), 13, 16. I follow Thrush, spelling the chief's name to indicate Whulshootseed pronunciation. *Native Seattle*, 37–38.

9 Thrush, *Native Seattle*, 51–53.

10 Laurie C. Donaldson, "Change in Economic Roles of Suquamish Men and Women: An Ethnohistoric Analysis," MA thesis, Western Washington University, 1985, 60–62.

11 G. A. Paige to M. T. Simmons, July 1859, ARCIA (1859), 249.

12 Alexandra Harmon, *Indians in the Making: Ethnic Relations and Indian Identities around Puget Sound* (Berkeley: University of California Press, 1998), esp. 96–98.

13 Notes, Suquamish Tribal Oral History Interview J.33.03, Celia Jackson, 1982.

14 Donaldson, "Change in Economic Roles," 64, 66; Robert B. Ross, Sr., "Story of the Port Madison Indians as They Were in 1871 When He Arrived Here from Australia," undated manuscript, Suquamish Tribal Archives; Forsman, "Dyes Inlet Communities," 14–15.

15 Donaldson, "Change in Economic Roles," 74.

16 Harmon, *Indians in the Making*, 103–24.

17 Correspondence regarding Port Madison Reserve, Charles J. Kappler, *Indian Affairs: Laws and Treaties*, vol. 1, *Laws*, Part 3, Executive Orders Relating to Indian Reserves (Washington, DC: Government Printing Office, 1904), 921, https://dc.library.okstate.edu/digital/collection/kapplers/id/27868/rec/2.

18 Correspondence regarding Port Madison Reserve.

19 Donaldson, "Change in Economic Roles," 70.

20 E. E. Riddell and North End Improvement Council, "History of Suquamish," *Kitsap County Herald*, Oct. 14, 1932, 1, 3, clipping in Suquamish Tribal Archives.

21 Riddell, "History of Suquamish"; Donaldson, "Change in Economic Roles," citing H. Exec. Doc. 1, 5, 43rd Cong., 2d sess.; Report of Superintendent Edward Miller, 1900, Suquamish Annual Reports, NA PAR RG 75, Tulalip Agency Annual Reports, 1863–1943, Box 1; Suquamish Tribe Cultural Program, "You Don't Make Farmers: The Failure of Indian Assimilation on the Port Madison Reservation," undated manuscript, 14–15, Suquamish Tribal Archives.

22 US Senate Subcommittee on Indian Affairs, *Survey of Conditions of Indians in the United States*, 72nd Cong., 1st sess., part 32 (1934), 17212–13.

23 Suquamish oral history interviews mention nine off-reservation "villages" or family settlements in Kitsap County. Suquamish Tribal Archives.

24 Deposition testimony, Duwamish et al. v. United States of America, No. F-275, UWL Microfilm A-7348, 404–8; notes, Suquamish Oral History Interview W.1.12, Lawrence Webster, 1982.

25 Donaldson, "Change in Economic Roles," 79; Report of Cyrus Pickrell, 1908, Suquamish Annual Reports, Box 1.

26 Notes, Suquamish Oral History Interview W.1.03, Lawrence Webster, 1980.

27 Julia Bandelean et al., *Seeing a New Day: A 150 Year History of Saint Peter Catholic Mission* (Port Madison Indian Reservation, Suquamish, WA: St. Peter Mission, 2005), 12.

28 Notes, Suquamish Oral History Interview W.1.16, Lawrence Webster, 1982.

29 Agreement ratified Mar. 3, 1905, 33 Stat. 1078.

30 "When I First Remember Suquamish: Lawrence Webster's Memories," March 1969, manuscript in Suquamish Tribal Archives; Report of Cyrus Pickrell, 1908; Suquamish Tribe Cultural Program, "You Don't Make Farmers."

31 Report of Cyrus Pickrell, 1908; Suquamish Oral History Interview W.1.12.

32 Minutes, meetings with CIA Emmons, Sept. 13 and 14, 1956, NA PAR RG 75 WWA Decimal Files 1950–1965, Box 18.

33 34 Stat. 1018, sec.6 (1905), 58th Cong., sess. 3, ch. 1479; Petitioner's Memorandum of Authorities, Exhibit 4, Oliphant v. Schlie; Cyrus B. Pickrell to Charles M. Buchanan, Sept. 6, 1909, Suquamish Land Sales Records, NA PAR RG 75, Tulalip Indian Agency, Land Sales Case Files, Summaries of Land Sales, 1902–1917, Box 2; Riddell, "History of Suquamish."

34 Suquamish Tribe Cultural Program, "You Don't Make Farmers," 21–22.

35 34 Stat. 182–83; Francis Paul Prucha, *The Great Father: The United States Government and the American Indians* (Lincoln: University of Nebraska Press, 1984), 2:873–79.

36 Suquamish Annual Reports, Box 3.

37 32 Stat. 275; Report of A. Bartow, 1906, Suquamish Annual Reports, Box 1.

38 Suquamish Annual Reports, Box 2; US Senate, *Survey of Conditions of Indians*, 17200.

39 Suquamish Cultural Program, "You Don't Make Farmers," 19–21.

40 North Kitsap Trails, map, www.northkitsaptrails.org/files/map_suquamish_poi.pdf; Riddell, "History of Suquamish."

41 William J. Egbert to Buchanan, July 28, 1917, Records of the BIA, CCF, 1907–1939, Series B, Indian Customs and Social Relations, Folder 002133-022-0798, Proquest.com/historyvault; notes, Suquamish Oral History Interview H.8.01, Holmes Hyland, 1981.

42 Advertisement, *ST*, Aug. 3, 1915, 18.

43 Egbert to Buchanan, July 28, 1917.

44 1920 Narrative Report, Suquamish Annual Reports, Box 5.

45 Report of A. Bartow, 1904, Suquamish Annual Reports, Box 1; notes, Suquamish Oral History Interview W.1.06, Lawrence Webster, 1982.

46 David Wilma and Walt Crowley, "Tacoma—Thumbnail History," History Link, http://www.historylink.org/File/5055; John Caldbick, "Bremerton—Thumbnail History," History Link, http://www.historylink.org/File/9583; Jennifer Ott, "Poulsbo—Thumbnail History," History Link, http://www.historylink.org/File/8359; F. A. Gross, [1926], "The Problem of Indian Administration," and Narrative Report for 1927, Suquamish Annual Reports, Box 5; Webster, "When I First Remember Suquamish."

47 Bandalean, *Seeing a New Day*, 13; Riddell, "History of Suquamish."

48 Suquamish Land Sales Records, NA PAR RG 75, Tulalip Indian Agency, Land Sales Case Files, Completed Sales, 1919–1932, Box 2, files "W. L. Gazzam, Misc. Correspondence" and "Completed Sales"; Charles P. LeWarne, "Townspeople of Poulsbo Vote to Create a Port District," History Link, www.historylink.org/index.cfm?DisplayPage=output.cfm&file_id=9716.

49 "Free Excursions to Suquamish," advertisement, *ST*, Aug. 3, 1915, 18; "Cherry Tree Planted by U.S. Gov't. at Suquamish," *ST*, June 8, 1912, 5.

50 Egbert to Buchanan, July 28, 1917; *Felix S. Cohen's Handbook of Federal Indian Law* (1942; repr. Albuquerque: University of New Mexico Press, 1971), 8, 361–62.

51 62 U.S. Stat. 757 (June 25, 1948), 18 U.S.C. 1151.

52 "Whites and Redskins Will Honor Seattle," *ST*, Aug. 30, 1912, 14.

53 "Service at Grave of Chief Seattle Prove Most Enthusiastic [*sic*]," *ST*, Aug. 27, 1911, 3; "Indians Are to Celebrate—Old-Time War Dances on Port Madison Reservation," *ST*, Aug. 19, 1921, 15; "Chief Seattle Day Will Be Celebrated at Suquamish Saturday and Sunday," *ST*, Aug. 25, 1927, 26; Harmon, *Indians in the Making*, 150; Thrush, *Native Seattle*, 126–27, 148.

54 "Suquamish Progresses," *ST*, Sept. 9, 1915, 13; 1920 Narrative Report, Suquamish Annual Reports, Box 5.

55 Bandelean, *Seeing a New Day*, 15, 18, 28; author's conversation with Leonard Forsman, June 19, 2018.

56 Suquamish Annual Reports, Boxes 1, 2, 6; Suquamish Economic Survey, 1933–34, NA PAR RG 75, Tulalip Indian Agency, Box 2.

57 Indian Census Rolls, UWL Microfilm BOT-496.

58 R. G. Stillman, "Suquamish Indians and Port Madison Reservation," Sept. 26, 1938, MS in Suquamish Tribal Archives. On Stillman, "A Picture of Northwest Indians," Library of Congress, http://lcweb2.loc.gov/mss/wpalh3/38/3807/38071813/38071813.pdf.

59 Wayne Suttles and Barbara Lane, "Southern Coast Salish," in *Handbook of North American Indians*, vol. 7 (Washington, DC: Smithsonian Institution, 1990), 485, 494–95.

60 Harmon, *Indians in the Making*, chapter 4.

61 E. C. Chirouse to J. Q. Smith, Nov. 13, 1874, NA M-2011, Reel 2; Report of the Tulalip Agency [D.C. Govan], 1895, and report of Allen Bartow, 1904, Suquamish Annual Reports, Box 1.

62 Report of Allen Bartow, 1904.

63 Suquamish Oral History Interview W.1.12.

64 Suquamish Oral History Interview W.1.18, Lawrence Webster, 1982; Harmon, *Indians in the Making*, 178–80; Thomas C. Bishop, "An Appeal to the Government to Fulfill Sacred Promises Made 61 Years Ago," 1915, UWL Special Collections.

65 Additional Memorandum of Authorities of Additional Respondents, Exhibit 1, Oliphant v. Schlie.

66 Notes, Suquamish Oral History Interview W.1.11, Lawrence Webster, 1982; Harmon, *Indians in the Making*, 180.

67 Harmon, *Indians in the Making*, 178–80.

68 Superintendent Dickens to Commissioner of Indian Affairs, June 27, 1925, NA PAR RG75 WWA, General Correspondence, Tribal Operations Branch, Box 259.

69 Notes, Suquamish Oral History Interview W.1.18.

70 Gladys Fowler et al., and Charles A. Alexis to Lynn Frazier, June 15, 1931, US Senate, *Survey of Conditions of Indians*, 11808–9.

71 F. A. Gross, "The Problem of Indian Administration."

72 Mary Carolyn Howard, testimony transcript, June 13, 1952, 9, Indian Claims Commission Docket No. 132, copy in Suquamish Tribal Archives.

73 F. A. Gross, "The Problem of Indian Administration."

74 O. C. Upchurch telegraph, April 25, 1935, and memorandum to BIA Indian Organization Division, April 10, 1935, NA RG 75, Records of the Indian Organization Division, General Records Concerning Indian Organization, 1934–56, Box 36; George P. LaVatta to Mr. Meiklejohn, Mar. 28, 1940, Records of the BIA, CCF, 1907–1939, Series B, Indian Customs and Social Relations, Folder 002133-012-0952, Proquest.com/historyvault.

75 O. C. Upchurch to George P. LaVatta, Feb. 14, 1940, Records of the BIA, CCF, 1907–1939, Series B, Folder 002133-012-0952.

76 Notes, Suquamish Oral History Interview W.1.12; O. C. Upchurch to George P. LaVatta, Feb. 14, 1940, and minutes by L. Webster, secretary, meeting of Suquamish Indians, Feb. 11, 1940, "for the purpose of voting on accepting Charter and By-laws proposed under the Wheeler-Howard Act," Records of the BIA, CCF, 1907–1939, Series B, Folder 002133-012-0952.

77 Questionnaires on Tribal Organization, May 15, 1953, NA PAR RG 75 WWA Decimal Files 1950–1965, Box 16.

78 Howard testimony transcript, 8, 11, Indian Claims Commission.

79 US House of Representatives, Committee on Indian Affairs, *Investigate Indian Affairs*, 78th Cong., 1st sess., Hearings on H. Res. 166, 1943.

80 F. A. Gross to Pete Henderson, Feb. 18, 1948, Suquamish Correspondence, NA PAR RG 75 WWA, Tribal Operations Branch, Tribal Files, ca. 1919–68, Box 289.

81 "Indian Affairs Badly Handled, Says Jackson," *ST*, Oct. 1, 1944, 18.

82 Bertelson, "Historic Indian Spot Wiped Out by Progress."

83 F. A. Gross to Jack Taylor, Sept. 6, 1950, Suquamish Correspondence, NA PAR, RG 75 WWA, Tribal Operations Branch, Tribal Files, ca. 1919–68, Box 289.

84 Minutes, meetings with CIA Emmons, Sept. 13 and 14, 1956; minutes, Suquamish Tribal Council, Feb. 19, 1956, NA RG 75, Portland Area Office, Tribal Operations Branch, Tribal Council Minutes ca. 1950–65, Box 1576.

85 Minutes, Suquamish Tribal Council, Feb. 19, 1956.

86 US Department of Health, Education, and Welfare, Public Health Service, Division of Indian Health, *Indians on Federal Reservations in the United States, a Digest*, Portland Area, Public Health Service Bulletin No. 615, Part 1 (1958).

87 Government Withdrawal Program 1953, NA PAR RG 75 WWA Decimal Files 1950–1965, 103.3, Box 15.

88 In 1959, the commission calculated the 1859 value of acreage ceded at $78,500, just over a penny an acre. In 1972, the tribe refused the ICC award of $42,170.49. The Suquamish Tribe of Indians v. the United States of America, Indian Claims Commission Docket No. 132, 24 Ind. Cl. Com. 34, 49 (1970) and 197 Ct. Cl. 775 (1972); minutes, Suquamish Tribal Council, Feb. 10, 1963, NA RG75, Portland Area Office, Tribal Operations Branch, Tribal Council Minutes ca. 1950–65, Box 1576.

89 Patricia C. Wilcox and Mary C. Howard to Melvin Robertson, January 12, 1955, NA PAR RG 75 WWA Decimal Files 1950–1965, 109, Box 17.

90 "State Jurisdiction to Cover 2 Tribes," *ST*, May 15, 1958, 21; RCW 37.12.02; Proclamation of Jurisdiction, Suquamish Tribal Archives.

91 "Suquamish Leaders Fear Backdoor Treaty Abrogation from Congress," *Kitsap County Herald*, May 5, 1960, 11, clipping in Suquamish Tribal Archives.

92 The Inter-Tribal Council of Western Washington Indians met in this period with BIA officials to discuss termination policy implementation. Harmon, *Indians in the Making*, 209.

93 "Jurisdiction over Tribes Left in Doubt by State Ruling," *ST*, April 19, 1972, 72; United States v. James Russell Lawrence, 595 F. 2d 1149 (9th Cir. 1979); RCW 37.12.010.

94 Notes, Suquamish Oral History Interview W.1.06.

95 Suquamish Indian Tribe Constitution and By-Laws, approved June 16, 1965, Suquamish Tribal Archives. A BIA official assumed that constitution drafters limited the territory to tribally owned land because the reservation was under state jurisdiction. R. D. Holtz to Tribal Operations, Dec. 4, 1964, Officer Files, NA RG 75, Box 40, "Suquamish" folder.

96 "Suquamish Indians O.K. Constitution," *ST*, June 3, 1965, 17.

97 "Chief Seattle Days," *ST*, July 7, 1963, 5 and 37.

98 ICAP Files, Box 57, Folder 2, Suquamish.

99 US BIA, "New Horizons": Indian Leaders Conference with Robert L. Bennett, Spokane, Oct. 17–19, 1966, UWL Special Collections, 352.

100 Burt Schorr, "Indian Landlords: Tribes Seek to Prosper by Leasing Reservations for Industry, Suburbs," *WSJ*, Oct 3, 1966, 1; "Indian-Owned Land Offered

Developers," *ST*, Feb. 6, 1966, 4; "Lots Are Offered on Reservation," *ST*, May 19, 1968, 109. Also, Business Lease, June 15, 1967, between Suquamish Tribe and Chief Seattle Properties, Inc. re: government lot in sec. 21, T 26N, Range 2 East of WM, Exhibit 5, Oliphant v. Schlie.

101 "Girl Laments Indian Land, Culture Loss," *Kitsap County Herald*, July 30, 1969, 1, clipping, Suquamish Tribal Archives.

102 The tribe made this one of my tasks when I served as on-reservation attorney, 1984–88.

103 "Kitsap Indians Cling to History," *Bremerton Sun*, May 16, 1969, 10-D.

104 "Suquamish Tribe Still Awaits Claim Decision," *Bremerton Sun*, Feb. 26, 1969, 17; "Kitsap Indians Cling to History," *Bremerton Sun*; transcript, Richard Belmont testimony, AIPRC hearing, Yakima, Washington, Feb. 2, 1976, 74–75, NCAI Records, pre-1994 accessions, Series 6, Box 258.

105 Author's telephone conversation with Richard Belmont, Jr., Feb. 1, 2012.

106 Denise Halette, "Port Madison Policies Could Influence Future," *Bremerton Sun*, April 16, 1973, 1.

107 Telephone conversation with Richard Belmont.

108 "Quinaults Close Beaches to White Men," *ST*, Aug. 24, 1969, 27; "Lummis Close Beach Area," *ST*, Oct. 24, 1969, 1.

109 Author's conversation with Bennie Armstrong, Jr., Suquamish, Mar. 26, 2012.

110 File: "Affiliated Tribes of the N.W. Indians, 8/30–9/1, 1966," NA PAR RG 75, Portland Area Office, Tribal Operations Branch, General Subject Files, 1953–67, Box 1521.

111 "Indians Ask Solons for More Control," *ST*, Mar. 19, 1971, 7.

112 Seabury Blair, Jr., "$100,000 Suit Lodged as Two Indian Tribes Continue War over Cigarettes," *Bremerton Sun*, Jan. 29, 1973, 1; Halette, "Port Madison Policies Could Influence Future."

113 Marjorie Jones, "Suquamish Zoning Bans Garbage Dump," *ST*, July 7, 1972, 31.

114 "Indians Sue for Land near Bremerton," *ST*, Jan. 11, 1973, 42; Hilda Bryant, "Tribe Wants Land near Bremerton," *Seattle Post-Intelligencer*, Jan.11, 1973, A10.

115 "Suquamish Decide Tribe to Operate Chief Seattle Days," *Bremerton Sun*, May 1, 1973, 2.

116 Tom Wilson, *Courage to Follow the Vision: The Journey of Lyle Emerson George* (Silverdale, WA: Red Apple Publishing, 2002), 98, 101.

CHAPTER 7: ENCOURAGING SIGNS

1 Transcript, 32nd Annual NCAI Convention Indian Litigation Panel, Portland, OR, Nov. 11, 1975, 25–26, NCAI Records, pre-1994, series 6, Box 277, Litigation Conference, File: "Lit. Comm."

2 Barry Ernstoff to Sasha Harmon, e-mail of June 14, 2011.

3 Transcript of argument, Jan. 9, 1978, Oliphant v. Suquamish Tribe, 55, 40.

4 Washington State Bar Association Lawyer Directory, https://www.mywsba.org/LawyerDirectory/LawyerProfile.aspx?Usr_ID=3876; Ernstoff, minutes of Puget Sound Indian Law Society, Oct. 26, 1972, Johnson Papers, General Correspondence; "Indians Bar Loggers at Barricade," *ST*, Sept. 16, 1971, 6; "Indians Continue to Bar Loggers," *ST*, Sept. 17, 1971, 58; "Quinault Indians Win Round in Dispute with Logging Firms," *ST*, Sept. 23, 1971, 32; "Quinaults in Accord on Logging Pact," *ST*, Sept. 25, 1971, 4; Don Hannula, "Quinaults Determined to Protect Land," *ST*, Sept. 26, 1971, 1.

5 Don Hannula, "Quinault Indians Now Run Reservation with a Firm Hand," *ST*, Sept. 26, 1971, 72.

6 John Bell, "Coast Indians Shun 'Warpath' but Assert Tribal Powers," *ST*, Mar. 18, 1973, 1; John Bell, "The Quinaults—a Rebirth," *ST*, Mar.18, 1973, 28.

7 Robert L. Beaty to Guy McMinds, Aug. 15, 1972, and Oct. 18, 1972, Johnson Papers, Box 2.

8 Shelby Scates, "Quinault Tribe Pushes for Sovereignty," *Seattle Post-Intelligencer*, Dec. 17, 1972, F 1.

9 Quinault Tribal Code of Laws, approved March 31, 1973, preamble and section 5.05.03.

10 Author's interview with Michael Taylor, Jan. 30, 2012, Camano Island, Washington.

11 DeLaCruz interview.

12 Trial transcript, United States of America, Plaintiff, Quinault Tribe of Indians, et al. Intervenor-plaintiffs v. State of Washington, Defendant, Civil No. 9213, US District Court, Western District of Washington at Tacoma, Sept. 13, 1973, 3490.

13 Barry Siegel, "Tribes Seek to Govern Non-Indians: Indians' New Powers Bring Gains, Conflicts," *LAT*, May 27, 1986, 4.

14 Author's interview with Michael Taylor; author's interview with Dan Raas, April 4, 2012, Bellingham, WA.

15 American Indian Lawyers Association, *The Indian Civil Rights Act, Five Years Later* (Denver, 1973), meeting record, May 11, 1973, 24–29; Rod Lewis to William Byler, Nov. 13, 1972, AAIA Papers, Series 2, Subject Files, 1851–1995, Subseries 2, Tribal, Box 199, Folder 2, Gila River Pima-Maricopa, 1957–1973; author's telephone interview with Rodney Lewis, May 1, 2012; US Senate, *Reform of the Federal Criminal Laws*, Hearings before Subcommittee on Criminal Laws and Procedures, Committee on the Judiciary, 93rd Cong., 1st sess., CIS-NO 74 S521-24, Part IX, July 25, 1973, 6496-6500.

16 Brief of amicus curiae Salt River Pima-Maricopa Indian Community, Oliphant. v. Suquamish Indian Tribe; Thomas Biolsi, *"Deadliest Enemies": Law and the Making*

of Race Relations on and off Rosebud Reservation (Berkeley: University of California Press, 2001), 143.

17 Brief of amicus curiae NCAI, Oliphant v. Suquamish Tribe.

18 Oliphant's family owned a plumbing business on the reservation. Malone was president of Chief Seattle Properties, Inc., lessee of the tribe's land for a residential development.

19 By 2012, law firm files on this case had been destroyed. Thomas P. Schlosser e-mail to author, Jan. 20, 2012.

20 Memorandum of Authorities of Amicus Curiae Suquamish Tribe, Oliphant v. Schlie.

21 Motion of Quinault Tribe and Queets Band to appear as amicus curiae, Oliphant v. Schlie.

22 Memorandum of Amici Curiae National Tribal Chairman's Association et al., and Memorandum of Amicus Curiae United States of America, Oliphant v. Schlie.

23 ATNI Resolution 74-23, NCAI Records, Series 4, Intertribal Organizations, Box 139, N–P, Folder: "Affiliated Tribes of Northwest Indians [1959–1975]."

24 Schlie was later dismissed as a respondent.

25 Petitioner's Memorandum of Authorities, 13 and ff., Oliphant v. Schlie.

26 Transcript of Proceedings, Oliphant v. Schlie, Jan. 25, 1974, 21, 28, 69.

27 Magistrate John L. Weinberg's Report and Recommendation, Case No. C74-683S, US District Court, Western District of Washington, in Ray Records, Box 2T-6-002, Folder "Indian Jurisdiction."

28 Ortiz-Barraza v. United States, 512 F. 2d 1176, 1179 (9th Cir., 1975); Quechan Tribe of Indians v. Rowe, 531 F. 2d 408 (9th Cir., 1976).

29 Oliphant v. Schlie, 544 F. 2d 1007 (9th Cir. August 24, 1976).

30 Daniel H. Israel, "The Reemergence of Tribal Nationalism and Its Impact on Reservation Resource Development," 47 *Colorado Law Review* 617 (1975–1976): 630–31n48.

31 "Honorable George H. Boldt," posted by Washington Department of Fisheries as *The Boldt Decision* at http://wdfw.wa.gov/fishing/salmon/BoldtDecision8.5x11layoutforweb.pdf; George H. Boldt obituary, UPI archives, www.upi.com/Archives/1984/03/19/Retired-US-District-Court-Judge-George-H-Boldt-a/3740448520400.

32 "Honorable George H. Boldt," 23; sample finding of a tribe's political status, 65.

33 Author's interview with Michael Taylor.

34 Guy McMinds, testimony, Department of the Interior and Related Agencies Appropriations for 1975, Part 5, House Committee on Appropriations subcommittee, 93rd Cong., 2d sess., CIS No. 74-H181-2, 271.

35 US Senate, *Constitutional Rights of the American Indian*, Subcommittee on Constitutional Rights of the Committee on the Judiciary, 89th Cong., 1st sess., June 22–24, 29, 1965, CIS-NO: 89-S1693, SUDOC Y4.J89/2:In2/5/965.

36 Ralph Reeser to Senator Joseph D. Tydings, April 25, 1968, AAIA Papers, Series 2, Subject Files, Subseries 3, Legislation, Box 311, Folder 8, Judicial System, 1962–1986.

37 Ralph W. Johnson, "Indian Justice Planning Project, 1971," 97–98, bound typescript, Gallagher Law Library, UW.

38 Opinion M-36810, 77 I.D., Aug. 10, 1970, cited in 1 *American Indian Law Review* (1973): 13.

39 Adams Papers, Box 81, Folder 3.

40 Biolsi, *"Deadliest Enemies,"* 149, and citation; Reid Peyton Chambers statement, US Senate Subcommittee on Indian Affairs, Committee on Interior and Insular Affairs, *Tribal Judicial Reform*, 94th Cong., 1st sess., Feb. 24, 1975, S. 441–53, 57; Robert L. Pirtle, *To Right the Unrightable Wrong: An Autobiography of Robert L. Pirtle, Tribal Lawyer* (Bloomington, IN: Xlibris, 2007), 422.

41 Morris Thompson to Deputy Solicitor, Sept. 3, 1976, NCAI Records, Pre-1994, Series 6, Box 170, File "Criminal Jurisdiction."

42 Indian preference laws applicable to Bureau of Indian Affairs and Indian Health Service positions, 25 U.S.C. 472a; Morton v. Mancari, 417 U.S. 535 (1974).

43 For example, Franklin Ducheneaux, "Tribal Jurisdiction over Non-Indians," *NCIO News* 1 (May 1971): 5, AAIA Papers, Series 2, Subject Files, 1851–1995, Subseries 1, General Correspondence, Box 128, Folder 10, Jurisdiction, 1961–1972.

44 Israel, "Reemergence of Tribal Nationalism," 630.

45 Author's interview with Alan Parker, Nov. 30, 2011, Olympia, Washington; Rennard Strickland and Charles F. Wilkinson, eds., *Felix S. Cohen's Handbook of Federal Indian Law*, rev. ed. (Charlottesville, VA: Michie Bobbs-Merrill, 1982); Margery H. Brown, "The 1982 Felix S. Cohen's Handbook of Federal Indian Law: A Review and Commentary," 44 *Montana Law Review* (Jan. 1983): 147–57.

46 Seth S. King, "Indian, Starting Job as Aide to Interior Secretary, Sees Backlash in Congress over Tribal Land Claims," *NYT*, Nov. 1, 1977, 16; Mark N. Trahant, *The Last Great Battle of the Indian Wars: Henry M. Jackson, Forrest J. Gerard and the Campaign for the Self-Determination of American's Indian Tribes* (n.p., 2010), 45; "Forrest Gerard, Blackfeet, Architect of Indian Self-Determination Has Walked On," Native News Online, Dec. 30, 2013, http://nativenewsonline.net/currents/forrest-gerard-blackfeet-architect-indian-self-determination-walked/.

47 James G. Abourezk, *Advise and Dissent: Memoirs of South Dakota and the U.S. Senate* (Chicago: Lawrence Hill Books, 1989),10, 200; "James Abourezk,"

Wikipedia, https://en.wikipedia.org/wiki/James_Abourezk; US Senate, *Tribal Judicial Reform*, 41–53, 1.

48 Abourezk implied that tribal criminal jurisdiction over non-Indians was fair recompense for "whites . . . , who had been accustomed to mistreating Indians all of their lives." *Advise and Dissent*, 220.

49 Resolution 73-17, April 13, 1973, and Resolutions 2 and 3, Sept. 11, 1970, NCAI Records, Series 4, Intertribal Organizations, Box 139, N–P.

50 William R. Baldassin and John T. McDermott, "Jurisdiction over Non-Indians: An Opinion of the 'Opinion,'" 1 *American Indian Law Review* (1973): 16, 19.

51 "[Transcript—Workshop Two: Tribal Government] [1974]," NCAI Records, pre-1994 accessions, Series 1, Conventions, Box 25 (two folders).

52 Transcript: National Conference on Jurisdiction and P.L. 280, Feb. 24 and 25, 1975, NCAI Records, Pre-1994, Series 6. Box 259. Emphasis added.

53 Long, Harry R., v. Quinault Tribe, Quinault Tribal Council, and the Honorable Frank Hall, a Judge thereof, No. C75-67T, NA RG 21, US District Court, Western District of Washington, Southern Division, Tacoma, Civil Files—Selected, 1968–1985, Box 31. Also, author's interview with Dan Raas.

54 AAIA Papers, Series 2, Subject Files, 1851–1995, Subseries 2, Tribal, Box 285, Folder 10, Makah.

55 "Utes Sue to Extend Tribal Law to Some Non-Indians," *NYT*, Oct. 18, 1975, 59; "Court to Test Utes' Policing of Lands," *Denver Post*, clipping attached to Jan. 27, 1976, AIPRC press release; "Court Will Hear Tribal Law Dispute," *Deseret News*, June 13, 1977, B-1, clipping in Tyler Papers, Box 119, Folder 9, News Clippings, 1971–1980.

56 James Robins, "Indian Jurisdiction Problem Brews," *Blackfoot, Idaho, News*, Nov. 1, 1975, n.p., Tyler Papers, News Clippings, 1971–1980.

57 NCAI Records, pre-1994 accessions, Series 1, Conventions. Box 30, 1975–1976, Folder: "[Speeches] 1975 Convention—Portland, Oregon, November 10, 1975."

58 US Senate, *Reform of the Federal Criminal Laws*, Part VII, June 12, 1973, 5888–90, 5901.

59 US Senate, *Reform of the Federal Criminal Laws*, 5895–96.

60 US Senate, *Reform of the Federal Criminal Laws*, 5898–99.

61 US Senate, *Reform of the Federal Criminal Laws*, Part IX, July 35, 1973, 6496–6500.

62 US Senate Subcommittee on Indian Affairs, Committee on Interior and Insular Affairs, Hearing on S. 2010, Indian Law Enforcement Improvement Act of 1975, 94th Cong., 1st sess., Dec. 3 and 4, 1975, Part 1, CIS-NO: 76-S441-28, 1–2.

63 US Senate, Hearing on S. 2010, 11–13.

64 US Senate, Hearing on S. 2010, 14–15.

65 US Senate, Hearing on S. 2010, 119–22.

66 US Senate, Hearing on S. 2010, 122–24.

67 Undated memorandum [1974], Sherwin Broadhead to James Abourezk, Broadhead Papers.

68 Lloyd Meeds, "American Indian Policy Review Commission," 40 *Law and Contemporary Problems* (Winter 1976): 9–11.

69 Abourezk, *Advise and Dissent*, 216–17.

70 Sherwin Broadhead Curriculum Vitae, Broadhead Papers; Colville Law and Order Code, adopted by Colville Business Council Resolution #683, Oct. 12, 1972.

71 Sherwin Broadhead et al., "Report on Tribal, State, and Federal Jurisdiction; Final Report to the American Indian Policy Review Commission (Washington, DC: US Government Printing Office, 1978); Native American Rights Fund, www.narf.org/profiles/donald-r-wharton/; US Commission on Civil Rights, "The Navajo Nation: American Colony," vii, https://babel.hathitrust.org/cgi/pt?id=mdp.39015012105964;view=1up;seq=1. The AIPRC invited specific tribes, including Quinaults, "to write their own policy review commission report" and called for other tribes to do the same. James Abourezk, speech transcript, NCAI Records, pre-1994 accessions, Series 1, Conventions, Box 30, 1975–1976, Folder: "[Speeches] 1975 Convention—Portland, Oregon, Nov. 10, 1975."

72 Mrs. H. A. Dewar to Lloyd Meeds, Feb. 23, 1976, Broadhead Papers.

73 Written statements, AIPRC public hearing, Yakima, Feb. 2, 1976, NCAI Records, pre-1994 accessions, Series 6, Box 258.

74 AIPRC hearing, Yakima, 121–29.

75 Michael Taylor, testimony, AIPRC Records, NA RG 220.17.8 (A1 Entry 38060), Box 60, Transcripts of Task Force Hearings, State of Washington, Vol. 2, 410–11, 413–14.

76 AIPRC hearing, Yakima, 75–103.

77 "Panel on U.S. Indian Policy Urges Tribes Be Recognized as Sovereign," *NYT*, Mar.16, 1977, 48.

78 AIPRC Task Force Seven: Reservation and Resource Development and Protection, *Report on Reservation and Resource Development and Protection* (Washington: US Government Printing Office, 1976), 25.

79 AIPRC Task Force Two: Tribal Government, *Report on Tribal Government* (Washington: US Government Printing Office, 1976), 30, 32, 159, 277.

80 Transcript of meeting Jan. 7, 1977, 130–31, AIPRC Records, NA RG 220.17.8 (A1 Entry 38060), Box 26, Transcripts, Commission Meetings, Nov. 20, 1976, to Jan. 6, 1977.

81 "Meeds Raps Increase in Tribal Powers," *TNT*, May 15, 1977, A1; "Solons Ask More Power for Indians," *TNT*, May 17, 1977, A3. In commission discussions, Meeds acknowledged Indian tribes' "sovereignty" over Indians on Indian land.

Transcript, AIPRC Records, NA RG 220.17.8 (A1 Entry 38060), Box 27, meeting Jan. 7, 1977, 32.

82 Alexandra Harmon, *Rich Indians: Native People and the Problem of Wealth in American History* (Chapel Hill: University of North Carolina Press, 2010), 230–48.

83 "Hill Cooling on Indians as Tribal Claims Grow," *WP*, Oct. 9, 1977, A1, A8, clipping, Meeds Papers, Box 218, Folder "Omnibus Indian Bill, 1977" and Box 174, Folder: "General Correspondence, 1977–78."

84 "Lloyd Meeds—American Indian Policy: Perspective on a Complex Issue," *WP*, Oct. 22, 1977, A2; "Rep. Bonker Joins Move to Revise Indian Treaties," *TNT*, Nov. 25, 1977, B16; "Redefinition Favored for Indian Sovereignty," *TNT*, Sept. 29, 1977, A10.

85 Meeds Papers, Box 218, Folder "Omnibus Indian Bill, 1977."

86 Lee Moriwaki, "Non-Indian-Rights Legislation Pushed," *ST*, Sept. 16, 1976, 25.

87 Clipping, "Indians, County Meet at Moclips," *Montesano Vidette*, Mar. 21, 1974, Johnson Papers, NAICJA correspondence file; "Zoning Jurisdiction: Quinault Hassle Aired," *North Beach Beacon* (Ocean Shores, WA), Aug. 22, 1974, 1; Cheryl Heinman, "Hearing Slated on Non-Indian Properties," *Daily World*, Mar. 29, 1974, clipping, Meeds Papers, Box 174, folder: "General Correspondence, 1977–78."

88 Warren King, "Lines Drawn in Suquamish Squabble," *ST*, Aug. 10, 1977, 15.

89 NCAI Records, Pre-1994, Series 6, Box 170, file "Cmtes & Special Issues: Policy Conference, 1974, NCAI and AOI National Indian Meeting, April 22–23, 1974—Washington, DC."

90 Richard W. Belmont, Jr., to Concerned Indians, Sept. 18, 1975, NCAI Records, Pre-1994. Series 6, Box 262, Jurisdiction, File: "Correspondence Chronological 1975 National Indian Litigation Committee."

91 Harmon, *Rich Indians*, 230 and notes; Ronald P. Erickson, statement before Senate Select Committee on Indian Affairs, Mar. 10, 1978, Broadhead Papers.

92 Meeds Papers, Box 174 (AIPRC stuff), Folder: "General Correspondence, 1977–78.

93 Moriwaki, "Non-Indian-Rights Legislation Pushed"; Christopher Dunagan, "Ballfield No Longer Just 'What Was Left of a Reservation,'" *Bremerton Sun*, Aug. 3, 1977, 2.

94 NCAI Executive Committee Resolution, Mar. 24, 1976, NCAI Records, Series 6, Pre-1994 accessions, Litigation Committee, Box 276, File: "Chronological Correspondence 1976—July 1 to December 31, 1976, National Indian Litigation Committee."

95 Marshall Wilson, "Indians Put Faith in Judicial System," *ST*, Dec. 5, 1976, D16 [75].

96 Linda Daniels, "Indians 'Have Always Had Jurisdiction,'" *ST*, Aug.10, 1977, 14; Al Ziontz, transcript of remarks, NCAI litigation conference, Mar. 1977, 126, NCAI Records, Series 6, Pre-1994 accessions, Litigation Committee, File: ["Proceedings: Litigation Conference, Vol. II, March 22, 1976] [1 of 2]; TNT staff and the Associated Press, "High Court Asked to Uphold Tribal Powers," *TNT*, Jan. 9, 1978, A-1.

97 Pirtle, *To Right the Unrightable Wrong*, 346.

98 NCAI Records, Series 6, Pre-1994 accessions, Litigation Committee, Box 277, File: "Litigation Conference [1976]."

99 NCAI Records, "Litigation Conference [1976]."

100 Author's telephone interview with Rodney Lewis; NCAI Records, pre-1994 accessions, Series 1, Conventions, Box 36, 1977–1978, Folder: "[Transcript—34th Annual Convention—Tape Four]," Dallas, Sept. 19–23, 1977; NCAI Records, Series 6, Pre-1994 accessions, Litigation Committee, Box 277, File: "[Proceedings: Litigation Conference, Vol. II, March 22, 1976] [1 of 2]," 121–24.

101 NCAI Records, "Litigation Conference [March 22, 1976]."

102 NCAI Records, "[Proceedings: Litigation Conference, Vol. II, March 22, 1976] [1 of 2]," 130.

103 NCAI Records, Series 6, Pre-1994 accessions, Litigation Committee, Box 278, File: "[Proceedings—NCAI Litigation Conference—March 24, 25, 1977, Volume I] [1 of 2]," 19.

104 Transcript, 32ndAnnual NCAI Convention Indian Litigation Panel, Portland, Nov. 11, 1975, NCAI Records, Series 6, Pre-1994 accessions, Litigation Committee, Box 277, file: "Lit. Comm. [NCAI Litigation Panel, 32nd Annual Convention & General Material on March '76 Litigation Conf.]," 14.

105 Austin Sarat and Stuart Scheingold. "What Cause Lawyers Do *For*, and *To*, Social Movements: An Introduction," in *Cause Lawyers and Social Movements*, ed. Austin Sarat and Stuart A. Scheingold (Stanford, CA: Stanford University Press, 2006), 4.

106 NCAI Records, "[Proceedings: Litigation Conference, Vol. II, March 22, 1976] [1 of 2],", 131.

107 NCAI Records, "[Proceedings—NCAI Litigation Conference—March 24, 25, 1977, Volume I] [1 of 2]," 37.

108 Author's interview with Justine James, Sr., Taholah, July 16, 2012.

109 In the Supreme Court, Brief of Respondents in Opposition to Petition for Writ of Certiorari to the United States Court of Appeals for the Ninth Circuit, Ray Records, Box 2T-6-002, Folder "Indian Jurisdiction."

110 Memorandum, Leo M. Krulitz to Cecil D. Andrus, with correspondence of Raymond V. Butler, Office of Indian Services, BIA, to Skip Skanen, Aug. 28, 1978, NCAI Records, Pre-1994. Series 6, Box 262, Jurisdiction, File: "Oliphant."

111 Author's interview with Rodney Lewis.
112 Barry Ernstoff, memorandum, Sept. 29, 1977, Johnson Papers, Box 3.
113 Cynthia Gorney, "Tribal Powers Challenged," *WP*, Feb. 20, 1978, A1.

CHAPTER 8: TELLING STORIES IN COURT

1 Kim Lane Scheppele, "Foreword: Telling Stories," 87 *Michigan Law Review* 2073 (Aug. 1989): 2080.
2 Milner Ball, "Stories of Origin and Constitutional Possibilities," 87 *Michigan Law Review* 2280 (Aug. 1989): 2309.
3 Malone incorrectly gave 1969 as the date of the lease.
4 Brief for Petitioners, Oliphant v. Suquamish Tribe, 9–13, 4a. See chapter 6 on the 1916 Suquamish constitution.
5 Brief for Petitioners, 21, 22, 29, and Reply Brief for Petitioners, 9, both in Oliphant v. Suquamish Tribe.
6 Brief for Petitioners, Oliphant v. Suquamish Tribe, 10, quoting McClanahan v. Arizona State Tax Commission, 431 U.S. 165 (1972).
7 Brief for Petitioners, Oliphant v. Suquamish Tribe, 96.
8 Brief for Petitioners, Oliphant v. Suquamish Tribe, 8–9.
9 Brief for Petitioners, Oliphant v. Suquamish Tribe, 19.
10 Brief for Petitioners, Oliphant v. Suquamish Tribe, 26, citing John Woodward, "*United States v. Washington*, A Last Stand for the Indians?," March 1973, UW Law Library; and Alvin Josephy, *The Indian Heritage of America* (New York: Knopf, 1968), 73–81.
11 Blackmun Papers; Briefs of Amici Curiae State of South Dakota and Kitsap County, Washington, Oliphant v. Suquamish Tribe. Joining South Dakota as amici curiae were Montana, New Mexico, Nebraska, North Dakota, Nevada, Oregon, and Wyoming.
12 Brief for Respondents, Oliphant v. Suquamish Tribe, 5.
13 Brief for Respondents, Oliphant v. Suquamish Tribe, 15.
14 Brief for Respondents, Oliphant v. Suquamish Tribe, 6–7.
15 Brief for Respondents, Oliphant v. Suquamish Tribe, 4, and Brief for the United States as Amicus Curiae, 2.
16 Brief for Respondents, Oliphant v. Suquamish Tribe, 64.
17 On Trentadue, see this law firm website, https://sautah.com/jesse-c-trentadue.
18 Reply Brief for Petitioners, Oliphant v. Suquamish Tribe, 41.
19 Reply Brief, Oliphant v. Suquamish Tribe, 8–9, citing U.S. v. Washington, 384 F. Supp. 312, 355, emphasis added by Malone.
20 Reply Brief, Oliphant v. Suquamish Tribe, 33.
21 Reply Brief, Oliphant v. Suquamish Tribe, 38–39.

22 Reply Brief, Oliphant v. Suquamish Tribe, 79.

23 Brief of Amici Curiae: The National Congress of American Indians, the Arapahoe Tribe of Wyoming, the Hoopa Valley Tribe of California, and the Confederated Salish and Kootenai Tribes of Montana, Oliphant v. Suquamish Tribe, 3–5.

24 Brief of Amicus Curiae National American Indian Court Judges Association, Oliphant v. Suquamish Tribe, 5–7, 16–21.

25 Brief of Amici Curiae Colorado Indian Tribes, et al., Oliphant v. Suquamish Tribe, 2–11.

26 Brief of Amici Curiae Quinault Indian Nation and Lummi Indian Tribe, Oliphant v. Suquamish Tribe, 2

27 The transcript identified a justice only if an attorney addressed him by name.

28 Transcript, Oliphant v. Suquamish Tribe, Transcripts of Oral Arguments, Records of the Supreme Court of the United States, RG 267, Entry 17, OT 1976, Box 63, 28–29.

29 Transcript, Oliphant v. Suquamish Tribe, 65–70.

30 Transcript, United States v. Anthony Robert Wheeler, Transcripts of Oral Arguments, Records of the Supreme Court of the United States, No. 76-1629, argued Jan. 11, 1978, 9.

31 Opinion, Oliphant v. Suquamish Tribe, 435 U.S. 191 (1978), 195.

32 Opinion, Oliphant v. Suquamish Tribe, 197–206, 208–11.

33 Opinion, Oliphant v. Suquamish Tribe, 207 and note 17.

34 Opinion, Oliphant v. Suquamish Tribe, 197.

35 Opinion, Oliphant v. Suquamish Tribe, 207–9.

36 Opinion, Oliphant v. Suquamish Tribe, 199–201 and note 11; Ex parte Kenyon, 14 Fed. Cas. 353 (W.D. Ark. 1878).

37 Morton Mintz, "Court Rejects Tribe's Right to Try Non-Indian," *WP*, Mar. 7, 1978, A4; "Tribal Governments Can't Try Non-Indian, Supreme Court Rules," *WSJ*, Mar. 7, 1978, 4; "Supreme Court Roundup; Justices to Rule on a Pennsylvania Law Limiting Abortions Decision," *NYT*, Mar. 7, 1978, 12; David Suffia, "'Not a Sovereign Nation': Ruano Hails Indian-Law Decision," *ST*, Mar. 6, 1978, A15.

38 Russel Lawrence Barsh and James Youngblood Henderson, "The Betrayal: *Oliphant v. Suquamish Indian Tribe* and the Hunting of the Snark," 63 *Minnesota Law Review* 609 (1978–79): 610; Alex Skibine, "Indians in the Courts" [notes], 6 *American Indian Journal* 10 (Jan. 1980). A less critical analysis: Richard B. Collins, "Implied Limitations on the Jurisdiction of Indian Tribes," 64 *Washington Law Review* 479 (1979).

39 Philip Lee Fetzer, "Jurisdictional Decisions in Indian Law: The Importance of Extralegal Factors in Judicial Decision Making," 9 *American Indian Law Review* 253 (1981): 263.

40 Barsh and Henderson, "Betrayal," 628, 635; Bethany R. Berger, "Justice and the Outsider: Jurisdiction over Non-Members in Tribal Legal Systems," *Articles and Working Papers, University of Connecticut School of Law* (2004): 11–12, http://lsr.nellco.org/uconn.wps/16; Sarah Krakoff, "*Oliphant v. Suquamish Indian Tribe*: Mark the Plumber v. Tribal Empire, or Non-Indian Anxiety v. Tribal Sovereignty?," in *Indian Law Stories*, ed. Carole E. Goldberg, Kevin K. Washburn, and Philip P. Frickey, 261–96 (New York: Foundation Press/ Thomson Reuters, 2011), 277.

41 Berger, "Justice and the Outsider," 11–12.

42 David E. Wilkins, *American Indian Sovereignty and the U.S. Supreme Court: The Masking of Justice* (Austin: University of Texas Press, 1997), 199, 201.

43 Wilkins, *American Indian Sovereignty*, 198; Berger, "Justice and the Outsider," 7–8.

44 Krakoff, "*Oliphant v. Suquamish Indian Tribe*," 279, 277.

45 Berger, "Justice and the Outsider," 3–14.

46 Barsh and Henderson, "Betrayal," 618. Emphasis in the original.

47 Robert N. Clinton, "The Curse of Relevance: An Essay on the Relationship of Historical Research to Federal Indian Litigation," 28 *Arizona Law Review* 36 (1986).

48 Barsh and Henderson, "Betrayal," 639.

49 Barsh and Henderson, "Betrayal," 622–23.

50 Wilkins, *American Indian Sovereignty*, 211.

51 Robert A. Williams, Jr., "The Algebra of Federal Indian Law: The Hard Trail of Decolonizing and Americanizing the White Man's Indian Jurisprudence," 1986 *Wisconsin Law Review* 219 (1986): 268. Also, Peter Maxfield, "*Oliphant v. Suquamish*: The Whole Is Greater Than the Sum of Its Parts," 19 *Journal of Contemporary Law* 391 (1992): 393.

52 Barsh and Henderson, "Betrayal," 635.

53 Clinton, "Curse of Relevance," 44; Stephen Winston, "Can Lawyers and Judges Be Historians? A Critical Examination of the Siemens Slave-Labor Cases," 20 *Berkeley Journal of International Law* 174 (2002).

54 Fetzer, "Jurisdictional Decisions in Indian Law," 253–72.

55 Winston, "Can Lawyers and Judges Be Historians?," 174.

56 Brief of the National Congress of American Indians, Oliphant. v. Suquamish Tribe, 7, 36.

57 Author's interview with Michael Taylor, Jan. 30, 2012, Camano Island, Washington.

58 Cherokee Nation v. Georgia, 30 U.S. (5 Peters) (1831) 1, 17; United States v. Kagama, 118 U.S. 375 (1886); Lone Wolf v. Hitchcock, 187 U.S. 553 (1903).

59 Lone Wolf v. Hitchcock, 565.

60 Russel Lawrence Barsh and James Youngblood Henderson, *The Road: Indian Tribes and Political Liberty* (Berkeley: University of California Press, 1980), 48, 56–59, 62–63, 83–90; David E. Wilkins and K. Tsianina Lomawaima, *Uneven Ground: American Indian Sovereignty and Federal Law* (Norman: University of Oklahoma Press, 2001), 109–11; Robert N. Clinton, "There Is No Federal Supremacy Clause for Indian Tribes," 34 *Arizona State Law Journal* 112 (2002): 168–75.

61 Petra T. Shattuck and Jill Norgren, *Partial Justice: Federal Indian Law in a Liberal Constitutional System* (New York: Berg, 1991), 92, 115, 124, 190, 194–95; Nell Jessup Newton, "Federal Power over Indians: Its Sources, Scope, and Limitations," 132 *University of Pennsylvania Law Review* 195 (1984).

62 Robert A. Williams, Jr., "The People of the States Where They Are Found Are Often Their Deadliest Enemies: The Indian Side of the Story of Indian Rights and Federalism," 38 *University of Arizona Law Review* 981 (1996): 997; Sidney L. Harring, "The Distorted History That Gave Rise to the 'So-Called' Plenary Power Doctrine: The Story of *United States v. Kagama*," in Goldberg, Washburn, and Frickey, *Indian Law Stories*, 182–83.

63 A search of the Hein Online database for pre-1978 articles critiquing the holdings in *U.S. v. Kagama* or *Lone Wolf v. Hitchcock* turned up nothing.

64 Brief for the Respondents, Oliphant. v. Suquamish Tribe, 6–7, citing Morton v. Mancari, 417 U.S. 535, 553 (1974).

65 Shattuck and Norgren, *Partial Justice*, 196.

66 Marshall Wilson, "Indians Put Faith in Judicial System," *ST*, Dec. 5, 1976, D16 [75]; Transcript of meeting Jan. 7, 1977, 130–31, AIPRC Records, NA RG 220.17.8 (A1 Entry 38060), Box 26, Transcripts, Commission Meetings, Nov. 20, 1976, to Jan. 6, 1977.

67 For example, Paul C. Rosier, *Rebirth of the Blackfeet Nation, 1912–1954* (Lincoln: University of Nebraska Press, 2001); James Robert Allison III, *Sovereignty for Survival: American Energy Development and Indian Self-Determination* (New Haven, CT: Yale University Press, 2015); Frederick E. Hoxie, *Parading through History: The Making of the Crow Nation in America, 1805–1935* (Cambridge: Cambridge University Press, 1995); Joshua L. Reid, *The Sea Is My Country: The Maritime World of the Makahs* (New Haven, CT: Yale University Press, 2015).

68 Alexandra Harmon, "Writing History by Litigation: The Legacy and Limitations of Northwest Indian Rights Cases," *Columbia: The Magazine of Northwest History* (Winter 1990/91): 5–15; Charles A. Miller, *The Supreme Court and the Uses of History* (Cambridge, MA: Harvard University Press, 1969), 4; John Phillip Reid, "Law and History," 27 *Loyola in Los Angeles Law Review* 193 (1993–94): 195–97, 202; Frederick E. Hoxie, "War of the Worlds: History versus

the Law in Charles Wilkinson's *American Indians, Time and the Law*," 13 *Law and Social Inquiry* 792 (1988): 799; Clinton, "The Curse of Relevance," 38, 35–39.

69 United Sates v. Washington, 384 F. Supp. 312 (W. Dist. Wash. 1974), 350.

CHAPTER 9: OBSTACLES, OPTIONS, AND OPPORTUNITIES

1 Bob Liff, "Suquamish: Who's in Charge Here?," *Seattle Sun*, Mar. 15, 1978, 8.

2 Scott R. Maier, "Life after Oliphant: Who Will Keep Peace on the Reservation?," *The Argus,* Mar. 31, 1978, 1.

3 Liff, "Suquamish."

4 Joe DeLaCruz message to General Council, Mar. 29, 1980, NCAI Records, Pre-1994 accessions, Series 6, Committees and Special Issues, Box 122, Tribal Files (Series 4), Qu–Se.

5 Maier, "Life after Oliphant."

6 Joe DeLaCruz testimony, *Jurisdiction on Indian Reservations*, Senate Select Committee on Indian Affairs, Hearings on S. 1181, S. 1722, S. 2832, 96th Cong., 2d sess., May 17, 18, 19, 1980 (Washington, DC: US Government Publishing Office, 1980), 94–95.

7 Maier, "Life after Oliphant."

8 Maier, "Life after Oliphant."

9 Liff, "Suquamish."

10 Maier, "Life after Oliphant."

11 Ralph Johnson to Northwest Region Tribal Court Judges, Mar. 13, 1978, Johnson Papers, Box 10, General Correspondence folder, NAICJA 1977–78; Liff, "Suquamish."

12 Maier, "Life after Oliphant."

13 See chapter 8.

14 Christopher Dunagan, "Indians Disappointed, Outraged," *Bremerton Sun*, Mar. 7, 1978, 1.

15 Charles A. Hobbs, Jerry R. Goldstein, and Robin A. Friedman, "Review of Developments in Indian Law in the Courts, September 1, 1977, through August 31, 1978," NCAI Records, Pre-1994, Series 6, Box 262, Jurisdiction, File: "Oliphant," 6.

16 "Who Controls Reservation Land? Non-Indian Landowners Protest Quinault Rules," *Daily Journal-American* (Bellevue, WA), Sept. 28, 1978, B7; Warren King, "Indians Seek Land Use Control," *ST,* July 30, 1977, 4; Warren King, "Lines Drawn in Suquamish Squabble," *ST,* Aug. 10, 1977, 15; Marjorie Jones, "Suquamish Zoning Bans Garbage Dump, *ST,* July 9, 1972, 31.

17 Liff, "Suquamish."

18 Robert Smith, "Muckleshoots vs. Auburn: Can Tribe Control Non-Indian Land," *ST* (South Times), Aug. 16, 1978, H1; Trans-Canada Enterprises, Ltd. v. Muckleshoot Indian Tribe et al., 634 F. 2d 474 (9th Cir., Dec. 24, 1980); Robert Smith, "Still Reservation? Jurisdiction Dispute Holds Up Mobile-Home Site," *ST*, Aug. 16, 1978, 117; Muckleshoot Indian Tribe et al. v. Trans-Canada Enterprises, Ltd., et al., 713 F.2d 455 (9th Cir. 1983).

19 See chapter 4.

20 Maier, "Life after Oliphant"; Washington v. Confederated Bands and Tribes of the Yakima Indian Nation, 439 U.S. 463 (1979).

21 United States v. Wheeler, 435 U.S. 313, 322–23 (1978) (permitting a Navajo court and a federal court to try an Indian for the same crime without violating the constitutional prohibition of double jeopardy); Santa Clara Pueblo v. Martinez, 236 U.S. 49 (1978), 65–66.

22 Bryan vs. Itasca County, 426 U.S. 373 (1976).

23 Catherine B. Stetson, "Decriminalizing Tribal Codes: A Response to *Oliphant*," 9 *American Indian Law Review* 51 (1981).

24 Michael Taylor, "State and Tribal Civil Jurisdiction: Washington's Decriminalized Traffic Infraction Scheme in the U.S. Supreme Court," *Indian Law Newsletter* (Washington State Bar Association) 2 (Mar. 1992): 1; Travis Baker, "What Can Tribal Officers Do with Non-Indian Speeders?," *Kitsap Sun* blog, July 10, 2009.

25 John S. Sledd, "The Blind Man and the Oliphant: Tribal Jurisdiction and the Civil-Criminal Boundary," paper for annual UW Indian Law Symposium, ca. 1992, in author's possession.

26 Montana v. United States, 450 U.S. 544 (1981), 563–67.

27 Matthew L. M. Fletcher, "A Unifying Theory of Tribal Civil Jurisdiction," 46 *Arizona State Law Journal* 779 (2014): 783; Joseph P. Kalt and Joseph William Singer, "Myths and Realities of Tribal Sovereignty: The Law and Economics of Indian Self-Rule," *Joint Occasional Papers on Native Affairs* no. 2004-03 (Cambridge, MA: Harvard Project on American Indian Development, 2004), 15.

28 Brendale v. Confederated Tribes and Bands of the Yakima Nation, 492 U.S. 408 (1989); United States v. Bourland, 508 U.S. 679 (1993).

29 Merrion v. Jicarilla Apache Tribe, 455 U.S. 130 (1982); Kerr-McGee Corporation v. Navajo Tribe of Indians, 470 U.S. 195 (1985).

30 Atkinson Trading Company v. Shirley, 532 U.S. 645 (2001), 654–59.

31 Michael Taylor, "A-1 vs. Strate—Tribal Court, Tribal Land," paper for UW Law School Indian Law Symposium, 1998, 1.

32 National Farmers Union Insurance Company v. Crow Tribe of Indians, 471 U.S. 845 (1985); Iowa Mutual Insurance Company v. LaPlante, 480 U.S. 9 (1987).

33 Strate v. A-1 Contractors, 526 U.S. 438 (1997); Nevada v. Hicks, 533 U.S. 353 (2001); Lisa M. Slepnikoff, "More Questions Than Answers: *Plains Commerce Bank v. Long Family Land and Cattle Company, Inc.* and the U.S. Supreme Court's Failure to Define the Extent of Tribal Civil Law Authority," 54 *South Dakota Law Review* 460 (2009).
34 Fletcher, "Unifying Theory of Tribal Civil Jurisdiction," 782–83 and cases cited.
35 Joe DeLaCruz keynote, National Fisheries Conference, Union of British Columbia Indian Chiefs National Indian Brotherhood 5/20/80, Fourth World Documentation Project Archives, Center for World Indigenous Studies, www.cwis.org.
36 Kenneth Snow, et al. v. Quinault Indian Nation, 709 F.2d 1319 (9th Cir. 1983), cert. denied 107 S. Ct. 2655.
37 Joseph B. DeLaCruz to Ken Smith, Jan. 16, 1984, NCAI Records, Pre-1994 accessions, Series 6, Committees and Special Issues, Box 122, Tribal Files (Series 4), Qu–Se; Scott Maier, "Small Tribe vs. Corporation," *The Argus*, Jan. 26, 1979, 4.
38 Sechrist v. Quinault Indian Nation, 9 Indian Law Reporter K3064 (W.D. Wash., May 7, 1982); Cardin v. De La Cruz, 671 F. 2d 363 (9th Cir. 1982).
39 "AILTP Conference on the Administration of Justice on Indian Reservations," *American Indian Journal* (Sept. 1979), 49.
40 Peter Fabish, "The Decline of Tribal Sovereignty: The Journey from Dicta to Dogma in *Duro v. Reina*, 119 S.Ct. 2053 (1990)," 66 *Washington Law Review* 567 (1991), 569n15.
41 Morton v. Mancari, 417 U.S. 535 (1974).
42 Duro v. Reina, 495 U.S. 676 (1990).
43 18 U.S.C. 1152.
44 Fabish, "Decline of Tribal Sovereignty."
45 68 U.S.L.W. 4843 (May 29, 1990).
46 Daniel K. Inouye et al., Select Committee on Indian Affairs, to Richard L. Thornburgh, June 12, 1990; 25 U.S.C. 1301 (2) and (4).
47 "Impact of Supreme Court's Ruling in Duro v. Reina," Hearing Report of Select Committee on Indian Affairs, 102 Cong., 2d sess., June 12, 1991, part 2, 45–57, 55.
48 "Impact of Supreme Court's Ruling in Duro v. Reina," 48–49.
49 United States v. Lara, 541 U.S. 193 (2004); Linda Greenhouse, "Court Upholds Tribal Power It Once Denied," *NYT*, April 20, 2004, A12.
50 Oliphant et al. v. Suquamish Indian Tribe, 435 U.S. 191, 212.
51 Linda Daniel, "Indians 'Have Always Had Jurisdiction,'" *ST*, Aug. 10, 1977, 14.
52 Maier, "Life after Oliphant," 1.
53 Joe DeLaCruz testimony, *Jurisdiction on Indian Reservations*, 96–97.
54 Charles Wilkinson, *Blood Struggle: The Rise of Modern Indian Nations* (New York: Norton, 2005), 268, 324; Kalt and Singer, "Myths and Realities of Tribal

Sovereignty," 1–2; Laura E. Evans, *Power from Powerlessness: Tribal Governments, Institutional Niches, and American Federalism* (Oxford: Oxford University Press, 2011). On April 29, 1994, President Bill Clinton issued an executive memorandum directing all departments and agencies to "operate within a government-to-government relationship with federally recognized tribes." "Governtment-to-Government Relations with Native American Tribal Governments," https://www.justice.gov/archive/otj/Presidential_Statements/presdoc1.htm.

55 Timothy Egan, "Embracing Self-Rule, 7 Tribes Begin a 3-Year Experiment in Sovereignty," *NYT*, Jan. 16, 1991, A16.

56 Geoffrey D. Strommer and Stephen D. Osborne, "The History, Status, and Future of Tribal Self-Governance under the Indian Self-Determination and Education Assistance Act," 39 *American Indian Law Review* 1 (2015): 29; Pub. L. 103-413 (Oct. 25, 1994).

57 "Great Tribal Leaders of Modern Times: Mel Tonasket," Tribal Leadership Forum, Institute for Tribal Government, videotape (interview, Nov. 2001), Portland State University, Portland, OR, 2005.

58 Andrew E. Serwer, "American Indians Discover Money Is Power," *Fortune*, April 19, 1993, 136–40; Alexandra Harmon, *Rich Indians: Native People and the Problem of Wealth in American History* (Chapel Hill: University of North Carolina Press, 2010), 249–51, 268–69.

59 "American Indian Leaders Plan Defense Strategies," *Indian Country Today* online, Oct. 3, 2001; David Melmer, "Law Enforcement Issues Were Brought to the Fore," *McClatchy-Tribune Business News*, Dec. 26, 2007, *Indian Country Today* online.

60 Department of Justice, "Violence against Women Act (VAWA) Reauthorization 2013," https://www.justice.gov/tribal/violence-against-women-act-vawa-reauthorization-2013-0; "Violence against Women: Fixing the Law," *American Indian* (Winter 2015): 35.

61 Louise Erdrich, "Rape on Reservations," *NYT*, Feb. 27, 2013, A25; Jonathan Weisman, "Measure to Protect Women Stuck on Tribal Land Issue," *NYT*, Feb. 11, 2013, A11.

62 Julie Muhlstein, "Tulalip Leader Speaks in D.C. for Protection for Women," *Everett Herald*, May 22, 2012.

63 US Senate Committee on Indian Affairs, *Native Women: Protecting, Shielding, and Safeguarding Our Sisters, Mothers, and Daughters*, hearing, July 14, 2011, CIS 2012-S411-6, SuDoc Y4.IN2/11: S.Hrg 112-311.

64 Weisman, "Measure to Protect Women Stuck on Tribal Land Issue"; Department of Justice, "Violence against Women Act"; "Violence against Women: Fixing the Law."

65 Lynda V. Mapes, "Tribes Regain Ability to Prosecute Criminals for Some Crimes on Their Reservations," *ST*, Feb. 28, 2013.

66 "Impact of Supreme Court's Ruling in Duro v. Reina."

67 Robert H. Keller, Jr., ed., "Washington State and Tribal Sovereignty: A 1979 Debate on Indian Law," *Pacific Northwest Quarterly* 78 (July 1988): 98–109, 103.

68 "AILTP Conference on the Administration of Justice." Also, "A Challenge for the 80's Political Unity," report of NCAI 36th Annual Convention, Albuquerque, Oct. 1–5, 1979.

69 RCW 10.92.020; Richard Roesler, "Bill Aims to Expand Tribal Cops' Authority," *Spokesman-Review* (Spokane), Feb. 27, 2008, A1; Washington State House Bill 24761 also discussed in "Northwest High Intensity Drug Trafficking Area, Criminal Exploitation of Washington State Tribal Lands, 2009," https://www2.kuow.org/specials/addicted/Criminal%20Exploitation%20of%20Washington%20State%20Tribal%20Lands%202009.pdf.

70 Agreement between Confederated Tribes of the Colville Indian Reservation and Department of Game, State of Washington, August 29, 1982, appended to materials prepared by Alan Stay—"Jurisdictional Agreements: Tribal/State/Federal"—for UW Law School Indian Law Symposium, 1990.

71 Gil Bailey, "A Drunken-Driving Dilemma: An Indian Tribe's Police See Non-Indians Freed," *Seattle Post-Intelligencer*, Mar. 24, 1986, D1.

72 The State of Washington v. David P. Schmuck, No. 58987-9, Supreme Court of Washington en banc, 121 Wn.2d 373 (1993), 850 P.2d 1332.

73 Richard Walker, "Agreement with County Would Clear Way for Suquamish Police to Enforce State Law," *Kitsap Daily News*, Dec. 1, 2015; Ken Alltucker, "Suquamish Casino: County, Tribe Squabble over Law Enforcement," *Kitsap Sun*, Dec. 1, 1995; JoAnne Marez, "Kitsap County: Sheriff Announces Retirement," *Kitsap Sun*, Mar. 28, 1998; David Schaefer, "Kitsap Prosecutor: Bully or Just Tough? Clem Faces Test in Re-Election Bid," *ST*, Sept. 15, 1994.

74 Editorial, "Suquamish Tribe: A Vital Part of Our Safety Net," *North Kitsap Herald*, May 17, 2016.

75 Richard Walker, "Suquamish Tribe's Economic Boom 'Breathtaking,'" *Kitsap Daily News* (Bremerton), Jan. 30, 2015.

76 Richard Walker, "10 Things You Should Know about the Quinault Nation: From Strong Leaders like Fawn Sharp to Stewards of the Environment," *Indian Country Today*, Jan. 30, 2017; Quinault Indian Nation website, www.quinaultindiannation.com/presidentsoffice.htm.

77 Paul Shukovsky, "Neighbors Sue to Disband Suquamish Tribe: Sovereign Powers Are Resented by Non-Indians in a Pattern Growing in the U.S.," *Seattle Post-Intelligencer*, Oct. 17, 2001, online.

78 Draft Complaint for Declaratory and Injunctive Relief (not signed or filed in US District Court, Western District of Washington at Tacoma), Association of Property Owners/Residents of Port Madison, et al. v. Individual council members of the Suquamish Tribal Council, et al., in author's possession.

79 Judgment, Association of Property Owners/Residents of Port Madison, et al. v. Individual council members of the Suquamish Tribal Council, et al., Ninth Circuit Court of Appeals, No. 02-35522, Sept. 9, 2003, National Indian Law Library document online, www.narf.org/nill/bulletins/cta/documents/aporpma.html.

80 Corrected Brief of Appellants and Brief of Respondent, Quinault Indian Nation, et al., Appellants, vs. Sea Crest Land Development Company, et al., Respondents, no. 37688-1-II, Court of Appeals for the State of Washington, Division II, July 7, 2008, https://www.courts.wa.gov/content/Briefs/A02/376881%20corrected%20appellant.pdf; "Lawsuit Seeks to Wrest Control of Lake Quinault from Tribe," *Indian Country Today*, Feb. 10, 2015.

81 Richard White, *The Republic for Which It Stands: The United States during Reconstruction and the Gilded Age, 1865–1896* (New York: Oxford University Press, 2017), 433.

82 Sally Engle Merry, *Colonizing Hawai'i: The Cultural Power of Law* (Princeton, NJ: Princeton University Press, 2000), 260.

83 Jeffrey R. Dudas, "Law at the American Frontier," 29 *Law and Social Inquiry* (2004): 884; Lisa Ford, *Settler Sovereignty: Jurisdiction and Indigenous People in America and Australia, 1788–1836* (Cambridge, MA: Harvard University Press), 2010.

84 *New Oxford Dictionary*, 3rd ed.; Sidney L. Harring, *Crow Dog's Case: American Indian Sovereignty, Tribal Law, and United States Law in the Nineteenth Century* (New York: Cambridge University Press, 1994), 14–15; Vine Deloria, Jr., "Self-Determination and the Concept of Sovereignty," in *Economic Development in American Indian Reservations*, ed. Roxanne Dunbar Ortiz (Albuquerque: University of New Mexico Native American Studies, 1979), 22.

85 Dudas, "Law at the American Frontier," 884; Abigail C. Saguy and Forrest Stuart, "Culture and Law: Beyond a Paradigm of Cause and Effect," *Annals of the American Academy of Political and Social Science* 619 (Sept. 2008): 154.

SELECTED ARCHIVAL COLLECTIONS

Adams, Hank. Papers. Included in Papers of Frederick Haley, University of Washington Libraries Special Collections, Accession 1988-005.

American Indian Policy Review Commission (AIPRC) Records. NA RG 220.17.8, A1 Entry 38060.

Association on American Indian Affairs (AAIA) Papers. Special Collections, Seeley G. Mudd Library, Princeton University. Call No. MC147.

Blackmun, Harry A. Papers. Library of Congress Manuscripts. Supreme Court File, Box 270, Folder 3, Opinions, 76-5729, *Oliphant v. Suquamish Indian Tribe.*

Broadhead, William Sherwin. Papers. University of Washington Libraries Special Collections, Accession 6177-001.

DeLaCruz, Joe. Interview, 1973. Tapes 5 and 6, Northwest Tribal Oral History Interviews, 1963–1973, Center for Pacific Northwest Studies, Bellingham, Washington.

Hansen, Julia Butler. Papers. University of Washington Libraries Special Collections, Accession 1501-001.

Indian Community Action Project Reservation (ICAP) Files. University of Utah Archives, Accession 0165.

Johnson, Ralph Whitney. Papers. University of Washington Libraries Special Collections, Accession 2320-5.

Lyman, Stanley D. Papers, 1923–1979. University of Utah, J. Willard Marriott Library Special Collections, Manuscripts, UU_Ms 0181.

Meeds, Lloyd. Papers. University of Washington Libraries Special Collections, Accession 2900-9.

National Congress of American Indians (NCAI) Records. National Museum of the American Indian Cultural Resource Center, Suitland, Maryland.

Officer, James E. Office Files. United States Bureau of Indian Affairs. National Archives Record Group 75.

Oliphant, Mark David, and Daniel B. Belgarde v. The Suquamish Indian Tribe, et al. (Oliphant v. Suquamish Tribe). Records of the Supreme Court of the United States, October Term, 1977, No. 76-5729.

Oliphant, Mark David v. Edward Schlie, Chief of Police of the City of Bremerton, U.S. District Court, Western District of Washington. Case No. 511-73C2. National Archives, Pacific Alaska Region, RG 21, Records of U.S. District Courts, Accession 21-79-0021, Location 99475, Transfer Box 32; Archives no. PT-000-2011-0684, Box 445.

O'Neil, Floyd. Papers. Indian Self-Rule Conference. University of Utah, J. Willard Marriott Library Special Collections, Accession 0890.

Price, Monroe. Interview, 1971. University of Utah, J. Willard Marriott Library Special Collections, Doris Duke Indian Oral History Transcripts, MS 0417, Item 1006.

Ray, Governor Dixy Lee. Records. Indian Affairs. Washington State Archives, Accession AR2-T-12.

Suquamish Tribal Oral History Interviews, Suquamish Tribal Archives, Suquamish Museum, Suquamish, WA.

Tyler, S. Lyman. Papers. University of Utah, J. Willard Marriott Library Special Collections, Manuscripts, UU_MS 0042.

Washington State Department of Fisheries (WDF) Central Files. Indian Affairs, Box 32, Quinault Files, Washington State Archives, Accession AR64-1-25.

INDEX

D

G

Q

R

T

V

EMIL AND KATHLEEN SICK SERIES IN WESTERN HISTORY AND BIOGRAPHY

The Great Columbia Plain: A Historical Geography, 1805–1910, by Donald W. Meinig
Mills and Markets: A History of the Pacific Coast Lumber Industry to 1900, by Thomas R. Cox
Radical Heritage: Labor, Socialism, and Reform in Washington and British Columbia, 1885–1917, by Carlos A. Schwantes
The Battle for Butte: Mining and Politics on the Northern Frontier, 1864–1906, by Michael P. Malone
The Forging of a Black Community: Seattle's Central District from 1870 through the Civil Rights Era, by Quintard Taylor
Warren G. Magnuson and the Shaping of Twentieth-Century America, by Shelby Scates
The Atomic West, edited by Bruce Hevly and John M. Findlay
Power and Place in the North American West, edited by Richard White and John M. Findlay
Henry M. Jackson: A Life in Politics, by Robert G. Kaufman
Parallel Destinies: Canadian-American Relations West of the Rockies, edited by John M. Findlay and Ken S. Coates
Nikkei in the Pacific Northwest: Japanese Americans and Japanese Canadians in the Twentieth Century, edited by Louis Fiset and Gail M. Nomura
Bringing Indians to the Book, by Albert Furtwangler
Death of Celilo Falls, by Katrine Barber
The Power of Promises: Perspectives on Indian Treaties of the Pacific Northwest, edited by Alexandra Harmon
Warship under Sail: The USS Decatur *in the Pacific West*, by Lorraine McConaghy
Shadow Tribe: The Making of Columbia River Indian Identity, by Andrew H. Fisher
A Home for Every Child: Relinquishment, Adoption, and the Washington Children's Home Society, 1896–1915, by Patricia Susan Hart
Atomic Frontier Days: Hanford and the American West, by John M. Findlay and Bruce Hevly
The Nature of Borders: Salmon, Boundaries, and Bandits on the Salish Sea, by Lissa K. Wadewitz
Encounters in Avalanche Country: A History of Survival in the Mountain West, 1820–1920, by Diana L. Di Stefano
The Rising Tide of Color: Race, State Violence, and Radical Movements across the Pacific, edited by Moon-Ho Jung
Trout Culture: How Fly Fishing Forever Changed the Rocky Mountain West, by Jen Corrinne Brown
Japanese Prostitutes in the North American West, 1887–1920, by Kazuhiro Oharazeki
In Defense of Wyam: Native-White Alliances and the Struggle for Celilo Village, by Katrine Barber
Gold Rush Manliness: Race and Gender on the Pacific Slope, by Christopher Herbert
Reclaiming the Reservation: Histories of Indian Sovereignty Suppressed and Renewed, by Alexandra Harmon